OUR TIMES

VOLUME I

William McKinley

WILLIAM MC KINLEY

FROM THE PAINTING BY W. D. MURPHY

MARK SULLIVAN

OUR TIMES

1900-1925

Introduction by Dewey W. Grantham

I

The Turn of the Century

New York

CHARLES SCRIBNER'S SONS

A-1.72 [C]

Printed in the United States of America
Library of Congress Catalog Card Number 70-138308
SBN 684-12354-1 (trade cloth)
SBN 684-12791-1 (college paper, SUL)

GENERAL INTRODUCTION

MARK SULLIVAN AND THE WRITING OF CONTEMPORARY HISTORY

By Dewey W. Grantham

The inimitable Mr. Dooley once expressed his dissatisfaction with the way history was traditionally written by remarking to his friend Hennessy: "I know histhry isn't thrue, Hinnissy, because it ain't like what I see ivry day in Halsted Sthreet. If any wan comes along with a histhry iv Greece or Rome that'll show me th' people fightin', gettin' dhrunk, makin' love, gettin' married, owin' th' groceryman an' bein' without hard coal, I'll believe they was a Greece or Rome, but not before." Historians were like doctors, explained Mr. Dooley. They told you "what a counthry died iv" but not what "it lived iv." Yet the writing of history was changing even as Mr. Dooley voiced his lament. The historian James G. Randall took note of this in 1929 when he referred to "the new garb which the historical muse is assuming." Clio was no longer "preoccupied with presidents, congresses, court decisions, and the like," observed Randall. "She is now concerned with mobs, crazes, fads, Jesse James, P.T. Barnum, the fabulous 'forties, the gay 'nineties, and a thousand other such things."

One of the American writers who employed the new approach to the writing of history was the well-known journalist Mark Sullivan. In 1923 Sullivan signed a contract with Charles Scribner's Sons to write a history of the United States during the first twenty-five years of the twentieth century. "It is not going to be a history in the usual formal sense," he pointed out in 1924, "for it is designed to be more a history of the people than merely of politicians, statesmen and wars." In the first volume, which appeared in 1926, the author stated that his purpose was "to follow an average American through this quarter-century of his country's history, to recreate the flow of the days as he saw them, to picture events in terms of their influence on him, his daily life and ultimate destiny." Thus Sullivan's focus, like that of Lord Macaulay and John Bach McMaster, whom he quoted approvingly, was "the history of the people" in all its variety. Politics, he noted in his discussion of the 1890's, "had less bearing than many other aspects of existence on the average man's capacity and opportunity to get comfort, satisfaction, and fun out of life."

Sullivan called his history *Our Times.* It was a singularly inviting title, for it communicated the writer's wholehearted commitment to his own time and place. The use of the possessive plural suggested, in the words of Stuart Sherman, "so much loyalty, so much affection, so much social and fraternal feeling, so keen a sense of the common lot." The first thing that caught the eye of the reader was the illustrations, which brightened the pages and provided contrast to the text. The pictures—an average of 230 per volume—might be cartoons from the old *Life* or *The New Yorker* that brought back the humor of the times. They might be sketches from *Vogue* and *McCall's* arranged to show the cycle of women's skirts. The narrative itself was a kaleidoscope in which one encountered not only Bryan, Roosevelt, and Wilson, not only the new American empire, the Great War, and the politics of normalcy, but also the Gibson girl, Billy Sunday, vaudeville, stereopticon views, "mutton-leg sleeves," the gags of Weber and Fields, Spencerian penmanship, "ragtime,"

Richard Harding Davis, the "Yellow Kid," John Philip Sousa, Ford jokes, the novels of Elinor Glyn, "The Birth of a Nation," Jack Dempsey, Teapot Dome, and the Jazz Age. The six volumes presented a fascinating panorama of early twentieth-century America. Published between 1926 and 1935, *Our Times* was an immense success (the first volume went through seven printings in 1926 alone), and its author quickly became identified with a new kind of history.

Mark Sullivan's ambitious venture in the writing of a large-scale contemporary history was a natural outgrowth of his successful career as a journalist during the first two decades of the twentieth century. There was an Alger-like quality about Sullivan's rapid rise to the top of his profession which inevitably colored his impressions of that era and reinforced his faith in its values. Born in 1874, the tenth child of Irish immigrants, Sullivan grew up on a small farm in southeastern Pennsylvania. He began to write for newspapers while still in high school and subsequently spent four years working for small-town papers. He eventually managed to attend Harvard College, from which he was graduated in 1900. He stayed on at Harvard to study law, supporting himself by writing stories for the *Boston Transcript*. Sullivan received his law degree in 1903, but he could not resist the lure of journalism in "a time of intellectual insurgency." He soon abandoned the law for the exciting world of magazine writing, working briefly for the *Ladies' Home Journal* and *McClure's Magazine* before joining the staff of *Collier's Weekly* in 1906. His progress from that point was incredibly fast. He soon became *Collier's* political expert, enjoyed the friendship and confidence of Theodore Roosevelt, and through his own political page achieved a national reputation almost overnight. Sullivan was an early muckraker, and he helped make *Collier's* one of the leading reform journals of the day. He attacked the political "standpatters," supported the Republican insurgents, and joined Roosevelt's Progressives in 1912. He served for a few years as editor of *Collier's* but left the magazine in 1919 to write a widely-syndicated political column for the New York *Evening Post*. Three years later he shifted to the *New York Tribune*, and he continued to write for that newspaper until his death in 1952.

Sullivan's career as a journalist had an important bearing on his entry into the field of historical writing. It gave him the perspective of the social commentator. It impressed upon him the value of entertainment as a feature of the appeal to a larger reading public. It also made him aware of the new audience for serious writing that was emerging in the United States, for the popular magazine that he knew so well was itself the product of a cultural revolution involving the growing middle classes, new developments in the graphic arts, and the broadening interests and tastes of ordinary people. Perhaps Sullivan sensed the yearning in this new audience for a panoramic treatment of the past that would provide some degree of order and stability in a changing world. He certainly realized that a new approach to the writing of history was needed to make such works more popular. He recognized the advantages his journalistic experiences would give him for the new undertaking. He had crossed and recrossed the United States, and, as Edward L. Weldon has written in an unpublished study, he had built up "an extensive network of bipartisan informants who kept him attuned to grassroot moods, helping establish him as a reliable reporter and an amazingly accurate political forecaster."

Over the years, moreover, Sullivan had become intrigued with "the relation between history as it happened and history as it is written." He once told Arthur M.

Schlesinger that he could "make an entertaining but highly explosive book by detaching passages from printed history and printing in a parallel column facts that I know about the true motives, the true point of view, and even the true actions of the principals who acted out the original facts." The idea of writing a more accurate chronicle of his own time based on personal observation as well as formal documents encouraged the journalist to turn historian. The concept of recent history that he devised seems to have been inspired in part by Harry Thurston Peck's *Twenty Years of the Republic*, an account of the years 1885-1905 which Sullivan read as a young reporter.

There were still other factors involved in Sullivan's decision to write *Our Times*. He was a man of prodigious energy and great self-discipline, able, as he put it, to "carry along two or three things at the same time." The three or four syndicated columns he wrote each week on national politics for the *Tribune* left him a good deal of leisure for magazine articles and other work. The times also had something to do with the crystallization of Sullivan's historical perspective. Although the years of normalcy had their compensations, the writer missed the heroes of the Progressive era and shared in the disillusionment of the postwar period. He was disturbed by many of the changes brought by the first World War, by the assault upon traditional values, by "the tendencies of literary and intellectual cults" to "jeer at America." He looked back to prewar America, to "the things that are traditionally and characteristically American."

The publication of *Our Times* created something of a sensation. "I am reading your gorgeous, delicious book," William Allen White informed the author in March, 1926. "It is like renewing one's youth." "I love the informality of your arrangement," Hermann Hagedorn wrote

Sullivan, "your avoidance of too strict an adherence to chronology, the conversational manner, the occasional irony, the biting comment here and there so gently phrased." Josephus Daniels was so impressed with the second volume that he read "most of it aloud" to his family. "Each new volume of *Our Times* fills me with a consuming envy of you for having done it," the historian Frederic L. Paxson said to Sullivan in 1930. "It represents something that I have had always in my mind; but I could never have executed it as you have." Frederick Lewis Allen, whose own popular history of the 1920's, *Only Yesterday*, was about to be published, wrote Sullivan in the fall of 1931 to express his indebtedness to the older man for having developed "a method of writing contemporary history which, to some extent at least, I have followed." Meanwhile, the successive volumes of *Our Times* found their way to the best-seller lists, and the series was frequently included in surveys of the best books published during the decade 1925-1935.

The numerous reviews of the series were generous. They emphasized its contemporary character, the space it gave to the unpretentious aspects of American life, and the freshness, vividness, and informality of its treatment. Almost all reviewers responded nostalgically to the evocation of manners and moods from the day before yesterday. Sullivan was somewhat disconcerted at the attitude of some "highbrows" who did not take him seriously and at the frequent description of his history as "scrap book-y," "journalistic," and "family album-y." He was also disappointed because a number of professional historians did not seem to regard *Our Times* as "sound history." According to one historian, "It is fascinating, but it is not history." In his own mind Sullivan was convinced that his work had modified both the writing of history and "the teaching of history in colleges."

Recognition of his achievement did come from many quarters—in the form of honorary degrees, membership on the Harvard Board of Overseers, and an invitation to teach at Columbia University in 1930. Two of the Pulitzer Prize judges on the history panel voted for his fifth volume in 1934. The following year—on November 18, 1935—he received *Time's* accolade when his picture appeared on the cover of that magazine. In the "six fat volumes and 3,740 pages" of his popular history, proclaimed *Time*, "Author Sullivan has presented a superb newsreel of the U.S. from 1900 to 1925—its heroes, its villains, its ideas, its sensations, its fun, fads & fancies."

Sullivan was not a trained historian, which proved to be a source both of weakness and of strength in his attempt to re-create the recent past. One of the most serious flaws in *Our Times* as a historical account is its lack of coherent and unified organization. It is more a series of informative and entertaining articles than an effective synthesis, and it shows little evidence of chronological sequence or progression. In places the work gave the appearance of having been thrown together, commented John D. Hicks, who was reminded of "the bewilderment of a dog turned loose in a field of rabbits and earnestly desirous of chasing them all." Some of the voluminous information in the six volumes is not well digested, and the chronological catch-all chapters at the end of each book have little relation to the main narrative. Sullivan neglected many important sources, particularly the more serious types of materials, and he was sometimes careless and undiscriminating in the use of those he did employ.

Our Times is guided by no theoretical or philosophical view of the historical process. Sullivan refers to the existence of "certain forces" in history which "determined much of what happened," but he does not clearly define what he means by the term or use it with any precision as a tool of analysis. He wrote a chronicle of events as they appeared to contemporaries, not necessarily as they actually happened. His explanations are often oversimplified and tend to stress a single factor. He doubts the influence of great men in history but emphasizes the feats of many individuals. His average American remains a rather nebulous figure (though one reviewer thought him "a combination of Theodore Roosevelt, Elbert Hubbard, Henry Ford, and Zane Grey"). While Sullivan avoids passing judgment and expressing his own opinion, his style is didactic and his account has much of the subjective quality of a memoir. It is capricious in its emphases, allocations of space, and omissions. Sullivan exaggerates the role of Theodore Roosevelt and is unfair in his interpretation of Woodrow Wilson. His orientation is toward the eastern part of the country, and he reveals a strong agrarian bias in favor of small-town, rural America. His focus is usually on the newsworthy events of the era. In short, as Charles Seymour pointed out, Sullivan was "probably too good a journalist to be a good historian. He cannot escape his own impressions of men and events, those impressions that give life to his pages."

Yet there is much to be said for Mark Sullivan's attempt to write a history of his own time. His conception of the project itself deserves comment, for it was as breathtaking in its imaginative sweep as it was uncomplicated in its design. If the work is uneven, it is also readable, informative, and unfailingly interesting. If Sullivan's "average American" is a somewhat shadowy figure and if his analysis of powerful "forces" is shallow, his chronicle nevertheless suggests how the average man was affected by certain movements and developments. If the author tends to concentrate upon the sensational and the dramatic, he does not rely upon newspaper headlines alone.

For "the spirit and flavor of the time," he turned to "the less obtrusive records on the inside pages, including the advertisements, where, as in the living-room and kitchen of a home, are to be found a more intimate reflection of the life of the period than is provided by the front porch or the first page." If Sullivan was sometimes partisan in his analysis of politics, he made a consistent effort to present both sides of a question. Although he was not a profound or a subtle thinker, he was a first-rate reporter with a remarkable instinct for the interesting and the significant. He wrote with clarity and force, and his appraisals were shrewd and perceptive.

The writing of *Our Times* took twelve years, but, as Sullivan said, "the time of preparation, the experience that went into the work, were the years of the author's adult life, of which substantially the whole was passed, with eager interest in the flow of the days, in continuously close contact with events and persons and forces in a considerable variety of fields." Thus *Our Times* is a mirror for the America Sullivan knew from his own experience. It reflects his strong commitment to the traditional culture—to liberty, nationality, progress, and faith in the universality of moral values. It celebrates the triumph of individualism and progress in what the writer called an era of "dynamic materialism" and "dynamic humanitarianism." The changes in postwar America, the mounting evidence of new cultural values and of increasing bureaucratization and standardization, caused Sullivan, with the passing years, to have some doubts about the beneficence of material progress. This mental tension undoubtedly heightened his nostalgia for the good years that antedated Sarajevo and explains some of the ambivalence toward the new order that found its way into the pages of the later volumes of his history. He was never able to decide whether, to use David Potter's concepts, his average American would end up as an idealistic individualist or a materialistic conformist.

"The professional historian," Allan Nevins observed in his review of the first volume of *Our Times*, "has always been too fearful that a record of the immediate past would be superficial and inaccurate, forgetting that no history is really definitive." This was not true of Mark Sullivan. He should be remembered as one of the pioneers in demonstrating the possibilities of writing contemporary history. There was a novel aspect in his technique. He made extensive use of newspapers ("diaries of history," he called them) and periodicals, as well as his own experiences. But the most notable feature of his use of sources was his reliance upon the records and recollections of his contemporaries—upon research in the memories of living participants.

Sullivan's practice was to gather all of the readily available evidence on a topic, with the assistance of Mabel Shea, his secretary, and William E. Shea, his research assistant. He would next write a draft and have it set in type. The galleys for these individual chapters would be sent for criticism and suggestions to as many as fifty people—"to literally everybody who had any close connection with events at the time." Thus Sullivan turned to Charles Dana Gibson for information and advice on popular art, to Edward W. Bok on fashions, to Orville Wright on early aviation, to Clarence S. Darrow on the Haywood trial of 1906-07, to Irene Castle on new dances, and to Ivy L. Lee on advertising. Virtually all of the surviving public figures on the national scene were invited to contribute in this fashion, and Sullivan estimated that the number of his collaborators ran into the thousands. "The whole scheme of this enterprise," he explained, "is built upon the idea that history will be laid before all or most of those who were actors in the events or who, living at the time, had judgment about the events."

Our Times is also significant in American historiography because it contributed to a more inclusive definition of what constitutes history. Sullivan complained that historians depended too exclusively for their materials upon "those who function in the traditional forums, those who write or fight, orate, or rule." He departed from that tradition. *Our Times*, as Heywood Broun asserted, "gives not only the bird's eye view of one looking down from the clear height of a distance, but also the worm's eye view of an observer who lay in the dust between the trampling feet." This approach was subversive, commented another reviewer. "It blows up the old Roman road and scatters the 'dignity' of history to the four winds of heaven." Sullivan was intent on describing the culture and recapturing the atmosphere of the period he was writing about, and in an effort to do that he concerned himself with what Frederick Lewis Allen called "the fads and fashions and follies of the time, the things which millions of people thought about and talked about and became excited about and which at once touched their daily lives."

Our Times is a classic in the field of popular history, and it is appropriate that it should be reprinted without change, with all of its blemishes and "typographical sins" as they originally appeared. It is, on the one hand, a jumbled, superficial, and journalistic narrative; but, on the other hand, it is an absorbing treatment of the first quarter of the twentieth century, enlightening, entertaining, and thoroughly delightful. As a shrewd piece of contemporary history, it helped to broaden the content of history and to increase its popular appeal in the United States. It is also noteworthy because it succeeds magnificently in evoking the spirit of that confident age that spanned the period between the 1890's and the 1920's. And most important of all, it is an extraordinary repository of raw material for the study and understanding of an epoch in our national life.

INTRODUCTION TO VOLUME I

THE TURN OF THE CENTURY

Mark Sullivan set out to write a new kind of American history, a history that would delineate the culture of the people and show how the average man was affected by the everyday circumstances of his environment. Sullivan's interest in the average American is clearly revealed in the first volume of the series, *The Turn of the Century*. In the opening chapter Sullivan tries to paint "a faithful and universal picture of the occupations and the interests, fads and recreations of the American people, in all parts of the country, small town and big, as of the beginning of the century." He does this by "stringing together" an illuminating selection of items from the American newspapers of January 1, 1900. The result is a vivid example of impressionistic recall and an ingenious way to begin a popular history.

In his attempt to characterize the American people and their major institutions, Sullivan introduces two themes that frequently reappear in later volumes: individualism and progress. Of all American characteristics, he maintains, "the most important was freedom of opportunity for the individual." Progress is also much in evidence. In order to show the dimensions of "material enrichment" during the period, Sullivan contrasts the situation in 1900 with that in 1925. In one place he declares that if McMaster, "writing in 1883 of American history up to that year, found it necessary and appropriate to use words of exaltation, we shall have to try to find super-superlative ones to describe the period of the present history, 1900-25." Politics and politicians are important in this book, but they do not dominate it. Well over half of the narrative is taken up with social, cultural, and scientific phenomena. It is significant that the author devotes forty pages to the work of William C. Gorgas ("A Modern Warrior") and only six pages to the second election of William McKinley.

Our Times portrays the surface manifestations of early twentieth-century life in the United States, but it fails to deal in any sustained way with the deeper currents of the national experience. This volume illustrates many of the limitations of the series. The political treatment of the years 1896-1903, organized around some of the more conspicuous national leaders, is episodic and journalistic. Many aspects of the period's politics, including the agrarian revolt and the Populist movement, are ignored or inadequately discussed. In his elaborate consideration of the money question, Sullivan advances a debatable theory as to the relation of politics in the nineties to the "increase of the population of the country out of proportion to the supply of gold." There is no real analysis of economic trends, of the labor movement, or of the more profound intellectual currents. Sullivan shows no awareness of the increasing stratification of American society, nor does he deal with the elaboration of the Jim Crow system in the South and other evidences of racism in the United States at the turn of the century.

However inadequate it may be by modern standards as a serious work of history, *Our Times*, as this first volume demonstrates, is a fascinating period piece. It has, as one reviewer noted, "all of the raciness of a fresh news story." The author's *dramatis personae*—Bryan, Roosevelt, Dewey, Gorgas—comprise a cast of remarkable and diverse leading characters. His sketches of these and other figures are skillfull and discerning. While he fails to analyze the underlying influences in turn-of-the-century politics, he does illuminate the political culture as it was experienced by the average American of the day. He also tells us something about the making—and destroying—of heroes in America.

This volume's contribution to an understanding of the emerging popular culture at the beginning of the period is more important. It has much to say about popular preoccupations, working habits, and patterns of leisure, about material objects that served and amused Americans, about arts that instructed, entertained, and inspired the people. Where else can one find easily available such an engaging essay as the one on "changing styles in dogs"? Sullivan wanted to include in his story "many things about the stage, popular periodicals, art, the rise of the short story, and the like." "To illustrate what I am trying to say," he wrote Charles Dana Gibson in February, 1924, "there is no better example than your own case. Your drawings not only had an immense vogue and therefore belong in a history of the period, as a mere record of the vogue they had; but in addition to that your art had some effect on the point of view of young people. It reflected itself . . . in their dress and their manners. So you can see how, as it seems to me, your art belongs in a history of that period."

A final observation about the first volume of *Our Times* may be appropriate. The book has an enormous cumulative impact upon the reader. Despite its rambling and disjointed character as a narrative, it somehow manages (perhaps Sullivan planned it that way!) to call forth much of the mood and outlook of the turn of the century. "It has been like living over most of my life," exclaimed "Ding" the cartoonist, after reading the section on the 1890's. The note of self-congratulation, the interest in probing the national future, the persistent moralism, the exaltation of material progress, the new awareness of the nation's larger role in world affairs, the sense of wonder and of infinite possibilities in the applications of science to technology and industry, even the beginnings of the American's love affair with the automobile—all of these aspects of that long-ago era are brought to life in the pages that follow.

Dewey W. Grantham
Vanderbilt University

AUTHOR'S FOREWORD

AVONDALE is a village in Southeastern Pennsylvania, in Chester County; it is about 40 miles west of Philadelphia and about 8 north of the Mason and Dixon line, where that historic boundary curves in an arc to the north, to make room for the "hundreds" of Delaware. (A "hundred" as the name for the smallest unit of government goes back to pre-Norman England; Delaware is, I think, the only place in America where it is preserved.) The streams about Avondale flow south into Delaware Bay; a little to the west is a slight rise in the land, a plain just high enough to make a water-shed, beyond which the streams flow into the Susquehanna River and Chesapeake Bay.

It is a countryside of soft, rolling hills and tranquil winding creeks; of old, well-tilled farms, many of them long held in the same families, with practically every farm preserving a wood-lot, a bit of the primeval wilderness, made up mainly of oaks, with some poplars and an occasional hickory, and, until a blight that came in the early 1900's, many chestnuts, out of which the farmers split the posts and rails for their fences, which here still resist the invasion of the iron post and steel wire. If the wood-lot is on low ground, there are beeches; on the edges the dog-wood salutes the spring with broad white petals. Along the streams are many willows, thriftily preserved to guard against loss of the soil by flood. In the meadows stand occasional black walnuts, some locusts, and here and there a gum tree; the gum tree is the herald of autumn: when its leaves begin to show red, the farmer knows that corn-cutting time is just ahead. The crops are much the same as those first planted on the virgin soil; wheat, corn and potatoes remain staples; clover and timothy for hay have given way to alfalfa; oats has diminished in proportion as the horse has retired before the automobile — when gasoline first appeared, local jest called it "oats for the car." By the side of each fat barn a tall silo is a comparative modernism; milk has become a principal "money crop."

It is a fertile land; a township near Avondale was named by the early settlers "New Garden." Those early settlers must have escaped a part, at least, of the pangs of home-sickness, for the Avondale countryside looked, and still looks much like some parts of the rural England from which they came. Their origin, and some of their institutions, are commemorated by the local place-names: Chatham, Oxford, Nottingham, Chesterville, London Grove, Penn Green, Kennett Square, Marlborough. (Two of the near-by villages kept Indian names, Toughkennamon and Hockessin.) Within five miles of Avondale are seven Quaker meeting-houses, nearly all dating back to the early settlement, some now disused, but all kept up in simple dignity, brooding upon the burying-grounds that surround them, in the older of which, according with Quaker tradition, the headstones rise no more than nine or ten inches above the trimmed grass. Like the churches, the farmhouses are well kept up, many of solid stone or brick. Three tall evergreens in front of the house is a local custom almost universally maintained. It is a lovely country, soft to the eye and sweet to the spirit, with appealing suggestions of comfort, security, a wholesome way of life, a tempo attuned to nature's own, traditions, affectionate attachment to the local soil. Had it happened to have, in its two and a half centuries, as many poets as New England, it might have been as well known. No part of America is more American, none more dependable to serve as the type of a settled, working, time-tested order of society.

On an old farm about a mile west of Avondale, I write these words in the room in which I was born. Through the south window, some ten miles away, I can see, and, when the wind is right, faintly hear, the airplanes whir by on their ten daily flights between Washington and New York. Yet as a boy I saw, on the road at the end of our lane, as a familiar spectacle, an institution now so extinct as the drover, he and his helpers, with many a "ho" and "hi," driving cattle "on the hoof" to the Eastern city markets. On the road — still dirt, improved enough to accommodate the automobile but not enough to incautiously invite the through bus or the speeding tourist — the first vehicle I saw not drawn by a horse was a steam "traction engine" (pronounced "en-gyne"), an amazing novelty which, at a pace much slower than a horse, though more powerful, drew the threshing-machine from farm to farm; ahead of it, at a distance of a hundred yards, rode a mounted man with a red flag to warn of danger. Of one form of transportation I have seen the complete cycle; the trolley-car came in the early 1880's, grew for a decade or two, was undermined by the automobile and bus, and, by the time I was fifty, was on the way to desuetude. In the field in front of the house I saw my father reap the wheat with a "cradle." When, at the end of one harvest, he hung the cradle beside the flail on a rafter of the barn, it remained there permanently, for the next year he drove a mechanical marvel called a "reaper." By the time the startling "reaper and binder" came, I was a schoolboy well grown.

Completing this foreword as the short winter afternoon wanes, I turn on the electric light. But this morning, in the attic, I fingered the candle-mould into which, as a boy, I saw my mother pour melted tallow; that was just before kerosene, which we preferred to call, less pretentiously, "coal oil." With a finger and thumb I turn on the steam heat, but in the kitchen is still the fireplace that once was the only source of warmth; on the inner sides are the hooks from which hung the crane.

But not all the span can be described by comparison of new with old. For some of the new is so utterly new that it had no predecessor. In the year in which I was born, there was no telephone, nor any other means of carrying the human voice farther than could be accomplished by a good pair of lungs in a favoring wind. There was no radio, no motion picture. The coming of these, and others like them, with the changes in point-of-view that accompanied them, composes a part of the theme of this history. Of much else with which it deals, the patient reader will be aware as he turns the pages. I hope that he will find as much pleasure in the reading, as I in the writing, of an America that was only yesterday, yet much of which is one with Nineveh and Tyre.

MARK SULLIVAN.

Avondale,
December 8, 1935.

CONTENTS

ILLUSTRATIONS

The Turn of the Century

1

THE TURN OF THE CENTURY

Some Aspects of the Surface of Life in America on New Year's Day, 1900, as Recorded in Those "Diaries of History," the Newspapers. Looking Backward and Looking Forward. The Principal Character in This History. The Picture That America Presented to the Eye in 1900. Old Ways of Life. The "White Man's Burden" and the "Little Brown Brother." High Estate of an Institution About to Fall Upon Evil Days. Some Words That Were Not Yet in the Dictionary and Some Institutions Not Yet in Being.

THE purpose of this narrative is to follow an average American through this quarter-century of his country's history, to recreate the flow of the days as he saw them, to picture events in terms of their influence on him, his daily life and ultimate destiny. The aim is to appraise the actors of history and their activities according to the way they affected the average man, the way he felt about them, the ways in which he was influenced by his leaders, and in which he influenced them.

As democracy in America has expressed itself, the period 1900–25 is unparalleled in the importance of the rôle played by the average man. He was the principal spectator; indeed, he was the whole audience. He not only watched the performance, but largely determined the actions of those who from time to time were upon the stage, regulated the length of their tenure in the spotlight, retired them to the wings, or summoned them back. It was his will or his whim, his applause, his disapproval or his indifference, that dictated the entrances and the exits. He himself was one of the performers — was in fact the principal performer in a more fundamental sense and more continuously than any of the actors; for the drama consisted essentially of the reactions of the average man to the actors and of the actors to him. This average man, this audience, was also in a true sense the author and the stage-manager. In short, he was, as he himself would express it, "pretty near the whole show."

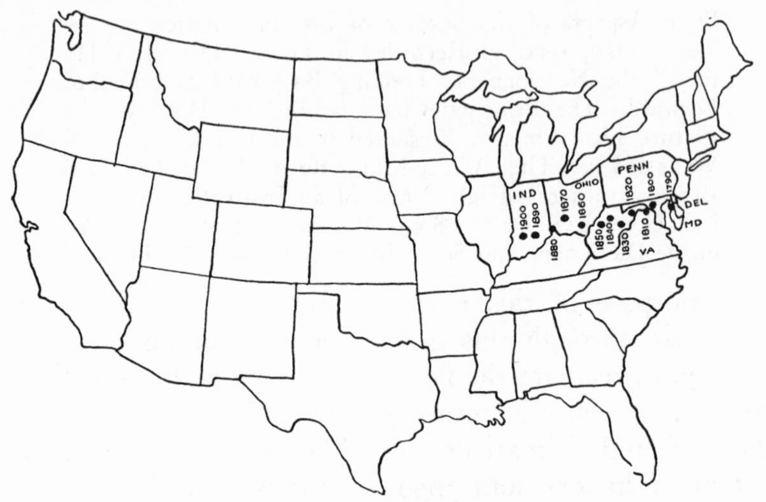

Western movement of the centre of population as determined by the Census Bureau for the decades 1790–1900. In 1900, the centre was six miles west of Columbus, Ind. By 1920, the centre had moved farther west, to the village of Whitehall, Ind.

In habitat this average American is universal. He may slur his r's in Georgia or grind them in Illinois; drawl the gentle r's of the Lone Sta' State, or describe himself as living in the Green Mount-in State. Geographically, he has no boundaries. But if the reader prefers to personify him and give him a local habitat, if he wishes to pick out one average American who shall typify all average Americans, he may take advantage of that statistical accident whereby every decade some small American community is elevated to a curious and, though irrelevant, nevertheless proud and interest-provoking conspicuousness, by emerging as the resultant of the labors of some hundreds of clerks in the Census Bureau. The town determined as the centre of population of the United States in 1900 was named, as it happens, Columbus, in Indiana.[1] It would be squeezing the last drop of significance out of a statistical coincidence to suggest that the town which happened to be the centre of population was also the typical dwelling-place, and had the typical surroundings, of the man who in the same year was the typical American. Yet a fair case might be made out to the effect that the typical American of 1900 had possibly more points of identity with the typical inhabitant of an Indiana community than with most other persons in other backgrounds. Socially, Indiana provided the dramatis personæ of the novels and plays of that American writer who, more nearly than any other during the period this history covers, reflected typical American life, Mr. Booth Tarkington, of Indianapolis.[2] Politically, this average

[1] The exact centre was six miles southeast of Columbus.

[2] "The Man from Home," by Tarkington and Harry Leon Wilson, contains, in the portrait of Daniel Voorhees Pike (who "would not trade the State Insane Asylum at home for the worst ruined ruin in Europe"), as good a picture as any writer may hope to make of the average American male: "His voice has the homely quality of the Central States, clear, quiet, and strong, with a very slight drawl at times when the situation strikes him as humorous, often exhibiting an apologetic character. His English is the United States language as spoken by the average citizen to be met on a day coach anywhere in the Central States. He is clean-shaven, and his hair, which shows a slight tendency to gray, is neatly parted on the left side. His light straw hat . . . like the rest of his apparel, is neither new nor old. His short 'lay-down' collar and cuffs are of white, well-laundered linen. . . . His trousers are . . . not fashionably cut, yet they fit him well and are neither baggy at the knees nor 'high-water.' His shoes . . . show a 'good shine.' In brief, he is just the average well-to-do but untravelled citizen that you might meet on an accommodation train between Logansport and Kokomo, Indiana."

Not only Daniel Voorhees Pike, but Squire Buckalew and the sardonic Mr. Arp in the "Conquest of Canaan"; Alice Adams, her ne'er-do-well brother, and her pathetic father trying to become a successful manufacturer after a lifetime as an employee; Dan Oliphant, of "The Midlander," Sheridan, of "The Turmoil" —these and scores of others pictured by Mr. Tarkington out of his own experiences, compose a gallery of American characters of whom the typicalness and the authenticity are, considering their number and variety, greater than the creations of any other contemporary American author.

Indianan, with his neighbor in Ohio, determined the occupant of the White House for nearly half of all the years from the Civil War to 1925. In politics, the representativeness, so to speak, of the citizen of Indiana and Ohio was universally recognized, and won for him something close to omnipotence; for his ideas, his prejudices, his economic interests, were universally considered and generally deferred to.

However, this suggestion is merely casual, and has no more purpose than to give some slight flesh-and-blood concreteness to what otherwise might be a rather indefinite abstraction, the average American. And in this narrative the average American is not a formless conception; he is the principal character. The reader may seem to lose sight of him for considerable stretches, but he is there, on every page.

II

The American of 1900, reading his paper on Monday morning, New Year's Day, or the Sunday paper of the day before, or almost any paper during the year, observed, with some uneasiness, that the head-lines continued to occupy themselves, as they had for a considerable time, with the Philippines, Cuba, Porto Rico, Guam, Aguinaldo, the Igorrotes; words which three years before had had no more meaning to him than to stir old memories of something he had seen in his schoolboy geographies — you couldn't even be confident how to pronounce the names. Now they came close. His favorite politicians demanded that he think about them. Bryan[1] told him we should put

[1] Annexation overseas was the principal issue of the presidential campaign of 1900. The Republicans called it expansion, the Democrats called it imperialism and militarism. Some details of it are covered in chapters 13, 20, and 21. The problem of devising a form of government for each of our dependencies, which troubled Congress and the Supreme Court for several years, was worked out in the "Insular Decisions" discussed in chapter 21. Other aspects of the Spanish War, its aftermath and effects, are described in chapters 21 and 22.

them away, Beveridge that we should embrace them. Some of his neighbors were infected with the pride that some newspapers and some orators conveyed in resounding phrases about America, the new world-power. Others, far from satisfied, felt it was an unanticipated result of

From "The Leader," Pittsburgh.

A twentieth-century prospect.
The expansion sentiment here pictured and the prediction made by the cartoonist reached its full tide in 1900 and later ebbed.

the war with Spain, not clearly announced on the programme, that had left these waifs of the world on our door-step. They didn't seem to fit the American idea of a family of States, didn't seem quite the sort of folks we could take fully into our family circle, as adopted children should be taken if they are taken at all. We weren't quite sure we wanted them, or what we should do with them. Would it be self-interest to refuse them? Should we follow those who preached that these orphans of the storm were a call to duty? Much advice and exhortation was afloat. It was in February of the year before, 1899, that Kipling had given out his poem:

> Take up the White Man's burden,
> Send forth the best ye breed . . .
> To wait in heavy harness,
> On fluttering folk and wild —
> Your new-caught sullen peoples,
> Half devil and half child.[1]

That poem had a powerful effect on sentimental minds, or minds responsive to the call of adventure; but the average American was probably as much impressed by the less exalted verse which Colonel Henry Watterson — with rather irresponsible neglect to discriminate among the divers varieties of people in our new acquisitions — called to the aid of a strong expression of editorial feeling in the Louisville *Courier-Journal:*

[1] "The White Man's Burden" was taken as being addressed partly to America in its adventure in the Philippines, and partly to Kipling's own country in its attempt to master the Boers. Some one said of it: "In winged words it circled the earth in a day, and by repetition became hackneyed in a week." Some one else, that it "revealed a necessary but thankless task to be performed by the white race under the restraints of conscience."

Of course the parodists did not fail to see the rich opportunity in Kipling's assuming the benevolence of the White Man's point of view. One, in the New York *Times*, voiced a possible point of view of the Burden, or those who, like the Boers, ardently resisted being made a Burden:

> "Take up the White Man's burden;
> Send forth your sturdy sons,
> And load them down with whiskey
> And Testaments and guns.
> Throw in a few diseases
> To spread in tropic climes,
> For there the healthy niggers
> Are quite behind the times.
> And don't forget the factories!
> On those benighted shores . . .
> They never work twelve hours a day,
> And live in strange content. . . ."

In the 1900 campaign of the Democrats against imperialism, Richard Croker, when asked for his definition of anti-imperialism, replied: "My idea of anti-imperialism is opposition to the fashion of shooting everybody who doesn't speak English."

But the riff-raff; Lord, the riff-raff: injun, nigger, beggar-man, thief —

"Both mongrel, puppy, whelp, and hound,
And cur of low degree."

The Philippines, we felt, were something vaguely Asiatic. As to them, the average American's sentiment was less accurately expressed by the benevolent phrase of the kindly Mr. Taft, "the little brown brother," than by the ballad which that phrase inspired an American soldier,

Some of America's newly acquired dependents—bow and arrow men from the mountains of Luzon, P. I.

made cynical by closer personal and hostile contact than Mr. Taft as Governor-General had had, to write:

He may be a brother of Big Bill Taft;
But he ain't no brother of mine.[1]

[1] This was a common word-of-mouth version. The original, by Robert F. Morrison, in the Manila Sunday *Sun*, began:

"I'm only a common soldier-man, in the blasted Philippines;
They say I've got Brown Brothers here, but I dunno what it means.
I like the word Fraternity, but still I draw the line;
He *may* be a brother of William H. Taft, but he ain't no friend of mine.

I never had a brother who would beg to get a drink
To keep himself from dying when he hovered on the brink;

III

Hardly less than in our own adventure in the Philippines, America in 1900 was interested in the British effort to conquer the Boers, which, during the early part

A Chicago *Inter-Ocean* cartoon reflecting pride in expansion.

of that year, was going badly. That fact gave strong satisfaction to the average American. In the form in

And when my Pal had give it him, and emptied out his sack,
Would take the opportunity to stick him in the back."

Another ditty that expressed soldier opinion of the Filipinos began with the simplest and most emphatic affirmation of disapproval:

"Damn, damn, damn the Filipino."

And included the exhortation:

"Underneath the starry flag,
Civilize him with a Krag."

which the conflict staged itself to the American eye, the Boer was kin to the American himself. He was a free man, economically independent; he was fighting against oppression by highly trained forces, greatly superior in numbers, equipment, organization, and the other leverages of power. The American inevitably thought of the analogy to his own struggle for independence. Recalling that most affectionately held group among all the traditions of his history, Bunker Hill, Valley Forge, George Washington, Israel Putnam, Nathan Hale, he thought of Oom Paul Kruger, Cronje, and De Wet in the same terms.

In the beginning the British papers had talked about the Boers as if they were a mere fly on the track of progress. They had said the British soldiers would eat their Christmas dinner in Pretoria — the Queen sent out chocolate specially stamped for that anticipated celebration. When the Boers administered defeat after defeat to the British, the average American jeered. He applauded stage travesties of the overconfident British. He laughed when the papers lampooned them, in such witticisms as: "The surprise party is the chief amusement of the Boer social season,"[1] and: "The Boers are good billiard shots — they are great at reversing the English." [2]

Even so austerely restrained a periodical as *The Review of Reviews*, one so habitually conscious of high responsibility for amity and good manners among nations, reflected, in this case, the emotion of Americans generally in a passage that pointed out "a ludicrous aspect to the heroics and hysterics of the London press":

> The very same London papers which a few days ago thought the Boers could not and would not fight, and that a few British regiments could go to Pretoria without firing a shot, have now

[1] The Memphis *Commercial-Appeal.*

[2] *The Tiger,* journal of undergraduate wit at Princeton.

gone to the opposite extreme of regarding the Boer armies as the most formidable ever known in the history of warfare, and are begging their readers to consider that the British Empire is engaged in a life-and-death struggle. . . . This tone merely invites the contempt of the world, while it also provokes the freer expression of enthusiastic admiration for the magnificent stand of the Dutch farmers against such overwhelming odds.

When the British finally conquered the Boers, *Life* (November 15, 1900) said: "A small boy with diamonds is no match for a large burglar with experience." This active sympathy which the average American had for the Boers, coupled with biting disapproval[1] of the British, his hero sentiment for Cronje and De Wet in their rough country clothes as against the spick-and-span military correctness of the British generals, his pleasure at the little armies of Boer irregulars administering defeat after defeat to the much larger armies of British regulars, was more than a mere incident of the news. It had permanent importance, because it was one contribution to a certain mood that was prevalent in America in 1900, a mood of championship for the under dog

[1] Because the present chapter aims to picture life in 1900 as the average American saw it, I have given the prevailing and characteristic point of view about the Boer War. Some thoughtful Americans, better informed about our foreign relations and world affairs, recalled the helpful sympathy we had received from Great Britain during our war with Spain. As John Hay, then the American ambassador to Great Britain, put it, in a letter to Senator Lodge: "[Great Britain] is the only European country whose sympathies are not openly against us." On May 13, 1898, twelve days after the battle of Manila Bay, Joseph Chamberlin, then a Cabinet Minister and outstanding leader of British thought, said in a public speech: "What is our next duty? It is to establish and to maintain bonds of permanent amity with our kinsmen across the Atlantic. . . . They speak our language. They are bred of our race." This gesture of support from England was of the highest importance to America. Recollection of it influenced thoughtful Americans and determined the official attitude of the American Government during the Boer War. This point of view was in the mind of the editor of *Harper's Weekly* who, when popular devotion to the Boers was at its height, courageously—though his phraseology was inept—reminded his readers: "Whether we think the war against the Boers was unjust or for the welfare of civilization, what sympathies we have to express should be for the mother country. . . . We cannot lose sight of the stupendous fact that British prestige is in mortal danger. Nor can we fail, if we have a proper pride of race, or a decent sense of gratitude . . . to mourn over their disasters.

against the upper, a disposition of the average American to see himself as an under dog in economic situations and controversies in his own country. That prevailing

From a drawing in "Black and White" (London).

General Piet Cronje, Boer leader.
American sentiment was prevailingly pro-Boer and supported Kruger, Cronje, De Wet, and other Boer leaders. Photographs of them and stories about them appeared almost daily in the American newspapers of 1900.

American mood of 1900 determined much that happened after 1900 in our politics and social organization.

IV

If the American, reading the papers of New Year's Day, 1900, was more than commonly reflective over the serious aspects of the news, it was only partly because the sporting page and the comic strip had not yet arrived to overbalance the American newspaper on the side of the merely diverting. It was due also to the presence in the newspapers of that day and in the sermons of the day before, of a spirit of solemnity, occasioned by the coming of a new year and, as some said, a new century.

Throughout 1899 there had been much discussion as to what day and year marked the close of the nineteenth century and the beginning of the twentieth. It was recognized by everybody as a turning-point, a hundred-mile stone. There was a human disposition to sum things up, to say who had been the greatest men of the century just closed, what had been the greatest books, the greatest inventions, the greatest advances in science. Looking forward, there was a similar disposition to forecast and predict. This appealed to nearly everybody; and to find people disputing the correctness of the date you chose for harking back or looking forward was an irritation. Wherever men met they argued about it. Editorials dealt with it, seriously or facetiously. Contentious persons wrote letters to the papers. School-children were set to figuring. It grew to the vogue of one of those puzzles like "How old is Ann?"

A learned editor, Doctor Albert Shaw, settled the question for his readers in his magazine[1] for January, 1900. With somewhat the air of an Olympian so wise he can afford to be tolerant, he gently rebuked those who were disputing about so clear a thing:

> There has been a curious misapprehension in the minds of many people, and even in print there has been a good deal of allusion to the year now ending [1899] as the closing one of the nineteenth century.

Having thus, in his capacity of commentator on events, recorded a dispute, which, because it existed, one must take account of, Doctor Shaw proceeded with an air be-

[1] *The Review of Reviews.*

coming to unassailable authority, an air which seemed to say: "Of course, you understand I'm not arguing with you; I'm merely telling you":

> A half-minute's clear thinking is enough to remove all confusion. With December 31 we complete the year 1899 — that is to say, we round out 99 of the 100 years that are necessary to complete a full century. We must give the nineteenth century the 365 days that belong to its hundredth and final year, before we begin the year 1 of the twentieth century. The mathematical faculty works more keenly in monetary affairs than elsewhere; and none of the people who have proposed to allow ninety-nine years to go for a century would suppose that a $1,900 debt had been fully met by a tender of $1,899.[1]

V

Among the more scintillating facets of the surface of life as reflected in the newspapers on January 1, 1900, the Indianapolis *Journal* recorded that "A. P. Hurst, a drygoods salesman from New York, interviewed at the Bates Hotel last night," assured the world that:

> The shirtwaist will be with us more than ever this summer. Women are wearing shirtwaists because they are comfortable, because they can be made to fit any form, and because they are mannish. Sleeves will be smaller, but still not tight.

[1] This pronouncement the present writer accepts as having mathematical soundness. Nevertheless this history chooses to be as illogical as those who differed with Doctor Shaw; and takes January 1, 1900, as its starting-point. It does so for much the same reason that animated those who did not agree with Doctor Shaw—a reason, that is, which is not a reason at all, and not within the world of reason but within the world of imagination. January 1, 1900, appeals to the human imagination, seems to the eye, and sounds to the ear, more like the beginning of a century than does January 1, 1901. January 1, 1900, therefore is taken as the date of the beginning of the quarter-century that this history covers. But, though one may go back a year farther at the beginning, one cannot be in the position of denying that the quarter-century ended December 31, 1925. Not twenty-five years, therefore, is the scope of this work, but twenty-six. Twenty-six, and yet considerably more, at the beginning, for events do not separate themselves into such smoothly cut sections as the calendar; nor do the characters of history come into being with any such accommodating regard for those numerical landmarks that are the convenience of historians. And so it has been necessary to include many things that trailed over from the nineteenth century.

"The shirtwaist," the confident Mr. Hurst assured a world too supine in its submission to the dogma that change is a cosmic law — "the shirtwaist has come to stay." [1]

The shirtwaist vogue of 1900.
Three patterns "specially designed" for the *Ladies' Home Journal* of May, 1899.

Concerning another institution there was an equally confident assertion of secure optimism as to the present and future state of trade. The advertisement of Budweiser — name potent and far-flung in those days —

[1] Not quite. This is an early and trivial example of a lesson that we shall find repeated rather often, and in more serious connections; namely, that permanence is a rare commodity. Within a little more than three years after this sanguine travelling salesman's prediction, a Chicago *Tribune* poet was writing, in March, 1903, under the caption "Vale the Shirtwaist":

"Sad news; bad news;
Anything but glad news!
What do you suppose they're saying
At the fashion show?— . . .
They declare the shirtwaist girl
Must pack her trunk and go."

Though its great vogue was destined to pass, the shirtwaist really was so popular, was so much talked about, as to seem to justify the expectation that it had "come to stay." While it was at its height, in June, 1900, a Detroit *Free Press* poet conscripted a presumably indignant muse to glorify it:

"When gentle June displays her wares,
And of her beauties boast [*sic*],
The contest shows beyond a doubt,
The shirtwaist's worn the most."

took the form of a congratulatory telegram from the manufacturer:

> NEW YEAR GREETING. IMPORTANT TELEGRAM
> St. Louis, Mo., Dec. 31, 1899.
>
> J. L. Bieler, Indianapolis, Ind.
>
> Prediction of our last year's message pale [*sic*] in the presence of our trade reports for 1899. We have reached the highest point in our history. Our motto "Nothing is too good for the American people" has found prompt and generous response. In return we send with a hearty goodwill our wishes for a Happy New Year.
>
> ADOLPHUS BUSCH, President,
> Anheuser-Busch Brewing Association.

The writer, having in mind a generation of readers of whom many were born after 1900, is puzzled whether he had better explain that the reference was to beer, real beer; to Budweiser, brand-word that once blazed ornately in the windows of 10,000 saloons, blurred the landscape with its billboards; which was a national institution in much the same sense as baseball, ice-cream, or the Ford automobile; which was the subject, a few years later, of a popular song:

Bud Budweiser's a friend of mine, friend of mine; yes, a friend of mine.
What care I if the sun don't shine while I've got Budweiser?
That's the reason I feel so fine, feel so fine; yes, I feel so fine;
For though Bill the Kaiser's a friend of Budweiser's,
Budweiser's a friend of mine.

Liquor in various aspects occupied a good deal of the attention of the newspapers of January 1, 1900. The Boston *Transcript* sedately deplored the city's record of 26,000 drunks in a year, but believed that "an evil sure to exist under any circumstances can better be kept within bounds by restriction than by prohibition." The

Raleigh, N. C., *News and Observer*[1] reported the sudden death from impure whiskey of "eight prime young negroes" — a phrase recalling slavery. (There were localisms such as that all over the not yet standardized America of 1900.) The Wichita, Kans., *Beacon* recorded that burglars in Davidson's saloon had robbed the slot machine of eight dollars, but "did not disturb the stocks of liquor"; a discrimination which did not at that time necessarily reflect extreme abstemiousness, but which in 1925 would be inexplicable on any commercial basis. In Utica, N. Y., a liquor-dealer offered through *The Press*, "rye, bourbon, and Canada malt whiskey, $2 per gallon; strictly pure California wines, 75 cents per gallon." The Fargo, N. D., *Forum* reported that "the blind pig situation in Mandan has reached the acute stage; the saloon men . . . have raised a fund of $1,800 to head off the prosecution." The Portland *Oregonian* reported a New Year's sermon: "The agitation against side entrances to saloons has not attained permanence and the recent organization of liquor-dealers to defeat reform has revealed the saloon in its true light as an institute of vice."

As an antidote to organization and money on the side of the liquor-sellers, there was just getting under way an organization on the other side, destined to be the Nemesis of the saloon. The Washington, Pa., *Reporter* carried this announcement:

> A meeting is called for Tuesday evening, January 2, 1900, at 7.30 at the First Presbyterian Church, to consider the question of the organization of an Anti-Saloon League.[2]

The Omaha, Neb., *World-Herald* printed advertisements of "sugar, 4c. lb.; eggs, 14c. a dozen." The

[1] All the newspaper quotations in this section are from issues of January 1, 1900, except the advertisement from the St. Louis *Post-Dispatch*, which was printed a few weeks before.

[2] The Anti-Saloon League, as a nation-wide institution, was organized through the union of some local leagues at Washington, D. C., December 18, 1895.

Williamsport, Pa., *Gazette and Bulletin*, "potatoes 35c. to 45c. a bushel, butter 24c. to 25c. a pound." The Dallas, Tex., *News*, "top hogs $4.15." Wheat was 70c. a bushel; corn, 33 cents; Texas steers, $4.25 a hundred.[1]

Liquor advertisements in the newspapers and magazines of 1900 were as common as those of any other business.

The Boston *Herald:* "Boarders Wanted; turkey dinner, 20 cents; supper or breakfast, 15 cents." In the Trenton, N. J., *Times*, the United States Hotel quoted rates of "$1 per day; furnished rooms 50 cents — horse sheds for country shoppers." In the Chicago *Tribune*, Siegel,

[1] While Texas readers will understand this terminology of the cattle market, it seems wise, for the benefit of the startled New York proofreader who queries the word "hundred," to explain that in this connection it means hundredweight.

Cooper & Co. advertised: "Ladies' muslin nightgowns, 19c.; 50-inch all-wool sponged and shrunk French cheviots, water and dust proof serges, all high-class fabrics, warranted for color and wear, 79c." In the same paper "The Fair" offered "women's shoes, worth \$3, for sale at \$1.97; misses' and children's shoes, \$1.19." In the Decatur, Ills., *Review* was advertised: "A good well-made corset in long or short style, all sizes; our price, 50 cents." Gingham was 5c. a yard; men's box-calf shoes \$2.50; "Stein-Bloch suits that were \$13 to \$17, now \$10"; men's suits that were \$8 to \$13, for \$5.50. "Ten dollar overcoats for six dollars." In the Los Angeles *Express* an advertisement said: "Wanted, Jan. 8, lady cashier for store; salary \$8 a week; name 2 or 3 references."

Help Wanted—Female.

GIRLS WANTED, over 14, to label samples, \$2.50. The National Cloak Co., 112 W. 24th st.

Help Wanted—Male.

STENOGRAPHER and typewriter for a downtown commercial house; salary about \$10 per week; preference given to one who can read and write Spanish. Address, giving age and reference, D. F. C., Export, P. O. box 2301, N. Y.

BOY WANTED to work in saloon & learn bartending. Apply 23 E. 17th st.

HELP WANTED—FEMALE.

Household Help Wanted—Female.

CHAMBERMAID wanted for nurses' training school, to live out; hours 7.30 A. M. to 2.30 P. M.; \$40 per month. Apply 1086 Lexington av. (near 76th).

GIRL, white, housework, plain cooking; small Christian family; afternoons and evenings only; sleep out. M 504 World, Harlem.

HELP WANTED—MALE

CLERK, with time-keeping experience, hours 6.30 A. M. to 2.30 P. M.; \$110 month; state age, experience; religion. F. 846 World.

A contrast between 1900 and 1925.

The advertisements in the left-hand column, offering such wages as ten dollars a week and less for stenographers, are reproduced from the New York *World* of January 4, 1900. Those in the second column appeared in the same paper just twenty-five years later, January 1, 1925.

The St. Louis *Post-Dispatch* received within twenty-four hours 725 answers to an advertisement that had read:

NIGHT WATCHMAN WANTED — Must be fairly well educated, neat of appearance, able-bodied, and if necessary be ready to furnish bond; none but those who can show absolute proofs of their honesty and sobriety in all senses of the word need apply; hours, 6 to 6, Monday to Friday (off Saturday nights); 1 P. M. Sunday to 6 A. M. Monday; salary $15 per week; state whether married or single and inclose references. Address in own handwriting, H 789, *Post-Dispatch.*

In the Chicago *Tribune* a patent-medicine advertisement proclaimed: "General Joe Wheeler Praises Peruna." Similar testimonials were by three United States senators. One, from a senator from Mississippi, read:

> For some time I have been a sufferer from catarrh in its most incipient stage. So much so that I became alarmed as to my general health. But hearing of Peruna as a good remedy, I gave it a fair trial, and soon began to improve. I take pleasure in recommending your great natural catarrh cure. Peruna is the best I have ever tried.

The Duluth, Minn., *News-Tribune* advertised a brand of tobacco as "not made by a trust," a form of commendation frequent in trade slogans of that time of anti-monopoly sentiment. In the Hartford, Conn., *Courant* the American Bicycle Company advertised: "The 1900 bevel-gear chainless; ideal mount for road or track." The West Chester, Pa., *Local News* reflected the pre-ammonia, pre-electric method of storing up coolness for the summer: "Horace Sinclair and William Tanguy are filling their ice-houses to-day with six-inch ice from the Brandywine." A Trenton, N. J., store, daringly unconventional, advertised a skirt, specially made for skating, "short enough to avoid entanglement with the skates." The fashion notes of the New Orleans *Item* praised light-weight skirts, "as they can be gathered up in the hand and kept clear of muddy pavements." The Tacoma, Wash., *News-Tribune* described the preparations of many Tacomans to join the rush to the new Alaska gold-field, at Nome. The Wichita, Kans., *Beacon* recorded a heated fight between those who wanted the proposed Arkansas River bridge wide enough to carry the street-car tracks, and those who claimed the street-cars would frighten the horses. In all the advertising pages of the Baltimore *Sun* the word "automobile" did not appear, but there were columns of advertisements of broughams, rockaways, Germantowns, opera wagonettes, phaetons, buggies, runabouts, tally-hos. In the same paper a dancing academy avowed its capacity to transmit "quick mastery of the waltz and German."

The Sacramento, Cal., *Union* (then *Record-Union*) printed a city ordinance in black-face type providing a fine of twenty dollars or imprisonment for fifty days as a safeguard against a suspected labor-saving device of the Chinese, principal purveyors of starched cleanliness in the days before mechanical washing and ironing:

> It shall be unlawful for any person owning, carrying on or conducting any public laundry in the city of Sacramento to spray the clothing of any person or persons being laundered therein with water or other fluid emitted from the mouth.

The Tulsa (then Indian Territory, now Oklahoma[1]) *Democrat*, at that time a weekly, had no January 1 issue, but on January 7, 1900, devoted itself to some self-congratulatory statistics. The population had reached 1340; President Kurn of the Frisco Railroad was quoted as saying Tulsa had become the biggest point of traffic origin in the Territory; the car-load business for the week was given as: "Receipts: 1 car bran; shipments: 2 cars hogs, 1 car sand, 1 car mules." In the world of matters less exclusively commercial, *The Democrat* chronicled the

[1] Of the contrasts within this quarter-century that are within my personal acquaintance, and which typify one of the outstanding characteristics of the period, namely the rapid material growth of America, one of the most vivid is illustrated in the person of James J. McGraw, of Tulsa, Okla. On the opening of the Cherokee Strip, September 16, 1893, Mr. McGraw, as a sixteen-year-old boy in a homeseeker family, saw the Territory as an open prairie on which there was not one human being, every one having been cleared off by the soldiers, who that day stood at spaced intervals in front of the long line of "sooners," each soldier with revolver pointed skyward, ready to fire at noon the signal for the homestead rush. Twenty-eight years later, Mr. McGraw was president of The Exchange National Bank of Tulsa, capital and surplus over $4,000,000, annual business over $40,000,000, housed in a twelve-story skyscraper, in a city of 110,000 people.

In 1900, Tulsa, Okla., was a straggling one-street town. Eleven years before it did not exist. This photograph was taken in 1893.

Tulsa, Okla., in 1924. In this year it was a city of 110,000.

The president of the Exchange National Bank (in the tall building at the left of the photograph) is James J. McGraw. As a boy, Mr. McGraw saw Oklahoma when, in the entire length and breadth of it, there was not one white man. He participated with his family in the first rush of settlers to the Cherokee strip in 1893.

approaching nuptials of Mary, daughter of Chief Frank Corndropper, the ceremony to include a transfer of several hundred ponies to the bride's father by the bridegroom (who must be a full-blood).

VI

In his newspapers of January 1, 1900, the American found no such word as radio,[1] for that was yet twenty years from coming; nor "movie," for that too was still mainly of the future; nor chauffeur, for the automobile was only just emerging and had been called "horseless carriage" when treated seriously, but rather more frequently, "devil-wagon," and the driver, the "engineer." There was no such word as aviator — all that that word implies was still a part of the Arabian Nights. Nor was there any mention of income tax or surtax, no annual warnings of the approach of March 15 — all that was yet thirteen years from coming. In 1900 doctors had not heard of 606 or of insulin; science had not heard of relativity or the quantum theory. Farmers had not heard of tractors, nor bankers of the Federal Reserve System. Merchants had not heard of chain-stores nor "self-service"; nor seamen of oil-burning engines. Modernism had not been added to the common vocabulary of theology, nor futurist and "cubist" to that of art. Politicians had not heard of direct primaries, nor of the commission form of government, nor of city managers, nor of blocs in Congress, nor of a League of Nations, nor of a World Court.[2] They had not heard of "muck-rakers," nor of

[1] The number of new words added to the dictionary between 1900 and 1925, and new uses of old words, is a reflection of the expanding of man's intelligence and the increasing complexity of civilization. Nearly a thousand were used to adjust the radio to the language. Hundreds were required for the automobile, its parts and associations; yet more hundreds for the popular and technical terminology of aviation.

[2] They had not heard of the World Court of the nineteen-twenties, but they had heard of a previous incarnation of the idea. It was in January, 1900, that

"Bull Moose" except in a zoological sense. Neither had they heard of "dry" and "wet" as categories important in vote-getting, nor of a Volstead Act; they had not heard of an Eighteenth Amendment, nor a Nineteenth, nor a Seventeenth, nor a Sixteenth — there were but fifteen amendments in 1900, and the last had been passed in 1869.

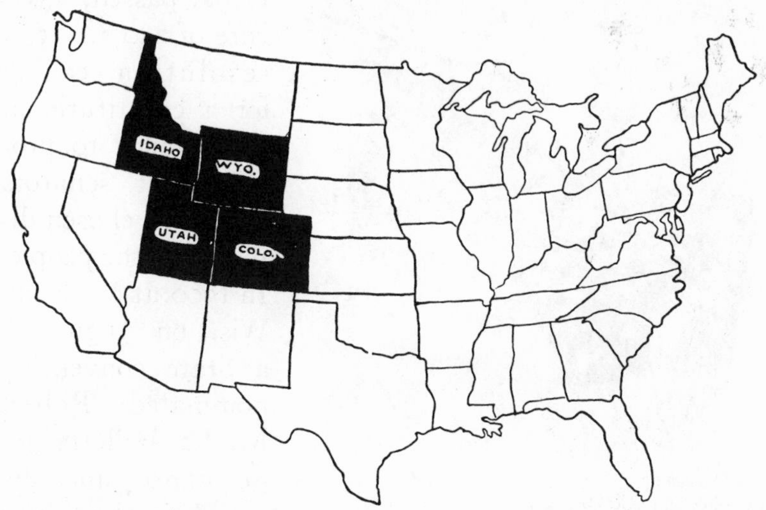

In 1900 woman suffrage had made only a beginning, in four thinly populated Western States: Wyoming, 1869; Colorado, 1893; Utah, 1896; Idaho, 1896.

In 1900 woman suffrage had only made a beginning, in four thinly peopled Western States. A woman governor or a woman congressman was a humorous idea, far-fetched, to be sure, yet one out of which a particularly fertile humorist, on the stage or in the papers,

the Senate debated ratification of The Hague Convention for the Settlement of International Disputes. In the January, 1900, *Review of Reviews*, the editor, Albert Shaw, was using phrases that later became familiar in another connection: "For the Senate to refuse to ratify the treaty, in this transitional year which is ushering in a new century, would be making history in the retrograde rather than the progressive sense. . . . We join . . . in respectfully asking the senators, without regard to party affiliations, to honor themselves . . . by voting cheerfully to make the United States a party to this international agreement."

could get much whimsical burlesque. In 1900, the Lower House of Congress, in the spirit of a popular slogan that said "Let the people elect their senators," and stimulated by two recent scandals in the naming of senators by State legislatures in Montana and Pennsylvania, passed, by a vote of 240 to 15, a resolution calling for a constitutional amendment to provide that senators should be chosen directly by the people. In 1900, at Madison, Wis., on August 8, a State convention nominated Robert M. La Follette for governor and demanded that the system of party conventions and caucuses for governor be abolished, and that nominations for political office be made by "direct primaries."[1]

Courtesy of Armour & Company.

In the old days the cattleman was often a peddler, taking his stock from one butcher to another for sale. This was still remembered in 1900.

The newspapers of 1900 contained no mention of smoking[2] by women, nor of "bobbing," nor "permanent

[1] The first "direct primary" was held in September, 1900, in Minneapolis. The law providing for it had been passed by the Minnesota State legislature during the session of 1899. It was so worded as to confine the first experiment to the largest city of the State, "with the purpose of bringing to light the merits and defects of the system before it should be applied to the entire State." The innovation was described by Senator Washburn as "the greatest political proposition ever introduced into American politics."

[2] Indeed there was a distinct movement against smoking by men. Three important railroads put in effect, on January 1, 1900, a rule against smoking, what the Washington, Pa., *Reporter*, in recording the edict, called "the nasty cigarette."

wave," nor vamp, nor flapper, nor jazz, nor feminism, nor birth-control. There was no such word as rum-runner, nor hijacker, nor bolshevism, fundamentalism, behaviorism, Nordic, Freudian, complexes, ectoplasm, brain-storm, Rotary, Kiwanis, blue-sky law, cafeteria, automat, sundae; nor mah-jong, nor cross-word puzzle.

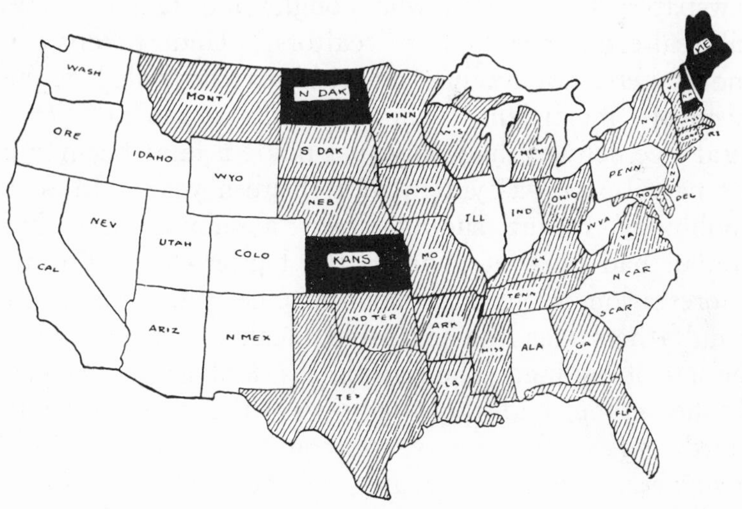

Prohibition had made little headway by 1900. Only the States in black were completely dry. The shaded ones were partially dry.

Not even military men had heard of camouflage; neither that nor "propaganda" had come into the vocabulary of the average man. "Over the top," "zero hour," "no man's land" meant nothing to him. "Drive" meant only an agreeable experience with a horse. The newspapers of 1900 had not yet come to the lavishness of photographic illustration that was to be theirs by the end of the quarter-century. There were no rotogravure sections. If there had been, they would not have pictured boy scouts, nor State constabularies, nor traffic cops, nor Ku Klux Klan parades; nor women riding astride, nor the nudities of the Follies, nor one-piece bathing-suits, nor advertisements of lip-sticks, nor motion-picture actresses, for there were no such things.

In 1900, "short-haired woman" was a phrase of jibing; women doctors were looked on partly with ridicule, partly with suspicion. Of prohibition and votes for women, the most conspicuous function was to provide material for newspaper jokes. Men who bought and sold lots were still real-estate agents, not "realtors." Undertakers were undertakers, not having yet attained the frilled euphemism of "mortician." There were "star-routes" yet — rural free delivery had only just made a faint beginning; the parcel-post was yet to wait thirteen years. In 1900, "bobbing" meant sliding down a snow-covered hill; woman had not yet gone to the barber-shop. For the deforestation of the male countenance, the razor of our grandfathers was the exclusive means; men still knew the art of honing. The hairpin, as well as the bicycle, the horseshoe, and the buggy were the bases of established and, so far as any one could foresee, permanent businesses. Ox-teams could still be seen on country roads; horse-drawn street-cars in the cities. Horses or mules for trucks were practically universal;[1] livery-stables were everywhere. The blacksmith beneath the spreading chestnut-tree was a reality; neither the garage mechanic nor the chestnut blight had come to retire that scene to poetry. The hitching-post had not been supplanted by the parking problem. Croquet had not given way to golf. "Boys in blue" had not yet passed into song. Army blue was not merely a sentimental memory, had not succumbed to the invasion of utilitarianism in olive green. G. A. R. were still potent letters.

[1] A very few motor-trucks of European make had come to America just before 1900. The first American-made gasoline truck was built and sold in 1900. Practically all the transformation of city streets and country roads that attended gasoline motive power came after 1900. Even for street-cars, horses were still much in use in 1900. That a time should come when horses would be a rare sight on city streets seemed, in 1900, one of the least credible of prophecies.

In 1900, the Grand Army of the Republic was still a numerous body, high in the nation's sentiment, deferred to in politics, their annual national reunions and parades stirring events, and their local posts[1] important in their communities. Among the older generation the memories and issues of the Civil War still had power to excite feeling, although the Spanish War, with its outpouring of a common national emotion against a foreign foe, had come close to completing the burial of the rancors of the war between the States. Such terms as "Rebel," "Yank," and "damn Yankee," "Secesh" were still occasionally used, sometimes with a touch of ancient malice. A few politicians, chiefly older ones, still found or thought they found potency in "waving the bloody shirt." Negro suffrage was still a living and, in some quarters, an acrimonious issue.

The passing of the questions arising out of the Civil War, and the figures associated with it, as major incidents of politics and life, was one of the most marked of the many respects in which 1900 was a dividing year.

[1] By 1917, there was but a tottering handful of them left to contribute a pathetic blessing to the ceremonies with which their grandsons, under the name American Expeditionary Force, left to fight in France, grandsons destined to substitute, in the newer generation's experiences, Belleau Wood for Gettysburg, St. Mihiel for Bloody Angle. In April, 1918, passing through Peru, Ind., on a train, I saw what was left of the local G. A. R. post come down to the station to see the local "draftees" off. The veterans, the youngest of whom necessarily were at least seventy, wore their army uniforms, and evidently had been at pains to get together what was left of the fife and drum corps that had played them off to war some fifty years before. Now once more it played "Rally 'Round the Flag, Boys," to old men who could no longer rally. As one watched them saying good-by to the younger men, one wondered how much the furtive tears in their eyes were for their own long-gone youth, how much for the fates that might await their grandsons. At least that and some other thoughts composed the reflections of one observer. The reaction of another, a travelling salesman from Chicago, who spoke with the accent of very recent Americanization, was expressed in a naïve question: "Who are them old guys?" In observing that unfamiliarity with our traditions, that unresponsiveness to sentiment about them, one had a glimpse of understanding of that anti-alien feeling which arose in America soon after the Great War, expressing itself in the immigration restriction law and in some other ways.

VII

In 1900, America presented to the eye the picture of a country that was still mostly frontier of one sort or another, the torn edges of civilization's first contact with nature, man in his invasion of the primeval. There were some areas that retained the beauty of nature untouched: the Rocky Mountains, parts of the Western plains where the railroads had not yet reached, and some bits of New England. There were other spots, comparatively few, chiefly the farming regions of eastern Pennsylvania, New York State, and New England, where beauty had come with the work of man — old farms with solid well-kept barns, many of heavy stone or brick; substantial houses with lawns shaded by evergreen trees that had been growing for more than a generation, fields kept clean to the fence corners — areas that to the eye and spirit gave satisfying suggestions of a settled order, traditions, crystallized ways of life, comfort, serenity, hereditary attachment to the local soil.

Only the Eastern seaboard had the appearance of civilization having really established itself and attained permanence. From the Alleghanies to the Pacific Coast, the picture was mainly of a country still frontier and of a people still in flux: the Alleghany mountainsides scarred by the axe, cluttered with the rubbish of improvident lumbering, blackened with fire; mountain valleys disfigured with ugly coal-breakers, furnaces, and smokestacks; western Pennsylvania and eastern Ohio an eruption of ungainly wooden oil-derricks; rivers muddied by the erosion from lands cleared of trees but not yet brought to grass, soiled with the sewage of raw new towns and factories; prairies furrowed with the first breaking of sod. Nineteen hundred was in the flood-tide of railroad-building: long fingers of fresh dirt pushing up and down the prairies, steam-shovels digging into virgin land, rock-blasting on the mountainsides. On the prairie farms, sod houses were not unusual. Frequently there were no barns, or, if any, mere sheds. Straw was not even stacked, but rotted in sodden piles. Villages were just past the early

Geronimo.

Group photograph taken at Omaha Exposition, 1897.
The older type of American Indian could still be seen in 1900. Geronimo was the last of the fighting Indian leaders.

picturesqueness of two long lines of saloons and stores, but not yet arrived at the orderliness of established communities; houses were almost wholly frame, usually of one story, with a false top, and generally of a flimsy construction that suggested transiency; larger towns with a marble Carnegie Library at Second Street, and Indian tepees at Tenth. Even as to most of the cities, including the Eastern ones, their outer edges were a kind of frontier, unfinished streets pushing out to the fields; sidewalks, where there were any, either of brick that loosened with the first thaw, or wood that rotted quickly; rapid growth leading to rapid change. At the gates of the country, great masses of human raw materials were being dumped from immigrant ships. Slovenly immigrant trains[1] tracked westward. Bands of unattached men, floating labor, moved about from the logging-camps of the winter woods to harvest in the fields, or to railroad-construction camps. Restless "sooners" wandered hungrily about to grab the last opportunities for free land.

One whole quarter of the country, which had been the seat of its most ornate civilization, the South, though it had spots of melancholy beauty, presented chiefly the impression of the weedy ruins of thirty-five years after the Civil War, and comparatively few years after Reconstruction — ironic word.

[1] "From the four quarters of the earth the people came, the broken and the unbroken, the tame and the wild—Germans, Irish, Italians, Hungarians, Scotch, Welsh, English, French, Swiss, Swedes, Norwegians, Greeks, Poles, Russians, Jews, Dalmatians, Armenians, Roumanians, Bulgarians, Servians, Persians, Syrians, Japanese, Chinese, Turks, and every hybrid that these could propagate. And if there were no Eskimos nor Patagonians, what other human strain that earth might furnish failed to swim and bubble in this crucible?"—Booth Tarkington, in "The Turmoil."

2

AMERICA IN 1900

The Background, the Stage, and the Characters. Some Characteristics That Distinguished the United States from Other Nations. America's Equipment for Producing Its Leaders. Some Men Destined for Leadership and Where They Were in 1900. The Origins of the People and of Their Language, Laws, Literature, Music, and Other Institutions.

In 1900 the United States was a nation of just under 76,000,000 people, with dependencies in the West Indies, off the coast of Asia, near the Arctic Ocean, and in the mid-Pacific, all acquired recently, except Alaska. The area of the mainland was 3,026,789 square miles. This expanse of territory reached from 25° north latitude to 49°. Its temperature varied from a winter extreme of 45° below zero in Bismarck, N. D., to a summer extreme of 117° in Phœnix, Ariz., its elevation from the 14,501 feet of Mount Whitney to the sea-level savannas of the Gulf Coast; its climate from the four months of immunity from frost that was good for hard wheat in North Dakota, to the practically frostless lands that would raise oranges in Florida and California.

Within this scope of land and climate there was such an abundance and variety of food and other natural resources as made it the most nearly self-sustaining compact nation that then was or ever had been. Within its own borders it reaped every variety of edible grain; raised every kind of vegetable food in common use, except bananas and a few condiments and stimulants, such as cocoa, coffee, tea, and pepper — and even some of these were raised to some extent, and practically all could be raised in any emergency. It produced every kind of meat for common use. From its streams, lakes, and shores it was supplied with nearly every kind of fish or fish product except a few epicurean delicacies, such as caviar from Russia and sardines from the Mediterranean.

Of material for clothing, it had five times as much

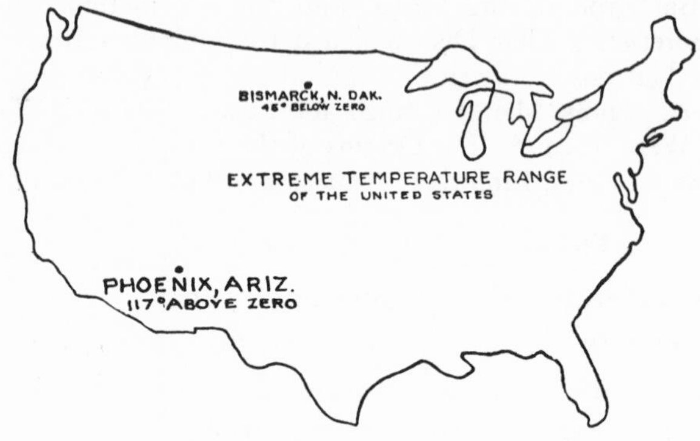

cotton as all the rest of the world, as much wool as the people desired to raise, and while it imported silk and some linen, it could produce these in any quantity necessary for its own use. Of the raw materials for shelter and for the most exacting and complex needs of modern manufacture of every kind, it had teeming stores. Of woods it had an abundance of all, except a few minor and dispensable ones like mahogany, teak, and balsa. Of minerals[1] it had an abundance of all the more important ones, and also some supplies of tin, manganese, vanadium, and platinum, though it imported most of these. Of vegetable products needed on any large or essential scale for manufacture, it had all except rubber; and it had the soil and climate to produce this if desired.

[1] The one conspicuous lack in the natural resources of the United States was nitrate deposits sufficient for fertilizer and explosives. This mineral had to be imported, chiefly from Chile. During the period 1900–25 processes were devised, chiefly under the urgency of war need, for extracting nitrogen from the air.

Not only did this nation have supplies of every kind of natural resource and raw materials abundant for its own use; of most of them, it had stores far greater than those of any other nation; and of many, more than all the rest of the world. Measured by annual output, in 1900

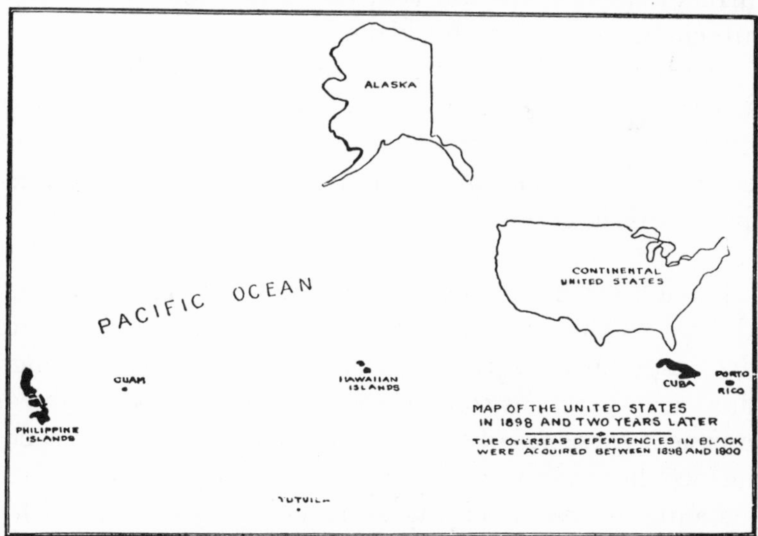

MAP OF THE UNITED STATES IN 1898 AND TWO YEARS LATER

THE OVERSEAS DEPENDENCIES IN BLACK WERE ACQUIRED BETWEEN 1898 AND 1900

America produced more than half the world's cotton, corn, copper, and oil; more than a third of its steel, pig iron, and silver; and substantially a third of its coal and gold.[1]

Of the physical facts about this country, two had more bearing on its welfare than any others. Externally, it

[1] The annual output as of 1900 was an incomplete picture of America's potential natural resources. The country was able to increase its output to a degree that was estimated by *The Manufacturers' Record*, in 1925, as:

80%	of the world's	sulphur.	55%	of the world's	cotton.
66%	" "	steel.	55%	" "	iron ore.
65%	" "	naval stores.	52%	" "	timber output.
64%	" "	zinc.	51%	" "	pig iron.
63%	" "	mica.	51%	" "	copper.
62%	" "	lead.	45%	" "	barytes.
62%	" "	petroleum.	43%	" "	coal.
60%	" "	talc and soapstone.	42%	" "	phosphate.

was widely separated from the two old and densely populated continents of the world; from Europe by the Atlantic Ocean; from Asia by the Pacific. Internally, within this nation's whole immensity of territory, there was no boundary, no customs barrier, no variation of language, currency or fundamental law, no impediment to the free interchange of goods and ideas.

The parts of this country were bound together for the purposes of trade and mutual intercourse by almost 200,000 miles of railroad, more than 200,000 miles of telegraph-lines, and more than a million miles of telephone-wire in service.

Though some portions of this country were not as well adapted to the propagation of human stock of the white race, especially to the preservation of infants through their early years, as some European countries less subject to violent extremes of heat and dryness; yet in this respect the people inhabiting this territory had practised much ingenuity in the inventing and perfecting of devices for making artificial ice, pasteurizing milk, heating their homes in winter, and otherwise overcoming local handicaps of climate; and also had equipped themselves generously with physicians and nurses, and institutions for training them, and with hospitals; so that on the whole this territory was admirably adapted to the physical well-being of the human stock that inhabited it.

This human stock was of the white (Caucasian) race, except: about 9,000,000 in whole or part of black (Ethiopian) blood, descendants of a strain originally brought to the country as slaves and later set free and made citizens; about 114,000 of Mongolian stock (90,000 Chinese and 24,000 Japanese); and 237,000 who were in whole or part of the aboriginal Indian blood.

A most important fact about the stock of this nation,

for which there was no parallel or precedent among great nations, either of its own time or of the past; an aspect that had many advantages, but which came to be regarded during this quarter-century as having possible perils in excess of its advantages, was the fact that alone among great nations its stock was not indigenous to the soil, was not homogeneous, had no long common history nor any body of common institutions arising out of its own experiences. Its people had come from other countries, either immediately or through near ancestors, all within a period of less than 300 years, and most within a much shorter period. Also, this people recruited its population as much through additions from overseas[1] as through births in its native stock.

As respects the origins of the dominant white race: in 1900, 41,000,000 were reckoned roughly as "native white stock," meaning descendants of stock which had been in America for at least one whole generation.[2] Of this native white stock a large majority derived from the early settlers, who had been chiefly British. Twenty-six millions, or 40 per cent of the total whites, had come very recently from Europe — were either direct immigrants or the children of immigrants. Of this class of recent increments, about 30 per cent were of British stock, 31 per cent of German stock, 4 per cent Swedish, 4 per cent Russian, 4 per cent Austrian, 3 per cent Italian. At this time, however, and for several years after 1900, immigration from Russia, Poland, and Italy was increasing very rapidly; whereas immigration from northwestern Europe was not. Consequently there was a measurable tendency for the British and other northwest European portions

[1] This statement requires amplification. The annual immigration to America was from a half to a third as large as the annual births. But of the births a disproportionately large number were in the families of recent immigrants, who had earlier marriages and much larger families than the native stock.

[2] This means children of parents born in America.

of the stock to decline from their numerical superiority in the composition of this people as a whole.

II

Most of the institutions of this people, their language, their religion, their fundamental laws, their point of view regarding organized society, the relations of the sexes, education and the like, were derived from the same European countries that were the sources of the people themselves. To a greater extent even than the people themselves were British, their institutions were based on British models. English was the common language, universal and mandatory in legislative proceedings, legal documents, and the like; and practically universal in daily use. Exceptions consisted of a few spots in Pennsylvania, where the language in daily use was "Pennsylvania Dutch," a patois derived from the early German settlers of those communities and modified by contact with the English tongue; some communities in the Southwest, where Spanish was in common use, a heritage from the early Spanish settlement of Mexico; a few spots, like part of the Gulf coast of Louisiana, where a remnant of Acadian exiles retained their French tongue after a hundred and forty years; a few other localities, chiefly in New England, where more recent immigrants from French Canada retained their French tongue. Some of the late immigrants from Europe continued to use their native tongues in a few settlements: Italian and Yiddish in New York and other cities of the East; German in some communities in the Northwest, as well as Swedish, Finnish, Polish, Greek. Indian tribal languages were in use in a few scattered places.

In jurisprudence the origin was wholly English, except in Louisiana, where the Napoleonic code of the early settlers was retained. The legislative institutions were based wholly on English models.

In education the traditions were prevailingly British, except that in higher university education there had been for some years a disposition to turn to German models and to import German teachers. Of the modern languages taught in high schools and colleges, other than English, there was more of German than of all others combined.

As respects literature, including poetry and the drama, the origins were almost wholly British. A few Latin and Greek classics were read in high schools and colleges. There was some literature from the French, chiefly novels and philosophy, with a few dramas; some from the Germans, mostly philosophical; little from the Spanish, except one or two classics; some from Italy; and the beginnings of a literature transplanted from Russia and the Scandinavian countries.

Classical music was an exception to the prevailingly British origins of this people's culture. The only British contributions that could be regarded as within the category "classic" were the comic operas of Gilbert and Sullivan. In this field there was a strong infusion from the German, chiefly the operas of Wagner and the instrumental music of Beethoven, Brahms, and some others. There was also a strong infusion from the Italian, consisting of such operas as Verdi's "Il Trovatore," "La Traviata," and "Aïda." There was some classic music of French origin, some of Russian, and a little of Spanish. A few experiments had been made, chiefly by Edward MacDowell, toward building up a characteristic American music based on Indian strains.

Popular music was largely British in origin, and more from Scotland and Ireland than from England. A considerable number of the melodies in popular use came from Negro sources or were based on Negro themes and the Negro imagination. In this particular year, 1900, there was, in instrumental popular music, a vogue for a type known as "ragtime" and the "cake-walk," of mongrel origin.[1]

The religious attachments of this people were almost wholly to denominations accepting the doctrine of the divinity of Jesus Christ. The exceptions, which differed utterly from each other and had nothing essential in common except non-acceptance of the divinity of Christ, were about 1,050,000 Jews, about 75,000 Unitarians, a few hundred believers in Buddhism or some other Oriental religion. A few Indians still followed their original rites.

Within the Christian religion about 12,000,000 were attached to the Roman Catholic faith; about 700,000 to the Episcopal, a few hundreds to the Greek Catholic. The remainder belonged to one or another evangelical or reformed denomination — about 6,000,000 Methodists, 5,000,000 Baptists, 1,500,000 Lutherans, 1,500,000 Presbyterians, 350,000 Mormons, 80,000 followers of Christian Science. Except the Mormons and the followers of Christian Science, which sects had originated in America,

[1] Ragtime and the cake-walk were commonly spoken of as Negro music. More accurately they were expressions of what some metropolitan artisans of music chose to attribute to the Negro. So far as the Negro practised them they represented not his taste, but the corruption of his taste, his deference to what the other race wanted, especially in New York, where vogues are made. The genuine contributions of the Negro have true beauty, and form a worthy and permanent contribution to the very small body of indigenous American music. Roosevelt once described the Negro "spirituals" as coming nearer to a true school of American music than anything else. The Negro "spiritual" is as moving a form of art as any race has devised to picture God, eternity, and man's ultimate destiny. The "spirituals" are so spontaneous, so much a part of the soul of the singer, that not until very recent years has it been possible to get them on paper. Most of them reflected a poignantly pathetic effort to reconcile the goodness, mercy, and justice of a God sincerely believed in, with the conditions of slavery. One, transcribed without too much effort to reproduce Negro pronunciation, ran:

"O Lord, remember the rich an' remember the poor.
Remember the bond an' the free.
And when you done rememberin' all 'round,
Then, O Lord, remember me."

most of these denominational affiliations had accompanied immigrants to America or been inherited from immigrants. All the immigrant stocks, except the Negro, tended to maintain the religions of the countries from which they came.

III

The distinctive characteristics of this people, marking them off from some or all other nations, included: a determined faith in the democratic organization of society and the representative form of government; a taboo against kings and aristocracy; separation of church and state; zeal for universal education; an indisposition to maintain a large standing army; a prevailing and growing trend toward the abolition of alcoholic drinks. There was a freedom — at that time — from much of the regulation by government[1] that was common in many other countries, and a vigilance against encroachment by government on the individual, a trait derived from the comparatively recent experiences of most of these people as voluntary exiles from monarchical and other exacting forms of government.

There was a freedom from stratification into castes, social or industrial, accompanied by the absence from the country's political system of any permanent or important labor or otherwise radical political party. Freedom from stratification also led to sociability, an easy approachableness and informality in human relations, not common in nations having one degree or another of

[1] When I imply there was greater freedom from regulation by government in 1900 than in 1925, I should add that the cause was not any change in the spirit of the individual American. Submission to greater regulation by government, the appearance of "verbotens" in America, was caused chiefly by increasing density of population. The more man was obliged to rub elbows against his neighbor, and to feel the rub of his neighbor's elbow, the more did regulation become inevitable. The tendency was accelerated by what may be called the increased velocity of man, brought about by the automobile and other developments of machinery. This is amplified in Chapter 8 and some subsequent chapters.

caste.[1] The people had independence of spirit, accompanied by the concession of equal independence to others — a trait due to exemption from caste, to the nature of the people, most of whom had been pioneers themselves or in their recent ancestors, and to immunity from great anxiety about making a livelihood, an immunity made possible by the natural wealth of the country. Another national trait was a responsiveness to idealism, greater than was common among older nations where the economic pressure of numbers made unselfishness less easy and where experience had brought disillusionment. The American temperament included adaptiveness,[2] a willingness more prompt than among other peoples to dismiss the old and try the new, a freedom from enthralment to the familiar, which accounted for much of the rapidity of their progress, especially in machinery.

Some minor distinctive institutions included: the celebration of a national holiday known as Thanksgiving, rocking-chairs, a greater fastidiousness about personal cleanliness as measured by the commonness of bathtubs as compared with other countries; ice-water, pie, New

[1] While exemption from caste was characteristic of the white race, it is also true that between whites and blacks there was a greater separation than characterized race relations in most other countries. S. S. McClure thinks the existence of a race problem in America, slavery and its aftermath, had a deep bearing on our national history, and accounted among other things for the lateness of our handling of social problems. Slavery was an anachronism in democracy, and the Negro so great a variation from homogeneity as to constitute an impediment to the acceptance of democratic ideals, and to putting them into effect. Moreover, during the first seventy-five years of the country's history, the slavery question consumed most of the country's capacity for handling social and political problems. Most tragically, the final solution of slavery took the form of civil war, so that during the next twenty-five years the aftermath of slavery was equally absorbing. It was only about 1890 that the country finally got itself free from the slavery incubus and was able to develop its talent for the democratic treatment of political, social, and industrial problems.

[2] Mr. Herbert Hoover thinks this point should be emphasized. Intellectual freedom and curiosity about the new, the instinct of the American mind to look into, examine, and experiment—this led to, among other things, a willingness to "scrap" not only old machinery but old formulas, old ideas; and brought about, among other results, the condition expressed in the saying that "American mechanical progress could be measured by the size of its scrap-heaps."

England boiled dinner, chewing-gum; baseball, a game calling for unusually quick reactions intellectually and prompt and easy co-operation muscularly; a diversion called poker, indigenous to this nation and containing definite elements of the interplay of psychology not found in ordinary card games.

IV

Of all the characteristics of this people, the most important was freedom of opportunity for the individual, which provided the nation with a constant, rapid, and generous supply of leadership in every line from its own ranks. A national habit of mind, social organization and education, made it as easy for the individual to arrive at leadership from the lowest ranks[1] as for those in the highest ranks to keep it. Certain handicaps, partly legal and partly in the intangible world of social point of view, denied to those already highly placed in wealth or position any great hereditary advantages or rights, or any other security of tenure except what they and their descendants could provide through energy

From a photograph by Underwood & Underwood.

William McKinley, President 1897–1901, taken at his desk in the White House.

[1] Mr. Herbert Hoover thinks this American trait should be emphasized and expanded. (In later chapters it is.) He regards it as accounting for much that is best in American social organization, and also for much of the rapidity of America's progress. Mr. Hoover pictures American society as a soiution in energetic ferment, with the particles rapidly seeking and finding, with the minimum of obstruction, their places of greatest adaptation and efficiency.

or talent. The same national point of view and practice, together with the great natural wealth of the country and the system of universal free education, made it easy for the talented and the energetic to rise.

From a photograph copyrighted by Tomlinson.

Mark Twain in front of his boyhood home. Taken on the occasion of his last visit to Hannibal, Missouri, 1902.

In 1900 the President of the United States, William McKinley, was the son of a country lawyer. The greatest ironmaster, Andrew Carnegie, was the son of a weaver — he had come to the United States as an immigrant and had spent his youth as a telegraph messenger-boy. Of the two men who were making the largest contributions to applied science, one, Michael Pupin, had been a shepherd-boy in Serbia, had come to America as an immigrant and worked as a farm-hand in Delaware; the other, Thomas A. Edison, had spent his youth as a newsboy and telegraph-operator. One of the outstanding geniuses in electricity, Charles P. Steinmetz, had come to America to escape persecution for his socialistic beliefs, and had had difficulty, because of physical defects, in passing the immigration authorities, who feared he might become a public charge. The leading railroad operator, James J. Hill, had begun as a clerk in a village store. The richest man in the country, John D. Rockefeller, had been a clerk in a commission house. One of the leaders of literature, Mark Twain, had got his pen-name from his experience as a pilot on a Mississippi River steamboat. A noted journalist, Joseph Pulitzer, had entered America as an immigrant, literally without dry clothes[1] on his back, for he had leaped from a ship in Boston Harbor and swum ashore in order to take advantage, for himself, of the bounty offered to volunteers in the Civil War.

William H. Taft in 1900.

[1] Pulitzer's biographer, friend, and lifetime business associate, Don C. Seitz, describes this apparently record-breaking entry into the United States without making it clear whether the immigrant entered merely with wet clothes or with none at all: "At this time Europe swarmed with agents seeking recruits, in the guise of emigrants, for the Union Army. The boy fell into the hands of one of these and was shipped to Boston. Arriving in port, in company with another who had been 'recruited' in this fashion, he decided to collect his own bounty, and slipped over the ship's side at night; being an expert swimmer, he safely reached the American shore some time in August or in September, 1864. The irregularity of his arrival obscures the date. . . ."

At the same time this American system provided abundant opportunity for those who had been born in the higher ranks to remain there, if they had the character, talent, and energy to endure the competition. In 1900 the man who was just becoming one of the leaders in public life, Theodore Roosevelt, had been born to wealth and in the social environment of the old Dutch families of New York. The man who in 1900 was intrusted with carrying our institutions to our first great dependency, and who was later to be President of the United States and chief justice of the Supreme Court, William H. Taft, was the son of a father who had been secretary of war and attorney-general in cabinets a generation before. The leading educator, Charles W. Eliot, president of Harvard University, had been born in the higher social and business circles of New England. The leading banker, J. Pierpont Morgan, although his power was due to the salience of his personality, had inherited the banking-house of which he was head. One of the leading businesses, the du Pont Company, had been in the hands of one family since its foundation, more than a hundred years before.

Calvin Coolidge just before 1900.

Among those who had not yet emerged in 1900 to leadership, but were destined to supply it within the

Herbert Hoover in 1900.

quarter-century to follow; among those who in the opening year of the century were being incubated for leadership through some of the processes which this democracy provided — among these: In 1900, Woodrow Wilson was a professor at Princeton, and had not yet written his history of the American people. William G. McAdoo was practising law in New York and writing the opening chapters of a book on poverty and its prevention, a work for which he had secured practical training through having spent a desperately poor boyhood in the devastated South of the post-Civil-War period, and through, also, his struggles to get a foothold in New York, where he was about to develop the idea of uniting the island of Manhattan with the New Jersey mainland by tunnels under the Hudson River. In 1900, Herbert Hoover, then twenty-five years old, and five years out of Leland Stanford University, through which he had worked his way, was making in China the beginnings of what was to be, before he was thirty-five, a world-wide reputation as an engineer. In

William Gibbs McAdoo in 1900.

1900, Charles Evans Hughes was in the ranks of young, hard-working, and comparatively unknown lawyers in New York City, spending some of his time as a lecturer in New York University Law School. William E. Borah, then thirty-five years old, was practising law in Boise, Idaho, where he had located because that was the terminus of the longest railroad trip he had been able to pay for when, nine years before, he had started West after completing his legal education. Calvin Coolidge was an obscure lawyer in a small New England town, making his beginnings in politics in fellowship with a local shoemaker.

3

1900–25

A Period Characterized by an Immense Elevation That Came to America as a Whole, Accompanied by an Immense Enrichment of the Individual American. The Nation Makes a Start Toward Imperialism, but Thinks Better of It. Later, Through an Unintended Stimulus from Europe, a Different Sort of World Dominance Is Thrust Upon Us. Enrichments That Came to the Average Man. Some Other Important Changes Which May Have Been Enrichments, or May Not. A Partial Roll-Call of the Worthies, and of Some That Were Less Worthy. The Most Important Character of All.

In 1900, on January 10, America read in its newspapers the accounts, heralded with grandiose head-lines, of a speech delivered in the Senate the day before by Albert J. Beveridge, of Indiana. Because of the speaker's youth — he was thirty-seven — because of certain qualities that went with his youth, because it was his first speech as a senator, and because of an aggressive policy he advocated, his speech received nation-wide attention. Senator Beveridge had just returned from a trip to the scene of the American army operations in the Philippines. His speech dealt with the question of annexing and retaining that distant archipelago, and, broadly, with the whole policy of territorial expansion for America, the leading political issue of the day. Some sentences (selected chiefly from his peroration) read:

> . . . We will not renounce our part in the mission of the race, trustee, under God, of the civilization of the world. . . . Mr. President, self-government and internal development have been the dominant notes of our first century; administration and the development of other lands will be the dominant notes of our second century. . . . He has made us [our race] the master organizers of the world to establish system where chaos

reigns. . . . He has made us adepts in government that we may administer government among savage and senile peoples. . . . And of all our race, He has marked the American people as His chosen Nation to finally lead in the regeneration of the world. This is the divine mission of America, and it holds for us all the profit, all the glory, all the happiness possible to man. We are trustees of the world's progress, guardians of its righteous peace. The judgment of the Master is upon us: "Ye have been faithful over a few things; I will make you ruler over many things." What shall history say of us? Shall it say that we renounced that holy trust, left the savage to his base condition, the wilderness to the reign of waste, deserted duty, abandoned glory, forgot our sordid profit even, because we feared our strength and read the charter of our powers with the doubter's eye and the quibbler's mind? Shall it say that, called by events to captain and command the proudest, ablest, purest race of history in history's noblest work, we declined that great commission? . . . Pray God the time may never come when mammon and the love of ease will so debase our blood that we will fear to shed it for the flag and its imperial destiny.[1]

The tone of Beveridge's speech was in the spirit of the times. It was a day of expansion and expansiveness: Great Britain pushing into Africa from north and south; France contesting Great Britain's advance at Fashoda and elsewhere; Russia pressing down into China; even Italy looking to get a foothold in Africa; Belgium beginning to exploit the Congo; Germany picking up unconsidered trifles everywhere. It was a day also of young

[1] Beveridge was alluding to the proposal of the anti-expansionists, including most of the Democrats, led by Bryan, and a fraction of the Republicans led by Senator Hoar, of Massachusetts. Their policy was that America should retire from the Philippines and bring home the American army. Beveridge and the Administration felt that the public advocacy of this policy in America was the chief obstacle to the army's work. Secretary of War Root said that Bryan was chiefly responsible for the deaths of American soldiers. The Republicans expressed outrage at this policy, which they called one of "scuttle and retreat." This spirit accounts for some of what now seems the flamboyancy of Beveridge's peroration. The quite temperate body of the speech included an account of his observations in the Philippines, of the work of the American army, and of the commercial possibilities for America in the Orient; a plea that it would be disaster to the Filipinos themselves for America to turn them loose; and a constitutional argument that the United States has the right "as an attribute of nationality" to acquire and administer dependencies. This contention was sustained by the Supreme Court in the "Insular Cases" decided in 1901.

Raising the flag over Santiago.

Drawn by F. C. Yohn from photographs and sketches made during the ceremony. Showing the squadron of Second United States Cavalry and Ninth United States Infantry and the group of general officers and their staffs.

men: Cecil Rhodes; Kitchener of Khartoum. Just a few months before, Kipling had given out his poem about taking up the White Man's Burden. So much was America

From The Brooklyn Daily "Eagle," January, 1900.

An anti-expansion cartoonist protests against Uncle Sam's following the counsels of Senator Beveridge.

infected by ideas about far-flung lines of empire that even the gentle, amiable William Allen White added a high-pitched note to the chorus about Anglo-Saxon "manifest destiny." On March 20, 1899, he wrote in the Emporia *Gazette:* "Only Anglo-Saxons can govern themselves. The Cubans will need a despotic government for many years to restrain anarchy until Cuba is filled with Yankees. Uncle Sam the First will have to govern Cuba as Alphonso the Thirteenth governed it. . . . It is the Anglo-Saxon's manifest destiny to go forth as a world conqueror. He will take possession of the islands of the sea. . . . This is what fate holds for the chosen people. It is so written. . . . It is to be."

The American people listened to Senator Beveridge's speech (it was a key-note of Republican administration policy and platform) and to other similar speeches as part of what guidance they could get in a new relation to the world that had been thrust on them unexpectedly by the Spanish-American War. They set up the policies involved in that new relation as a political issue in the

Courtesy of U. S. Signal Corps.

American officers in the Philippines in 1900.
The tall man at the extreme left of the second line is Major, later General, John J. Pershing.

presidential campaign of 1900, under the name "expansion," as it was called by the Republicans, who favored it, or "imperialism" and "militarism," as it was called by the Democrats, who opposed it. They debated it, and heard it debated. They decided, apparently, in favor of expansion by electing the Republican ticket, McKinley and Roosevelt, over Bryan and Stevenson, and proceeded to the business of making adjustments with their new possessions and with the world in a manner that seemed at the time to constitute the kind of answer Senator Beveridge's rhetorical questions pleaded for.

During 1900 the United States maintained in the Philippines an army of 60,000 officers and men, and at the same time sent there William H. Taft and four others as a commission to set up civil government; maintained in Cuba a temporary governor-general in the person of

General Wood and other officials at the review of the Street Cleaning Department on the Alameda.

General Leonard Wood, and began the work of fixing the permanent relations of that island with the United States; devised a form of civil government for Porto Rico, and otherwise cleaned up the débris of the Spanish-American War. Brought 1,280 Cuban school-teachers to Boston to study at Harvard University; abolished polygamy in the Island of Guam, and ordered the Sultan of Sulu to liberate his slaves. Adopted a territorial form of government for Hawaii; ratified the annexation of the Island of Tutuila, in the Samoas; carried on negotiations for the purchase of the Danish West Indies; made inquiries looking to the purchase of the Galapagos Islands; negotiated with England, France, Germany, Italy, Russia, and Japan for the open-door policy in China, and

From "The Rocky Mountain News," Denver, 1900.

Uncle Sam: "By gum, I rather like your looks."

secured adoption of it; sent 2,400 troops to China to participate with the troops of European nations and Japan in the suppression of the Boxer Rebellion; negotiated the Hay-Pauncefote Treaty looking to the construction of an Isthmian canal by the United States; entered into reciprocity treaties with Germany and Italy; entertained President McKinley's recommendation that Congress take "immediate action on the promotion of American shipping and foreign trade"; sent 5000 tons of corn to relieve a famine in India; sent more exhibits to the Paris Exposition than any other nation; and won sixteen out of the twenty-one contests in the international athletic games at Paris.

All this America did in 1900. These events having to do with America's relation to the world, and especially the ones having to do with expansion, with the new possessions that came to us as a result of the Spanish War, constituted the most important activity of the United States in that year. Reading them in the impressiveness

From the San Francisco "Chronicle."

The cxpansion rooster.
Cartoon of America during the period of its expansion ambition, 1900.

of their aggregate, or witnessing them at the time, one might have assumed that they marked a new departure in American history. And from the standpoint of the past, they did. But so far as one might have inferred something about the future, so far as one might have assumed — as many in 1900 did assume — that this striking coincidence of many activities in the field of foreign relations was an augury of further expansion overseas, and that we were about to add ourselves to history's long procession of empires — so far as that was assumed, the forecast was not borne out. It so happened that these various annexations, in all of which important steps were taken in 1900, were the only annexations of land off our own continent that America had ever made, excepting only the four diminutive islands of Samoa, and distant Guam, all taken two years before, in 1898; and none were made thereafter. We completed later the purchase of the Danish West Indies, and we completed the steps for the ownership[1] of the Panama Canal Zone; but we never made another annexation.

The entire history of American overseas expansion is compressed practically within the year 1900 and the two years preceding. We took the path of Senator Beveridge's "imperial destiny" far enough to complete the commitments we had become involved in, as unanticipated and rather disturbing incidents of a war we had begun only to rescue the Cuban people from the cruelties of Spanish rule. Then we stopped. For the change of emotion we went through, the cooling down from a hectic and rather artificially stimulated ardor, there is no phrase that conveys the picture quite so precisely as the slang one: we concluded to forget it. The American people, after about 1902, not only had a distinct disinclination for further expansion but were inclined to regard the annexations we had already made as embarrassing liabilities.[2] By

[1] Strictly, a perpetual lease. We paid $10,000,000 down and $250,000 yearly.

[2] Some thoughtful persons believe this later mood of America was merely a halting, and that ultimately we shall take the course of expansion. They regard twenty-five years as being a mere interlude in history, considered from the standpoint of centuries. These persons base part of their argument on precedent, pointing out that the entire history of America up to 1900 had been a succession of impulses of expansion. This is true; but I make two distinctions: one between an expansion which consisted of absorbing more or less unoccupied lands on our own continent, and expansion overseas. The other distinction is between an expansion which is chiefly of land and takes in very few people; and one

1919, so great was our disinclination for responsibilities that when they were strongly urged upon us by other nations in the form of "mandates" over some of the former German dependencies, we rejected them with an emphasis that was clear evidence of an overwhelming and definitely crystallized public opinion in favor of America remaining at home.

II

Nine days before Senator Beveridge's address, the world heard from another young man. On January 1, 1900, another speech on "imperial destiny" was delivered in another country; a speech less heralded by American newspapers and utterly unnoticed as having any meaning for America. In its ultimate bearing on America's relation to the world and on the lives of individual Americans, it was of far more consequence than Senator Beveridge's summons to adventure. This speech, delivered on foreign soil by a man who was not an American and never saw America — this speech, in the train of events that followed and accompanied it, resulted in thrusting upon the United States, eighteen years later, a dominance not foreseen or thought possible by even so

which takes more or less the Roman form of asserting sovereignty over large bodies of people alien in stock, language, and institutions. It is this latter form of expansion which our people embarked upon and seemed to approve in 1900; but as to which, as it seems to me, our people have taken a different view since 1900. The American was a frontiersman and a settler on land. He liked and practised for a century the form of expansion that gave him opportunity to stretch himself on new land, after driving off the aborigines. But as soon as he found that expansion in the West Indies and the Philippines did not mean free land, but meant administering government for crowded communities—at that point the average American lost interest. This latter form of expansion appealed to Great Britain, and Great Britain practised it because she had an important mercantile and shipping class, whose economic interests were served by dominance in overseas territories. America's economic interest in expansion looked chiefly to free land. Possibly America may some time approximate the conditions that gave Great Britain an economic motive for overseas expansion in the other sense. If so, America may then resume expansion. For the present, that is matter for prophets; not until a good many years from now will it become matter for historians.

expansive a dreamer as Senator Beveridge; a dominance which did not rest on physical expansion or on imperialism or on militarism; or on any sort of aggressiveness; which included no annexation of territory — which was

The German Kaiser in 1900, as Admiral of the German fleet. His announcement, on January 1, 1900, of his purpose to have a great navy was one of the important steps leading to the Great War.

attended, indeed, by a definitely considered refusal on our part to accept new territory — a dominance which not only was unplanned and unsought, both in its means and its outcome, but which actually we tried to put aside.

It was in 1900 and, dramatically, on New Year's Day that the German Kaiser, Wilhelm II, then within three years of Senator Beveridge's age, and having some of the same qualities of youth, including the temperament that sometimes identifies personally held national ambitions with the purposes of God — the German Kaiser proclaimed, and his minister transmitted to the Reichstag, his purpose of building the German navy up to a parity with his army:

> The first day of the new century sees our army — in other words, our people — in arms, gathered around their standards, kneeling before the Lord of Hosts. . . . Even as my grandfather labored for his army, so will I, in like manner, unerringly carry on and carry through the work of reorganizing my navy, in order that it may be justified in standing by the side of my land-forces and that by it the German Empire may also be in a position to win the place which it has not yet attained. With the two united, I hope to be enabled, with a firm trust in the guidance of God, to prove the truth of the saying of Frederick William the First: "When one in this world wants to decide something with the pen he does not do it unless supported by the strength of the sword."

Von Buelow, transmitting the Kaiser's purpose to the Reichstag, said:

> . . . If we neglect to provide a fleet now, we will never be able to make up for lost time. . . . There are some groups of interested people, perhaps of nations, who find that they lived more at their ease when the German permitted them to treat him as the arrogant cavalier treats his tutor. . . . But those days of political impotence and economic submissiveness are past, and shall not return.[1]

[1] The Kaiser's speech was delivered before the officers of the Berlin garrison. "His Majesty," cabled a correspondent, "delivered his address in a high-pitched, strident voice. Each syllable was emphasized." In its editorial comment of the day following, January 2, 1900, the New York *World* said: "If Emperor William had sought to wear a costume appropriate to the speech he made at Berlin yesterday, the latest possible style he could have adopted would have been a suit of early mediæval armor. . . . He and his pose and his speech are melancholy reminders of a past whose lessons have been all too imperfectly learned."

In the same year, 1900, the Kaiser, sending his soldiers to the scene of the Boxer Rebellion in China, directed them to "give no quarter and to conduct themselves so like Huns that for a thousand years no Chinaman will dare look askance at a German," an injunction to *schrecklichkeit* that fifteen years later came back to Potsdam to roost.

That determination of the German Kaiser on January 1, 1900, with the rest of the events of which it was a part — that act, in its train of consequences, brought it about that the United States should have, at the end of the quarter-century, the world dominance, economic and in other respects, which previously had been Great Britain's, and which, being Great Britain's, had been coveted by the Kaiser as Germany's rightful "place in the sun"; which, before being Great Britain's, had been Spain's; and so on back, through a long and colorful succession of dominant nations, to Tyre. Germany, coveting the place, tried to take it away from Britain; failed, and saw it fall to an innocent and uncovetous, even a reluctant, bystander.[1]

III

That change in the relation of America as a nation to the rest of the world was only one of the undreamed changes that came to the United States and its people during the period 1900 to 1925. The elevation of America internationally was important, but it entered less into the daily life of the average man than some other advances during the same period — advances that came, not through political leaders, nor wars, nor the other agencies that constitute the materials of most histories, but from men of science and practical industry.

[1] In the cases of most of the earlier nations, dominance was attended by naval supremacy. Naval supremacy would have come to the United States after the Great War. Every other nation was too poor to compete with us. The United States had actually started on a programme of naval construction that would have given us a leadership on the sea corresponding to our position in the world, when the Washington Conference for the Limitation of Naval Armament intervened, in 1921. In that conference we took a step unique in history. Instead of going on to take our appropriate leadership on the sea, we agreed, and the other nations agreed with us, that naval supremacy should no longer be held by one nation, that there should be no competition in naval armament; naval supremacy was, so to speak, "trusteed" in a mutual agreement, with America and Great Britain having equal shares, and the other nations appropriate lesser shares.

The war, and all that accompanied it and resulted from it, was not the most important thing that happened during this period, except as respects international relations. Undoubtedly the war was a supreme adventure to the millions who went to fight, and had a profound influence on the other millions who remained at home. But even measured by the yardstick of human life, the losses occasioned by the war were far outbalanced by the salvaging of life effected by new discoveries of medical science and the application of new principles in sanitation. Due chiefly to medical progress between 1900 and 1925, man was enriched in the thing he prizes most — his security of tenure on life, his defense against disease and death. The average age of the people who died in 1900 was forty-nine years; of those who died in 1925, fifty-five years.[1] A dozen Great Wars could not counteract the beneficence of this progress. The Great War thrust upon us world leadership, economic, financial, and, to the extent that we accepted it, political; but this elevation had little concrete effect on the life of the individual, compared with the blessings showered on him by medical science.

At the beginning of 1900 it had not yet been proved that yellow fever is transmitted by a mosquito, typhus by a louse, bubonic plague by a flea. Gorgas had not yet demonstrated that mosquitoes may be eliminated from any portion of the earth's surface and man's only weapon against malaria was quinine. Neither these facts nor the fundamental fact underlying them was known; and these plagues were as uncontrollable, except by the expedient of isolation, as they had been since the beginning of history. It was not known that typhoid and cholera come from germs in unclean water and milk; these diseases

[1] This increase, roughly 12 per cent, applied to the whole population of the United States, gives a total aggregate years of human life several times greater than the 120,000 American lives charged to the war.

were still the scourges they always had been. Insulin for diabetes, vaccination against typhoid, emetin for dysentery, adrenalin — all were still unknown. Antitoxin for diphtheria and the X-ray were only just coming into use. Ehrlich had not yet made those 606 patient experiments that resulted in the remedy for syphilis. Radium had not yet been used in the treatment of cancer. All these and many other advances in medicine, surgery, and sanitation came between 1900 and 1925. They effected a six years' postponement of death, and that was but one enrichment among many.

Man was enriched in the outward reach of his senses. It is true by 1900 the telephone had been developed to a point where one man could talk to another over 1400 miles of space, from New York to Omaha. That was already a marvel. But in 1900 men still under middle age could remember the time when the farthest distance one man could throw his voice was limited to what a good pair of lungs could do in a favoring wind, hands cupped megaphone-like, and "a whoop or a holler." In 1921, when President Harding delivered his speech at the burial of the unknown soldier, the distance his voice could carry was multiplied by the De Forest tube 3,000,000,000,000,000,000,000,000,000,000 times; by 1925 the radio made the human voice audible half-way round the world.

Man was similarly enriched in the outward reach of his sight, or in the number of things that were brought within his vision, and the facility with which they were brought, by increases in the capacity of the telescope, through which more of the universe was brought within his understanding; by increased power of the microscope, through which man's knowledge of the minute forms of life was multiplied; by the perfection of the motion-picture and its use in education and entertainment.

Man was enriched in the quantity of power brought to his service, and in the lowered cost of this power brought about partly by increased production and partly by the growing efficiency of the engines devised for converting coal, gas, petroleum, and waterfalls into power. One advance alone, the perfection and wide-spread application of the internal-combustion engine, which is the outstanding single achievement of the quarter-century in the field of mechanical advance, added to the service of man not less than half a billion horse-power.[1] In 1900 the average American farmer had, as the only supplement to his own muscles, the power of two or three horses to carry on his work. By 1925, practically every progressive farmer had an automobile of at least twenty horse-power. Many had tractors of between twenty and fifty horse-power, stationary gas-engines of from two to ten horse-power, and electrical connection with near-by generating plants which put at their command practically unlimited power. By the harnessing of rivers for the development of electrical power, by immense increases in the size of the units of steam and electricity man can now manufacture and control, the quantity of power brought to his service was multiplied enormously. In 1900 there was but one generating station exceeding 5000 horse-power; in 1925 there were more than fifty stations exceeding 100,000 horse-power. In the total electric power produced in the country the growth was from an aggregate of 3,343,000,000 horse-

[1] The gasoline-engine is an instrumentality about which almost any superlative can be used. Here—in the form which it finally reached in the Liberty airplane motor—is a mechanism of metal weighing 806 pounds, less than the weight of a horse, but having 400 times the power of a horse. As used in the automobile, one manufacturer, Henry Ford, furnished to each of the more than 12,000,000 buyers of his automobile twenty to thirty times as much power as the English king in Shakespeare longed for when he said "My kingdom for a horse"—and at a cost little more than was the price of a good horse in 1900.

The extension of the gasoline-engine until it became available to everybody was the great characteristic of the first quarter of the twentieth century. In 1925, the promise seemed to be that the similar diffusion of electricity would be the characteristic of the second quarter-century.

power hours in 1902 to 74,576,000,000 horse-power hours in 1923, a twentyfold increase.

Man was enriched in his knowledge of the universe. In one field of pure science,[1] understanding of the nature of matter, the advances made between 1900 and 1925 were greater than the sum of all the advances made in all time before.

Man was enriched in his leisure. In 1900 the Saturday half-holiday was practically unknown, and the ten-hour working day for six days a week was still common. It was in 1901 that the Federal Government gave sanction to the eight-hour day by decreeing it for work on government contracts. In 1900, golf was a diversion of the rich, somewhat under disapproval as being effete. A winter trip to Florida or California was yet more exclusively a rare prerogative of the well-to-do. Even the two weeks' summer holiday had barely begun to get under way.

Man was enriched — fabulously enriched — in his access to material goods — comforts, conveniences, luxuries. In 1900 the automobile was a dubious novelty. There were in all less than 8000 in the United States; by 1925 there were more than 17,000,000. In 1900, there were less than 10 miles of concrete road; by 1925, more than 20,000. In 1900, there was but one telephone for each 66 people; by 1925 it was of practically universal access, with one for each 7 people In 1900, it was recorded that the number of silk stockings sold in the United States was 12,572 dozen pairs a pair for one person to each 2000 of the population; in 1921, the number of pairs of silk or artificial silk was 18,088,841—one for each 6 of the people—an increase of access to luxury which, expressed in percentages, almost invades higher mathemat-

[1] "It sounds incredible, but nevertheless it is true, that science up to the close of the nineteenth century had no suspicion even of the existence of the *original sources of natural energy*. . . . The vista opened up by these new discoveries of the *radio-active properties* of some substances admittedly is without parallel in the whole history of science."—Professor J. J. Thomson, "Outline of Science,"

ics—and destroyed the ancient significance of "a silk-stocking."

Man was enriched in his knowledge of the surface of the earth. During this period both the North Pole and the South Pole were reached. By 1925 there remained no considerable portion of the earth's surface that had not been explored. By the airplane man achieved his age-long ambition to fly; by the submarine, he achieved the capacity to remain under water and direct his movements there at will. By the wireless he was enriched in his safety on the sea.[1]

In 1900 the great Texas oil-fields were still undiscovered. Radium, helium, the use of vanadium in steel, argon gas, electrolytic waterproofing, high-speed tool steel, the long-distance transmission of photographs, were undiscovered or undeveloped. The Marconi wireless was unperfected. The "loading coil" for long-distance telephoning, the multiplex telephone, the vacuum-tube amplifier were unknown. The tungsten electric light was not yet made. In 1900 there were no oil-burning locomotives, no flotation process for recovering copper, no vacuum cleaners, no self-starter, no electric cook-stoves or electric irons, no fireless cookers, no disk phonographs.

(This section has dealt with the material enrichment of man, only. Whether he was spiritually enriched also; what use man made of his increased years upon the earth, his increased leisure, the energies released by machinery from the need of getting a livelihood — the whole question of the spiritual experiences of man during this period is one about which it is not possible to speak so broadly or so confidently. That, with the speculations that must accompany it, awaits consideration later.)

[1] It would be interesting to compare, item by item, man's earliest longings for those things he deemed impossible, the fancies with which his imagination played in the Arabian Nights Tales and other myths and fairy-stories, with the things that became actualities between 1900 and 1925.

IV

There came in America during this period certain changes in government, certain legislative, political, and judicial innovations. Whether these were all enrichments is a subject of debate, as the changes in science and industry are not. Some would refuse to concede that all the changes in government were advances. In any event they were innovations, the fundamental importance of which warrants almost any superlative. The thirteen[1] most important, and their dates, were:

The *Direct Primary*, beginning in 1900. (Accompanied in some States by the initiative, referendum, and recall.) This gave the people increased control over the selection of their officials; and greatly reduced the power of party machines.

The "*Insular Cases*." 1901. The decisions of the Supreme Court in these cases made the adjustments whereby the American Government was enabled to possess and administer dependencies.

Conservation, beginning with the Reclamation Act, in 1902. This reversed the government's previous policy of expediting the transfer of public lands into private ownership. An incident of the adoption of conservation was an extension of the power of the executive branch of the government by Roosevelt, who established the precedent that the President can do whatever he is not expressly forbidden to do by the Constitution or the laws.

The "*Lottery Case*." 1903. This decision of the Supreme Court opened the way for a Federal police power, later

[1] This summary is the result of much consideration and checking up by men of authority in the field it covers. To some readers, additions will occur. Decisions under the Sherman Act were ruled out because they had to do with an innovation that came before 1900. The decision in the Oregon School case, 1925, was important; but it did not introduce an innovation — it prevented one. Similarly, there are reasons for ruling out other decisions and legislation from the classification adopted here. All these subjects will be covered more fully as they occur.

exercised in the Pure Food Act, the Meat Inspection Act, and several other important "public welfare" laws. The power was limited subsequently by the decisions in the "Child Labor cases."

The *Direct Election of United States Senators.* 1913. This reduced the status of the States and, like the direct primary, increased the control of the people over the selection of their representatives.

The *Graduated Income Tax.* 1913. This was an extension of the power of the Federal Government over private property.

Elevation of Organized Labor, illustrated by the Adamson eight-hour law, 1916.

The *Draft* as a mechanism for providing man-power for a war to be carried on abroad. 1917. This was an increase of the power exercised by the government over the individual.

National Prohibition. 1919.

National Woman Suffrage. 1920.

The *Limitation of Naval Armament* by agreement with other nations at the Washington Conference. 1921.

Extension of Federal Control. When radio and aviation came in, the assumption by the Federal Government of the function of control was uncontested by the States. This constituted an advance in the regulatory power of the Federal Government.

Immigration Restriction and Selection. 1921 and 1924. The adoption of the principle of limiting the immigration from each country to a fixed ratio of the natives of that country already here, was the first American assertion of intention to control the composition of its human stock.

Those thirteen stand out. Some in one way, some in another, some combined and some working in diverse ways, this group of innovations during the period 1900–

25 worked a political revolution, altered fundamentally the American conception of representative government, altered fundamentally the American conception of the relation of the individual to the government, altered America's relation to the world, changed measurably the basis of organized society in America, reflected the passing of some of the oldest of America's ideals, and either gave or reflected a new direction to social evolution in America.

V

1900 to 1925 included the greater part of the activities of Bryan, almost all the national career of Roosevelt, and all the public life of Wilson. It comprised the whole of the stirring history of the birth, growth, and death of the Progressive party. It covered practically all the national career of William H. Taft, and all that of Warren G. Harding, who when the quarter-century began was an obscure editor in a little Ohio town. These were the years of the principal activities of Robert M. La Follette and Henry Cabot Lodge; they included the periods of two picturesque speakers of the House of Representatives, Joseph G. Cannon and Champ Clark. Elihu Root, Charles Evans Hughes, and Philander Chase Knox all made the beginnings of their national careers after 1900. This period saw the apotheosis of the political boss in Senators Mark Hanna (who first defined Republican policy as "stand pat"), Matthew S. Quay, Arthur Pue Gorman, Thomas C. Platt, and Nelson W. Aldrich — and the passing of that type with the death, at midnight of the closing day of 1922, of Senator Boies Penrose, high-stand graduate, first of Harvard College and later of Pennsylvania politics, who in the first edition of Bryce's "American Commonwealth" was mentioned as an eminent leader of municipal reform, and in the second edition was discreetly unmentioned.

Into some or all of the years of this quarter-century overlapped several whose early achievements became so familiar that by 1925 they already seemed almost legendary: Edison, whose early invention gave promise to his own phrase, "press the button"; Alexander Graham Bell, inventor of the telephone; Collis P. Huntington, the transcontinental railroad-builder, whose epitaph was that he had reduced the breadth of the American continent from six weeks to six days; John D. Rockefeller; Mary Baker Eddy, one of the two Americans who have founded considerable religions.

1900 to 1925 saw, in its opening year, Doctor Walter Reed's determination of the cause of yellow fever, and Doctor Gorgas's discovery and practice of the means of exterminating it — by 1925, these two pioneers of science and sanitation had already reached whatever is science's equivalent of canonization. Theirs were only two of the many advances in medical science which made that field one as to which, indisputably, this could be said to be the golden age.

1900 to 1925 included the riper years of J. Pierpont Morgan, and the complete history, so far, of the most striking of his promotions, the United States Steel Corporation, the largest unit of organized business in the world. It included practically all the publicly noticed career of Edward H. Harriman, who, because of the greater public attention focussed on his financial operations, and because of his failure to see the light of a new day in the relations between capital and politics, was called, inadequately, a mere manipulator; he was also one of the ablest practical railroad men of his generation, an outstanding example of rich constructive imagination, coupled with capacity for execution on as large a scale as human minds often comprehend. In the less elevated worlds of finance, these years embraced the career of Thomas W.

Lawson, one of those curious characters that plunge for one mad day or so into the very centre of history at a time when history has somewhat the form of an unusually fast-moving whirlpool; he practised frenzied finance most frenziedly, and then exposed it more frenziedly yet, thereby contributing to an enlightenment of the public that led to certain legislative, social, and financial reforms.

Other characters were in the crowded and varied gallery of 1900 to 1925: Samuel Gompers, whose lifetime coincided with the whole history of successful labor organization in America; James J. Hill, Admiral Dewey, Admiral Peary, Doctor Cook, Carry A. Nation, Chancellor Day, Ben Tillman, Billy Sunday. But one may fall back on the words in which Saint Paul, similarly pressed, took refuge when he found himself unable to complete, fully, the "roll-call of the worthies,"[1] and of some not so worthy: "For the time would fail me to tell of Gideon, and of Barak, and of Samson, and of Jephthah; of David also and of Samuel, and of the prophets: . . . Wherefore seeing we also are compassed about with so great a cloud of witnesses, let us lay aside every weight . . . and let us run with patience the race that is set before us."

And, finally, in the way that play producers sometimes put the name of the principal actor in the emphasis of heavy type at the end of the list of dramatis personæ, let us recall that character who is often ignored but never should be, the average American, who in this narrative plays the principal rôle. Professor William G. Sumner of Yale once published a lecture about the average American, entitled "The Forgotten Man," which, in spite of some high-pitched overstatement, has become a familiar passage, in a sense a classic, in American political economy:

[1] Eleventh chapter of the Epistle to the Hebrews.

> Wealth comes only from production, and all that the wrangling grabbers, loafers, and robbers get to deal with comes from somebody's toil and sacrifice. Who, then, is he who provides it all? Go and find him, and you will have once more before you the Forgotten Man. You will find him hard at work because he has a great many to support. Nature has done a great deal for him in giving him a fertile soil and an excellent climate, and he wonders why it is that, after all, his scale of comfort is so moderate. He has to get out of the soil enough to pay all his taxes, and that means the cost of all the jobs and the fund for all the plunder. The Forgotten Man is delving away in patient industry, supporting his family, paying his taxes, casting his vote, supporting the church and school, reading his newspaper, and cheering for the politician of his admiration, but he is the only one for whom there is no provision in the great scramble and the big divide. Such is the Forgotten Man. He works, he votes, generally he prays — but he always pays — yes, above all, he pays.

This forgotten man, the principal character in this narrative, had come, just preceding the period of this history, to think he was being forgotten entirely too much, and arrived at a resolution destined, with other factors, to carry him far. The enrichment that subsequently came to him was less dependent on politics than on some other forces; but that purpose of the average man to make himself heard was part of a mood which determined much of the political and social history of this quarter-century; a mood in which the average American thought of himself as the under dog in a political and economic controversy, in which he was determined to fight for himself, but also felt the need of a big brother with a stick. Into that mood of 1900, Theodore Roosevelt fitted like the clutch of an automobile into the gear.

4

ROOSEVELT GETS HIS START

Through the Popularity Which the Spanish War Brought Him, He Is Made Governor of New York. Thereafter His Enemies, Wishing to Get Him Out of New York, "Kick Him Up-stairs" to the Vice-Presidency, Much Against His Own Will. A Typical Story and Picture of the Boss System.

ON January 1, 1900, Theodore Roosevelt was governor of New York. To that office he had come as a result of the part he had had in the Spanish-American War.

The popular heroes developed by the Spanish War were: Dewey, Hobson, Schley, Sampson, Roosevelt, Wood, and Lawton. The two outstanding ones were Dewey and Roosevelt. Both, immediately after the war, became the beneficiaries of the public disposition to honor war heroes[1] with high political office. Dewey sought the presidency, managed his effort rather badly,[2] and ceased forever to be a political personality. Roosevelt was thrust into a political career which, with the benefit of an accident, carried him not only to the presidency but to such political potency as not more than two other Americans have ever had.

[1] It is a striking fact that the Great War developed no such American military and naval heroes as either the Spanish War or the Civil War. Neither Pershing, who was the military commander in the Great War, nor Sims, who was the naval leader, had any great popular following. At the time there was much discussion of the reasons for this. Probably one reason was psychological, the fact that the Great War was not fought through to a finish. Indeed, the fact that that war was inconclusive, that just about the time America was getting into the stride of its intense fighting emotion, the Germans quit on us and left us no one on whom to take that emotion out—possibly this aborting of a national emotion may have accounted not only for the failure of the people to come to the point of hero-worship but also for a good many of the other rather unusual psychological conditions that developed among us during the period following the Armistice.

[2] See Chapter 12.

II

Roosevelt, at the time the Spanish War was brewing, was assistant secretary of the navy. As such, and in all his relations to the public, he was strong for bringing on the war. He was impatient about the hesitancy of Presi-

From a photograph by Brown Bros.

Theodore Roosevelt, as colonel of the Rough Riders, 1898.

dent McKinley,[1] and the even greater hesitancy of Senator Mark Hanna of Ohio, who was the dominant personality in the McKinley administration and in the Republican party.

At the private Gridiron dinner of March 26, 1898, less than three weeks before the Spanish War began,

[1] Roosevelt said: "McKinley has no more backbone than a chocolate eclair."

Mark Hanna spoke against it. Hanna "was out of tune with the prevailing idea which permeated the country at that time." He showed this in everything he said. He

Officers' mess of the Rough Riders in Texas soon after their organization. Colonel Wood left, and Lieutenant-Colonel Roosevelt right, at head of table.

talked about the great loss of life that would ensue, the cost of war, the necessity for moving slowly in all great undertakings. At the end of Hanna's speech, the president of the club remarked: "At least we have one man connected with this administration who is not afraid to fight — Theodore Roosevelt — assistant secretary of the navy." Roosevelt then spoke: "We will have this war for the freedom of Cuba, Senator Hanna, in spite of the timidity of commercial interests." [1]

As the war approached, Roosevelt hurried the preparations of the fleet to a degree that rather disturbed his superior, the secretary of the navy.[2] When the declara-

Roosevelt surrounded by the pride of his heart, the Rough Riders, at the point where they charged over the hill at San Juan.

[1] Arthur Wallace Dunn, "Gridiron Nights."

[2] "Mr. Long was at the head of the Navy Department for a year before the war came and never saw the shadows that were cast before, but Assistant Secretary Theodore Roosevelt saw them, and every time the Secretary's back was turned he would issue some kind of an order in the line of military preparedness and prevail upon Congress to do something toward meeting the inevitable. One day, when the Secretary had left the department to prepare for a trip to Boston on the evening train, Roosevelt hurried up to Congress and had an amendment inserted in an appropriation bill providing for the furnishing of war materials, and the Secretary, learning of this action, gave up his trip and hurried back to his department to checkmate his hot-headed young assistant, but all to no purpose." —David S. Barry, "Forty Years in Washington."

Drawn by Howard Chandler Christy from sketches made on the scene.

Grimes's Battery at El Poso.

The third Spanish shell fell in among the Cubans in the blockhouse and among the Rough Riders.

tion came, Roosevelt resigned from his executive office in the navy in order to get into the actual fighting. He brought together one of the most picturesque aggregations of soldiers, amateur and professional, that ever fought in any American war. In his regiment, in the kind of men he sought and the kind who gravitated to him, one could see echoes of Roosevelt's own past, his reading, his writing, all his interests. The Rough Riders reflected Roosevelt's experiences and associations as a rancher and hunter in the West, his college associates, his "highbrow" friends — and to an even greater extent those of Roosevelt's friends who would much prefer to be called "lowbrow"; and the interests and preoccupations he had picked up in his books, "The Winning of the West," "The Wilderness Hunter," "The Boone and Crockett Club Series."

The picturesqueness of the regiment thus brought together was the first of several aspects of Roosevelt's participation in the Spanish War that attracted to him the interest and, generally, the approving attention of the public. The performance of the regiment at the battle of San Juan Hill was another. Yet another was his part in a public demand on the War Department for action to conserve the health of troops.

III

At the end of the war Roosevelt was the principal leader whose politics were Republican. That caused him to fit into a situation which was gravely troubling the Republican boss of New York State, Senator Thomas C. Platt. Platt was typical of the boss domination which then existed in most States, in both parties. This story of Platt and Roosevelt can stand as a sufficient picture of the system as it was just before it began to be undermined by the substitution of direct primaries[1] for party conventions as the mechanism for nominating candidates. The bosses stood, one foot in the world of politics and one in the world of big business, and were the medium through which each served the other. Of this system, and of the specific case of Platt, there is an adequate picture penned by Elihu Root in his later years of mellow statesmanship:

> They call the system — I do not coin the phrase, I adopt it because it carries its own meaning — the system they call "invisible government." . . . The governor did not count, the legislature did not count, secretaries of state and what not did not count. . . . Mr. Platt ruled the State. For nigh upon twenty years he ruled it. It was not the governor, it was not the legislature, it was not any elected officers; it was Mr. Platt. And the capital was not here [in Albany]; it was at 49 Broadway, with Mr. Platt and his lieutenants.[2]

In New York the Republicans were in power, but the State administration had been discredited by extravagance in connection with the Erie Canal. If Platt and the Republicans were to retain power, it was necessary to put forward the strongest possible candidate for governor. Inevitably, Roosevelt's name suggested itself to Platt's need. But there were drawbacks that caused the situation to trouble Platt greatly.

To nominate Roosevelt would insure success — certainly it would go farther toward insuring success than any other choice. But, after election, what kind of governor, from Platt's point of view, would Roosevelt make? Platt was entirely familiar with Roosevelt's previous career. As he reflected back on Roosevelt as a member of the New York legislature, as a national civil service

[1] The first direct primary was held in Minnesota, this very year, 1900. The following year it was introduced in Wisconsin by La Follette. The boss as an institution lingered until nearly 1925. Penrose, of Pennsylvania, who died in 1922, was the "last of the barons," the last boss with a State-wide domination.

[2] Elihu Root, "Addresses on Government and Citizenship." This speech was made at a New York State Constitutional Convention.

commissioner, as police commissioner of New York, and otherwise, he was compelled to admit to himself that Roosevelt had been sufficiently regular to entitle him to good party standing. And yet Roosevelt had seemed again and again to be just at the outer edge of party

Chauncey Depew posed in his office, Grand Central Station, in 1895, for Alexander Black's first picture-play, "Miss Jerry." The play was pictured with a succession of still photographs.

regularity. Platt could not think of him as such an out-and-out reformer as to be definitely disqualified; and yet he knew that Roosevelt had repeatedly been close enough to party insurgency to make his choice a gamble. If Platt had felt he could win comfortably with any good candidate, he would not have given Roosevelt a moment's thought. But Platt had to make a delicate balance between the imperative need of a strong candidate in order to win and the possibility that Roosevelt, if he should win, might be a disturbance. Platt sent for Chauncey M. Depew, who, to Platt and the Republican organization generally, had the relationship of a kind of emeritus boss and all-round provider of sage counsel. Platt asked Depew for advice. Depew said:

> Mr. Platt, I always look at a public question from the view of the speaker's platform. . . . Now, if you nominate Governor Black and I am addressing a large audience — and I certainly will — the heckler in the audience will arise and interrupt me, saying: "Chauncey, we agree with what you say about the Grand Old Party and all that, but how about the canal steal?" I have to explain that the amount stolen was only a million, and that would be fatal. But if Colonel Roosevelt is nominated, I can say to the heckler with indignation and enthusiasm: "I am mighty glad you asked that question. We have nominated for governor a man who has demonstrated in public office and on the battle-field that he is a fighter for the right, and is always victorious. If he is elected, you know and we all know from his demonstrated characteristics — courage and ability — that every thief will be caught and punished, and every dollar that can be found restored to the public treasury." Then I will follow the colonel leading his Rough Riders up San Juan Hill and ask the band to play the "Star-Spangled Banner." [1]

Platt listened to Depew's rosy vision of how the election could be won, and said impulsively: "Roosevelt will be nominated." [2]

But Platt was a subtle person. He had made up his mind to nominate Roosevelt; but, being a master of the arts by which one man gains advantage over another, he sent out a fishing expedition to see if he could exact some

[1] Chauncey M. Depew, "My Memories of Eighty Years."

[2] This episode was merely the final incident in a long period of mental turmoil on Platt's part and pressure on him from some of his younger lieutenants. Probably the person who had worked hardest to persuade Platt to take Roosevelt was Benjamin B. Odell, later governor of New York. Odell at this time was a comparatively young man and had just become chairman of the Republican State Committee. He wished to make good in his new responsibility by success in the coming election for governor. He doubted if the Republicans could win if they should renominate Governor Black, as Platt and most of the organization wanted to do. Odell, feeling strongly the desirability of nominating Roosevelt, urged that course on Platt in frequent and persistent interviews.

sort of promise from Roosevelt. A henchman of Platt, Lemuel Ely Quigg, went to Montauk, where Roosevelt's Rough Riders were recuperating, and told Roosevelt that Platt was disposed to nominate him, but that Platt would like to feel sure Roosevelt, when governor, would not "make war on him." Roosevelt replied that he had no intention of making "war on Platt or on anybody else, if war could be avoided."[1]

That being the best Quigg or Platt could get, and just so much more than the nothing at all with which they would have been satisfied perforce, Quigg reported the conversation to Platt. Roosevelt was nominated, won the election, and took office on January 1, 1899.

IV

Roosevelt had not been elected a week before his actions justified Platt's apprehensions. Roosevelt was to Platt and the party organization just what he had been before, almost regular, but yet seriously distant from regularity in its political implications. Roosevelt used to defer to Platt, used to go to his hotel for breakfast with

[1] It must not be supposed that Roosevelt was unnecessarily truculent to Platt's emissary. It can be taken for granted he avoided putting his reply in words or in a manner that would have made his nomination impossible. Roosevelt wanted the governorship, and already had the ambition to be President. One of the strongest of Roosevelt's political arts was his capacity to make no sacrifice of essential principle, nor of his own reasonable independence, and at the same time work with the party organization. Roosevelt's own account of his reply to Quigg, written in his "Autobiography" fourteen years later, reads: "I said I should not make war on Mr. Platt or anybody else if war could be avoided; that what I wanted was to be governor and not a faction leader; that I certainly would confer with the organization men, as with everybody else who seemed to me to have any knowledge of or interest in public affairs, and that as to Mr. Platt and the organization leaders, I would do so in the sincere hope that there might always result harmony of opinion and purpose; but that while I would try to get on well with the organization, the organization must, with equal sincerity, strive to do what I regarded as essential for the public good; and that in every case, after full consideration of what everybody had to say who might possess real knowledge of the matter, I should have to act finally as my own judgment and conscience dictated and administer the State government as I thought it ought to be administered."

him; but it was the deference of a younger to an older man, not of a creature to his maker nor of a political lieutenant to his boss. The relations between the two caused Platt constant uneasiness. Roosevelt did many things on his own account as to which another governor under the same circumstances would have consulted Platt. But these matters were never of sufficient weight to give Platt occasion to make an issue. On the other hand, Roosevelt did some things at Platt's suggestion, made some appointments that he recommended. But here again these appointments were such as Roosevelt might readily have made on his own initiative. For some months there was not any break; but at no time could Platt sleep comfortably o' nights. He could not feel that sense of security that is normal for a boss to have about a governor of his own creating. This early period is illustrated by a comparatively unimportant appointment, commissioner of public works. As Roosevelt tells it in his "Autobiography":

> Senator Platt asked me to come and see him. . . .[1] On arrival, the Senator informed me that he was glad to say that I would have a most admirable man as superintendent of public works, as he had just received a telegram from a certain gentleman, whom he named, saying that he would accept the position. He handed me the telegram. . . . I told the Senator very politely that I was sorry, but that I could not appoint his man. This produced an explosion, but I declined to lose my temper, merely repeating that I must decline to accept any man chosen for me, and that I must choose the man myself. Although I was very polite, I was also very firm, and Mr. Platt and his friends finally abandoned their position. . . . It must be remembered that Mr. Platt was to all intents and purposes a large part of, and sometimes a majority of, the legislature.[2]

[1] At this point Roosevelt interjects a parenthetical explanation of why he went to Platt: "He was an old and physically feeble man, able to move about only with extreme difficulty." Roosevelt was a little sensitive about the jibes of some of the more critical newspapers concerning his "breakfasts with Platt."

[2] Theodore Roosevelt, "An Autobiography."

Platt swallowed that, and the status of polite truce went on. Roosevelt initiated and later put through a good deal of legislation of his own inspiration, about workmen's compensation, conservation of forests and wild life, a tenement-house commission, hours of labor, safety devices on railroads, sweat-shop labor. So long as it was a matter of this kind of humanitarian legislation, Platt "eased along" with Roosevelt. He and the other bosses had an idea it didn't amount to much. They counted on, and tried to insert, "jokers" in the statutes to make them impotent; or expected to be able to beat them in the courts or otherwise to get around them.

But there was one appointment that was of most vital importance to Platt and the big financial interests he represented. The office of superintendent of insurance in New York had jurisdiction over the great insurance companies located there, which companies were the principal customers for securities issued by the corporations and sold by the banks.[1] Between these insurance companies and corporations, on the one hand, and the political organizations there had been for years the kind of relation which later was an incident of the sensational exposures dealing with the Equitable and other insurance companies.[2]

The reappointment of the superintendent of insurance then in office, Louis F. Payn, was so vital to Platt that he came to a show-down with Roosevelt. "Mr. Platt," Roosevelt wrote, "issued an ultimatum to me that the incumbent must be reappointed or else that he would

[1] ". . . The superintendent of insurance, a man whose office made him a factor of immense importance in the big business circles of New York. . . . These operations had thrown him into a peculiarly intimate business contact of one sort and another with various financiers with whom I did not deem it expedient that the Superintendent of Insurance, while such, should have any intimate and secret money-making relations."—Roosevelt's "Autobiography."

[2] Out of these scandals, in 1905, Charles E. Hughes got his start in public life, as counsel for the legislative committee that conducted the investigation.

fight." But, after a prolonged strain, Platt yielded. Roosevelt concluded: "I never saw a bluff carried more resolutely through to the final limit."

Payn poured out his soul to Platt in the trite refrain of I-told-you-so. "I warned you," Payn said, "that this fellow would soon have you dangling at his chariot wheel. You would not believe me. He has begun by scalping members of your 'Old Guard.' He'll get you, too, soon." [1]

But the hardest fight between Roosevelt and Platt was over what was known as the "franchise tax." That proposal cut so deep into Platt's interests, into his very hold on political and financial life, that he could not yield. The franchise tax was a measure designed to make street-railway corporations pay taxes on the value of their franchises. It was opposed, naturally, by the whole fraternity of big business interests, and by the political machines and bosses who reflected these interests. Roosevelt, on the contrary, espoused it as "a matter of plain decency and honesty." He continues: "Senator Platt and the other[2] machine leaders did everything to get me to abandon my intention. As usual, I saw them, talked the matter all over with them, and did my best to convert them to my way of thinking. Senator Platt, I believe, was quite sincere in his opposition." [3]

Roosevelt, having listened to all the protests, ignored them. On April 27, 1899, he sent a special message to the legislature, certifying that the emergency demanded the immediate passage of the bill. There followed some rapid action. The Speaker actually tore up the message

[1] Thomas Collier Platt, "Autobiography."

[2] Benjamin B. Odell, then chairman of the Republican State Committee, later governor, wrote me, July 21, 1925: "I was in sympathy with Roosevelt on this [franchise] bill. . . . Notwithstanding the pressure brought upon me as chairman of the State Committee to exert my influence against the bill, I refrained, because Roosevelt had . . . made it his pet measure. . . . Senator Platt was very much annoyed . . . and it nearly caused a break between Platt and myself."

[3] Theodore Roosevelt, "Autobiography."

without reading it to the Assembly. That night the leaders were busy trying to arrange some device for the defeat of the bill — which did not seem difficult, as the session was about to close. At seven the next morning Roosevelt was informed of what had occurred. At eight he sent in another special message, in which he said: "I learn that the emergency message which I sent last evening to the Assembly on behalf of the Franchise Tax Bill has not been read. I therefore send hereby another message on the subject. I need not impress upon the Assembly the need of passing this bill at once."

Roosevelt sent with this message an intimation that if it were not promptly read he would go up in person and read it. At that, the opposition collapsed and the bill went through with a rush. But the end was not yet.

Platt now realized fully that he had a bear by the tail, a most energetic, impulsive, rampant bear. He tried sweet reasonableness. He wrote Roosevelt a letter:

> When the subject of your nomination was under consideration, there was one matter that gave me real anxiety: . . . I had heard from a good many sources that you were a little loose on the relations of capital and labor, on trusts and combinations, and, indeed, on those numerous questions which have recently arisen in politics affecting . . . the right of a man to run his own business in his own way, with due respect, of course, to the Ten Commandments and the Penal Code. . . . I understood from a number of business men, and among them many of your own personal friends, that you entertained various altruistic ideas, all very well in their way, but which before they could safely be put into law needed very profound consideration. . . . At the last moment [of the recent legislature], and to my very great surprise, you did a thing which has caused the business community of New York to wonder how far the notions of Populism, as laid down in Kansas and Nebraska, have taken hold upon the Republican party of the State of New York.

This sweetly reasonable protest — at least, it was sweetly reasonable up to the last sentence, when Platt just simply could not help exploding — did not move Roosevelt.

V

Platt was now in an acutely distressing position, with disaster behind him, trouble all about him, and ahead of him a dilemma of such a sort as few political bosses have ever had to face. For his own purposes he had made use of Roosevelt by taking advantage of the latter's Spanish War popularity and nominating him for governor as the only candidate likely to insure success for Platt and his party. Roosevelt as governor had promptly justified the worst of the doubts Platt had had when he made the choice. Not only that; Roosevelt, by the very fact of his defiance of Platt, had added to his previous popularity, had accumulated such a wide-spread public support that it was a question — if indeed there was any — whether it was Roosevelt or Platt who had command of the Republican party in New York. To Platt the worst of this situation was not in its present disaster, but in the complications placed immediately in front of him by the necessity of giving consideration to the next nomination for the governorship. The normal thing would be to renominate Roosevelt. To do otherwise would be such a pointed calling of public attention as to invite the State to go Democratic. But to Platt and the interests he represented that was far less to be feared than the

"Tom" Platt in 1900.

other alternative. Two more years of Roosevelt as governor would destroy Platt, the Republican organization, and the whole interlocking of politics and big business which was the basis of the existence of the boss system in both parties. Roosevelt wanted the renomination and frankly said so. For Platt to find an excuse for denying it to him seemed an impossible problem. But Platt saw a way out.

Mark Hanna.
In 1900, as national boss of the Republican party, he resisted the effort to nominate Roosevelt for Vice-President. Hanna died in 1904.

There was also approaching another nomination, that of Vice-President, at the Republican National Convention in June, 1900. For President, McKinley would be renominated. The vice-presidency was open, and in that opening Platt saw his opportunity to ship Roosevelt out of New York. There were difficulties. But Platt went about it with a characteristic combination of persistence and slyness.

Roosevelt declared he would not be side-tracked off to Washington. He did not want to be Vice-President. He wanted to go on being governor of New York. Roosevelt's New York friends and following wanted him to continue. As the public became aware of the paradoxical situation the New York *World* printed a cartoon in which Roosevelt, riding a horse, was grinning and saying "Nay! Nay!" to Platt, who was holding out a bucket of feed to lure Roosevelt into the vice-presidential stock-yard. That picture of Roosevelt, avoiding the trap with a grin of gay self-confidence, while it portrayed the essentials of the situation accurately, was rather distant from Roosevelt's private state of mind. He was unusually serious and troubled.

Roosevelt's resistance was not the only difficulty that embarrassed Platt. Resistance came also from Mark

From "Harper's Weekly," June 28, 1900.

Roosevelt's being forced into the Vice-Presidency against his will appealed irresistibly to the cartoonists.

Hanna, and in the nature of things was formidable. Hanna was the national [1] boss as Platt was the New York boss; and Hanna did not want Roosevelt in Washington any more than Platt wanted him in New York.

[1] Hanna's dominance of the Republican party in the nation was practically unquestioned. He was senator from Ohio, chairman of the Republican National Committee, and, most potent of all, intimate friend of President McKinley. While Hanna and Platt were both bosses, while the power of each rested to a large degree on the union between politics and big business, Hanna was of a higher order, both as politician and as man.

Hanna had much the same notion about Roosevelt's "various altruistic ideas" that Platt had expressed in his letter. Between Platt and Hanna there now ensued something like one of those card games in which the art consists in so manœuvring as to cause an undesirable card to turn up in your opponent's hand. Some one said that every time Platt and Hanna met and parted, Hanna used to search his pockets carefully to make sure Platt had not dropped Roosevelt into one of them.[1]

These were the complexities that bothered Platt. There were other complexities that played into Platt's hand — and bothered Roosevelt. Roosevelt's popularity had become not only local to New York, but had spread throughout the country. Republicans everywhere, especially in the West, of the sort who liked Roosevelt, took kindly to the idea of nominating him for Vice-President, which office they saw merely as a titular honor higher than governor. The people who held this sentiment were the same who loathed Platt and all Platt's purposes. Their motive for liking Roosevelt and wishing to elevate him was admiration for the fight he had made against Platt. Nevertheless, their attitude at this moment was most helpful to the one purpose closest to Platt's heart — and correspondingly embarrassing to Roosevelt.

Platt was shrewd and had the whip-hand. He knew that if he could get Roosevelt nominated for Vice-President, the strength of the national ticket would carry his own State ticket through; he would be able to put any one he chose on his State ticket for governor and resume his interrupted boss-ship. Thus could he, by a single

[1] James Ford Rhodes, brother-in-law of Senator Hanna, writes: "Hanna regarded Roosevelt as erratic and 'unsafe,' and was emphatically opposed to his nomination as Vice-President. . . . And President McKinley in an unobtrusive way let it be known that he did not want Roosevelt as a running-mate." (Hanna's early intention was to nominate Jonathan P. Dolliver, of Iowa.)

move, get rid of Roosevelt, put Roosevelt where he did not want to be, and at the same time make use of Roosevelt's popularity for ends that Roosevelt abhorred. As Platt manœuvred it, the situation became far more embarrassing to Roosevelt than to Platt, and in all its aspects became a curious comedy of paradox.

VI

Roosevelt knew Platt's motive perfectly. In a letter to Senator Lodge, February 3, 1900, he described the reasons Platt had for wishing to get him out of the State:

> The big moneyed men . . . have been pressing him very strongly . . . . The big insurance companies . . . to a man want me out. . . . The great corporations affected by the franchise tax have also been at the Senator.

Henry Cabot Lodge.
For thirty-nine years the close personal friend and political adviser of Roosevelt, Lodge was almost alone among Roosevelt's friends in advising him he would do well to accept the Vice-Presidential nomination.

If it had been merely a case of resisting Platt on a clear issue like that, Roosevelt would have rushed into the fight joyously, and in all likelihood would have had his way. But the situation was full of complexities, public and personal, which pulled Roosevelt in diverse ways, so that as the decisive day (June 21, 1900) approached, he was driven into a frame of mind hardly duplicated in his career of normal decisiveness. He was almost in what New Englanders call a "state."

His central thought at all times was that he did not

want the vice-presidency, but preferred to remain governor. To Senator Lodge he wrote in various letters during the early months of 1900 repeated expressions of his disinclination to take "a position in which there is not any work at all and . . . no reputation to make. . . . In the Vice-Presidency I could do nothing . . . I am a comparatively young man and I like to work. I do not like to be a figurehead. . . . As Vice-President, if I did anything, I should attract suspicion and antagonism. The office [of Vice-President] is merely a show office. . . . It would not entertain me to preside over the Senate. . . . The chance for a Vice-President to do anything is infinitesimal. I suppose I should have leisure to take up my historical work again but that is about all. . . . I have not sufficient means to run the social side of the Vice-Presidency as it ought to be run. I should have to live very simply and would be always in the position of a 'poor man at a frolic.' . . . So, old man, I am going to declare decisively that I want to be Governor and do not want to be Vice-President." To Herman Kohlsaat he wrote of his determination not "to take an office for which I really have no special fitness and where there is nothing for a man of my type to do." To Platt he wrote: "I would a great deal rather be anything, say a professor of history, than Vice-President." To many friends he wrote and spoke in the same strain.

If Roosevelt had been able to confine himself to that clear thought, to his distaste for the functions of the vice-presidency, his preference for the governorship of New York, in that case the disturbance of his ease of mind and of his ordinarily strong clarity of thinking would have been comparatively little. If even the problem had presented itself to Roosevelt as one of simple self-interest, Roosevelt's judgment could have been clear. So far as he looked toward the presidency, as a later ambition, he shared the view of most persons about the vice-presidency.[1] At that time the vice-presidency was regarded as of little account, as a political graveyard. Instead of being a stepping-stone to the presidency, it was normally, except in the accident of death to the President, a traditional bar. Since Martin Van Buren, no man who had been Vice-President had later been elected President. To accept a vice-presidential nomination was regarded as writing "finis" to a man's political career. The whole psychology tended to make Roosevelt himself, and many of his thoughtful friends, agree with his enemies that to nominate him for Vice-President would end his political career and draw those formidable teeth. Roosevelt told his sister that he had no notion of becoming the principal character in a "vice-presidential burial-party," and wrote to Lodge: "I should be simply shelved as Vice-President."

That line of thought also, the course based on what he and most others regarded as self-interest, would have saved Roosevelt many of his perplexities if he had been free to follow it. But there were several considerations that pulled in other ways, at bewildering angles. Roosevelt had to take account of his relation to several differ-

[1] To this view, there was one important exception. Senator Lodge, Roosevelt's intimate friend, steadily combated the latter's view that the vice-presidency would bury him. In letters covering a period of six months before the nomination, Lodge wrote to Roosevelt:

"Your interests and your future have been constantly in my mind. The general impression of course is that you would be very foolish to take the Vice-Presidency. . . . My own opinion has not changed. I can put it most tersely by saying that if I were a candidate for the Presidency, I would take the Vice-Presidency in a minute at this juncture. . . . I daresay everybody else is right, they probably are, and I am wrong. . . . My belief in your taking it arises from my conviction that it is the true stepping-stone for you, either toward the Presidency or the Governor-Generalship of the Philippines. I think it is the best road to the former. . . . I think the Vice-Presidency is the better path to better and more important things. . . ."

Lodge's practically solitary conviction that Roosevelt ought to take the vice-presidency, his certainty that events would so turn out as to make him take it, is a story in itself.

ent groups, having diverse points of view, and likely to have differing reactions to his accepting or not accepting the vice-presidential nomination. He had to take account also of different possible aspects of the manner in which the offer of the vice-presidency should come to him, the public appearance of it, whether it should come to him through pressure of the progressive Republicans of the West, who sincerely admired him and wanted to elevate him, or as a device of the New York boss to get rid of him, or of the national bosses reluctantly to make use of him. All sorts of shadings contributed to Roosevelt's perplexity.

Roosevelt's rapidly growing popularity in the West weighed much with him. He was fond of the West and kin to it politically. If he was ever to run for the presidency, it would be as the representative of Western ideas. For human reasons and political ones, he disliked to take a course that might seem to the West to be selfish or cowardly. To Odell he said, reluctantly: "If the West nominates me, I will take it." On the other hand, he had to consider his New York following. To Lodge he wrote: "All my friends in the State would feel I was deserting them and are simply unable to understand my considering it." And again: "If I am now nominated for Vice-President it will be impossible to get it out of the heads of a number of people that the machine had forced me into it for their own sinister purpose, and that I had yielded from weakness, as they know I do not want the position of Vice-President."

There was a similar contradiction leading to inevitable mental confusion in his relation to the organization. He would hate to take the vice-presidency as the successful conclusion of Platt's plot to get him out of New York and out of politics. At the same time, if the national organization, under pressure from the West, and in order to save McKinley, should offer him the vice-presidency, and if he should refuse what was presented to him as an opportunity to serve the party — in that event, would they ever offer him, or let him have, anything again? In spite of Roosevelt's rapidly growing popular strength, that time was, as Roosevelt put it, "the zenith of the power of the bosses," and Roosevelt had not yet sufficient confidence in his personal strength, and was too much a party man, to hope to go higher against a determined hostility from the organization. The direct primaries had not yet come, and political advancement was still in the hands of the bosses. Finally, Roosevelt had to give thought to the possibility of missing both targets. If he should refuse the vice-presidential nomination in June, then Platt might deny him the renomination for governor in September.

On April 23, Roosevelt wrote to Lodge: "I did *not* say that I would not under any circumstances accept the Vice-Presidency. I have been careful to put it exactly as you advised." But on June 12, nine days before the convention, he wrote in a private letter to Francis V. Greene: "I will not accept under any circumstances and that is all there is about it." In reality, however, Roosevelt was far from being in the state of decision that those words proclaim, and he refrained from making that statement publicly. If he had been clear in his mind, if he had been determined not to take the vice-presidential nomination, he could have avoided it. Odell told him if he would "remain away from the Philadelphia convention and state positively and explicitly that he would not accept the nomination if tendered, he might be certain, with my [Odell's] help and influence, that he would not be nominated. Roosevelt refused pointblank to keep away from the convention and I [Odell] told him he would be nominated in spite of himself." Lodge told

The kind of Vice-President some persons expected Roosevelt would make. Cartoon on the left from the Washington *Times;* on the right from the Washington *Post.*

him the same: "If you go to that convention . . . you will be nominated . . . and if you are nominated . . . you will be unable to refuse. . . . If you stay away with your absolute declination, which you have already put out, I do not think you will be nominated."

That, instead of settling Roosevelt's mind, added another complexity. He feared that if he stayed away from the convention he would, as he expressed it to Lodge, "be looked upon as rather a coward." He gave some thought to whether he could refuse after being nominated, and looked up an old precedent, the case of Silas Wright.

The outcome was finally determined by the pressure of those followers of Roosevelt throughout the country, especially in the West, whose devotion to him was more ardent than penetrating. They saw no deeper than that the vice-presidency seemed an honor higher than the governorship of New York.[1] They, unaware of what was going on between Platt and Hanna, regarded the nomination to the vice-presidency as an elevation of their hero. In that mood their pressure grew to a point where Hanna had to take account of it. At the convention, Western delegations marched up and down the corridors in front of Hanna's door, chanting "We want Teddy." There were mutterings that if the wish of the Republican voters in the West to have Roosevelt for the vice-presidential nominee were denied by Hanna, the result might so exasperate them as to endanger success for the national ticket, including Hanna's beloved McKinley. Under that

[1] Roosevelt's more discriminating friends wanted him to become President ultimately. But they thought, and Roosevelt himself thought, that the surest way to the White House was to remain governor of New York, continue to make a good record, and thus qualify himself for the presidential nomination four years later, in 1904. To let the vice-presidential nomination be forced on him in 1900 was to accept a gamble, of which one outcome, the more probable one by far, was political desuetude; and the other, the only one that could be profitable, was the chance of McKinley's death.

pressure Hanna became willing to discuss the matter.[1] The same pressure was exerted on Roosevelt himself. He was told that his refusal to accept the nomination for Vice-President might endanger the election of Mc-

From "The Tribune," New York.

Is he setting the switch for the Roosevelt flyer?

Kinley, might bring about the risk of defeat by the Democrats. He was told that only his presence on the ticket could beat Bryan; that Bryan might beat McKinley, but could not beat him if Roosevelt were running on the same ticket as the candidate for Vice-President.

[1] One who was close to this situation wrote me, in March, 1925: "The night before [the nomination] Platt, who was laid up in his room with a broken rib, sent for Hanna, who had just gone to bed. Hanna dressed and came to Platt's room. Up to that moment, Hanna was absolutely scornful of Roosevelt being on the ticket, but Platt used his best talents in persuading Hanna it was the only thing to do. Hanna then issued a signed statement to the Associated Press advocating Roosevelt's nomination." To the newspaper men he said: "Boys, you can't stop it any more than you could stop Niagara."

Especially, it was argued that if Roosevelt should not be put on the ticket, after the West had demanded it, Bryan might win.

Lodge, who kept at Roosevelt's side during the con-

By Davenport.

Platt's hope of getting Roosevelt out of New York is here the theme of both cartoonists. (See opposite page.)

vention, who for six months had foreseen that just this situation would arise, and who almost alone among Roosevelt's friends had believed the vice-presidency to be "the better path to better and more important things" — Lodge now "bucked him up" with a saying that became much talked about: "Theodore, the way to break a precedent is to make one."

To that sort of argument and pressure Roosevelt listened — and yielded. A man who saw him an hour after he made the decision said: "His tail-feathers were all down. The fight had gone out of him and he had changed his former tune to that of: 'I cannot disappoint my Western friends if they insist. . . . I cannot seem to be bigger than the party.'"[1]

VII

Roosevelt was named for Vice-President. Hanna took over from Platt the tail of the obstreperous bear. The New York *Tribune* printed a cartoon showing Platt as a railroad workman throwing the switch which turned the Roosevelt flyer off the governorship track and onto the vice-presidential siding. The New York *Journal* printed a cartoon entitled "Rounded Up," in which Platt, riding triumphantly on his cow-pony, had thrown his lariat, entitled "Vice-Presidency," so as to catch Roosevelt's foot and throw him.

After the deed was securely completed by the actual election of Roosevelt, some one asked Senator Platt if he were going to attend the inaugural exercises at Washington. Platt replied: "Yes, I am going down to see Theodore Roosevelt take the veil."[2]

And but for a remote chance, the insane whim of the poor creature who murdered McKinley, Roosevelt would have been safely veiled into political sterility. Roosevelt himself felt so. On November 22, 1900, twenty days after he was elected Vice-President, he wrote to a friend, Edward S. Martin: "I do not expect to go any further in politics." Believing his political career ended, he took steps to utilize the energy for which the vice-presidency provided no outlet, by studying law, to equip himself for a new career.

[1] Ascribed to Nicholas Murray Butler by Herman Kohlsaat.
[2] H. H. Kohlsaat, "McKinley to Harding."

5

THREE POLITICAL LEADERS

In that 1900 campaign Roosevelt came into direct conflict with Bryan, Roosevelt as the Republican candidate for Vice-President campaigning[1] against Bryan as the Democratic candidate for President. This was the only occasion when Roosevelt and Bryan faced each other at the polls. But for twelve years, from 1900 until 1912, these two were the dominant leaders in their respective parties. (Bryan had been dominant since four years before, in 1896.) They, with Woodrow Wilson, were in a class apart, and above, in the political history of this quarter-century. For twelve years after 1900 Roosevelt and Bryan competed side by side. Then Woodrow Wilson arose and for the following eight years eclipsed both. No other political figures of the time approached these in the stature of their relations to their parties and to the public. In the six presidential elections from 1896 to 1916, always one of these and sometimes two were among the candidates. In 1896, Bryan ran for President; in 1900, Bryan ran for President and Roosevelt for Vice-President; in 1904, Roosevelt for President; in 1908, Bryan for President; in 1912, Roosevelt and Wilson ran; in 1916, Wilson again. When any one of them was not the candidate himself, he usually had a controlling hand in the selection of whoever else was, and in determining the issues.

Bryan nominated himself three times, and in 1912 determined the nomination of Wilson. (Bryan's career is

[1] Roosevelt travelled and spoke for eight weeks, covering 21,000 miles in twenty-four States; McKinley repeated his 1896 "front-porch" campaign.

unique in that he is the only man who was given his party's nomination for the presidency three times, in spite of repeated failure to win an election; Grover Cleveland was given the Democratic nomination three times, but he contributed to his party the asset of two successes.) Roosevelt nominated himself in 1904, nominated Taft in 1908, and again in 1912 nominated himself as the candidate of a third party that cast more votes than the Republicans. Wilson, having received the nomination in 1912, renominated himself in 1916, and in 1920 only prevented the nomination from being made in accordance with his wishes by preserving the most austere silence, and sternly ordering his secretary not to attempt to influence the convention "by so much as the lifting of a finger." To illustrate the position Roosevelt had, it can be said fairly that the personal relations between him and one man, Taft, first friendly and then hostile, determined the presidency three times and gave a definite bent to history.

Roosevelt, Wilson, and Bryan during the greater part of this quarter-century supplied America with its political leadership. In them the people personified their convictions, visualized their aspirations. Then within a single year all three passed off the scene in one way or another, and left America with a lack of accepted leaders, which accounted for much that happened thereafter.[1] In January, 1919, Roosevelt died. In September, 1919, Wilson became incapacitated. And the same year may be

[1] This passing of outstanding leaders, so striking in the field of politics, also took place in other fields of public thought. In the opening years of this quarter-century there had been such leaders as Joseph Pulitzer, E. L. Godkin, and Henry Watterson in journalism; Cardinal Gibbons, Lyman Abbott, and T. Dewitt Talmadge among clergymen; Charles W. Eliot, then in his prime, and Andrew D. White in education. By 1920 and after, there were none who could be called equivalents of these. The passing of so many accepted spokesmen in the various fields of public thought, the rather sudden poverty of leadership after great riches, was one of the striking phenomena of the times.

William Jennings Bryan in 1900, the year of his second campaign for the Presidency, at the age of 40.

From a photograph by United News Pictures.

Bryan at the Democratic National Convention in 1924, prematurely old at sixty-four.

named, without stretching the facts too much for the sake of emphasizing a coincidence, as the time when Bryan came to be generally recognized as, so to speak, shopworn — as having been too long on the shelf, and offered to the public too many times, unsuccessfully. When, in 1925, Bryan died, and in the same year La Follette,[1] an American era unusually rich in leadership, in forceful personalities, was ended completely.

Roosevelt, Bryan, and Wilson were in a class apart. Their leadership had one important basis in common. They represented, each within his party, a common political mood, a mood that arose in America during the nineties and continued, with some changes of objective, into the present century, until displaced by the coming of the Great War in 1914; a mood in which the common man regarded himself as oppressed, as in danger of becoming stratified economically; a mood of revolt against organized wealth, of resentment against the union of "big business" and the boss system in politics. But aside from being children and prophets of that common mood, Roosevelt, Bryan, and Wilson were quite unlike. They were unlike to some extent in the reforms they advocated to meet the common discontent, and even more so in their political methods. In intellect, in temperament, in practically every attribute that enters into personality they were utterly unlike. Decidedly it is desirable to make clear that the grouping of these three here is restricted to their

[1] Bryan in his three campaigns received respectively 47, 46, and 43 per cent of the popular vote; in the 1896 election, less than 50,000 added votes, if distributed among the States just right, would have given Bryan victory. Roosevelt received 57 per cent of the popular vote in 1904; in 1912 as the candidate of a third party he received 27 per cent. If he had permitted himself to be a candidate in 1908 he would have received an overwhelming majority. If he had lived until 1920 it is practically certain he would have been the Republican candidate, and would have received probably a larger popular vote than the 60 per cent that went to Harding. Wilson received 41 per cent of the popular vote in 1912 and 49 per cent in 1916. La Follette, as a third-party candidate in 1924, received 16 per cent of the popular vote.

From a photograph by Pach Bros.

Theodore Roosevelt, 1898.

From a photograph by Underwood & Underwood.

Roosevelt, shortly before his death in 1919.

contemporaneousness, the sustained leadership of each over scores of millions of people, and the fact that they sprang from a common political mood. It would be most misleading if carried further. To point out the differences of each from each, to contrast and compare them, is not called for at this point. That constitutes practically the whole political history of the period.

One is obliged to smile at the thought of how each of the three, and especially Roosevelt and Wilson, would have regarded being classified with the others. Roosevelt called Wilson a "Byzantine logothete," an epithet which, although literally meaningless when applied to Wilson, nevertheless, by the very reason of its mystical suggestion, called attention to what Roosevelt regarded as the extreme tenuity of substance in some of Wilson's writings and speeches. This was one of Roosevelt's characterizations of his great rival that the public got the benefit of; privately, Roosevelt's emotions toward Wilson were sometimes clothed in language less classic and less urbane, more "short and ugly." Wilson, on the other hand, carried out a policy of ignoring Roosevelt, because he thought that was the best way to meet, or avoid, the kind of public controversy Roosevelt frequently tried to force on him; to which reason of public policy there was the added motive that Wilson got personal satisfaction out of this course, since he shrewdly thought that to be silent, to have the air of gazing at the stars over Roosevelt's head, was the thing that would most exasperate a rival with the kind of temperament, and temper, that Roosevelt had.

Both Roosevelt and Wilson had less hotness of feeling toward Bryan than toward each other. Bryan, although he got more presidential nominations than either, and dominated his party for a longer period, must be classified apart from and a little below the others. A superior consciousness of that fact enabled the others to be more

From a photograph by Pach Bros.

Woodrow Wilson in 1900.

From a photograph by Wide World Photos.

Wilson in the closing year of his administration.

amiably genial toward Bryan than they ever could be toward each other. Wilson once expressed the wish that Bryan might be "knocked into a cocked hat," but later made him secretary of state. The relations between Roosevelt and Bryan included much good-natured jibing about the proprietorship of issues. Bryan used to paint a satirical picture of Roosevelt stealing plank after plank of his platform until he had nothing to stand on, a picture which the cartoonists sometimes translated into Bryan reduced to the protection of a barrel while Roosevelt, grinning, ran off with his clothes.

Of the three, it was Bryan and Roosevelt who arose most directly out of the political and economic mood of America during the 1890's. As between Bryan and Roosevelt, Bryan was the first child of that mood.

6

BRYAN

The Heredity, Background, Education, Environment, and Early Triumphs, and the Last Phase, of a Born Orator.

IN this history there will be many contrasts — some of them sensational, considering the shortness of the span. One of the most appealing consists of two newspaper despatches by correspondents who wrote of the same man, in the same setting — but in scenes a generation apart.

In January, 1924, a Washington correspondent, Clinton W. Gilbert, picturing a meeting of the Democratic national committee, wrote of William Jennings Bryan that "most of the time he was wandering about the lobby of the hotel, attracting no attention"; that at the sessions he was merely "a spectator pressed against the back wall of the meeting-room, wedged between a fat woman and a cub reporter." This correspondent made a cutting comparison: "The committee went in a body to pay its respects to Woodrow Wilson,[1] but it did not even ask Mr. Bryan to make a speech or have a chair." This account of Bryan at the 1924 meeting of the Democratic national committee did not leave to the reader, or to Mr. Bryan, any leeway to assume that the ignoring of him might be due to political reasons, to the fact that the committee had departed from his leadership and wanted to emphasize the separation. No such comforting assumption was left to the imagination. The situation was made cruelly clear: "Bryan is not ignored by design; he is ignored because he no longer counts." Most poignant of all, this

[1] This visit, in January, 1924, was, as it happens, the last that Mr. Wilson received from any group. Within less than three weeks he was dead.

1924 despatch goes on: "Occasionally a white-haired man would totter up to the hotel desk and ask respectfully for 'Mr. Bryan.' Mr. Bryan would come forward, his scant hair hanging down over his coat collar, and lean his big ear against the lips of his superannuated admirer. A few words would be exchanged, and Mr. Bryan would hurry away — nowhere, too important to waste his time on a ghost from the past and too unimportant to command the time of any one in the present."

This picture of Bryan of the last phase, while serviceable for the purpose of contrast, is oversardonic. The correspondent who wrote it was one of the joint authors of that vivacious volume "The Mirrors of Washington"; and this picture of Bryan tints the facts, which were sardonic enough, with the same temperament that made "The Mirrors of Washington" one of the most cynically disillusioning books of its time.[1] There may be equal truth, and a slightly different point of view, in a despatch that I myself sent from the 1920 Democratic convention at San Francisco, where Bryan made a plea for prohibition enforcement: "His first act was to wave aside the amplifier. Bryan was plainly an elderly man, but he scorned any help to that long-experienced voice. . . . His plea had eloquence, but it was the spirit of an elder admonishing a newer generation. One thought of the Prophet Isaiah. . . . The audience listened closely and gave him affectionate applause. But it was deference to his years, and contained no hint of indorsing his plea. . . . Bryan seemed like an elderly uncle in a black alpaca coat who comes to visit us in the city. We give him the easiest chair; we treat him with affection; when he ad-

[1] I hope I have made it clear that this picture of Bryan was extreme. Mr. Bryan was elderly, but not as old as the picture makes him out. While he had no vital relation to the national committee of his party, he still was able to make himself important to it if he should choose.

vises us about our affairs, we listen respectfully — but we go our own way." [1]

This latter picture had the more accurate shading, I think. Nevertheless, Mr. Gilbert's picture was merely too heavily drawn. The fundamental assertion was true. Bryan in his later years had little authority over his party organization, little deference from it, and decreasing deference from the rank and file. In March, 1925, he was the target of very general newspaper jibes because of his delivering daily lectures as an incident of a lot-selling campaign at a real-estate development in the suburbs of Miami, Fla. In July, 1925, at Dayton, Tenn., in a field other than politics, he became the central figure in a controversy almost as acrimonious, quite as potent to make for him intensely loyal partisans and intensely bitter opponents, as the political controversy that first gave him fame. In the conflict between Fundamentalism and Modernism, Bryan thought of himself as entering upon a new crusade, dreamed of eclipsing his former fame. Just as he was getting under way, before he had had time to deliver a speech prepared in the belief that it would have an even greater popular reception than his oration of twenty-nine years before, he died.

Bryan, in the year of his death, 1925, though only sixty-five, was, to more than half his fellow citizens, the Bryan of the last stage — an elderly man in baggy trousers and a black alpaca coat; mostly bald, except for a few stringy strands of graying hair that hung, a little untidily, over his coat collar; that once superbly clear and musical voice a little marred by a slightly hissing sound that came of age's imperfect teeth; the eyes, though they still flashed, flashing now with rather the cold hardness of an old fighter who has been denied success rather frequently, and lacking the warmth and depth that once

[1] Mark Sullivan, in the New York *Evening Post*, July, 1920.

they had, the quick mobility through the widest range of feeling from satirical humor to tense earnestness.

This later Bryan was the only one known in 1925 to more than half his fellow citizens; for a generation as measured in familiarity with public characters is short. As respects reading the newspapers with any real interest in public affairs, we must measure a generation as beginning at the age of sixteen to twenty. And so, in the closing year of this quarter-century, probably we should have to say that only those over forty could remember the early Bryan. Only those of middle age or older could have known, as a personal experience, the sensation with which Bryan first burst upon the country.

II

One read that picture of Bryan's later years as painted by Mr. Gilbert — one read it, or one saw the actual scene at the national committee meeting of 1924. And then one's mind went back to another scene, twenty-eight years before, at the national convention of 1896 — and reflected on some sombre aspects of time and change which various poets and Old Testament prophets have put into familiar and sufficient words. Could that Bryan of the 1924 picture be the same Bryan of whom at the Democratic National Convention of 1896, the correspondent of the New York *Sun*[1] had written:

> From all parts of the convention hall a great roar went up for Bryan, Bryan, Bryan. These cheers were continued and rolled on and on. . . . Mr. Bryan is a smooth-faced man of early middle life and his dark hair is long and wavy. . . . His rhetoric and English and his oratorical gestures were almost superb. . . . His voice is clear and resonant, and his bearing graceful. He is the idol of the silver camp, and if a vote could have been taken immediately after he had finished, he would,

[1] July 10, 1896. This despatch has the more force when it is remembered that *The Sun* was extremely hostile to Bryan.

without the slightest doubt, have been nominated for President by acclamation.

Or the same Bryan of whom, in his prime, John Clark Ridpath, fired by the ecstatic exaltation that was common at the time of his 1896 triumph, wrote:

> That unanswerable oration of William J. Bryan . . . was one of the few inspired utterances of the human soul rising to a great occasion, and pouring out the vehement river of truth. Bryan was on that day a chosen instrument. . . . He vaulted like an athlete into the wild arena, drew his sword, and stood defiant, blazing with wrath in the very face of an enemy that durst not attack him with anything but contumely and falsehood. . . . We intend that the patriot and statesman, William Jennings Bryan, shall be, as he deserves to be, the President of the United States . . . and that under his wholesome and patriotic administration a new century of peace shall be ushered in, in the splendor and revival of which the evil powers which have dominated American society for the last quarter of a century shall wither and perish from the earth.

III

That early Bryan, the Bryan of that picture and that ecstatic prophecy — how shall we make him live again for a generation that did not know his prime? How shall one tell, by what device of words can another generation be made to feel, the thrill that Bryan gave to the America of 1896? He was "beautiful as Apollo," said Stone of Missouri; he was young, he was dashing, he was magnetic.[1] In nominating him, the Honorable Henry T.

[1] Mr. R. L. Metcalfe, an associate of Bryan in his early Nebraska days, and for many years a coworker with Bryan on the latter's newspaper, *The Commoner*, wrote me feelingly of the hold Bryan's personality maintained over those who came into intimate personal contact with him: "If he had lived in any year, in any age, and had retained the capacity for leadership and the power of drawing men to him which he had in the early days he would have been THE leader. In those days it was not only his oratory but his loving and magnetic personality, his unfailing sense of humor, his practical attitude toward things of life generally, and so many things that I can feel right now but cannot name, that made him a real leader and brought men around him so that they would have been glad to die for him. That is all so true that I can't even tell about it in words."

Hardly any superlative one might use to suggest the exaltation many persons

Lewis, of Georgia, used the words applied by Prentiss to Henry Clay: "His civic laurels will not yield in splendor to the brightest chaplet that ever bloomed upon a warrior's brow." There was romance in the mere fact that one so young should win such fame, and in the daring of his ambition; for in the year in which he seized the nomination he was only a year over the age which the Constitution fixes as the youngest at which a man may aspire to the presidency, and younger by nine years[1] than any man who had reached the office.

Most of all, there was romance in the dramatic swiftness of his leap. On July 9, 1896, the name of Bryan meant nothing to probably nine hundred and ninety-nine out of every thousand people in the United States. Even to those who knew him at all, he was merely a Western ex-congressman who had served two terms and turned to editing a newspaper in Omaha. On that day, July 9, 1896, the correspondent of the New York *World*, writing of the Democratic National Convention at Chicago, said:

felt about Bryan in his prime would be too great. It might be unreasonable, it might even verge on impiety, but it would be an accurate description of the way some of Bryan's followers sincerely felt at the time he emerged and for some years later. One day in April, 1918, riding with Bryan on an interurban car in northern Indiana, as we passed through a town (I think it was Warsaw) Bryan told me of a family there that used to think of him as the second coming of Christ. To compare him, favorably, to St. Paul, was not uncommon. One Bryan zealot pointed out that St. Paul was not under the handicap of having to overcome the steady disparagement of hostile newspapers. Who can say what might have been Bryan's place in history if he had emerged not in the nineteenth century, and not in sophisticated America, but in a community unfamiliar with the simplest facts of science, interpreting some of the ordinary phenomena of nature as supernatural, still thinking of thunder, for example, as the voice of Jehovah; a community highly imaginative, given to mysticism, tending to exalt unusual personalities, susceptible to leadership, with a tradition of voices from on high?

[1] The youngest President before 1896 was Grant, who was forty-six when inaugurated in 1869. Grover Cleveland was forty-seven when inaugurated in 1885. Franklin Pierce was forty-eight when inaugurated in 1853. James K. Polk was forty-nine when inaugurated in 1845. Subsequent to 1896, Roosevelt was forty-three when he took office on McKinley's death in 1901, the youngest President we have ever had.

The Silverites will be invincible if united and harmonious; but they have neither machine nor boss. The opportunity is here; the man is lacking.

"The man is lacking"! That was printed on the morning of July 10, 1896. Before night of that day, before a

From a photograph by A. & P. Photos.

William Jennings Bryan (on the right), aged eleven, with his two brothers (Charles in centre). The year after this picture was taken, Bryan's "political career began at Centralia (Illinois). . . . The audience first became quiet and attentive, then wildly enthusiastic. . . . He was carried from the platform and about the town on the shoulders of cheering men."

good many subscribers to *The World* had had time to read it, William Jennings Bryan, through a single speech, had made himself spokesman and master of the silver wing of the party; had utterly routed the shrewd, hard old leaders who had commanded the Democratic party for a generation; and, in the confident self-possession with which he handled himself in victory, was restraining the exalted delegates from changing the order of the programme so as to give him the presidential nomination instantly, a day before the balloting was scheduled. Bryan forbade the change: "If my boom will not last until tomorrow, it certainly would wilt before Election Day."

Bryan in his bearded youth. Taken when he was eighteen.

Then he left the convention, went to his modest hotel,[1] and remained away while the convention took the action he knew was certain — actually, he was being shaved when the news of his nomination came next day.

Between these two extremes of Bryan, his radiant prime and his somewhat shuffling age, there lay as dramatic a personal career, as colorful a panorama, as we have had in American history. We turn now to his youth, and the comet-like blaze of glory with which he came upon us in 1896.

IV

(Bryan's wife wrote a biography of him in 1896. From it the facts in this section dealing with Bryan's youth are taken. All the quotations used here are from Mrs. Bryan, except one, which is from the family physician.)

[1] Bryan records in "The First Battle": "My entire expenses while in attendance at the convention were less than a hundred dollars."

Bryan's father was a "devout Baptist" who "prayed at morning, noon, and night, and was a firm believer in providential direction in the affairs of life"; "a fluent speaker" whose "mind was philosophical and his speeches argumentative," and who used to say that "the guest-chamber of his home was reserved for 'politicians and divines.'"

From a photograph by A. & P. Photos.

William Jennings Bryan as valedictorian of the class of 1881 at Illinois College.

"William Jennings Bryan was born at Salem, Ills., March 19, 1860. He learned to read quite early; after committing his lessons to memory, he stood upon a little table and spoke them to his mother. This was his first recorded effort at speechmaking. . . . His appetite, which has since been a constant companion, developed very early. The pockets of his first trousers were always filled with bread, which he kept for an emergency. . . . His father's congressional campaign in 1872 was his first political awakening, and from that time[1] on he always cherished the thought of entering public life. . . ."

"The lad's political career began at Centralia, only a few miles from Salem, where his father took him in his twelfth year to a great Democratic rally. Among the orators were some of the most distinguished men in the State. He listened to them all with flushed face and blazing eyes. His little body became a perfect volcano of

[1] He was then twelve.

enthusiasm. . . . Finally he mounted the platform and began to talk. Many laughed outright at the idea and all smiled. He was undaunted, however. He did not appear to see his auditors or to hear their laughing remarks at the start. As he proceeded the laughter ceased. In forcible and eloquent language, with the energy and diction of the born orator, he pursued his argument. . . . The audience first became quiet and attentive, then wildly enthusiastic. Cheer upon cheer rent the air. . . . When he closed there was a tumult of applause and he was carried from the platform and about the town on the shoulders of cheering men." [1]

"A prize contest always fired William's ambition. . . . During his first year at the Academy[2] he declaimed Patrick Henry's masterpiece." The second year he entered with "The Palmetto and the Pine." Later "he declaimed 'Bernardo del Carpio' and gained the second prize." Finally, with an essay on "Labor," he achieved first prize. The following year he won first prize with an oration on "Individual Powers." In an intercollegiate oratorical contest he won a second prize of $50 for an oration on "Justice." General John C. Black, of Illinois, was one of the judges and marked Mr. Bryan one hundred in delivery. Upon invitation of Mr. Black the young man called at the hotel and received many valuable suggestions upon the art of speaking. At his graduation he was class orator and delivered the valedictory.

He studied law, and on July 4, 1883 — Mrs. Bryan

[1] This quotation is from the physician of Bryan's father's family, Doctor William Hill. It is clear that Bryan had a hereditary bent toward spontaneous speechmaking, that this was accentuated by his surroundings in his early imaginative years, and that he became a personality which reacted in the form of instinctive oratory to situations with which he came in contact. Modern psychologists would be apt to find much significance, much explanation of Bryan's later career, in the oratorical personality of his father, the early and perhaps excessive forcing of that trait in Bryan's childhood by a family and friends less wise than loving, and the overemphasis on oratory in his education.

[2] Whipple Academy, preparatory department of Illinois College, Jacksonville, Ills.

specifies this Independence Day date as if it had some kind of symbolical significance — he began, in Jacksonville, Ills., not far from his birthplace, a law practice which shared his time — shared it rather generously — with active participation in every local political campaign. In

From a photograph copyrighted by Brown Brothers.

W. J. Bryan practising law in Jacksonville, Ills.

the summer of his twenty-seventh year, a law case took him to Kansas and Iowa. On the trip he spent a Sunday with a law-school classmate practising in Lincoln, Neb. Mrs. Bryan says he "was greatly impressed with the advantages which a growing capital furnishes for the young lawyer. He returned to Illinois full of enthusiasm for the West and perfected plans for our removal thither."

V

By this change, Bryan's talent found ideal soil. He was now at the very heart of the area of economic distress, a community where farmers and others were burdened with debt, among whom raged political issues arising out of their discontent and out of proposed cures, of which the principal one was free coinage of silver.[1]

Bryan had not been in his new home a year before he was in the thick of local politics. He became a delegate to the Democratic State Convention. He canvassed the congressional district in behalf of the Democratic candidate, who was defeated by 3400. Two years later,[2] Bryan got the congressional nomination and turned this large Republican majority into a Democratic majority of 6713. This really sensational victory, in Bryan's first candidacy before the people, was due largely to sheer personal power as a speechmaker, in a series of joint debates with his Republican opponent.

Bryan, elected to Congress, dropped his law work,[3] never to resume it. When his first term ended he had to run in a new district, the State having been reapportioned. He repeated his previous feat, changing a Republican majority of 6500 to a Democratic majority of 140.

Bryan's congressional experience was active. He served on the Ways and Means Committee, an unusual distinction for a new member; made speeches against the rules of the Republican Speaker, "Czar" Reed; against Cleveland's sales of government bonds to replenish the gold in the Treasury; and in favor of the income tax. He did not, however, attain anything approaching national fame, although a prepared speech he made on the tariff re-

[1] Though Bryan at once became the exponent of the local political discontent, he did not take up free silver specifically until a few years later, after he was in Congress.

[2] 1890. Bryan, on this date of his first election to public office, was thirty years old.

[3] Bryan's income as a lawyer had never exceeded $1800 a year and was generally much lower. For him, and at that time, election to Congress at $5000 a year and some perquisites was an elevation.

ceived wide attention from the newspapers and was circulated by Democratic congressmen to the extent of a hundred thousand copies. The most important influence Bryan's congressional experience had on his career was his contacts with other men who led him to think about bimetallism as the chief cause of economic distress in the West.[1]

In 1894 he declined to run for another term in the Lower House, and stood as the Democratic candidate for United States senator. He repeated his previous feats at speechmaking, talking, Mrs. Bryan tells us, "four or five hours each day and sometimes riding thirty miles over rough roads between speeches."[2] As the possibility of a Democratic legislature being elected in November was small, Bryan knew when he undertook it that his fight for the senatorship was futile. Nevertheless he conducted his campaign energetically, not so much in the hope of election as to rally and consolidate his following for the attempt to wrest control of his party in the State from

[1] One such contact arose out of his tariff speech, March 16, 1892, which was the most noteworthy effort of his career in Congress. (Mr. R. L. Metcalfe, Bryan's lifelong friend and associate, who has read the proofs of this chapter, believes the tariff speech "was the greatest Bryan ever made on any subject.") At the close of this speech, Bryan discussed it with Joseph W. Bailey, then a young Democratic congressman, later senator, from Texas, "sitting on one of the sofas that were then kept in the hall of the House just back of the seats." Bailey told Bryan that the latter's explanation of the fall in prices, as due to "improved processes of production," could not be sustained. Bryan, a little resentful, and using a method of argument characteristic with him, asked Bailey if he "agreed with the Republicans in thinking the protective tariff had resulted in reducing prices." Bailey promptly replied that he "did not accept that theory any more than I accepted his." Later in the conversation Bailey said that "what we were in the habit of calling a fall in prices was really nothing more or less than an appreciation in value of gold." Bryan replied, "I see you have given a good deal of study to that subject, and I am going to take up the question right away." "He then asked me"—I quote from a letter Senator Bailey sent me September 7, 1925—"what were the best books on the subject and I gave him the names of several. . . . About the time the House was adjourning that afternoon he came to me and asked me if I would go with him down to the bookstore and help him select the best books in relation to the money question."

With Mrs. Bryan, who had studied law after her marriage in order to be of help to her husband, Bryan devoted his leisure to study of bimetallism.

[2] This was in the days of horse-drawn wagons and crude dirt roads.

the "gold bugs." Foreseeing defeat, he became editor of the Omaha *World-Herald*.[1] From that date until the national convention at which he became famous, he divided his time between writing for *The World-Herald* and speechmaking, rather more the latter than the former. Mrs. Bryan says: "The contest for supremacy in the Democratic party had begun in earnest, and calls for speeches were so numerous and so urgent that it seemed best to devote his time to lecturing and to the public discussion of the money question."

VI

In his lecturing up and down the West, Bryan kept experimenting with a speech he was weaving, a speech in which phrases like "cross of gold," "crown of thorns," and other figures gradually fell into place. Also, on his travels, he kept in touch with former associates in Congress, local Democratic leaders, and persons likely to be sent as delegates to the 1896 Democratic National Convention, then approaching. To ex-Senator Charles S. Thomas, of Colorado, he wrote on April 16, 1896, nearly three months before the national convention:

> . . . I don't suppose your delegation is committed to any candidate. If we succeed in getting a sixteen-to-one plank in Chicago, our delegation may present my name. Whether it goes further than a compliment will depend upon the feeling of other States. I am not saying this to the public but write you in confidence. . . .[2]

[1] His salary was $1800 a year.

[2] Bryan's ambition struck Senator Thomas as it would have struck the public, if Bryan had not been "not saying this to the public." Senator Thomas read the letter and read it again. Years later, he recalled: "I then laid it down and wondered whether I would ever again encounter such superlative assurance. Here was a young man barely thirty-six, living in a comparatively unimportant Republican State west of the Mississippi River, audaciously announcing his probable candidacy for the presidential nomination of the national Democracy. The very seriousness of the suggestion emphasized its absurdity."

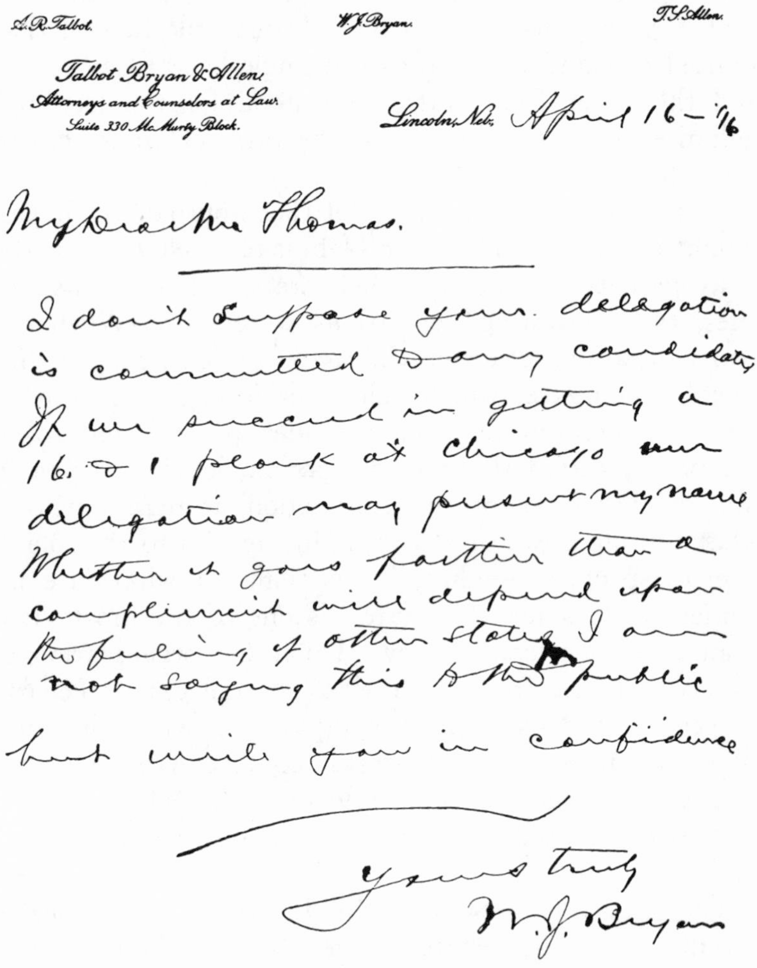

A. R. Talbot. W. J. Bryan. T. S. Allen.

Talbot Bryan & Allen.
Attorneys and Counselors at Law.
Suite 330 McMurty Block.

Lincoln, Neb. April 16 – '96

My dear Mr. Thomas.

I don't suppose your delegation is committed to any candidate. If we succeed in getting a 16 to 1 plank at Chicago our delegation may present my name. Whether it goes farther than a compliment will depend upon the feeling of other states. I am not saying this to the public but write you in confidence.

Yours truly
W. J. Bryan

This is the earliest statement in writing, so far as the writer of this history has been able to discover, of Bryan's candidacy for the 1896 nomination. The date, April 16, is nearly three months before the convention. The letter controverts the generally accepted legend that the nomination came to Bryan as a surprise. Charles S. Thomas, to whom the letter was addressed, was at that time Delegate-Elect from Colorado, and member of the National Committee.

Throughout this period of politics and speechmaking, the issues arising out of currency,[1] and especially the free-

[1] These are described and explained in Chapter 9.

silver question, were acute. The contest for supremacy that Mrs. Bryan mentions was between the faction that wanted to stand by gold, as the single basis of currency, and the silver Democrats, who stood for the free and unlimited coinage of silver in the ratio of 16 ounces of silver to 1 of gold.

As the national convention of 1896 approached, Bryan sought a place as one of the Nebraska delegates. In the cleavage between the gold Democrats and the free-silver ones, two contesting delegations were sent. When the two delegations reached Chicago, the Democratic National Committee, which held over from four years before, and therefore reflected the older, pro-gold control of the party, seated the gold delegation, leaving Bryan in the opening days of the convention a mere outsider. That turning down of Bryan, reducing him to the rôle of a mere spectator — that, in the light of what fate intended to do a few days later, is one of the most vivid ironies in American history. Upon the organization of the convention itself, composed of delegates recently chosen, and consequently sympathetic with the new silver sentiment, the Nebraska contest was reviewed. The gold delegation was rejected; the silver delegation was accepted; Bryan got his seat — and his opportunity.

The opportunity came in the debate on resolutions — specifically, in the debate on the currency plank. It was bitterly acrimonious. The audience was turbulent. Ben Tillman, of South Carolina, making the opening speech in behalf of silver, got a reception that gave him occasion to utter the reproof: "There are only three things in the world that can hiss — a goose, a serpent, and a man." The arguments in favor of gold were made by Senator Hill, of New York, Senator Vilas, of Wisconsin, and ex-Governor Russell, of Massachusetts.

Then, to make the closing speech,[1] came Bryan.

Of Bryan's speech that day, of Bryan in his prime, of Bryan when he was not "a spectator pressed against the back wall of the room, wedged between a fat woman and a cub reporter," but an actor, the principal actor; of

From "The Advertiser," New York.

"Which way, Miss Democracy?"
A cartoonist's portrayal of the quandary of the Democrats prior to the 1896 convention.

Bryan when he was magnificent, commanding, dominant; of Bryan on this day of his highest reach, there is an unforgetable picture by Harry Thurston Peck:

Until now there had spoken no man to whom that riotous assembly would listen with respect. But at this moment there appeared upon the platform Mr. William Jennings Bryan, of Nebraska. . . . As he confronted the 20,000 yelling, cursing, shouting men before him, they felt at once that indescribable, magnetic thrill which beasts and men alike experience in the presence of a master. Serene and self-possessed, and with a

[1] To get the opportunity, strategically important, of making the closing speech, Bryan had asked ex-Senator Thomas, of Colorado, to intercede for him with the chairman, Senator Jones, of Arkansas. Mr. Thomas made the request and the chairman granted it.

smile upon his lips, he faced the roaring multitude with a splendid consciousness of power. Before a single word had been uttered by him, the pandemonium sank to an inarticulate murmur, and when he began to speak, even this was hushed to the profoundest silence. A mellow, penetrating voice, that reached, apparently without the slightest effort, to the farthermost recesses of that enormous hall, gave utterance to a brief exordium. . . . The repose and graceful dignity of his manner, the courteous reference to his opponents, and the perfect clearness and simplicity of his language, riveted the attention of every man and woman in the convention hall. . . . He spoke with the utmost deliberation, so that every word was driven home to each hearer's consciousness, and yet with an ever-increasing force, which found fit expression in the wonderful harmony and power of his voice. His sentences rang out, now with an accent of superb disdain, and now with the stirring challenge of a bugle call. . . . The great hall seemed to rock and sway with the fierce energy of the shout that ascended from twenty thousand throats. . . . The leaderless Democracy of the West was leaderless no more. Throughout the latter part of his address, a crash of applause had followed every sentence; but now the tumult was like that of a great sea thundering against the dikes. Twenty thousand men and women went mad with an irresistible enthusiasm. This orator had met their mood to the very full. He had found magic words for the feeling which they had been unable to express. And so he had played at will upon their very heart-strings, until the full tide of their emotion was let loose in one tempestuous roar of passion.

This account of Bryan's "Cross of Gold" speech fails to give adequate emphasis to his voice. Ex-Senator Thomas of Colorado speaks of it as "glorious," and the use of that word means much from a man who is austerely intellectual on all subjects, and as to Bryan is even a little cynical. It was not merely that Bryan's was the first voice that day to be able to fill the big hall. The music of it was memorable. Years afterward, men who were there talked of Bryan's speech in ways that showed it was a high spot in their emotional experiences. It was as an emotional experience that it was remembered, like hearing Patti or Jenny Lind. Ex-Senator Thomas says that Bryan brought tears to the eyes of men and caused women in the gallery to become hysterical.

Of what followed that speech of Bryan's — for a picture of the Democratic party when it was not ignoring Bryan, but rather was in a frenzy to get at him and lick his hands — read this from Charles Warren:

> There was a pause. Then occurred a wild and hysterical uprising; waves of deafening cheers and yells swept from end to end of the building and back again, unceasing in their tumult. Delegates stood on chairs, uncontrollable, frenzied. A Georgia delegate suddenly tore away the State's blue-tipped rod, raised it high aloft, and started to rush toward the Nebraska delegation. Indian Territory raced down to follow him with its stick. Illinois, South Dakota, Missouri, Virginia, Alabama, Kentucky, Ohio, Iowa, Tennessee, Mississippi, Michigan, Utah, Nevada, California followed. A grand procession of State rods and delegates started around the delegates' enclosure. Bryan was hoisted upon the shoulders of his followers and carried with it. . . . It was fully thirty-five minutes before quiet was restored.

VII

That speech, in which Bryan won his nomination and burst flaming upon the country, is one of the great orations of American history — great, that is, in the light of its purpose and its superb adaptation to that purpose. Decidedly it is not great in the sense of an orderly intellectual exposition, as a well-reasoned argument for bimetallism. Of that the speech contains practically nothing. Bryan did not intend the "Cross of Gold" speech to be that. On other occasions he made arguments for the free-silver theory which reflected the working of his mind in the field of exposition. But the "Cross of Gold" speech was oratory wholly, and oratory of the highest order.

The speech was meant to get the nomination for the presidency. Within that larger purpose, it had to quiet a turbulent mob, to so appeal to the emotions of a majority of the crowd as to cause them to turn to the speaker as their leader; and to carry a similar inspiration to those outside the convention who composed the rank and file of the silver party. To these purposes, the speech was magnificently adapted, and was so designed in advance. At the time, it was widely thought the speech was improvised. Even yet, when people talk about outstanding examples of spontaneous oratory, they frequently refer familiarly to "Bryan's 'Cross of Gold' speech" as the classic American example. It has almost become, indeed in many quarters it has actually become, one of the legends of history that that speech is one of the conspicuous examples in literature of spontaneous oratory extemporized under the pressure of high emotion and the stimulus of a great occasion; and that the presidential nomination which followed was one of the most dramatic surprises in American politics. As to the first of these legends, it is only true in the sense that the speech had not actually been put into manuscript for that occasion; as to the second, the nomination of Bryan was a surprise to the country and even to most of the politicians and delegates. To Bryan it was no surprise.

Almost every paragraph of the "Cross of Gold" speech had been delivered scores of times to audiences up and down the Missouri valley, during two years preceding. The speech, as delivered at the convention, was extemporaneous only in the sense that the order of its parts was arranged to fit the occasion, and enough sentences improvised to form an introduction, to supply connections between the parts, and to adapt the whole to the particular audience and circumstances. The essential parts of the speech, those sonorous sentences, those emotion-rousing phrases, rolled out from Bryan's lips that day as familiar to Bryan himself as the Lord's Prayer. Every one he had tried again and again on country schoolhouse audiences.

Bryan had long held to himself the belief that he was the only man on whom the silver Democrats could agree, and through whom they could control the convention. The intention that he should get the Democratic nomination and that this speech should get it for him had been in his mind for months. Bryan wanted the nomination, and he went after it.[1]

VIII

As what it was, that speech was a consummate work of art. The opening sentences were most subtly devised to serve several purposes: to placate an audience that was angrily turbulent; to express courtesy to the speakers whom he was answering, all of whom were well-known public characters of long experience; to ingratiate himself with the audience by assuming modesty — to suggest, by indirection, that he was as conscious of his youthfulness as he well knew the audience would be. The opening was artfully devised to accomplish all these placatory offerings, made necessary by the conditions and the atmosphere, and yet at the same time to give, within the first three sentences, a sufficient hint of the passion that was

[1] Bryan, in the mellow memory of twenty-nine years later, did not see this as clearly as the evidence of the facts at the time shows it to be. Having read what I have here said, Mr. Bryan on May 6, 1925, wrote me, among other things:

"I think you have discovered more adroitness in my convention speech than I knew was in there. While I regarded the nomination as possible and had so stated to a few friends, I regarded it only as a possibility and counted upon the logic of the situation rather than my speech. I had no thought of my speech having the effect it did. I was fighting for a principle and found, as Jefferson once expressed it, that 'firm adherence to a principle is the best handmaiden to ambition.'"

I think it is true Bryan did not fully anticipate the immensity of the effect of his speech. At the same time, I think he did not fully recall how much assistance he gave to "the logic of the situation." At other times in the past, he told me, with humor, of conferences he held with State delegations the evening before the speech—delegations which, at that hour, decidedly did not share Bryan's views about his chances, or about the "logic of the situation," whichever you choose to call it. The letter Bryan wrote to ex-Senator Thomas nearly three months before the convention (quoted in this chapter) is sufficient evidence; and there is much besides that. After the nomination, Bryan, meeting ex-Senator Thomas, ventured a pun: "Are you still a doubting Thomas?"

to come, a hint necessary for creating an atmosphere of attentive expectation:

> Mr. Chairman and Gentlemen of the Convention: I would be presumptuous indeed to present myself against the distinguished gentlemen to whom you have listened, if this were a mere measuring of abilities; but this is not a contest between persons. The humblest citizen in all the land, when clad in the armor of a righteous cause, is stronger than all the hosts of error. I come to speak to you in defense of a cause as holy as the cause of liberty — the cause of humanity.

Having thus thrown out a hint, but only a hint, of passionate earnestness to come, he adroitly changed his gait for a moment, in order to disarm the hostility that might arise among many of the delegates if he were too strongly emotional at the start. He dropped back into a neutral mood to speak a few words about the parliamentary situation, explaining the alternative resolutions on which the delegates would be called to vote. Then again he put forth the hint of high eloquence to come:

> The individual is but an atom; he is born, he acts, he dies; but principles are eternal; and this has been a contest over a principle.

Yet once more he fell back to the mood of unargumentative quiet, giving an extended review of the conflict between the gold Democrats and the silver ones. By this time he was ready to begin to soar into eloquent passion:

> Then began the conflict. With a zeal approaching the zeal which inspired the crusaders who followed Peter the Hermit, our silver Democrats went forth from victory unto victory, until they are now assembled, not to discuss, not to debate, but to enter up the judgment already rendered by the plain people of this country.

He was still careful not to remain overlong, at too early a stage of the oration, in the mood of harsh insistence.

From that height of sternness he fell ingratiatingly back to the disarming mood of tolerance for his opponents:

> It is not with gladness, my friends, that we find ourselves brought into conflict with those who are now arrayed on the other side.

Then once more he returned to tense earnestness and, through a plausible device, managed, without being glaringly obvious, to name the classes of the community to whom he was appealing; managed to make a roll-call of the classes whose support he was seeking; and to suggest subtly the contrast between these humble classes on his side and the classes on the side of gold:

> When you [turning to the gold delegates] come before us and tell us that we are about to disturb your business interests, we reply that you have disturbed our business interests by your course. We say to you that you have made the definition of a business man too limited in its application. The man who is employed for wages is as much a business man as his employer; the attorney in a country town is as much a business man as the corporation counsel in a great metropolis; the merchant at the crossroads store is as much a business man as the merchant of New York; the farmer who goes forth in the morning and toils all day, who begins in the spring and toils all summer, and who by the application of brain and muscle to the natural resources of the country creates wealth, is as much a business man as the man who goes upon the board of trade and bets upon the price of grain; the miners who go down a thousand feet in the earth, or climb two thousand feet upon the cliffs, and bring forth from their hiding-places the precious metals to be poured into the channels of trade, are as much business men as the few financial magnates who, in a back room, corner the money of the world. We come to speak for this broader class of business men.

Then followed, similarly adroit in its indirection, an appeal designed to stir strong and homely sentiments, associations with home, religion, nature, youth, death:

> The pioneers away out there [pointing to the West], who rear their children near to Nature's heart, where they can

mingle their voices with the voices of the birds — out there where they have erected schoolhouses for the education of their young, churches where they praise their Creator, and cemeteries where rest the ashes of their dead — these people, we say, are as deserving of the consideration of our party as any people in this country. It is for these that we speak.

By this time Bryan was ready for challenge, defiance:

We do not come as aggressors. Our war is not a war of conquest; we are fighting in the defense of our homes, our families, and posterity. We have petitioned, and our petitions have been scorned; we have entreated, and our entreaties have been disregarded; we have begged, and they have mocked when our calamity came. We beg no longer; we entreat no more; we petition no more. We defy them.

Bryan now brought in the device of a direct personal challenge to an individual, a challenge of a sort most likely to excite the fighting spirit of his audience. It was a challenge difficult to make, considering the known high character of the individual he was challenging and the affection in which he was held. Bryan managed it:

Mr. McKinley was the most popular man among the Republicans, and three months ago everybody in the Republican party prophesied his election. How is it to-day? Why, the man who was once pleased to think that he looked like Napoleon — that man shudders to-day when he remembers that he was nominated on the anniversary of the battle of Waterloo. Not only that, but as he listens he can hear with ever-increasing distinctness the sound of the waves as they beat upon the lonely shores of St. Helena. Why this change? Ah, my friends, is not the reason for the change evident to any one who will look at the matter? No private character, however pure, no personal popularity, however great, can protect from the avenging wrath of an indignant people a man who will declare that he is in favor of fastening the gold standard upon this country; or who is willing to surrender the right of self-government and place the legislative control of our affairs in the hands of foreign potentates and powers.

From this Bryan passed to the gradual working up of his peroration:

You come to us and tell us that the great cities are in favor of the gold standard; we reply that the great cities rest upon our broad and fertile prairies. Burn down your cities and leave our farms, and your cities will spring up again as if by magic; but destroy our farms and the grass will grow in the streets of every city in the country.

Then came the superbly conceived conclusion, glowing with the atmosphere of Biblical memories Bryan evoked:

Having behind us the producing masses of this nation and the world, supported by the commercial interests, the laboring interests, and the toilers everywhere, we will answer their demand for a gold standard by saying to them: You shall not press down upon the brow of labor this crown of thorns, you shall not crucify mankind upon a cross of gold.

7

LEADERS AND FORCES

THAT "Cross of Gold" speech, and the reception it had, was not a comet, a mere isolated burst of oratory. It drew its materials from the conditions of the time, and found the response ready in the hearts of millions.

The rise of Bryan, and also so much as has so far been given of the rise of Roosevelt, has been told in terms, chiefly, of their individual actions, as if these men did certain things and the rest followed. But there is another theory of how history is made. Bryan had a relation to certain forces that were in motion during his time. So had Roosevelt. Some forces were common to both. And it is important to identify these forces — especially, at this stage, the ones that had most to do with Bryan.

II

As to any period, there must be, so to speak, a pattern of its history. We are compelled to believe so, no matter how great or how little our faith in one form or another of — whatever we shall call it, whether divine purpose, or orderly evolution, as the mainspring of the universe. We are compelled to believe so, because any other hypothesis would assume mere accident as one of its premises, and chaos as its most probable outcome, a chaos that presumably would have arrived long ago if there were any probability in this kind of hypothesis. And so, one of the problems of the historian who tries to get far below the surface may be stated: to find, after the event or period, what would have been, before it, the pattern in the mind of Omnipotence — the Engineer's blue-print, so to speak.

One supposes there must be such a thing. One takes it for granted that every historian must have searched for that pattern, with one degree of zeal or another. And yet, one has never heard of any historian as to whom subsequent historians said that this particular one had succeeded in finding, indisputably, the true pattern; and had constructed his history on the lines of the original blue-print.

What really happens in every history is that the writer sets up a hypothetical pattern of his own, has his own theory of why this happened, and why that followed. But that, after all, is merely one man's guess about the sequences of events, the relations of cause and effect. It is indeed one large guess made up of many small ones — guesses about men's motives (which, by the nature of the case, are practically universally a matter of surmise, and frequently not clearly known to the man himself); about laws of nature, some of them discovered only after the historians have made their guesses, and some not discovered yet; guesses that inevitably had to be guesses, because the evidence was not all in.

However, all that is rather deep. Let us say that there are two ways (at least) in which you can conceive of events as being brought about:

One is that the pattern of history is made by the strong men[1] of the period. One strong man goes after something. Another goes after something else. A multitude of other men of varying strengths go after various other objectives with varying degrees of momentum. These men come into contact with each other in an infinite variety of ways. Sometimes they meet in a direct head-on collision, and

[1] Carlyle: "All things that we see standing accomplished in the world are properly the outer material result, the practical realization and embodiment, of Thoughts that dwelt in the Great Men sent into the world." Walt Whitman: "Produce great persons; the rest follows." Eli Thayer said, and Edward Everett quoted: "Personal presence moves the world."

The classic examples of the two schools are Carlyle, who put the emphasis on the individual leader, and Buckle, who emphasized the philosophy of forces.

then you have a case such as that of Roosevelt and Bryan in their competition for the leadership of the American people during several years, or Roosevelt and Wilson during later years. Sometimes the course of one strong man having one purpose coincides with the course of another strong man having a different but not competing purpose; in which event their momentum is united and they accelerate each other. To some extent, this also is the case of Bryan and Roosevelt; for the appeals of both were in behalf of the under dog, and each gave momentum to the other, competitors though they were. In other cases strong men come together at an infinite variety of angles. The net resultant, as the engineers would say, of these various men coming together at every sort of angle of incidence, would determine what happens. That, if one could plot it all out, might be the pattern of history.

That is one of the more convenient possible theories of how history is made. Another is that there are certain forces in the world, some of which we can identify, others we cannot: economic conditions, forces of nature, developments of science and industry, laws of crowd psychology, psychic forces, waves of popular emotion, the power of ideas that get afloat, forces arising out of the influence exerted upon men by climate and other variations of nature. It is these forces,[1] this theory would say, that really determine the actions of the men we call leaders. According to this, the so-called leaders are mere chips on the surface. They become leaders chiefly by the mere accident of happening to be at a certain place at a certain time. About the farthest degree of credit this theory would concede to individual leaders would be merely that some had the astuteness to see one of these

[1] Bernard Shaw, in his preface to "Saint Joan," speaks of the world as being "finally governed by forces expressing themselves in religions and laws which make epochs, rather than by vulgarly ambitious individuals who make rows.

forces when it was beginning to get under way, and the energy to jump aboard it.[1] "The coach-dog school of economists," John Morley called some of these.

Between these two theories (because a historian, in order to achieve clearness, is more or less compelled to build along one line or the other) most historians incline toward the former, which puts the emphasis on the importance of individual personality, the leader. Probably they do so partly because that is the formula easier for the writer to conform to, and simpler for the reader to follow; and partly because, in the world of politics especially, the theory of human leadership seems to explain more things than the more recondite philosophy of forces. A conspicuous politician who arose during the period of this history, Will H. Hays, had an aphorism which was for him both a law of political action and a practicable rule of thumb for foresighted success: "Things don't happen; they are brought about."

However this may be, at the beginning of the period of this history and just before, there were certain forces in motion, economic phenomena and waves of human feeling, which, in their increasing momentum and widening scope, determined much of what happened. It was the nature of these forces that made it possible for Bryan[2] to come to the top, and possible, later, for the sort of leadership represented by Roosevelt to grow, while the type represented by Joe Cannon and Mark Hanna was defeated and subsided; made it possible for the causes Roosevelt advocated to be commonly accepted and to come to

[1] "Marchez à la tête des idées de votre siècle, ces idées vous suivent et vous soutiennent. Marchez à leur suite, elles vous entraînent. Marchez contre elles, elles vous renversent."—Louis Napoleon, 1841, quoted by Philip Guedalla.

[2] Mr. Bryan wrote me May 6, 1925: "You are entirely correct in describing public men as the creatures of their age. I have often used the same explanation in regard to myself. I lived in the very centre of the country out of which the reforms grew, and was quite naturally drawn to the people's side."

fruit in action, while the policies believed in by the standpat leaders were rejected and perished. One might assert, and reasonably defend the argument, that if Bryan had lived in a different period, he might have passed all his days as an obscure country lawyer in Lincoln, Neb.; and that if Roosevelt had come to maturity a decade earlier, say in 1870, when the spirit of the times was different, he might have gone to his grave with no greater record than having run for alderman in his district on a mugwump reform ticket half a dozen times unsuccessfully. As against this, the other school of thought would argue that a personality so dynamic as Roosevelt's or Bryan's would have given birth to the atmosphere and currents of popular emotion necessary to carry his purposes and himself to their goal.

However, one might bring this to the futile basis of that whimsy about the relative priority of the hen and the egg. During the nineties and just before, there were in the United States certain forces which gave rise to Bryan. Later, certain forces gave impetus and support to Roosevelt. To a considerable extent, the forces that gave rise to Bryan and those that gave rise to Roosevelt overlapped. Some had application to Bryan only. As to all these forces, I shall try to identify them, to trace the causes of them, and to follow their effects in the political and social movements of the quarter-century from 1900 to 1925.

8

FORCES THAT GAVE RISE TO UNREST

The State of Feeling in Many Parts of the Country and Among Large Numbers of the People. "What's the Matter with Kansas?" A Country Editor, by a Spontaneously Spirited Description of the People's Mood, Becomes Famous. Passing of the Era of Free Land. End of "Going West" in the Earlier Significance of that Phrase. "O'er the Mountains, Westward Ho." The Romance of the Covered Wagon. "Off to Oregon." Placing the Blame, or, in Some Cases, Misplacing It. Other Causes of Disquiet. The Financial and Currency Issues Out of Which Bryan Rose.

THERE was in America, during the years preceding 1900 and for many years thereafter, a prevailing mood. It was a mood of irritation. The average American in great numbers had the feeling that he was being "put upon" by something he couldn't quite see or get his fingers on; that somebody was "riding" him; that some force or other was "crowding" him. Vaguely he felt that his freedom of action, his opportunity to do as he pleased, was being frustrated in ways mysterious in their origin and operation, and in their effects most uncomfortable; that his economic freedom, as well as his freedom of action, and his capacity to direct his political liberty toward results he desired, was being circumscribed in a tightening ring, the drawing-strings of which, he felt sure, were being pulled by the hands of some invisible power which he ardently desired to see and get at, but could not. This unseen enemy he tried to personify. He called it the Invisible Government, the Money Interests, the Gold Bugs, Wall Street, the Trusts. During the first Bryan campaign, the spokesmen of the West spoke of the business men of the East, collectively, as "the enemy."

That mood was the source of most of the social and political movements of the years succeeding 1900. Of that mood, when it was at its angriest, there is a classic description.

II

One day[1] in 1896 a young editor twenty-eight years old in Emporia, Kans., being about to go on a trip, hurriedly wrote some editorials, which he left on his desk to fill the columns during his absence. On one he wrote the caption "What's the Matter with Kansas?" The young editor had no thought that it stood out from the others; but this particular editorial had a spontaneity which hurried writing sometimes has, when done under certain conditions. The inhibitions, the cautions, the considerations of tact about hurting people's feelings, those restraints which frequently attend more careful writing, had fallen away from this young man in haste to get away on his journey, and his free mind poured itself out. What he had been observing in his community, his reflections, convictions, dammed-back indignations, burst out in a hot flood.

The editorial appeared. A copy of the paper fell into the hands of Paul Morton,[2] a Chicago man, who, as a native of the country west of the Mississippi, took pains to keep informed about conditions in that territory. Morton, happening to meet Herman Kohlsaat, publisher of the Chicago *Times-Herald*, told him he had just read an editorial in a little Kansas paper giving a striking picture of conditions which, Morton said, Chicago and the East ought to know about. Kohlsaat asked Morton to send him the paper. The next day Kohlsaat reprinted the editorial in *The Times-Herald*. As soon as that edition of

[1] The date was August 15 and the paper was the Emporia *Gazette*.

[2] Son of J. Sterling Morton, a citizen of Nebraska, who was famous in his day as the first secretary of agriculture, and as the pioneer of Arbor Day. The son, Paul Morton, was later secretary of the navy in Roosevelt's administration.

The Times-Herald reached New York, *The Sun* gave it a second impetus.[1]

As a result of this sequence of merit, accident, and appreciation, there trickled in to the young man, on his vacation in the Colorado mountains, news that he had become famous. He had the substance to live up to the reputation that came so adventitiously. As William Allen White he became and remained a national character, as much beloved for his friendliness and whimsicalness[2] as admired for his devotion to every fine ideal; with a reputation not only as a spokesman of his local community and a political philosopher, but also as a novelist and short-story writer with a high place in the American literature of his time.

"What's the Matter with Kansas?" introduced a humorous, wise, and able man to leadership in American life and letters. Its pertinence to the present history lies in the vivid picture its lightning-like phrases give of the mood which was destined to give birth to many of the social and political movements of our time. "What's the Matter with Kansas?" was the epitome of an era. It was instantly recognized, went all over the country, and was discussed in a way that made it an event in American history.[3] One paragraph of it read:

> What's the matter with Kansas? We all know; yet here we are at it again. We have an old mossback Jacksonian who snorts and howls because there is a bathtub in the State House. We are running that old jay for governor. We have another shabby, wild-eyed, rattle-brained fanatic who has said openly in a dozen speeches that "the rights of the user are paramount to the rights of the owner." We are running him for chief justice, so that capital will come tumbling over itself to get

[1] These facts about the start of "What's the Matter with Kansas?" toward fame were told the writer by Mr. Kohlsaat.

[2] When over fifty he was occasionally called "the Peter Pan of the Prairies."

[3] Mark Hanna immediately circularized it, and used it in the campaign for McKinley more widely than any other pamphlet.

into the State. We have raked the ash-heap of failure in the State and found an old human hoop-skirt who has failed as a business man, who has failed as an editor, who has failed as a preacher, and we are going to run him for congressman-at-large. . . . Then we have discovered a kid without a law practice and have decided to run him for attorney-general. Then for fear some hint that the State had become respectable might percolate through the civilized portions of the nation, we have decided to send three or four harpies out lecturing, telling the people that Kansas is raising hell [1] and letting the corn go to weeds.

That outcry, if read in the absence of its background, might seem merely a profoundly disgusted editor's pungent description of a community indulging a perverse disposition to put incapable men in its public offices. But what is pictured in those nervous, high-pressure sentences was merely a symptom. Mr. White's editorial is a picture of the patient raving, and did not undertake to be a diagnosis of his disease; a description of the patient's hysteria rather than an analysis of his affliction.

What we must have is a statement of the sources of that frenzy, because those sources, those conditions preceding 1900, were the causes that determined the social and political movements of the nineties and of the fifteen years succeeding 1900. They gave rise to Bryan; and they were the causes of that public mood — that wish on the part of the average man for an elder brother with a big stick — in response to which Roosevelt rode into power and remained intrenched for half a generation. Some of the conditions were local to the West; some extended to other parts of the country and gave rise to a similar spirit; some similar conditions were local to other parts of the country. All contributed to the same mood of revolt. That mood was, speaking broadly, characteristic of the American people as a whole during anywhere

[1] It was Mrs. Mary Elizabeth Lease, "the Kansas Pythoness," who first said: "Kansas had better stop raising corn and begin raising hell."

from ten to thirty years preceding 1900; and for several years after. To have adequate understanding of Bryan and his rise, of the Roosevelt era, of the birth of the Progressive party, and of the first phase of Wilson; to understand these characters and movements of our own time, we must take some pains to identify the causes of that earlier mood.

There were these forces operating to strangle economic freedom, which the average American vaguely felt and loudly cried out against. Some of them proceeded from, or were directed by — or at least were taken advantage of by — persons, or organizations, with malevolent purposes, or, more accurately, selfish purposes. But many of these forces proceeded from no one individual, or corporation, or organization, malevolent or selfish or otherwise. Some arose out of causes no more malignly devised than the mere fact that the average man himself had increased greatly in the numbers of him residing upon the American continent. The individual average man was being circumscribed in his freedom by the mere increase in his own numbers.

III

The principal cause of the loss by the average American of a degree of economic freedom he had been accustomed to enjoy since the first settlement of the country was the practical coming to an end of the supply of free, or substantially free, virgin land. Put more accurately, it was the increase of population in proportion to the amount of land and other natural resources. During the 1890's occurred the last important one of those openings of Indian reservations to settlement, which were the principal means by which the Federal Government gave opportunity to landless men to acquire farms at small cost. That marked the end of that gloriously prodigal period of our national history during which a man with a family of sons need give little concern to their future, knowing that when the urge of manhood came, they could go out and acquire a farm by little more than the process of "squatting" upon it. The time had come to an end when a man of independent spirit, feeling distaste

Drawn by Howard Chandler Christy.

Officer firing the signals for the rush of land-seekers on an Indian Reservation opened to settlement.

for going to work as any one's hired man in a factory or elsewhere, could go West, settle upon a quarter-section of public land, and in course of time possess himself of it without being called on to pay more than a nominal sum. The average American, who had been able to look out on a far horizon of seemingly limitless land, now saw that horizon close in around him in the shape of the economic walls of a different sort of industrial and economic organization, walls which, to be sure, could be climbed; but which called for climbing.

This economic limitation which came with the end of

free land and the irritation of spirit arising out of it was felt not only in the West. It was felt even more in the East, where, for generations, the course of ambitious youth had been to "go West" and "take up" a quarter-section of land. For a generation of American life the phrase "go West" was universal, and had the meaning of promise implied in Horace Greeley's slogan "Go West, young man, go West."[1]

It would hardly be possible to exaggerate either the economic and social effects of the end of the period of free land, or the generous, colorful romance of that period while it lasted. The successive movements of American families and communities from the East toward the West were as picturesque as any of the great migrations of all time. In appeal to the imagination, the motion-picture of "The Covered Wagon," if realized as merely one example of a migration that included hundreds of thousands of people, can at least suggest comparison with De Quincey's "Flight of a Tartar Tribe." The records of those successive waves of American settlers taking up land can be traced by following the trails of family names and place-names, beginning in New England and reappearing at the outer edges of successive tides in New York and northern Pennsylvania; in northern Ohio and Indiana; in Wisconsin; in Kansas and Nebraska; in Oregon and Washington. The Southern movements went both west and northwest.

Vivid pictures of these migrations form, as it is fitting they should, the background of some of the best American novels. Herbert Quick's "Vandemark's Folly" is a picture of one caravan crossing the Mississippi River into Iowa, which, as history, is much more vivid, and probably

[1] To a later generation, the phrase "Go West" again became current; but this time with a very different significance, as a euphemism for death on the battlefields of France.

quite as accurate in fidelity to truth in the broad sense, as any formal, academic narrative of documents and dates. James Lane Allen's "Choir Invisible," dealing with an earlier era, contains an unforgetable picture of one of the westward paths. The most beautifully done of these epics of the free-land era is in Hamlin Garland's "Son of the Middle Border," in which he traces the migrations of his own family from Maine to Wisconsin, to Iowa, to North Dakota, and some to Southern California. The "Son of the Middle Border" not only is one of the fine American books of its time in all respects; as an intimate, a sometimes poignantly personal, story of a typical American family that made two of these migrations in one generation — as such, it is the truest and best of histories. Any reader with imagination can share the exultant, throat-catching thrill of the individual settler "going West" to free land, and recognize in the songs of the day the spirit that pervaded the whole country in that already long-gone time:

> My father . . . turned his face toward the free lands of the farther West. He became again the pioneer. Dakota was the magic word. The "Jim River Valley" was now the "land of delight," where "herds of deer and buffalo" still "furnished the cheer." Once more the spirit of the explorer flamed up in the soldier's heart. Once more the sunset allured. Once more my mother sang the marching song . . . at once a bugle-call and a vision.
>
> "O'er the hills in legions, boys,
> Fair freedom's star
> Points to the sunset regions, boys,
> Ha, ha! ha-ha!"
>
> And, some time in May, I think it was, father again set out . . . to . . . the land of the Dakotas which had but recently been wrested from the control of Sitting Bull.

Again:

> "As soon as Dad and Frank are settled on a farm here, I'm going west also . . . I want a place of my own." . . . As

the women came in, my father called out: "Come, Belle, sing 'O'er the hills in legions, boys!' Dave, get out your fiddle, and tune us all up." . . . And we all joined in the jubilant chorus:

"Cheer up, brothers, as we go,
O'er the mountains, Westward ho!"

By courtesy of Paramount Pictures.

"Going West," from the motion picture, "The Covered Wagon."

And at another point:

When my mother's clear voice rose on the notes of that exultant chorus, our hearts responded with a surge of emotion akin to that which sent the followers of Daniel Boone across the Blue Ridge, and lined the trails of Kentucky and Ohio with the canvas-covered wagons of the pioneers:

"When we've wood and prairie land,
Won by our toil,
We'll reign like kings in fairy-land,
Lords of the soil."

That sort of thing, as pictured by Hamlin Garland out of his own memory, was the common expression of the free, exultant spirit that attended "going West" to take up land and become an independent farmer. A youth about to take a job in a factory, or become a clerk in a bank, does not have just that emotion nor does his family feel moved to express itself in song.

That is the change that came upon America with the

Chorus from "Oh! Susanna."

end of free land. When one saw, in the motion-picture of "The Covered Wagon," [1] that bearded, Old-Testament-looking leader of the caravan, at the end of the long trail, stick into untouched Oregon sod the point of the plough he had brought in his ox-drawn wagon all the dangerous way from the Missouri River — when one saw his exaltation, the prayer, the ceremonial quality that he and his family and the other emigrants put into it — when one saw that, one wondered if all the audience realized how

[1] In this, too, there was one of those songs of "going West," written in the characteristic, mellow mood of confident hope and romantic adventure. The use of this melody as a recurring refrain in scene after scene was one of the features that made "The Covered Wagon" so appealing. ("The Covered Wagon" really redeemed and justified the motion-picture art.) One refrain was:

> "Don't you cry, Susanna,
> Don't you cry for me.
> I'm going off to Oregon,
> With my banjo on my knee."

full of meaning it was, not only as romance, but as the symbol of things that lie deep in the social, economic, and political history of America.

The free land had been for a hundred years the outlet for restlessness, the field for ambition. When that came

One of the last openings of government land to settlement.
Photograph of Hobart, Oklahoma, taken twelve days after the opening, in 1901.

to an end, restlessness turned in upon itself and fermented into something a little bitter. Ambition, compelled to do its pioneering in more complex fields, frequently failed to find satisfaction. Adventure and initiative, instead of finding free scope on a hundred and sixty acres of virgin land, had to turn to fields where men's elbows bumped each other, fields crowded and highly competitive, in which adventure was frequently thwarted, and initiative deprived of its chance — not merely of its chance to come to fruit, but even, sometimes, of its chance to get a start.

So long as there was free land, every man had the opportunity to create new wealth for himself by the simplest and oldest means known to humankind. With the end of free land, American men for the first time had occasion to look with envy upon the wealth of others, or with jealous scrutiny upon how they had acquired it. The end of free land was the beginning of those political issues which had to do, in one form or another, with "dividing up," or with curbing those who had much.

The end of free land was the largest one of those causes which, in the years preceding 1900, gave rise to a prevailing mood of repression, of discomfort, sullenly silent, or angrily vocal. Opulent America, generous, full-teated mother, was beginning to wean her children, and they were restless. It is doubtful if any considerable portion of those who were fretful recognized this intangible, inexorable thing as the cause of it. It took time to pass from easy-going assumption that our land, our forests, all our natural resources were unlimited, to uncomfortable consciousness that they were not. The average American, more readily visualizing a personified cause for his discomfort, dwelt more upon causes that proceeded from persons, or organizations of persons — corporations, "trusts," or what-not. There were such causes. But they were minor compared to the ending of the supply of free land.

I have expressed this as the "ending of the supply of free land." I might have put it: increase of population in proportion to the quantity of land. Increase of population worked for other similar changes in the mood of America. It brought a diminishing of natural resources, which in turn led to regulation, the beginning of "verbotens" in America. In 1900, many men could remember when they could take their rifles, go out among the buffalo-herds, and get as much meat as they wanted, without let or hindrance. To men with that memory, regulations, hunters' licenses, were irksome. This is a small illustration of what happened in many fields. The frontiersman had hardly ever encountered law or regulation. With increase of population came limits on liberty, "verbotens," "forbidden by law," "no trespassing." Later, with machinery, came another variety of regulation. In the days of the horse-drawn vehicle, "keep to the right" was about the only traffic code. With the coming of the automobile, stringent traffic rules came into being. One might suggest there is here something like a law of physics: the amount of regulation the individual must endure is in direct relation to density of population multiplied by velocity of its units.

IV

To be specific, the most important of the causes that gave rise to the mood of social and political discontent during the nineties and on until about 1914, were:

The ending of free land.

The ending, or the realization of the limitation, of other natural resources. (This led to the Roosevelt policy of conservation.)

The increase in population, out of proportion to the increase in gold supply.

The cutting in half of the volume of currency.

The immense increase in production of the silver-mines, faster than the increase in population, and very much faster than the increase in gold supply.

The action of the Supreme Court in 1896 in declaring invalid the income-tax law of that time.

The oppressive practices of the early railroad managers.

The rise of trusts and monopolies.

The growth of factories and factory life.

The protective tariff.

The power of organized wealth in politics.

Immigration.

The rise of the labor-unions and the treatment of them by corporation employers.

All these contributed to the rise of Bryan. But the three which had most to do with Bryan, which he picked out as his issues, were the ones having to do with currency: the diminished output of gold-mines; the increased output of silver-mines; and inflation of the currency, followed by deflation.

Most of the others of these causes of the American mood had to do more closely with Roosevelt, and will be discussed in connection with the Roosevelt era. We will examine now the ones that Bryan was associated with — gold, silver, currency. In every issue that Bryan, in his first phase, had, in practically every speech he made, these words appeared.

9

CONDITIONS THAT GAVE RISE TO BRYAN

Failure of the Gold-Mines to Supply Gold in Proportion to the Increase of Population and the Increased Demand for Gold for Monetary Purposes. Increase in the Purchasing Power of the Dollar, Which Is the Same as to Say, Increased Difficulty for Debtors to Get Money with Which to Pay Their Debts. How the Silver-Mines, in Contrast with the Gold-Mines, Increased Their Production Enormously and Thereby Provided the Materials for Political Commotion. The Income Tax Act of 1894. The Literature of Dissent, of Utopianism, and of Fallacy. "Coin Harvey" and His Book.

THE greatest single cause of the mood of irritation and unrest in America that expressed itself, successively, in Bryan, Roosevelt, and Wilson was the end of the free land and of other natural resources. To put it more exactly, it was the increase in the population of the country in proportion to the quantity of land. The same amount of land was there — but the number of people who wanted it had increased and was continuing to increase greatly.

That contributed to the rise of Bryan. But the more direct cause of Bryan's rise was the increase of the population of the country out of proportion to the supply of gold.[1]

II

The state of public feeling that gave rise to Bryan is comparable to a dough. Merely to lay hands on it, for the purpose of finding what of it had been yeast and what flour, is to change the appearance of it. To try to reduce it to its parts is instantly to transform it. Necessarily,

[1] This way of putting it is found subject to fault by some economists who agree with the essential thesis and with this chapter as a whole. Certain qualifications will appear in the later amplification of the subject.

therefore, any analysis of it is certain to provoke dissent from those who saw it only as a whole, and from others whose analyses run along different lines. At best, currency and finance is the field which, among all the aspects of human affairs, is the most difficult to be clear in, the most hospitable to fallacy, most crowded with pitfalls, both those of honest error and those prepared by sleight-of-hand intellects.

The conditions that gave rise to Bryan were brought about partly by man's imperfect management of man's common affairs, especially of his medium of exchange, and partly by nature. To try to identify these, and to show the part each had in the general result, is like analyzing a mixture that has fermented furiously and thrown up foam. To reduce it to its elements is to make it seem different from what it appeared as a whole, and invites controversy from those who lived through the period, saw it when it was in active ferment. Dissent comes also from those who, using other methods of analysis, have reached different conclusions.

The present effort has ease of understanding as its principal aim. Because clarity is the aim, it is desirable to treat each of the main elements separately. But in operation, these elements were not separate. On the contrary, it was the reacting of each upon the others, and the fermenting of the whole, that constituted the essence of the condition out of which Bryan rose.

The principal elements were: decrease in gold supply, increase in silver supply, and variations in the quantity of currency in circulation. There were other elements upon which some economists would put primary emphasis. Also some economists would phrase differently the causes I have named as fundamental. Finally, at times there was a psychological factor, the apprehension of the public about what the government was going to do — hope from some that the government would keep the gold standard which at times was nominal; fear from others that it would not. This psychological factor, it seems to me, was an outcome of the past actions of the government, rather than primarily a cause of what the government did. The whole condition was an endless chain,[1] and, in analysis, much depends on which link you examine first.

III

Decrease of Gold Supply

Gold was and is the practically universal standard of money. It was and is the thing men commonly think of as the standard of money. A good many persons thought gold ought not to be the standard of money. But the fact is, it was. Among others, Mr. Bryan wished this were otherwise. He strongly considered it ought to be otherwise. He imperiously demanded it should be otherwise. But it did not become otherwise.

Because gold was the standard of money, it was, next to land, or equally with land, the thing which everybody most desired to get.

Now, the amount of gold in the world was not a fixed quantity, as the amount of land was. And so it is more difficult to explain about gold, in relation to increase of population, than land.

[1] I have shown this chapter to several persons who lived through the events, including Mr. Bryan, and to several economists; and have taken account of many of the points they raised. As the chapter stands, it conforms to the theories of some; others would say it is merely one tenable analysis. One of the scholars with whom I have had discussions qualified his statement of his views, differing at some points from mine, with one of the few indisputable generalizations possible to be made within this field; namely, that there is no man who can say, and no authoritative scholar who will pretend to say, as to changes in the purchasing power of the dollar, what were all the factors causing them, and the relative weight of each. One of the two or three ablest among the men in political life who were on the side of bimetallism, having read this chapter, holds to his theory and to his version of the motives of men and the sequence of cause and effect, but concedes that the present narrative is a fair statement.

If we imagine, for convenience of explanation, that the amount of gold in the world were fixed, like the amount of land, then we could see readily that great increases in population, in proportion to the quantity of gold, lead to just the same sort of discomfort as the increase of population in proportion to the quantity of land. Just as increase in population makes it more difficult for the individual to acquire land, so does that same increase in population make it more difficult for the individual to obtain gold, or money based on gold.

And precisely that is what happened in the United States from the year the Civil War ended until the year Bryan first ran for public office; that is, from 1865 to 1890. For, while it was true that each year, from the mines of the world, some more gold was added to the world's stock, it was also true that — and this was the most important economic fact, next to the ending of free land, in the United States from 1865 to 1890 — the year to year additions to the amount of gold in the world were much smaller proportionately than the year to year additions to the population of the United States.[1] During these years the gold-mines of the world, so to speak, "loafed on the job"; while during the same years the social and economic forces (including immigration), which made for increases in our American population, were very active. Also, during the same years, several European countries went on a gold basis, thus adding to the demand for gold for currency purposes.

[1] Some who have read the proof of this chapter think I lay too much emphasis on increase of population. One points out that "population may increase but industry become stagnant." The latter condition of course would lead to a diminished demand for currency. But the fact is, in our modern Western civilization increase of population itself makes for increased activity in industry, and therefore increased demand for currency. An economist whose soundness of thought I respect writes me: "As I see it, it was not so much the failure of gold production to increase, as the increase in the demand for gold for monetary uses in other countries and in the United States, and the deflation of our currency following the Civil War, that made trouble." To me, this seems like saying the same thing I have put in other words.

What was going on in the world's production of gold from the end of the Civil War to the year Bryan first ran for office — 1865 to 1890 — is shown statistically in the following table:

1866	$129,614,000
1871	115,577,000
1876	103,700,000
1881	103,023,100
1886	106,163,900
1890	118,848,700

"Statistical Abstract of the United States," 1922.

That is a remarkable set of figures. Here was a period of twenty-five years in which the annual output of gold-mines did not increase — actually, indeed, decreased, for, as the table shows, the output in 1890 was less than the output in 1866. The output in every single year of the period was less than the output in the first year, 1866.

This record of gold's lagging is an exception to the course of the world. The period was one in which everything else went forward with immense momentum. (I say everything else; I can think of no exception.) Wheat-crops increased; copper increased; silver increased enormously; oil output grew; manufacturing expanded; railroad-building trebled. Only gold lagged.

But the particular thing whose increase is most relevant was the population of the United States. The large increases in the population of the United States during this period are shown by the following tabulation of annual increases for the same years considered in the table dealing with gold production:

1866	721,000
1871	996,629
1876	1,186,000
1881	1,160,217
1886	1,256,000
1890	1,333,250

Compiled from census returns and intermediate estimates of the actuary of the Treasury, found in the "Statistical Abstract of the United States," 1904.

That is to say, in the year 1890, while the addition to the world's gold supply was actually less than the addition in 1866 had been, the addition to the population of the United States in 1890 was almost twice that of 1866.

This increase in the number of people who wanted gold for currency to pay their debts and for other reasons, coupled with the failure of the gold-mines of the world to increase their output, was one of the two principal causes of the mood of social and political discontent out of which Bryan was incubated. It was at the root of the third-party movements: Greenback party, Populists, Silver party; of the free-silver movement; of distress among farmers who had mortgages on their land, and of all who owed money. It was a cause inherent in nature; but many of the people annoyed by it thought they could cure it by politics. Of these the leader was Bryan.

Actually, it was mainly cured finally by two men who came, not from the world of politics, but from the world of science. Their names were MacArthur and Forrest. They invented the cyanide process of extracting gold from low-grade ore. As if by some ironic whim of destiny, MacArthur and Forrest made their discovery in the very year in which Bryan was first elected to public office, 1890. After they got under way, the annual production of gold more than doubled within eight years, after having lagged for more than thirty years. Although Bryan probably never heard of these two mining engineers, it was they who frustrated his political career.[1]

[1] Doctor Edwin F. Gay, of Harvard University, thinks that even more important than invention of the cyanide process was "the transition from placer to lode mining in the 1890's, made possible by the discovery of the Rand mines of South Africa, the first development on a large scale of lode-mining. Edward Suess, in his book, 'Die Zukunft des Geldes,' written in 1877, had declared definitely, on the basis of a careful survey of all the gold-mining regions in the world, that since no largely remunerative reefs or lodes had ever been found, and since the washing of alluvial deposits (placer-mining) would ultimately and fairly soon come to an end, gold would therefore become scarcer and prices would fall. It was this con-

This is the first of many examples we shall have which show that the really fundamental history of America during this period was the history of the achievements of men of science, men who discovered more and more of the laws of nature, and brought those laws to the service of man, in industry, in medicine, in learning. The currents that flowed from the activities of scientists were the real history. Compared to the scientists and the inventors, the politicians were merely what H. G. Wells says the ancient kings and dynasties were — bubbles that bobbed along upon the surface, merely "showing the swirl of the forces beneath."

IV

Inflation Followed by Deflation

If the phenomenon of the lack of increase in the world's production of gold, happening at the same time as a rapid increase in the population of the United States, had stood alone, it would have accounted for much of the economic and political history of the time. But it did not stand alone. It was accompanied by and very intimately associated with another phenomenon equally apt to produce the same sort of economic and political result. That phenomenon was a decrease in the amount of currency in the country, relatively to the quantity of population. The result, to the average individual, was that in 1878 he had just about half as many dollars as he had had in 1864.

The reasons for this begin with the Civil War. While

clusion of the eminent geologist which was one of the factors that led Adolph Wagner, of Berlin, and other eminent economists to espouse bimetallism. I remember well sitting in the lecture-room in Berlin before the height of the free-silver controversy, in 1895, and hearing Wagner explain that the recent news of the development of deep-level reef-mining in South Africa had undermined the foundation of his advocacy of bimetallism. It was with irony that he heard that his name was being used in behalf of bimetallism in the political controversy in America."

the Civil War was on, the government, as one aid to paying the cost of the war, issued more and more dollars, directly and indirectly. Practically all governments try to help pay for all wars by this device of issuing, or otherwise creating, more currency. The addition made to the number of dollars circulating in the United States is shown in the following figures for the last year preceding the Civil War, and for the last year of the duration of the war:

1860 — Number of dollars in circulation	435,407,252
1865 — " " " " "	1,081,540,514

"Statistical Abstract of the United States," 1922.

Here we see the total quantity of money in circulation more than doubled in five years. Now, where the number of dollars in circulation is more than doubled in a short time, it follows that each person in the country has, on the average, twice as good a chance to get his hands on them. This is clearer when we look at the increase in terms of per capita circulation; that is, the number of dollars in circulation for each man, woman, and child. The figures are:

1860 — Number of dollars in circulation per capita	13.85
1865 — " " " " " " "	31.18

"Statistical Abstract of the United States," 1922.

That more than doubling of the number of dollars in circulation for each person might seem, superficially, a very good thing. To most persons, it did seem good. An appearance of prosperity, business activity, was created. But fundamentally this quick doubling by the government of the number of dollars in circulation had effects which wrought serious and gravely disturbing changes among men in their relation to each other, especially in the relation of debtor and creditor. These disturbing effects I shall explain a little later.

This mere doubling of the number of dollars caused each

dollar to have a decreased purchasing power. In addition, many of the new dollars were paper bearing the legend "The United States will pay." The date when payment would be made was not specified, but even the most optimistic felt it would be a long way in the future. Neither was it stated what the United States would pay in — whether gold, silver, or merely some new form of promise. In consequence, the public came to doubt whether all these dollars would be redeemable in gold, whether the government could get enough gold to redeem them all, and whether the government would maintain the determination to redeem them in gold. It followed that a paper dollar became worth less than a gold dollar — at one time less than half as much.[1]

So the doubling of the currency during the Civil War had two effects running parallel. The first was: each one dollar would purchase a smaller amount of goods. The law stated in that last sentence is simple and fundamental; and yet is so difficult to follow, in the ramifications of its effects, that failure to grasp it is at the bottom of nearly all financial and economic heresies.

The second effect of adding several hundred millions of paper dollars to the existing stock of dollars was that a paper dollar became worth less than a gold dollar, or, at that time, a silver dollar.

This more than doubling of the number of dollars in circulation was inflation. It had, I say, deeply disturbing effects on the relation of debtors to creditors, and otherwise on the relation of man to man and class to class. Let the more extended explanation of these effects wait for a moment. For the present let us turn to what the government did after the war ended, in 1865. This was a reduc-

[1] During this period of inflation those who were pleased by its effects had a doggerel that ran:

"You can say what you please of the fifty-cent dollar;
But I tell you, it beats none at all, all holler."

tion in the number of dollars — a reversal of the first process. This latter is called deflation.

Immediately after the Civil War, the government began to undo what it had done during the war, began to try, fitfully yet prevailingly, to get back to the gold standard; began to withdraw from time to time many of the paper dollars it had issued. This was deflation. The figures which show the reduction, the deflation, during a period of thirteen years following the Civil War are:

1865 — Number of dollars in circulation	1,081,540,514
1878 — " " " " "	773,379,295

"Statistical Abstract of the United States," 1922.

Expressed in terms of the number of dollars in circulation for each man, woman, and child of the population, the decrease is shown in the following figures. I give them for each of the thirteen years following the Civil War:

1864	$29.60	1872	$20.43
1865	31.18	1873	19.35
1866	26.49	1874	18.82
1867	23.73	1875	17.65
1868	20.88	1876	17.17
1869	19.61	1877	16.39
1870	20.10	1878	16.25
1871	20.08		

"Statistical Abstract of the United States," 1922.

That is to say, in 1878 the number of dollars for each person in the country was only about half what it had been in 1865. In other words, it was about twice as hard in 1878 for any person to get his hands on a dollar as it had been in 1865.

That gradual cutting in half of the number of dollars available to each person in the country had the effect on considerable numbers of the people of slow, grinding discomfort. In that table of figures is the vivid story of increasing difficulty for the debtor who owed dollars to get them; and, at the same time, increasing advantage for the creditor who had it in his power to demand dollars.

It should be borne in mind, too, that this same period of reduction in the number of dollars in circulation was also a period of increased activity in industry and commerce. That is to say, a time of increased need for currency was actually the time when the per capita circulation was cut, roughly, in half.

Also, for another reason, the number of dollars actually in circulation and available for those who needed and sought them was less. When more than one kind of dollars are in circulation — for example, metal dollars and paper dollars, and the public has doubts about either the capacity or the intention of the government to keep them on a parity, it follows that the public begins to hoard the dollar that is more intrinsically valuable. For this and other reasons, the more valuable dollars tend to disappear from circulation. In 1873, gold and silver were both at a premium and not in general circulation, prices being on the basis of depreciated paper currency.

As these paper dollars, the greenbacks, became the chief circulating medium for a decade and a half following the Civil War, prices of commodities were determined partly by the optimism or pessimism felt by the people concerning the future of these notes — and partly, also, of course, by the factor of the quantity of them in circulation. The capacity of each dollar to purchase a given quantity of goods fluctuated with increase and decrease in the number of dollars, and with the value of each dollar in terms of gold. To state it the other way around, the number of dollars required to purchase a unit of goods, let us say a bushel of wheat, went up with the increase in the number of dollars and down with the decrease. The variations in the number of dollars required to pay for a given unit of goods, taking 1860 as par, are shown in the accompanying tables:

Year	Retail prices
1860	$1.00
1861	.94
1862	1.09
1863	1.48
1864	2.25

That is, in 1864, it took $2.25 to buy as much goods as could have been purchased in 1860 with $1.00.

Next, the decrease in the number of dollars required to pay for a given unit of goods which took place during post-war deflation, from 1865 to 1880:

Year	Retail prices	Year	Retail prices
1865	$2.24	1873	$1.43
1866	2.03	1874	1.44
1867	1.77	1875	1.34
1868	1.80	1876	1.20
1869	1.72	1877	1.17
1870	1.56	1878	.99
1871	1.44	1879	.93
1872	1.38	1880	1.07

That is, by 1879, ninety-three cents would purchase as much goods as would have cost $2.24 fourteen years before.

There once more, in those figures, is the story of what took place from the close of the Civil War onward; namely, increasing advantage for those who had dollars, or contracts payable to them in dollars, and increasing difficulty for those who had to get dollars to pay their debts; increasing advantage for those who loaned money; increasing difficulty for those who borrowed.

Because of the economic and social effects of this policy of reducing the number of dollars in circulation, it was violently opposed by large numbers and classes of persons. The conflicts arising out of this opposition composed the major portion of the politics of the period from 1865 until the year Bryan first ran for office, 1890. What animated the opposition was the wish for more dollars, paper dollars, any kind of dollars. Of this wish, the chief exponent in the latter year was Bryan, who proposed to meet the wish by an unlimited coining of silver dollars.

V

Effects of Changes in the Number of Dollars

Of all the causes that give rise to discontent, which undermine the good faith and comity of man in relation to man, and class in relation to class, the greatest is fluctuation in the purchasing value of the unit of the currency.[1] When the value of the dollar goes downward, as happens during a war, one portion of the people is distressed and feels it has a grievance toward the other portion. When the value rises, as after a war, the other portion is distressed and has a corresponding sense of grievance.

For many of the thirty years after the Civil War the purchasing value of the dollar rose. This meant that the man in possession of dollars or having documents — mortgages, bonds, contracts of one sort or another — which enabled him to demand dollars from others, was in good fortune; while the man without dollars, or under obligation to get dollars in order to pay them to another, was in evil fortune. To the one, the good fortune came without effort or merit on his part; to the other, the evil fortune came with the same lack of deserving. For the most part the farmers of the West, and to some extent elsewhere

[1] Lecky said of such change in the basis of currency that it "beyond all others affects most deeply and universally the material well-being of man." He might have added something about the effect on the moral stability and spiritual elevation of man; for there is hardly anything so disturbing to the spirit of equity between man and man as for the debtor to see his creditor become the beneficiary of an arbitrary advantage over him, or vice versa, through a cause not blamable on himself, but proceeding from changes in the value of the unit of currency.

also, were in the latter class, the ones who suffered evil fortune through deflation.

During the Civil War, when the quantity of dollars was increased, the purchasing power of a single dollar went down. At one time during the Civil War a dollar was worth less than fifty cents, in comparison with what it had been worth normally. Let us then take what was common at the time, the case of a farmer who borrowed money on the security of a mortgage on his farm; or one who bought land, paying only partially for it and giving in the form of a mortgage a promise to pay the rest five, ten, or twenty years later. The farmer (the same thing applied to some classes besides farmers) who in 1865 or thereabouts gave a mortgage for, let us say, $5000, received from the money-lender 5000 dollars, which were really 50-cent pieces. Then, after the war, the government pursued the policy of bringing the paper dollar up to the standard of the gold dollar, by retiring some of the paper dollars, and otherwise. This process was hard on the farmer, who had given a mortgage and received from the money-lender in return for it 5000 dollars, which at the time were, in reality, 5000 50-cent pieces. By the time the mortgage came due, let us say, in the seventies, eighties, or early nineties, the farmer had to produce 5000 real dollars — gold dollars, or an equivalent of gold dollars.

To state this typical transaction in terms frequently used — and these were the terms in which the farmer saw it — the farmer, when he borrowed the money, had received 2500 bushels of wheat; but when the mortgage came due, had to pay back 5000 bushels. It is little wonder the farmer felt he had been treated badly.

Now, of the two parties to this typical transaction, the borrower, who fared badly, was generally of the West; while the money-lender, who did well, was of the East.

It was natural, then, that the farmer, feeling he had been cheated, and feeling also it was the government that had done it, began to associate his painful experience with the fact that the government was for most of that period in the hands of men who reflected the big business interests of the East rather than the Western farmers' own community.

This process — it was partly a phenomenon associated with gold supply and partly a condition brought about intentionally — this process, occurring in a wide variety of forms and an infinite number of cases, was one of the main causes of that mood of discontent, that feeling of being "gouged," which characterized great numbers of average Americans. It was chiefly responsible for the politics and legislation and third parties associated with currency, the free-silver movement, the Greenbackers. These were movements which had as their purpose to cause the government to increase the number of dollars in the country, or to prevent it from reducing the number.

VI

Increase of Silver Supply

I have told how the gold-mines of the world fell behind in production from year to year for twenty-five years; how that falling off had certain economic consequences; and how those consequences led to political effects.

Now the curious coincidence is that the silver-mines of the world, chiefly those of the United States, took precisely the opposite course — took it prodigally. During the same twenty-five years the silver output leaped upward from year to year. This rapid increase of silver contributed to the same political phenomena that had been caused by the falling off of gold and the deflation of the currency.

Let us look at the silver production of the United States for the same years for which we have already seen the decreasing gold production:

1855 —	Silver produced in the U. S.	$52,000
1860 —	" " " " " "	156,800

Then came the beginning of immense production:

1865 —	Silver produced in the U. S.	$11,642,200
1870 —	" " " " " "	16,434,000
1875 —	" " " " " "	30,485,900
1880 —	" " " " " "	34,717,000
1885 —	" " " " " "	42,503,500
1890 —	" " " " " "	57,242,100

"Statistical Abstract of the United States," 1922.

These figures show that the annual production of silver in the United States during the period of thirty-five years from 1855 to 1890 increased by about a thousand times what it had been at the beginning — by over 100,000 per cent. That phenomenon of nature was bound to have economic and political effects. And it did.

During the early years of the period, there had been silver coinage; that is, officially, we had a silver coinage. But, because silver was so scarce, it resulted that the amount of silver metal in a silver dollar was worth more as bullion than as a dollar. Consequently, people used the silver dollars as bullion. Silver dollars disappeared, practically, from circulation. So much had silver gone out of use that in 1873 Congress, in putting through a routine law to systematize the currency, omitted silver.

Soon after this law was passed, the greatly increased production of the silver-mines[1] began to make its influence felt in a variety of ways. One way was a desire on the part of the silver-mine owners for a market for their output. They wanted the government to be a large cus-

[1] A Nevada silver-mine that in 1873 produced $645,000, produced two years later, in 1875, about $16,125,000, about twenty-five times as much.

tomer for their product. They wanted the government to buy their silver and coin it into dollars. Whereas before 1873 they hadn't cared much whether the government bought their silver, by 1875 they were very excited about it. They set up the cry that the omission of silver dollars from the coinage act of 1873 had been the result of a conspiracy.[1] They called it "The Crime of '73," and that phrase figured large in American politics until almost as late as 1900. If the silver-mine owners had been alone in the demand, they might not have got so far as they did, but they were joined by that much larger and politically more potent class who wanted more dollars in circulation.

These two oddly assorted bedfellows, with an interest in common — the indigent Western farmer having a need for more dollars and the rich Western silver-mine owner having a need for a market — these two, seeing the trend toward a currency based on gold, combined to set up a great clamor. They[2] organized several formidable political movements, in which the silver-mine owners, for the most part, furnished the funds, while the farmers furnished the

[1] One can understand the point of view of the silver-mine owners. Since the beginning of the Republic, the government had been a potential market for silver for coinage purposes; but the operators of silver-mines had not cared to patronize it, because, owing to relative scarcity of silver, there had been more profitable ways to dispose of it. Then, when the enormously increased output of silver made the government as a market desirable, the silver-mine owners discovered that Congress had taken the government out of the market as a buyer of silver.

[2] Some quite conservative economists, statesmen, and scholars were also believers in bimetallism—among them Mr. (afterward Lord) Goschen and A. J. Balfour, in Great Britain; and in the United States, General Francis A. Walker, Charles Francis Adams, S. Dana Horton, and President E. B. Andrews, of Brown University. Among the editors of the East who held to this belief was Doctor Albert Shaw, who wrote in *The Review of Reviews* just prior to the Chicago Convention of 1896: "The dispassionate student of the financial and monetary history of the United States since the war must conclude that the great array of citizens now fighting for the coinage of silver are contending for a cause that has been logically evolved, and that owes the strength of its support to circumstances which can rationally be explained. . . . The East has never given the Western supporters of silver credit for the strength of their logical and historical argument for silver."

fervor. Together they acquired enough power in Congress to pass a law providing that the government buy every month enough silver bullion to coin not less than 2,000,000 nor more than 4,000,000 silver dollars. It was vetoed by President Hayes but passed by Congress over his veto.[1]

Later these two groups went farther. They caused Congress to direct the government to purchase every month 4,500,000 ounces of silver and to issue against it paper notes which should be legal tender and which should be redeemable on demand in "coin," either gold or silver, in the discretion of the secretary of the treasury.[2] What these interests wanted at all times was the "free and unlimited" coinage of silver, and the two acts passed were compromises made with them. The chief exponent, in the latter part of the period, for the "free and unlimited" coinage of silver was William Jennings Bryan; and on that issue the election of 1896 was fought.

Now, the addition of hundreds of millions of silver dollars and silver certificates to the circulating currency of the country, coupled with the psychological effect of the demand for yet more dollars, in the shape of the "free and unlimited" coinage of silver, had effects quite different from that prosperity which the proponents of free silver hoped for. There came into effect an old economic law, more potent than any law of Congress could be: when there is more than one kind of money in circulation, the more valuable kind — in this case, gold — tends to disappear. The government tried to keep up the gold basis;

[1] The Bland-Allison law, enacted February 28, 1878.

[2] The Sherman Act, passed in 1890 and repealed in 1893. Ex-Senator Charles S. Thomas, of Colorado, says that the silver interests did not really want either the Bland or the Sherman Act, and were not satisfied with them. What they wanted was the status preceding what they called "The Crime of '73"—the status that had existed from the beginning of the Republic until the silver demonetization act. They accepted the Bland and Sherman Acts under protest, as a part of what they demanded.

i. e., tried to maintain the idea that the country was on a gold basis, and that every dollar of any kind in circulation should have the same value as a gold dollar, and should be convertible into one. The government tried to keep in its vaults enough gold to be able, within reasonable limits, to meet every probable request from the owner of a silver or paper dollar to convert it into gold. But the effort was vain. Everybody who could get a gold dollar, by the simple device of handing in a silver one or a silver certificate at the United States Treasury, did so; and having got the gold dollar, proceeded to put it away in a bank vault, or in a stocking, or behind a chimney somewhere. By 1892 the amount of gold in the Treasury vaults was a very small fraction of the total stock of money in existence in the country, as is shown by the Treasury statement for September 1, 1892:

	General stock coined or issued	In Treasury	Amount in hands of public Sept. 1, 1892
Gold coin	$577,737,991	$166,583,580	$411,154,411
Standard silver dollars	414,966,735	357,343,849	57,622,886
Subsidiary silver	77,472,912	13,575,773	63,897,139
Gold certificates	152,234,589	23,847,210	128,387,379
Silver certificates	331,068,304	2,779,159	328,289,145
Treasury Certificates Act, July 14, 1890	109,382,637	5,268,551	104,114,086
United States notes	346,681,016	29,132,596	317,548,420
Currency Certificates Act, June 8, 1872	22,770,000	560,000	22,210,000
National bank notes	172,656,429	6,623,311	166,033,118
Totals	$2,204,970,613	$605,714,029	$1,599,256,584

About this time the creditor classes of the East and Europe became uneasy. They wanted that the debts due them should be paid, or payable, in gold. Consequently they wanted that the monetary system of the United States should be absolutely and unequivocally based on gold. But, with the growing strength of the Silverites, and the extension of their demand that the coinage of silver dollars be unlimited; and with the growing scarcity of gold in the government Treasury, these creditor classes of Europe and the East became apprehensive. Holders of American securities, fearful that if bimetallism should be established, they would receive interest and dividend payments in silver, began to sell. Debtors were harried for payments, securities were sold for what they would bring.

Then one day India joined the several European countries that had abandoned bimetallism. On the day India suspended its unlimited coinage of silver, June 26, 1893, the intrinsic value of the American silver dollar fell from sixty-seven cents to below sixty cents gold. This climax to a long accumulation of events was followed by one of the worst panics in American history.

This panic, in its ramifications, was one of the most direct causes of the economic distress among great masses of average Americans during the early 1890's. It was one of the immediate causes of the rise of Bryan.

VII

President Cleveland's Bond Issues

The chaos of the country's monetary system, resulting from the acts for the purchase and coinage of silver, confronted Grover Cleveland when he took over the presidency on March 4, 1893. It was the most serious of his problems. On the day he took office he found outstanding paper dollars to an extent five times as great as the amount of gold in the Treasury. Every paper dollar was, in theory, payable in gold. Further than that, under the practice of the Treasury, every silver dollar outstanding was exchangeable for one in gold. The integrity of the country's currency was appallingly threatened. Following Cleveland's inauguration the situation grew rapidly worse. It culminated in the "currency famine" which succeeded the demonetization of silver by the government of India on June 26. Four days after that event President Cleveland summoned Congress to meet in extra session on August 7, for the purpose of dealing with the alarming state of the nation's business, which he pronounced in his message as "largely the result of a financial policy which the executive branch of the government finds embodied in unwise laws — laws which must be executed until repealed by Congress."

In his message sent to the newly elected Congress on August 8, 1893, President Cleveland made a strong plea for the immediate repeal of the Sherman Act, which he said had been responsible, during its three years on the statute-books, for a depletion of the government's gold stocks of more than $132,000,000.

Meantime, Cleveland, in order to get more gold into the Treasury, sold bonds to two firms of New York bankers, who undertook to provide the government with gold in exchange for the government bonds. One of these issues was sold to the bankers at 104½. The bankers at once offered the bonds to the public, and the price went up to 118. This large and quick profit increased the resentful feeling of many classes that the money-lenders of Wall Street were profiting by the necessities of the government and the people; and profiting generally by Mr. Cleveland's gold policy. This incident gave great impetus to the free-silver movement, and to Bryan.[1]

[1] It should be remembered that the bankers who bought this particular issue of bonds undertook not only to deliver gold to the government, in exchange for them but also to stand steadily back of the government with efforts to prevent further depletion of the government's supply of gold.

VIII

Supreme Court's Invalidation of the Income-Tax Law of 1894

Another proposal, not directly within the field of currency and government finance, but related to it and put forward with the fervor that characterized discussion of gold and silver, was the "graduated income tax." The demand for it came especially from the farmers of the West and South, whose argument was expressed in the platform of one of the third parties: "A graduated income tax is the most equitable system of taxation, placing the burden of government upon those who can best afford to pay, instead of laying it upon the farmers and producers and exempting millionaire bondholders and corporations."

That a tax should be paid on incomes was a mere addition to things taxed. In that there was nothing strikingly novel. But the demand was that the tax should be "graduated." The advocacy of this innovation frequently took the loosely worded form that it would "compel the rich to pay their just proportion of the expenses of government." Essentially the demand was that the rich should pay more than their proportion. A tax on incomes, not graduated, if placed at, let us say, 2 per cent, would take $20 a year from a man with an income of a thousand dollars, and exactly twenty times $20, or $400, from a man with an income of $20,000. What was really demanded was that the second man in this illustration should pay twenty times as much as the first, and then, that this twenty should be multiplied again. As advocated, and as in effect in 1925, the graduated income tax took a larger ratio from large incomes and a smaller ratio from small incomes. An example, well below the extremes the United States has actually practised, would be 2 per cent, or $20, on incomes of a thousand dollars;

and 10 per cent, or $2000 a year, on incomes of $20,000. Essentially the demand was that the rich man should pay far more, proportionately, than the man with a small income.

On January 30, 1894, with the Democrats in control of both the legislative and executive branches of the government, an income-tax bill was reported as part of the Wilson tariff bill.[1] Of it Representative De Armond of Missouri, said:

> The passage of the bill will mark the dawn of a brighter day, with more of sunshine, more of the songs of birds, more of that sweetest music, the laughter of children well fed, well clothed, well housed. Can we doubt that in the brighter, happier days to come, good, even-handed, wholesome democracy shall be triumphant? God hasten the era of equality in taxation and in opportunity! And God prosper the Wilson bill, the first leaf in the glorious book of reform in taxation, the promise of a brightening future for those whose genius and labor create the wealth of the land, and whose courage and patriotism are the only sure bulwark in the defense of the Republic.[2]

The author of the bill asserted that it would "diminish the antipathy that now exists between the classes" and get rid of the "iconoclastic complaint which finds expression in violence and threatens the very foundations upon which our whole institution rests." In the Senate the bill met with an acrimonious attack by Eastern senators, of whom Hill, of New York, a Democrat, was the leader. Congressman J. H. Walker of Massachusetts opposed

[1] It was very mild, compared to what was to come twenty years later. It provided for a tax of 2 per cent on incomes over $4000. It was only graduated in the sense that incomes below that amount were exempt. This bill was drafted in part by William Jennings Bryan, then one of the junior members of the Committee on Ways and Means of the House of Representatives.

[2] Congressman De Armond's speech is in *The Congressional Record* for June 30, 1894. He was an example of a familiar type who believes and says that by political actions birds can be made to sing sweeter, skies to shine more brightly, and that nature can be made more beneficent to man. Just at that moment some processes were under way by which the riches of nature were to be made available to man as they never had been before. But these processes were being wrought by scientists, not by politicians.

the law for the reason, as he phrased it, that "The income tax takes from the wealth of the thrifty and the enterprising and gives to the shifty and the sluggard." Senator Sherman of Ohio said: "This attempt to array the rich against the poor . . . is socialism, communism, devilism."

After the measure became law, test cases to determine its constitutionality were brought before the Supreme Court. During the hearings, Joseph H. Choate expressed fears, curious to read now, that if such a law should be approved, and if "the communistic march" went on, there might come a time when as high an exemption as $20,000 might be made, and a rate of as high as 20 per cent imposed.[1] Mr. Choate told the court it ought to declare the law unconstitutional "no matter what the threatened consequences of popular or populistic wrath may be." Some of the justices were not free from the heat of language that characterized less responsible persons. Justice Field, in his opinion, said: "The present assault upon capital . . . will be but the stepping-stone to others larger and more sweeping till our political conditions will become a war of the poor against the rich; a war growing in intensity and bitterness." The court, after two hearings, declared the law unconstitutional,[2] by a five to four decision.

The New York *World* characterized the decision as "the triumph of selfishness over patriotism . . . another victory of greed over need. . . . The people at large will bow to this decision as they habitually do to all the decrees of their highest courts. But they will not accept law as justice."

Conservatives were ecstatic. The New York *Sun* said:

[1] Actually, twenty-four years later, in 1919, the income taxes imposed to defray the costs of the Great War went as high as seventy-three per cent on incomes of $1,000,000 or over.

[2] May 20, 1895.

"There is life left in the institutions which the founders of this republic devised and constructed. . . . The wave of socialistic revolution has gone far, but it breaks at the foot of the ultimate bulwark set up for protection of our liberties." The New York *Tribune* said: "Thanks to the

Passion-rousing pictures such as this played a large part in the political controversies about currency.

court, our government is not to be dragged into communistic warfare against rights of property."

The invalidation of the income tax was fresh fuel to the popular discontent, which the following year, 1896, flamed up in the shape of the Bryan campaign.

IX

The Literature of Dissent, of Utopianism, and of Fallacy

Popular thought, during the years Bryan was getting his start, was focussed on social and economic inequalities by two books. Henry George's "Progress and Poverty," [1]

[1] Nelson's Encyclopædia says it "was the most popular book on economics ever published." This is interesting, and, one assumes, must be true. I should like to compare the aggregate distribution of Adam Smith's "Wealth of Nations."

a plea for the restoration of economic opportunity to the individual, was so confident in argument and lucid in language as to give almost the effect of being impassioned. Edward Bellamy's "Looking Backward," an imaginative picture of an ideal commonwealth, had, to many minds, the effect of a plea for Socialism.

Another book, not to be compared with either "Progress and Poverty" or "Looking Backward," but actually taken most seriously by great numbers of Americans, was a curious little paper-covered volume, cheaply printed and illustrated with crude woodcuts, "Coin's Financial School," by W. H. Harvey. It was an ingenious and plausible presentation of fantastic fallacies about money, written in such a manner as to be persuasive to minds not well equipped for clear thinking in that one among all the fields of human thought which is most fruitful of errors.

Of "Coin's Financial School," Bryan said: "It is safe to say that no book in recent times has produced so great an effect in the treatment of an economic question." Since Bryan was both a believer in the book and a beneficiary of it, his judgment may be interpreted as not having convincing evidential value. Probably it was literally true. So responsible a publication as *The Review of Reviews* said in August, 1896 (the month after Bryan's attempt at the presidency on the free-silver issue began):

> About two years ago there appeared in Chicago a little book entitled "Coin's Financial School." Its author was a certain Mr. Harvey, at that time unknown to fame. Mr. Harvey's fame, however, is now secure enough.[1] As a man of letters he may not be enshrined in the American pantheon, and as a monetary scientist and publicist his reputation may prove only ephemeral.[2] But as a disturber of old parties, a pathfinder where political issues were mixed and hazy, an agitator with a genius for exposition so great as to sway public opinion from the Alleghanies to the Pacific and from the Great Lakes to the

[1] Not quite. In 1925, how many Americans recognize the name? [2] It did.

Gulf of Mexico, Mr. Harvey has made it certain and inevitable that his name must be forever[1] connected with one of the most remarkable chapters in the political history of his country. . . . Several very important things, doubtless, had conspired to

One of the illustrations with which "Coin" Harvey argued by ingenious but fallacious analogy.

bring about a revolution in the leadership and spirit of the Democratic party; but it may well be claimed that as a precipitant and a crystallizing reagent, nothing else was half so effective as the entry of Mr. Harvey with his little yellow-covered book.

In the preparation of this history, the writer has read many books not before read by him and reread many others. In all that reading, "Coin's Financial School"

[1] "Forever" ?

stands out with a few others (one was Carry Nation's "Autobiography") as having a unique interest, as reflecting an intense and vivid, though eccentric, personality. Harvey gravely represented himself as "Professor Coin," a young financier and teacher, establishing in Chicago a school for instruction in the theory of money. In drawing after drawing, he pictured himself as an extraordinarily

Another of "Coin" Harvey's illustrations of his financial theories.

good-looking young man in the most royal-looking knee-breeches and the most correct of dress coats. To his suppositious school there came as pupils — so he said — the leading bankers, business men, and editors of the Middle West: Lyman J. Gage, later secretary of the treasury; Philip D. Armour, Marshall Field, Levi Leiter, Franklin MacVeagh, also later secretary of the treasury; Editor Medill, of the Chicago *Tribune*, and the other editors of Chicago papers. Harvey printed their names, and pictured these men, some the most powerful figures of their time, as humbly sitting at his feet, eagerly imbibing from him instruction in the science of finance. Occasionally he pictured them as asking questions or putting forward arguments — in which exchanges Professor Coin always won, with the bankers and merchant princes gratefully accepting correction; or, if they did not waive their own ideas in favor of the professor's, suffering a defeat in the argument, to the enthusiastic approval of the other distinguished pupils.

Harvey wrote it all out, dialogue and all, as if it had

"Coin" Harvey's illustration of the rising value of the dollar.

actually happened, with a vividness that even to-day makes it necessary for one occasionally to call himself back from thinking that it all really took place; and which suggests that Harvey as a dramatist or novelist might have achieved the enduring figure which, as an economist, he hoped to achieve but did not. No doubt millions of those who read the book at the time took its verisimilitude for actuality; literary verisimilitude went hand in hand with the innately seductive deceptiveness of financial heresy plausibly stated, to make simple readers think the dialogues actually took place. "Coin's Financial School," with its abundance of cartoons and diagrams, is one of the curiosities of American history. One wonders if Harvey's is — for he is still living at this writing — a case of a vivid, expansive personality, reaching out almost abnormally for power and distinction, but defeated and suppressed by the realities of his surroundings; and, unable actually to be the great man he hoped to be, turning to find satisfaction in a literary outlet in which he pictured himself as greater than the great, a teacher of the great.[1]

X

Of the fervor fanned by such writing as "Coin's Financial School," and based mainly on the issues of gold, silver, and currency; of a people in revolt, there is an unforgetable picture by William Allen White:

> It was a fanaticism like the Crusades. Indeed, the delusion that was working on the people took the form of religious frenzy. Sacred hymns were torn from their pious tunes to give place to words which deified the cause and made gold — and all its symbols, capital, wealth, plutocracy — diabolical. At night, from ten thousand little white schoolhouse windows, lights twinkled back vain hope to the stars. For the thousands who assembled under the schoolhouse lamps believed that when their legislature met and their governor was elected, the millennium would come by proclamation. They sang their barbaric songs in unrhythmic jargon, with something of the

[1] In the year 1924 I tried to get a copy of "Coin's Financial School." Not even could one be supplied by the author himself, to whom I wrote. In that year he was running a hotel in Monte Ne, Ark. He was describing himself as the "chief executive officer" (and also, one suspects, the bulk of the active membership) of the World's Money Educational League. The curiously bizarre vitality of personality was still expressing itself, this time through the building of a huge concrete pyramid 130 feet high, on a peak in the Ozark Mountains, which was designed to preserve at its centre, for the benefit of the archæologists of 10,000 years from now, a document telling why American civilization fell. One suspects that those future Carnarvons and Carters, digging down to our contemporary Tutankhamen, will discover that American civilization fell because it failed to listen to the financial teachings of William H. Harvey.

It is an addition to the sum of querying doubt about permanence in this unstable world, to have lived as a boy through a quick succession of years in which there was on every tongue first Henry George's "Progress and Poverty," then Edward Bellamy's "Looking Backward," and later William H. Harvey's "Coin's Financial School"; and then, on undertaking to write a history of the period, to find one of these books, "Coin's Financial School," not easy to procure; another, "Looking Backward," almost equally unknown; and even Henry George's "Progress and Poverty," not widely read.

same mad faith that inspired the martyrs going to the stake. Far into the night the voices rose — women's voices, children's voices, the voices of old men, of youths and of maidens, rose on the ebbing prairie breezes, as the crusaders of the revolution rode home, praising the people's will as though it were God's

One of the pictures by which "Coin" Harvey aroused the West.

will, and cursing wealth for its inequity. It was a season of shibboleths and fetiches and slogans. Reason slept; and the passions — jealousy, covetousness, hatred — ran amuck; and whoever would check them was crucified in public contumely.

Out of that Bryan sprang. That, to an audience surprised and almost crazed with delight to find its passions voiced so truly and so eloquently in the "Cross of Gold" speech — that nominated Bryan. That state of mind, the fruit of nearly thirty years of controversy about currency and related questions, came to its climax in the Bryan campaign of 1896. In that campaign the issues associated with currency were fought out, and thereafter disappeared. The later discontent, that was associated with Roosevelt, arose out of different causes, and expressed itself in another group of issues.

10

THE NINETIES

This Chapter Deals with Other and More Cheerful Aspects of Life in America Just Before 1900. The Bicycle Built for Two. The Gibson Girl. Remington's Cowboys. Kemble's "Coons." Moody and Sankey. "The Ninety and Nine." The Four Hundred. The Klondike. The White City. The International Copyright Law, Which Gave a Lift to American Fiction. Owen Wister's "Virginian" and "Lin McLean." "Silas Lapham." "Wolfville." "Colonel Carter of Cartersville." Old Cap Collier, and Mr. Beadle's Entrancing Library. "Fables in Slang." Victor Herbert. "Brown October Ale." "Songs from Vagabondia." Kipling's Poems. "The Old Moulmein Pagoda." "Mr. Dooley." "Daisy Bell." "Sweet Rosie O'Grady." "Grandfather's Clock." "Gentleman Jim" Corbett. Li Hung Chang. "Casey at the Bat." "The Purple Cow." "Fin de Siècle." Richard Mansfield. "Cyrano de Bergerac." Julia Marlowe in Her Youth. Weber and Fields. The Pat and Mike Joke Gives Way to the Two Jews Joke. "The Old Homestead." "Uncle Tom's Cabin." "The Count of Monte Cristo." "Erminie." "Florodora." Sherlock Holmes. "Sag Harbor." And others, as they say, "too numerous to mention."

We have been dealing with the political aspects of the nineties, picking out deliberately those conditions that caused the average American to be in a mood of resentment, to feel that he was, politically and economically, in the position of the little dog being mauled by the big dog. We have been dwelling on these because they were the conditions that gave rise to the politics and the humanitarian movements of the early part of the present century.

It is true that in politics the nineties was a period of deep feeling, often angry feeling. There was truculence, talk of strife, actual strife. When Jacob S. Coxey found himself unable to approve some things being done in politics, the form of protest that occurred to him was military. "Coxey's Army," that started from northeastern Ohio to march to Washington and take control of the government in the interest of the people — or what Coxey[1] thought was the people's interest — was one of the most colorful episodes of the nineties. Even civil war was talked. Governor Waite, of Colorado, having been quoted as saying, "I am prepared to ride in blood up to my bridles," the New York *Sun*, then at the height of its brilliance under Charles A. Dana, harped wittily on "Bloody Bridles Waite." Threats of arms and blood were characteristic of the political and class contentiousness of the early nineties. No such angry intensity of feeling accompanied any of the political conflicts that came after 1900.

But politics, even under the hectic conditions of the nineties, had less bearing than many other aspects of existence on the average man's capacity and opportunity to get comfort, satisfaction, and fun out of life. There was plenty of enjoyment in the nineties, both high-spirited and the quieter sort that went with a more leisurely way of life. That slower pace of living was just beginning to be disturbed and speeded up by new standards. Just as certain economic conditions of the nineties determined much that happened in politics after 1900, so did other conditions give birth to much that happened after 1900 in literature, the drama, entertainment, diversion, culture.

[1] For those who want to read about it, there is a picture in Garet Garett's novel "The Driver." Coxey himself, in the year 1924, was engaged in the quite peaceful operation of a sand-quarry at Massillon, Ohio, and turning up at national political conventions, a most unobtrusive, rather shy man, who hung about the edges of the crowds, hoping to find some one who would listen to certain novel ideas he had about finance, and urge them upon the platform committees.

II

Several writers, lured by the picturesqueness of the nineties, have tried to characterize them in a word, occasionally a word of color. Stuart P. Sherman used the "Yellow 90's," though there is nothing in his text to suggest why he saw aptness in that adjective. Possibly the reason lies in the especial familiarity of Mr. Sherman as a man of letters with an artistic and literary movement that started in Europe and was expressed partly by Aubrey Beardsley in the "Yellow Book." Henry L. Mencken was thinking of this movement when he spoke of the nineties as a period of intellectual war, "essentially a revolt against academic authority, against the dull, hollow dignity of pedants, who continued to teach the Hawthornes and Emersons, and were anæsthetic to the new literature coming to flower all around them." The characterization Mr. Mencken arrived at is the "Electric 90's." Richard Le Gallienne's phrase, the "Romantic 90's," fits some of the literature and other forms of art that prevailed and otherwise carries an implication of the mood of those who lived through the period, that mood of memory which usually thinks of the past as "golden." W. L. Whittlesey, of Princeton University, spoke of them as the "Moulting Nineties," a characterization that would be seriously inept if it referred only to appearance, but having aptness as an intellectual characterization, since it implies the emergence from old ways, the dropping of old standards, old ideas, old political allegiances, old concepts of human relations, old disciplines of religion and family life. "Moulting" suggests a lusty, youthful hospitality to the new which came crowding in every field: new ways of life, new standards in art, a new spirit in literature, new inventions in machinery, new styles in clothing, new con-

Sports for girls, as recommended by *The Ladies' Home Journal* for June, 1890.

Butterick's bicycle fashions for women in 1899.

Left—Young girl's evening gown of muslin.—From *The Ladies' Home Journal* for February, 1894.
The model in the centre appeared in *The Ladies' Home Journal* for February, 1893.
Right—Two dainty bridesmaids.—From *The Ladies' Home Journal*, March, 1894.

ventions in human relations. We were dropping the hand-made, taking up the machine-made; leaving the farm to enter the factory; dropping the issues associated with the Civil War and its aftermath and thinking about questions arising out of new economic conditions; edging away from classic Greek and Latin ideals of education to

By courtesy of "Life."

A recollection of the nineties pictured in *Life* in 1925.

take up science. Johns Hopkins, founded in 1876, had the first adequately equipped physical laboratory in America, supplanting the ancient dynasty of the clergyman college-president with the economist and the administrator. In short, we were sprouting new coats, physical and mental, whose mature nature was not to be seen clearly until well after 1900.

III

The World's Fair at Chicago in 1893 was one of the most far-reaching stimulants to men's imaginations

America has ever seen. It was the largest, the most generally attended, and in practically every respect the best of the many America has had. The mood it evoked in the average American was one of awed exhilaration. Chicago, seen for the first time by millions of Americans, caused them to realize the miracle of the West's growth. Less than a mature lifetime before, in 1837, wolves had howled in what, by 1893, were to be Chicago's[1] principal business streets, and the largest enterprise of civilization west of the Alleghenies had been John Jacob Astor's fur-trading business.

The reproductions of the *Pinta*, *Niña*, and *Santa Maria*, sent to the World's Fair by the Queen of Spain to recall that adventure of Columbus which was the beginning of our history, caused us to think of ourselves as having traditions, made us nationally self-conscious. The reproduction of an early railroad-train alongside a Pullman of the day, together with models of what were in the nineties the grandest ocean ships, the *Teutonic* and *Majestic*, and the foreign villages and folk along the Midway, stimulated Americans to travel to an extent they had not before. The assembling from America and Europe of new models of machinery and architecture, the Court of Honor, the rich collections of statuary and paintings, caused nearly every person of the millions[2] who visited the Fair to go home with his soul enriched, his mind expanded and more flexible.

The picture written by Harry Thurston Peck was not too highly colored. He described the competition of St. Louis, New York, and other cities for the honor of cele-

[1] Julian Street writes me: "The Chicago house in which I lived as a baby was on a street following the old Indiana trail by which, in 1812, the remnants of Fort Dearborn's garrison retreated after the massacre toward Detroit. That was 67 years, the lifetime of a not very old man, before my birth."

[2] Rollin Lynde Hartt says I should emphasize that "it was 'Main Street' that went to the Fair—the 'best people' had a slight disdain for it." This was one reason for its wide-spreading beneficence.

brating the 400th anniversary of the discovery of America, the jeering predictions that a city so new as Chicago, so material in most of its aspects, could not rise to the spirit of the occasion. Then:

On the lakeside, a rough, unkempt, and tangled stretch of plain and swamp became transmuted into a shimmering dream

The Administration Building at the World's Fair on Chicago Day.

of loveliness under the magic touch of landscape-gardener and architect and artist. No felicity of language can bring before the eye that never saw them those harmonies which consummate Art, brooding lovingly over Nature, evolved into that maze of beauty. Not one of the 12,000,000[1] human beings who set foot within the Court of Honor, the crowning glory of the whole, could fail to be thrilled with a new and poignant sense of what both Art and Nature truly mean. The stately colonnades, the graceful arches, the clustered sculptures, the

[1] This is a conservative estimate after deducting duplicate admissions. It represents more than one out of every six of the population of the United States.

gleaming domes, the endless labyrinth of snowy columns, all diversified by greenery and interlaced by long lagoons of quiet water — here were blended form and color in a symmetrical and radiant purity such as modern eyes, at least, had never looked upon before. It was the sheer beauty of its wonderful

The earliest thousand-mile conversation.
In the presence of a company of experts Alexander Graham Bell opened the New York-Chicago telephone circuit in 1893.

ensemble, rather than the wealth of its exhibits, that made this exposition so remarkably significant in the history of such undertakings, and especially in its effect upon American civilization. . . . The importance of the Columbian Exposition lay in the fact that it revealed to millions of Americans whose lives were necessarily colorless and narrow, the splendid possibilities of art and the compelling power of the beautiful. . . .

The far-reaching influence of the demonstration was not one that could be measured by any formal test. But a study of American conditions will certainly reveal an accelerated appreciation of the graces of life and a quickening of the æsthetic sense throughout the whole decade which followed the creation of what Mr. H. C. Bunner most felicitously designated as the White City.

Not merely for a decade, as Mr. Peck was able to record in 1905, but unto this day the Chicago World's Fair left its mark in heightened appreciation of art, and all the fruits of an immense stimulation of the American mind. It brought the change from chromo art to higher forms on the walls of American parlors, and gave birth to what later came to be called "city planning." To the World's Fair more than one American city[1] owes the greater beauty of its avenues, parks, and ornaments; thousands of American homes the greater beauty of their architecture, furniture, and decorations; millions of American individuals their greater appreciation of beauty and their greater opportunity to enjoy it.

A more rhapsodical description, but one probably not far distant from the impression made on the average American, came from Halsey C. Ives, chief of the Department of Fine Arts at the Exposition:

Never, since the first gray dawn of time, has there been such a collection of works of genius, such an assembly of master

[1] Mr. Ernest I. Lewis, United States interstate commerce commissioner, whose judgment is valuable because of his eager curiosity about the significant in contemporary history, and because of his well-stocked mind acquired through much travel and long newspaper experience, writes: "I think the World's Fair at Chicago did fully as much as you indicate. All through the last twenty-five years there has been a wonderful registration of its effect. You find it in architecture, in community centres; in parking systems and playgrounds; Kansas City, Washington, Indianapolis, Cleveland, Pittsburgh, are good examples. The Chicago Fair was the first popular demonstration of the beauty of orderliness, of proper proportions, of classical lines—it was the death-blow, in short, to the Queen Anne and other flamboyant and helter-skelter concepts that had previously existed. The World's Fair, plus the Christian Science Church's adoption of the classical as its standard of construction, plus a better planning of Federal buildings through the country, has made the U. S. A. a decidedly better-looking place in which to live. This has been worked out principally in the first quarter of the present century."

spirits of the world, as that brought together by the grandest civic event in history, the World's Columbian Exposition. Here was a "spectacle of the centuries" . . . whose like men now living may never hope to see again. All the highest and best achievements of modern civilization; all that was strange, beautiful, artistic, and inspiring; a vast and wonderful university of the arts and sciences, teaching a noble lesson in history, art, science, discovery, and invention designed to stimulate the youth of this and future generations.

That appreciation, from an American source, may seem to have some rawness in its exaltation. But the same idea was expressed by an American of the most æsthetic type. Henry Adams, historian of French cathedrals and of American life, who usually was petulant about most aspects of America, said of the Chicago Fair: "As a scenic display, Paris had never approached it."

European authorities had the same high appreciation. The French *Gazette des Beaux-Arts* spoke of "the really extraordinary impression produced by this creation so boldly conceived and so clearly and unaffectedly realized." A writer in the Swiss *Bibliothèque Universelle*, having seen our World's Fair, made public repentance of some things he and other Europeans had previously thought and said about us, in an almost lyrical description which ended: "And we have been reproaching the United States with their barbarism!"

IV

To mention only one of many, many effects, I think it was the World's Fair, the heightened and more discriminating appreciation of art which it brought, that made possible the vogue that Charles Dana Gibson began to have about 1895. Preceding the nineties, the art that found its way to the walls of average American homes was a familiar type, in which high vividness of color was the most striking quality. During the later nineties,

Charles Dana Gibson's drawings in sheer black-and-white largely displaced the chromo and achieved an almost universal vogue. Gibson's characters, always clean and fine, composed the models for the manners of a whole genera-

From a drawing by C. D. Gibson, copyright by "Collier's Weekly."

A drawing that included both the "Gibson Girl" and the "Gibson Man."

tion of Americans, their dress, their pose, their attitude toward life. For years the walls of American homes, of students in colleges, were decorated with "His Move," "You Are Going on a Long Journey," "The Widow and Her Friends," "Pictures of People," "Americans." The Gibson Girl was pinned up in rude mining cabins in the Klondike and in freight-train cabooses; the Gibson Man decorated the rooms of girls in boarding-schools. "Fifth Avenue is like a procession of Gibsons," said Joseph Pennell, the illustrator.

Here was an example of art that at once pleased the

crowd and satisfied the critical.[1] Gibson could express more with a single line of black on white than any other artist of his generation. Beyond that he had what Augustus Thomas called "wide and deep understanding

One of E. W. Kemble's negro types.

of the human family." Gibson, with a single picture, including only two characters, could tell a whole story. A

[1] ". . . Gibson has drawn the true American girl. He is the American Du Maurier. . . . Before Gibson synthetized his ideal woman, the American girl was vague, nondescript, inchoate; there was no type of her to which one could point and say 'That is the typical American girl.' As soon as the world saw Gibson's ideal it bowed down in adoration, saying: 'Lo, at last the typical American girl.' Not only did the susceptible American men acknowledge her their queen, but the girls themselves held her as their own portrait, and strove to live up to the likeness. Thus did nature follow in the footsteps of art, and thus did the Gibson girl become legion, and the world take her to its heart as the type of American womanhood. . . . Gibson also created a type of man, the square-shouldered, firm-jawed, clean-shaven, well-groomed, wholesome youth—for which he and his friend Richard Harding Davis were the models; and the American young man, less self-consciously than the American girl, set himself to imitate the type. It was Gibson's pen which sent mustaches out of fashion and made the tailors pad the shoulders of well-cut coats."—New York *World.*

competent dramatist could take one of Gibson's pictures and build on it as much human comedy as would fill a one-act play. Out of the series of pictures which Gibson called "The Education of Mr. Pipp," Augustus Thomas

By courtesy of "Life."

A. B. Frost was unexcelled in drawing rural types.

actually made a comedy of the same name, in which Digby Bell played Mr. Pipp. Thomas said: "Nothing that I remember writing was more fun to do."

The nineties was also the time of E. W. Kemble's "coons," types of the real negro and of the Old South; types still close to the ingratiating deference of the slave, still carrying in dress and features a faint but recognizable echo of the original African; types that had charm, grace, picturesqueness; types which a quarter of a century of education, including migration to the North and its effects, was to make smarter but also to make flat in the common standardization of the time; types which, by 1925, Kemble would have been compelled to seek only

By courtesy of "Life."

In the nineties Frederic Remington could still see real Indians and save them on canvas for future generations.

among the elder negroes and in the remoter hamlets of the South. The nineties were the time also of A. B. Frost's rural types, destined like Kemble's coons to flatten and

Copyright by Charles Scribner's Sons.

The Land of Counterpane.
Jessie Willcox Smith was beginning her portrayal of types of American children.

merge in the standardization of Hart, Schaffner and Marx clothes.

Frederic Remington could still find true cowboys in their authentic background, and make them permanent[1] in "The Broncho Buster" and "Pony Tracks"; could still see the Indian in some of his primitive dignity and

Copyright by Dodd, Mead & Co.

One of Maxfield Parrish's drawings for "The Golden Age," by Kenneth Grahame.

picturesqueness. The nineties were the time of Maxfield Parrish's fantasies of "The Golden Age"; of Howard

[1] Remington was a true historian of the old West. On canvas, in bronze, and in words he seized the rapidly passing opportunity to immortalize the vanishing Indian riders, cow-punchers, soldiers, prairie ponies. The New York *Herald*, in 1920, eleven years after Remington's death, said: "Many artists and laymen found the color of Remington's Western paintings hard and unpleasant. They didn't realize that in his studies of the desert and the bad lands he set down the landscapes as he saw them, in the hard, dry light of the region—the light that made everything burn into the brain of the observer. What was once regarded as a fault is now regarded as a virtue in the painter. He is exalted as a realist, a sort of Courbet of the Southwest, the Indians and the big empty spaces. . . ."

Pyle's reproductions of early American history; of Zogbaum's pictures of American army life; the time when Jessie Willcox Smith could find and picture those unso-

Benjamin Franklin and Richard Oswald discussing the Treaty of Peace at Paris following the close of the American Revolution.
Drawn by Howard Pyle for "The Story of the Revolution," by Henry Cabot Lodge, in *Scribner's Magazine*.

phisticated children her pencil made immortal. In popular illustration the nineties were, in short, a time, distinctly a time, of naturalness and truth. That vogue continued a while after 1900, but came to be first overlapped and then superseded by a smarter, more glossy, more wooden school, the stiff collar-and-cuff starchiness of Leyendecker, and the unwrinkled slimness of the silk stockings which Coles Phillips pictured girls wearing as they rode in high-priced automobiles.

V

The nineties was definitely a time of budding for American interest in American writers and American types in fiction. This had, to some extent, an economic basis. Before the International Copyright Act of 1891, American publishers could watch what English books were successful, and then print them in America without the expensive royalty arrangements involved in the case of American authors. A New York publisher testified before a Senate committee that "the effect of absence of international copyright on the opportunities of American authors to get into print is most disastrous. I have unused manuscripts in my safe and have sent back manuscripts which ought to have been published. The market would not support them." A Boston publisher testified: "For two years I have refused to entertain the idea of publishing an American manuscript." After the passage of the new law, in 1891, the effect "in encouraging the production of American rather than of foreign books has been little less than marvellous." [1]

But the change was only partly a result of the International Copyright Act. There was in the nineties an expansion of national self-consciousness, a new spirit in our broadly national life, of which *The Bookman* said: "Americans have at last really learned to stand upon their own feet and to accept their own standards as the best for them. . . . Perhaps it has been hastened by the thrill of national sentiment which stirred the American people through our war with Spain. American writers

[1] *Literary Digest*, January 13, 1900.

until now have nearly always kept an eye on England and on English models; and the result has been a lack of independence fatal to originality. Now they have turned their backs resolutely upon everything extraneous and are able to see our own life in its real significance."

Not only the authors, but the readers also, came to "see our own life in its real significance," and that was the beginning of realism in American fiction. The American reader came to realize[1] there could be as much drama, and more verifiable truth, in the lives of his own neighbors, as in romances of English titled life; that a Boston paint-manufacturer named Silas Lapham, as portrayed by William Dean Howells, could be as interesting, and closer to life as the American himself knew it, than the more gilded English creations of Mrs. Humphry Ward; that Mark Twain's Missouri boy, Tom Sawyer, and Bret Harte's gambler, Jack Hamlin, and Edward Noyes Westcott's country banker, David Harum, could be as fascinating as the European characters of Ouida and Marie Corelli. This change in the nationality of the characters the American read about contributed to the rise of realism.[2] You might fool him about dukes and foreign-legion soldiers, but when he read about the people he knew, he demanded the truth and could not be deceived by literary wooden Indians.

The changing taste of the reader encouraged the author; the author catered to the taste of the reader. As a result, an American publisher was able to say that in the year 1899 not a single foreign work of fiction had

[1] "All at once, America found that she was full of materials for fiction."—Fred Lewis Pattee, in "A History of American Literature Since 1870."

[2] "Realism . . . was simply a demand for truth, an insistence that all characters and backgrounds be drawn from nature, and that no sequence of events be given that might not happen in the life of the average man. . . ."—Fred Lewis Pattee, in "A History of American Literature Since 1870."

been a sensational success in America; while the same year witnessed such a series of American successes as, taken collectively, had never before been approached. This change, a kind of literary declaration of independence a hundred and twenty years belated, is vividly portrayed in two contrasting lists four years apart.

In December, 1895, the six books most widely read in America were:

Days of Auld Lang Syne................Ian Maclaren
The Red Cockade.................Stanley J. Weyman
Chronicles of Count Antonio............Anthony Hope
Sorrows of Satan........................Marie Corelli
The Bonnie Brier Bush..................Ian Maclaren
The Second Jungle Book.............Rudyard Kipling

Those were all of British authorship.

Four years later, in December, 1899, the six most widely read were all by American authors:

Janice Meredith...................Paul Leicester Ford
Richard Carvel.....................Winston Churchill
When Knighthood Was in Flower........Charles Major
David Harum................Edward Noyes Westcott
Via Crucis.......................F. Marion Crawford
Mr. Dooley in the Hearts of His Countrymen
Finley Peter Dunne

The new stimulus, spiritual and economic, turned to characteristic American types, contemporary American communities, American history. Hamlin Garland pictured pioneer life on the prairies; Mary E. Wilkins, the New England spinster; Sarah Orne Jewett — a very great writer — a whole gallery of rural New England characters. No single American type has ever been more accurately and sympathetically portrayed than the true American cowboy, then beginning to pass away, in Owen Wister's "Lin McLean." Thomas Nelson Page in "Marse Chan" and Francis Hopkinson Smith in "Colonel Carter of

Cartersville" were making imperishable certain characters of the Old South who, as flesh and blood, were fast falling away before the noise and speed of a more hectic age — wrapping the faded skirts of their long frock coats about their thin figures, taking with them their horses and their dogs, their dignity and their gentle manners, they retreated from the automobile, the safety razor, and the intimations, already beginning to be disquieting, of the Volstead Act. Richard Harding Davis, both as an author and as an athletic out-of-doors personality, was at the height of a popularity based on high romance in the field of clean adventure, "Gallegher," "Van Bibber," "Soldiers of Fortune." The vogue for clean romance that Davis implanted in young people, who were his devoted readers, contributed to the distaste that same generation had twenty years later when they had become parents, for some of the very different sort of novels which, becoming popular during the period of this history, set changed standards for young folks.

In humor, the America of the nineties was so rich, both in productivity by writers and appreciation by the public, that one is tempted to say no other decade equalled it. Mark Twain had done the best of his humorous writing before 1890; in the nineties his characters were on every lip. Everybody had among his acquaintances a Colonel Mulberry Sellers, and identified him as such, familiarly spoke of him as such. In day-to-day life, in business and social affairs, situations were pictured by analogies in Mark Twain's stories. The aphorisms of his characters were quoted as settling disputes. His books were a standard American folk authority, a source for familiar wisdom and common sense.

"Mr. Dooley" (Finley Peter Dunne) was at his prime in the late nineties and early nineteen hundreds. His mechanism for weekly instalments of humorous philosophy about the news was composed of two characters, a Chicago saloonkeeper, "Mr. Dooley," and his friend "Mr. Hennessy." One could picture the conversations: The scene would be in the late afternoon when there was no trade to interfere with philosophy. Mr. Dooley would have read the news,[1] read it slowly, with adequate reflection, each sentence completely digested before he would pass on to the next. To him would come Hennessy, probably a man of leisure based on tiny savings invested in a house or two. "Well," Mr. Dooley would say, "I see Congress has got to wur-ruk again."

Mr. Hennessy's rôle was restricted to merely the obvious, the brief, the completely serious, the appropriate remark to lead Mr. Dooley on. He would utter the perfunctory formality his friend's observation seemed to call for: "The Lord save us fr'm harm." Then Mr. Dooley would be off with two or three pages about the Panama Canal, "Teddy Rosenfelt," immigration — as to which Mr. Dooley had sound American views, being himself "a Pilgrim father that missed the first boat." A distinction between Republicans and Democrats was explained:

> Ye ought to know th' histhry iv platforms. . . . Years ago, Hinnissy, manny years ago, they was a race between th' dimmycrats an' th' raypublicans f'r to see which shud have a choice iv principles. Th' dimmycrats lost. I dinnaw why. Mebby they stopped to take a dhrink. Annyhow, they lost. Th' raypublicans come up an' they choose th' "we commind" principles, an' they was nawthin' left f'r the dimmycrats but th' "we denounce an' deplores." I dinnaw how it come about, but th' dimmycrats didn't like th' way th' thing shtud, an' so they fixed it up between thim that whichiver won at th' iliction shud commind an' congratulate, an' thim that lost shud denounce an' deplore. An so it's been, on'y the dimmycrats has had so little chanct f'r to do annything but denounce an' deplore that they've almost lost th' use iv th' other wurruds.

[1] The nearest 1925 equivalent of "Mr. Dooley" was Will Rogers. Ring Lardner had a more direct similarity to George Ade.

. . . Billy Bryan . . . he's out in Lincoln, Neebrasky, far fr'm home, an' he says to himself: "Me throat is hoarse, an' I'll exercise me other fac'lties," he says. "I'll write a platform," he says. An' he sets down to a typewriter, an' denounces an' deplores till th' hired man blows th' dinner-horn. Whin he can denounce an' deplore no longer he views with alarm an' declares with indignation.

Of the acrimoniousness of politics in America during the nineties Mr. Dooley said: "If ye ar-re a tired la-ad an' wan without much fight in ye, livin' in this counthry is like thryin' to read th' Lives iv the Saints at a meetin' iv th' Clan-na-Gael." Of Senator Beveridge's oratory he said: "Ye could waltz to it." When Roosevelt wrote an appreciative book about the experiences of himself and his Rough Rider regiment in the Spanish War, Mr. Dooley said: "If I was him I'd call th' book 'Alone in Cubia.'" At another place Dooley suggested as titles: "Th' Biography iv a Hero be Wan who Knows"; "Th' Darin' Exploits iv a Brave Man be an Actual Eye-Witness, th' Account iv th' Desthruction iv Spanish Power in th' Ant Hills, as it fell fr'm th' lips iv Teddy Rosenfelt an' was took down be his own hands."

Mr. Dooley was not only a popular but a definitely useful institution to a whole generation of American life. To the people he supplied true philosophy, wisdom, compact common sense; to the public characters he supplied the corrective of satire, which the latter accepted, and were grateful for. Mr. Dooley, in the actuality of Finley Peter Dunne, was one of the few human beings toward whom, in personal contacts, Roosevelt habitually bore himself with a smiling but nevertheless serious deference, an attitude made up less of apprehension of Dunne's pen than of sincere appreciation of his deep-reaching wisdom.

Most useful of all, Mr. Dooley supplied the softening solvent of humor to the American atmosphere in times of acute controversy. Just when we were getting worked

From a photograph by Burr McIntosh.

Richard Harding Davis.

From the Albert Davis Collection.

George Ade.

Finley Peter Dunne (Mr. Dooley).

up into factional passion, with everybody searching the cellar of his vocabulary for verbal lumps of coal, Mr. Dooley would come out in the Sunday papers with a picture of the situation that made every reader laugh at it, and at himself. A remark that Dooley made in the nineties suggests some effects that have accompanied popular education, and could have been applied, twenty-five years later, to the 1925 controversy between the Fundamentalists and Modernists:

> Whin I was growin' up, half th' congregation heard mass with their prayer-books tur-rned upside down, an' they were as pious as anny. Th' Apostles' Creed niver was as con-vincin' to me afther I larned to r-read it as it was whin I cudden't read it, but believed it.

George Ade started on the Chicago *Record* in the early nineties with very simple stories of the realistic kind. In 1895 he wrote "Artie," sketches in the chatter of a fresh young gentleman employed in a business office. The popular demand for more of the vernacular of the day pulled him, against his inclination, away from realistic story-telling. In 1898 he wrote a fable combining the archaic form of Æsop with the most modern and barbaric idioms and street jargon. This putting wisdom and entertainment into the dress of hilarious, unconventional American talk led to more fables, of which probably the most popular was one which under the title "The Two Mandolin Players and the Willing Performer" conveyed the old truth that the self-confident youth often succeeds where the bashful lover fails. While that moral found most favor with the American temperament of the day, Ade was too profound a person to overstress it; most of his fables brought the overconfident characters to disaster. Some of the most widely read were "Lutie the False Alarm," who took music lessons; "The Preacher Who Flew His Kite," using language his congregation could not understand, and "The Two Vaudeville Actors," named "Zoroaster" and "Zendavesta." Ade's daring innovation lay in using the vernacular, the new catchwords and phrases heard in the street. He deliberately gathered them up, hung them about ancient axioms of

Equipment of a business office, *The Dramatic Mirror*, including a stenographer in the mode of the day. Photographed in 1898.

common sense, labelled the output so that none could be misled, and reached a public that was not thrilled by the correct writing of the magazine and editorial page. Hundreds of his phrases passed into the currency of compact wisdom.

In the nineties, Alfred Henry Lewis made those frankly overdrawn and richly picturesque characters of the Southwest, the Wolfville denizens who used to reckon the passing of the hours and identify the time of important events as "along about second drink time after breakfast." Into the mouth of "The Old Cattleman," Lewis put his own gift of characterization: "You can smell 'bad' off Silver Phil, like smoke in a house, an' folks who's on the level — an' most folks is — conceives a notion ag'in him the moment him an' they meets up." Lewis told in the local vernacular a bereft husband's appreciation:

> "Shore!" says old Glegg; "been out an' gone these two years. She's with them cherubim in glory. But folks, you oughter seen her to onderstand my loss. Five years ago we has a ranch over back of the Tres Hermanas by the Mexico line. The Injuns used to go lopin' by our ranch, no'th an' south, all the time. You-all recalls when they pays twenty-five dollars for skelps in Tucson? My wife's that thrifty them days that she buys all her own an' my child Abby's clothes with the Injuns she pots. Little Abby used to scout for her maw. 'Yere comes another!' little Abby would cry, as she stampedes up all breathless, her childish face aglow. With that, my wife would take her hands outen the wash-tub, snag onto that savage with her little old Winchester, and quit winner twenty-five right thar."

Some "best sellers," or otherwise widely read books, American and foreign, of the nineties were:

The Damnation of Theron Ware	Harold Frederic
Hugh Wynne	S. Weir Mitchell
The Choir Invisible	James Lane Allen
Quo Vadis?	Henryk Sienkiewicz
Sentimental Tommy	James M. Barrie
When the Sleeper Wakes	Herbert G. (later H. G.) Wells
The Greater Inclination	Edith Wharton
Main-Travelled Roads	Hamlin Garland
Stalky & Co.	Rudyard Kipling
The Gentleman from Indiana	Booth Tarkington

William Dean Howells, in all his more than thirty novels, was rarely, if ever, a "best seller" to the public; but to writers, especially to younger ones,[1] he was all that

[1] Howells recognized reality and genuine talent, even when its form was distant from his own austere propriety of word and idiom. George Ade writes me: "My sponsor and encouraging friend at that time [1893] was William Dean Howells." Scores of the best of the generation that followed Howells would give the same testimony.

"best seller" implies, and more. Writers, recognizing Howells as of the very best in craftsmanship, took him as a model, accepted his influence spontaneously and gladly. That brought it about that Howells, more than any

William Dean Howells.

other, was the father of the natural school in American fiction. Howells, in a scene in "Silas Lapham," pictured the embarrassment of a self-made paint-manufacturer invited to a formal dinner in an unaccustomed circle; his middle-aged purchase of his first dress suit; his uneasy doubt and watchfulness to find out whether one keeps on his white gloves during dinner; and, worst of all, the problem of good form presented by the wine on the table; his decision to abandon lifelong teetotalism in deference to what he generously thought was courtesy, and the disastrous consequences; the transition from shy and silent lack of self-confidence to boastfully loquacious excess of it, while the others at the table took on the silence of embarrassment — and then the self-reproach of "the cold gray dawn of the morning after" [1] — Howells pictured all that in a way that brought to the reader a literal, vivid, burning blush of sympathy. That illustrates Howells's strength, and also his defect, which was the making of serious tragedy out of mere mishaps in contact between those who were socially elect, in the Boston sense, and those who were not. Howells never quite freed himself from the consciousness that he was the son of an Ohio country printer, received — magnanimously received, as Howells seemed to feel — by Beacon Street and *The Atlantic Monthly*. Howells's very great importance lies in his leadership in realism, a realism[2] which in his case meant conjuring up reality through painstaking workmanship. (The word, and the practice, meant something less elevated to a later school.) Howells, after the lapse of a generation, stands out in a class by himself. He was the principal exponent of the new spirit in American literature, its master craftsman, the apostle of it, the model who inspired more of the best young writers of the present century than any other.

From William Dean Howells to Laura Jean Libbey is the farthest possible cry. They were alike in that both wrote many books — and in practically nothing else. The nineties was the time of the widest following of one

[1] A George Ade phrase that entered into widely popular usage.

[2] It cannot fail that Howells's novels "will be valued in years to come as historical documents. As a picture of the externals of the era they portray there is nothing to compare with them."—Fred Lewis Pattee, in "A History of American Literature Since 1870."

whose death in 1924 evoked this tribute from the New York *World:*

So Laura Jean Libbey is dead. What recollections her name calls up! School-days, strawride days, days when the bees bumbled outside and the smell of flowers floated in; days when boys, as though by psychic agreement, stoutly refused to work and hid "Nick Carter" and "Dick Merriwell" behind their geometries. And those terrifying, mysterious, alluring creatures across the aisle, those perverse creatures with ribbons on their hair and ringlets to their waists — what were they hiding behind their geometries? Laura Jean Libbey. Laura the incomparable, the delightful; Laura who could evoke pink-and-lavender glamour right from page 1; Laura who never failed to deliver the loving couple into each other's arms, while bells banged the nuptials and friends wept into their kerchiefs. She is said to be the author of eighty-two novels and forty plays. She once said she never had any trouble writing; no halting or doubt, no tramping the floor at midnight to capture an elusive concept, no temperamental fits, starts, or sulks, no waiting for inspiration. She always knew where she was going; right always conquered might, wrong, or what-not, and right was always perfectly easy to perceive. Well, all honor to her. Her works may not be great literature, but they were in key with youth. If she was not profound, girls found her readable; and who will say that her influence was not as good as the movie, which has usurped her place?

Laura Jean Libbey.

VI

There was another field of indigenous American fiction which, while inferior in dignity, was decidedly not inferior in popular interest, as measured by numbers of readers. An American who in 1925 was in the neighborhood of forty, had lived through two periods; in the first, the nineties, he saw the "dime novel" scourged into furtive hiding-places; in the second, after 1920, he saw it the diligently pursued prize of collectors and libraries. An engaging picture of the dime novel and the lure it held for the youth of the nineties is in Mr. Irvin S. Cobb's "A Plea for Old Cap Collier":

> I read them at every chance; so did every normal boy of my acquaintance. We traded lesser treasures for them; we swapped them on the basis of two old volumes for one new one; we maintained a clandestine circulating-library system which had its branch offices in every stable-loft in our part of town. The more daring among us read them in school behind the shelter of an open geography propped up on the desk. Shall you ever forget the horror of the moment when, carried away on the wings of adventure with Nick Carter or Big-Foot Wallace or Frank Reade or bully Old Cap, you forgot to flash occasional glances of cautious inquiry forward in order to make sure the teacher was where she properly should be, at her desk up in front, and read on and on until that subtle sixth sense which comes to you when a lot of people begin staring at you warned you something was amiss, and you looked up and round you and found yourself all surrounded by a ring of cruel, gloating eyes? . . . And at home you were caught in the act of reading them, or — what from the parental standpoint was almost as bad — in the act of harboring them? I was. Housecleaning times, when they found them hidden under furniture or tucked away on the back shelves of pantry closets, I was paddled until I had the feelings of a slice of hot buttered toast somewhat scorched on the under side. And each time, having been paddled, I was admonished that boys who read dime novels — only they weren't dime novels at all but cost uniformly five cents a copy — always came to a bad end, growing up to be criminals or Republicans or something equally abhorrent.[1]

[1] Mr. Cobb did not say, but it may well have been, that some of that stimulus to his youthful imagination which has happily enriched America may have come

That was the attitude parental authority had toward boys who read dime novels. But, compared with some accepted two-dollar novels of 1925, the dime novel of the nineties was "chaste, ethical, and overflowing with rectitude" — I quote Mr. Edmund Lester Pearson,[1] of the New York Public Library. Because his parents had not

From a photograph by Wide World Photos.

In June, 1925, at Bryn Mawr College the class which had graduated in 1900 revived the costumes of their commencement day.

forbidden him to read dime novels, he never took enough interest to look into one until after he was thirty. He then found that "the rules of delicacy in the treatment of elegant females — and there were never any inelegant ones — were still those of a refined seminary for young

through his early reading of the "nickul libruries." Zane Grey recites that he had a complete collection of Beadle's Dime Novels in a secret cave, which he and some of the neighbor boys had dug in a brier patch in the orchard, "the reading of which could be earned only by a deed of valor." It was in this cave, and by this inspiration, that Mr. Grey wrote his first story.

[1] The extremely engaging book from which I have borrowed some of this description of a phase of life in the nineties is "Books in Black or Red."

ladies. Heroines in the most distressing danger still kept the folds of their long skirts trailing upon the ground; they hunted jaguars in the South American jungles

BEADLE'S

Dime New York Library

COPYRIGHTED BY BEADLE & ADAMS.

Vol. XVIII. Published Every Week. Beadle & Adams, Publishers, No. 225

ROCKY MOUNTAIN AL; or, Nugget Nell, the Waif of the Range.

BY "BUCKSKIN SAM"—Major Sam S. Hall,

THE BLACK STEED OF ROCKY MOUNTAIN AL, WITH A SNORT OF MADNESS AND FURY, SPRUNG INTO THE AIR.

primly seated upon a side-saddle, and wearing a habit which would have been correct in Central Park in 1868. Their bathing costumes might cause their persecution for prudery to-day, but nothing else." Consequently, Mr. Pearson was moved to reflect on the absurdity that children should have been forbidden to read them. But the ban may have been as much economic as moral.

The dime novels were crude. Everything about them suggested crudeness — indeed proclaimed it. But the ban against them that Irvin Cobb describes, and of which every other youth of the nineties had knowledge, frequently purchased at the expense of going to bed supperless, or other forms of punishment aimed at a sense more directly susceptible to acute pain — that ban could not be justified, though frequently justification was attempted, on the ground that they were immoral. Were children forbidden to read them because their morals would be impaired? Or because the reading would consume time that might be devoted to the superior purpose — superior, that is, in the minds of their elders — of bringing in wood, going on errands? It is not without precedent in history that superior races have set up, as to their inferiors, a moral taboo on certain enjoyments for the purposes of economic advantage accruing to the superior race.[1]

The principal publisher of dime novels was Erastus F. Beadle.[2] He issued the first in 1860. The firm of Beadle and Adams continued the business until 1897. After the vogue passed, and the business ended, Mr. Beadle retired, appropriately enough, to Cooperstown, N. Y., and ended his days in the atmosphere of James Fenimore Cooper's "Deerslayer" and "Spy." A few of the titles of the dime novels with which Mr. Beadle entranced more than two generations of American boys were: "The Pirate Priest,

A friend writes me that in the community where he was a youth, Oregon, the ban against dime novels was based on their falsity—"They were lies!"

[2] In 1923 Mr. Pearson watched the preparation of an exhibition in the New York Public Library of more than 1300 publications of the house of Beadle, together with some specimens from followers and imitators. These cherished literary treasures were, writes Mr. Pearson, "books which within my own recollection had been considered an abomination, books which librarians had regarded with a shudder, to be sprinkled, metaphorically, with holy water and thrust into the *index librorum prohibitorum.* [Now they] were unblushingly, nay, proudly, placed on show, and duly ticketed as 'Dime Novels,' for all to see. . . . The old gentlemen who slipped in, looking somewhat furtively about (as if father, with his trunk-strap, hovered near by), and went with increasing delight from one show-case to the next, as they recalled one old friend after another—these visitors were a continual pleasure to the planners of the exhibition."

or The Planter Gambler's Daughter"; "The Gambler Pirate, or Bessie, the Lady of the Lagoon"; "The Double Daggers, or Deadwood Dick's Defiance"; "Double Dan, the Dastard, or The Pirates of the Pecos." They dealt with the trapper, the scout, the road-agent, the pony-express rider, the bison, and the grizzly. Among the characters were Old Sleuth, Nick Carter, Old Cap Collier, Deadwood Dick. Of the style, a few characteristic passages are sufficiently typical: "Hold, Captain Forrester! surrender or you die!" "God above! You risen from the deep, Mabel Mortimer!"

The innocuous harmlessness, nay the virtuous elevation, of the morals of the dime novel — and some other qualities it had — are illustrated in the opening page of "Night Scenes in New York; In Darkness and by Gaslight," by Old Sleuth (H. P. Halsey):

In a plainly furnished room in the upper part of the city were two persons, a young girl and a fierce, bad-looking man.

The girl speaks:

"Back! Back! On your life stand back!"

To which uningratiating remark the bad-looking one makes a singularly unresentful reply:

"Adele, I love you."

With a cool accuracy of argumentation not common under such circumstances, Adele responds:

"And you would prove your love by acts of violence?"

The gentleman protests:

"You are wrong. I would only persuade you to be my wife."

Whereupon the lady:

"Hear me, Lyman Treadwell; I am but a poor shop-girl; my present life is a struggle for a scanty existence; my future a life of toil; but over my present life of suffering there extends a rainbow of hope. . . . Life is short, eternity endless — the grave is but the entrance to eternity. And you, villain, ask me to change my present peace for a life of horror with you. No, monster, rather may I die at once!"

Upon which Mr. Pearson observed: "How tame compared with 'The Sheik'!" Or, we might add, with "Cytherea," or with many other accepted two-dollar novels of the "sex school" of the 1920's.

VII

Even more than in the field of fiction, the nineties were the flowering time of American drama, the most fecund period it had ever known. As in the case of fiction, one reason was economic. Until the International Copyright Act of 1891, American managers could produce the successful plays of famous foreign writers, such as Dumas, without needing to pay royalties. Naturally they preferred to do so, rather than produce new plays by unknown American writers, to whom they would have to pay royalties.

In 1890 there was still alive the man who was the first professional dramatist in the United States; that is, the first author who devoted himself to writing plays and did nothing else to earn his living. Bronson Howard, author of "Saratoga," was the first, and at the beginning of the nineties was the only one. "Saratoga" was produced in 1870. Howard lived until 1908. Of him, and the significance of his solitary eminence at the beginning of the nineties, an American critic, Clayton Hamilton, said in 1924, when in his forty-third year: "That a person of my age should have known with some degree of intimacy the earliest professional dramatist in this country, affords an indication of how very recent is the development of dramatic authorship in America." During the nineties Bronson Howard was joined by some ten or twelve others, among them William Gillette, James A.

Herne, Clyde Fitch, Augustus Thomas, David Belasco, Charles Hoyt.[1]

This beginning having been made in the nineties, the continuation of it afterward gave America, by 1925, not less than 200 dramatists, each of whom had had at least one play produced professionally. New York had passed from its twenty first-class theatres of the nineties, each open for about thirty weeks of the year, to, in 1925, more than sixty that aimed to keep their doors open fifty-two weeks each year. The change was not one of mere quantity. From its position of 1890, New York had become by 1925 the theatrical metropolis of the world.[2]

In that group of American dramatists who wrote during the nineties[3] two can be classified as the most im-

[1] Walter Prichard Eaton, who knows the stage well, says I should make a distinction here. He admits the American national awakening during the nineties, the number of plays written, the number of playwrights who developed; he concedes the importance to America; but he doubts the greatness of the drama produced. He writes: "It may truthfully be said that in the nineties, America became dramatically self-conscious. That can fairly be emphasized. But you should not give the impression that this outburst of individual drama was great drama; it wasn't. It was interesting because it showed our national awakening in the field of the theatre and made the profession of playwriting a dignified one. Don't minimize its importance to *us*. But don't imply our drama in the nineties was important as lasting literature. . . . Bronson Howard, Augustus Thomas, Clyde Fitch, Charles Hoyt, Harrigan and Hart, were of course doing good work in getting us used to skilfully made plays about American life; but only to the extent that they were forerunners of the renaissance, and their plays have perished. It was the productions of the Englishmen, Bernard Shaw, A. W. Pinero, Henry Arthur Jones, and especially the then frequently despised Ibsen, which chiefly marked the '90's as a door to the Twentieth Century."

[2] Speaking of the period that began in the early nineties and considering it in connection with the continuation up to 1924, and including not only native American drama, but that which came to us from England and other foreign sources, Clayton Hamilton, in "Conversations on Contemporary Drama," says: "We are living in a very wonderful period of dramatic creativity—a period more vast and varied, more wide-spread and more versatile in productiveness, than even those other great periods, the Greek, the Spanish, the Elizabethan, and the Classic French. . . . Living in the present period, I have actually attended the world-premières of several plays that seem destined to endure . . . for centuries to come. In New York . . . we have frequent opportunities to observe the first production anywhere, or at least the first production in America, of plays that are immeasurably more important than any that were written in all the twenty centuries between Sophocles and Shakespeare."

[3] Most of them were still living in 1925, but they were entitled to a designation of antiquity: they were "early American dramatists."

portant. In that classification they stood together; in all things else they were very far apart. Even the respective reasons for their importance were different, almost antagonistic.

On the opening night of "Sherlock Holmes," Novem-

From the Albert Davis Collection.

Richard Mansfield introduced Edmond Rostand's "Cyrano de Bergerac" to the American stage in October, 1898.

William Gillette dramatized and played "Sherlock Holmes."

ber 6, 1899, the playwright and actor of the part, William Gillette, told the applauding audience: "About a year ago it seemed to me the drama was insufficiently supplied with scoundrels." Gillette and Conan Doyle between them created a scoundrel as the foil for a Nemesis who will live as long as the English tongue. They added to the common speech a symbol for the frustration of villainy as definite in its meaning and as universally understood as the word "scoundrel" itself — one of the extremely rare cases, like Hamlet, Shylock, and Don Quixote, where characters out of literature pass into the language as practically common nouns. Conan Doyle of course had the incomparable inspiration; he was the original creator of Holmes in fiction. But the character of drama that Gillette made of him is hardly to be thought of as the dramatization of a story in the ordinary sense; it better deserves to be regarded as practically independent. The play with which Gillette personified Sherlock Holmes and set him before the eyes of delighted millions had the stamp of Gillette's individuality, one of the most inventive, various, adroit, and successful stage talents of his generation in any country. Gillette was a genuine personality, had wide range of understanding of art and fecund creativeness in it. He set himself the task of writing a classic melodrama[1] — and succeeded. In the title rôle, his "metallic tenor" and unconcerned air in the midst of situations that gave the audience a vicarious terror, was a triumph of acting equal to that of creation. Some of Gillette's other plays were "Secret Service," "Too Much Johnson," "The Private Secretary," and "Held by the Enemy."

James A. Herne's distinction rested on a wholly different kind of reason. Possibly Herne could have written "Sherlock Holmes," for he was skilled in stage-craft—but it is quite certain he would not if he could. Herne's importance rested on his distaste for melodrama, for every sort of artificiality. He was to the stage what Howells was to fiction, the pioneer American realist. Also, like Howells, he gave encouragement to younger dramatists having the same tastes and convictions, became the idol of a school of them. Much of the realism that had made headway on the American stage by the 1920's had its in-

[1] Norman Hapgood acknowledged "unchecked admiration for this frankly melodramatic masterpiece. . . . He [Gillette] took the good old honest thrills of melodrama . . . an undiluted dose of lurid detective . . . and handled his materials so skilfully that it sends shivers of delight up and down the spinal cords alike of urchins and philosophers. . . . It may be doubted whether anything so uncompromisingly melodramatic has ever, at least in our day, been so well done."

spiration in Herne. Herne never made any such success as "Sherlock Holmes," and the two of his plays that were most faithful to the school of realism, "The Reverend Griffith Davenport" and "Margaret Fleming," were also the least successful, in a popular sense. "Griffith Davenport" was the last important play, so far as I can remember, written about slavery, the last (except "Uncle Tom's Cabin") that depended on slavery for its interest. (In Herne's play when an escaping slave committed suicide the owner said: "There goes $1500.") William Dean Howells thought the waning public interest in slavery, a full generation after the Civil War, accounted for "Griffith Davenport's" relative failure. Herne also played "Uncle Nat" Berry in his own "Shore Acres" and wrote and played in "Hearts of Oak" and "Sag Harbor." He was one of the few dramatists of the nineties, or of any time, as to whom the most austere critics, such as Walter Eaton and Norman Hapgood, agreed with the more amiable master-craftsmen of the stage itself, such as Augustus Thomas. They all regarded Herne as outstanding in his generation.[1] From an even more competent judge of the fidelity of Herne's plays to actual life came a more spontaneous tribute to his realism: When "Sag Harbor" was on the New England stage, an authentic resident of that Long Island village said: "By gosh, sir, it was us and no mistake."

The playgoing America of the nineties gave appreciation to several varieties of appeal, including the very best. It was in the dramatic season of 1898–99 that

[1] Clayton Hamilton thinks a third dramatist of the nineties should be mentioned. Writing me colloquially in September, 1925, he said: "Clyde Fitch came so darn near being important that I think you ought to mention the fact that he was cut off at the early age of forty-four, just when it appeared that he was about to embark upon a new and mature career." Fitch wrote "Barbara Frietchie" and "Nathan Hale," and many plays of contemporary life. The fidelity of the latter to the minute details of the life of his time was Fitch's chief distinction.

Ellen Terry, writing from Boston to a friend, said: "I believe there was more money in the house one night than there ever had been before, and do you know what the play was? The dear old 'Merchant of Venice'!" Miss Terry's Portia was described by Norman Hapgood: "Her gait, her voice, her face, the wave of her hand, the toss of her head, all glow with the quick, warm throbbing life of spring, of buds and inspiring air!" Another beloved actress of the nineties who played in "The Merchant of Venice" and "The School for Scandal" was Ada Rehan. She inspired the austere Hapgood to speak of her "beautiful simplicity, matchless elocution, and quiet, melting poetry."

In the nineties Minnie Maddern Fiske played "Becky Sharp" and Ibsen's "A Doll's House." Mrs. Fiske could, if she chose, project no more than the profile of her nose and chin beyond the edge of the wings and, with as little as that, direct as much personality out upon the audience and excite as much emotion as some other actors using all their resources. No actress ever did more with the concentration of a fine, strong mentality into a richly vibrant voice than Mrs. Fiske in a single sentence: "It's too late, Becky Sharp!"

In October, 1898, Richard Mansfield played "Cyrano de Bergerac" at the Garden Theatre, New York. That event of the nineties was the introduction to America of what turned out to be "the most successful play that has ever been produced at any time in the history of the drama. . . . No other play in history has been so immediately and so enormously successful in every country of the world." Those words are Clayton Hamilton's.[1]

[1] I wrote to Mr. Hamilton about the inclusiveness of this judgment, and he replied: "I mean that it was the most instantaneously and universally popular play in the history of the theatre. It is not the greatest nor anything near the greatest, but it is, I think, the most contagious—and Walter Hampden ranks equally with Coquelin and Mansfield in the playing of the hero."

In the nineties Julia Marlowe was playing rôles of exquisite youth.

From a photograph by Brown Brothers.

Josef Hofmann in the early nineties.

From a photograph by Brown Brothers.

Mrs. Minnie Maddern Fiske in the nineties.

So far as they compose a judgment, they are subject to difference of opinion. But Mr. Hamilton has also set down, not as judgment, but as recollection of vivid fact, the way in which Rostand's words moved the youth of the nineties: Rostand "taught me in my teens to love the loveliness of words, an affection I have not as yet outlived. I remember how when I was sixteen I used to walk the streets repeating the verses of Rostand over and over to myself. I find myself doing it to this day. . . . No other man has ever shown a greater mastery of words."

That was Clayton Hamilton — and many, many other American youths of the time of Mansfield's production of "Cyrano" in the 1890's. More than a quarter of a century later, in the fall of 1924, Walter Hampden restored "Cyrano" to the American stage[1] and proved that, with respect to this play at least, the taste of 1924 did not differ from that of 1898. Hampden was advised by nearly every friend he had among producers not to court

[1] When Hampden's 1924 tour brought him to Washington I had occasion to observe the effect of the magic of Rostand's verse on another lad, one whose youth did not depend on mere years, but on temperament, and was permanent. Joseph P. Tumulty, after going to Washington as Secretary to President Woodrow Wilson, had a table in the Shoreham dining-room for lunch every day, a table that became an institution. One day as I entered the dining-room I observed that the casual lunchers, travellers and strangers, had their eyes on Tumulty's table, with an expression partly amusement, partly wonder. Tumulty was alone, his big horn spectacles on his nose, in one hand a book, the other busy with gestures of scorn. His voice rapt, sonorous, and considerably louder than his utter preoccupation realized, rolling out the dramatic shadings of

"What would you have me do?
Seek for the patronage of some great man,
And like a creeping vine on a tall tree
Creep upward, where I cannot stand alone?
No, thank you! . . . Be a buffoon
In the vile hope of teasing out a smile
On some cold face? No thank you!
Make my knees
Callous, and cultivate a supple spine—
Wear out my belly grovelling in the dust?
No, thank you!"

As I sat down, Tumulty asked me if I had seen Hampden in "Cyrano" the night before. Too rapt to wait for an answer, he cast me, without my will, in the rôle of Le Bret; and now having adequate dramatis personæ for the scene, raised his disaster with so hazardous a revival. He was told that times had changed during the hiatus of a quarter-century, and the piece would seem old-fashioned; that twentieth-century American audiences did not care for costume dramas, and would not sit through a play in verse. Hampden reasoned, however, that "Cyrano," being of the seventeenth century — being, more accurately, of all time and no time, being of the date that one identifies merely as long ago — Hampden reasoned that its popularity did not depend on any element of timeliness — it would be no more out of date in 1924 than it had been in 1898. He reasoned also that it would be new to all theatregoers under thirty, and that its high-spirited exuberance would appeal to youth. Most of all, Hampden took counsel of his own feeling for what is fine. His courage was rewarded. At the opening performance, November 1, 1924, the audience stood up and cheered;

voice to a still higher vehemence, and directed his withering "No, thank you's" at me:

"Scratch the back of any swine
That roots up gold for me? Tickle the horns
Of Mammon with my left hand, while my right,
Too proud to know his partner's business,
Takes in the fee? No, thank you! Use the fire
God gave me to burn incense all day long
Under the nose of wood and stone?
No, thank you! . . . Publish verses at my own
Expense? No, thank you!
Calculate, scheme, be afraid,
Love more to make a visit than a poem,
Seek introductions, favor, influences?
No, thank you! No, I thank you,
And again
I thank you!"

While I, trying to seem not to shrink from his gestures of outraged scorn, had occasion to wonder uneasily how many of the listening lunchers had seen "Cyrano" the night before, or were otherwise equipped to understand that the vehemence of which I was the object had been evoked as merely the vicarious echo of a poet in the French tongue, translated by Brian Hooker and declaimed by Walter Hampden. Tumulty was a man of forty-five, a seasoned theatregoer, but he—and many others, youths either by the almanac or by the permanent license of temperament—thrilled like a sensitive, romantic child to the translation of Rostand's verse, of which Brander Matthews said: "It is utterly impossible to translate 'Cyrano de Bergerac' into English verse; and Brian Hooker has done it."

in its fourth month it was playing to twenty thousand dollars a week.[1]

Richard Mansfield's introduction of "Cyrano de Bergerac" to America was one of his many services to the theatre, many pleasures to the public. He produced the first of Bernard Shaw's plays to be brought to America, "Arms and the Man," in 1894; and the second, "The Devil's Disciple," in 1897. He wanted to play "Candida," and put it in rehearsal, but abandoned it because, Shaw said, the actor could not embody the poet physically. Mansfield also played in "Dr. Jekyll and Mr. Hyde," "Henry V," "Beau Brummell," "A Parisian Romance."

In the nineties, Julia Marlowe was playing in rôles of exquisite youth, "The Countess Valeska," Rosalind in "As You Like It." Of Miss Marlowe as she was in these and others of her early impersonations, Augustus Thomas, out of his wide experience, says: "She had every requisite for success in star parts on the stage that a girl could need — youth and health, with their attractiveness; facial and physical beauty; stature, poise, carriage, voice, diction, proper pronunciation, mobile expression, definite and graceful gesture, and competent, well-shaped, responsive hands. Her mental equipment included gaiety, hospitality for humor, self-reliance, ready emotions under fair control, a capacity for attention. . . . Her voice, then as now, the best woman's speaking voice on the American or English stage." Norman Hapgood, recalling the glamour of his own youth during the nineties, and that of one of the most beautiful women who ever played on any stage, said of Miss Marlowe: "She burst upon the students of Harvard College like each one's personal dream."

Joseph Jefferson was playing "Rip Van Winkle,"

[1] For much about Hampden's revival of "Cyrano" I am indebted to Clayton Hamilton, who was closely associated with him.

Maude Adams played "Babbie" in "The Little Minister," Augustus Thomas wrote "Alabama," "In Mizzoura," and "Arizona," and dramatized "Beside the Bonnie

Richard Mansfield as Dick Dudgeon in "The Devil's Disciple."

Brier Bush." David Belasco presented Mrs. Leslie Carter in "The Heart of Maryland" in 1895 and Blanche Bates in "Naughty Anthony" in 1899. James O'Neill, later to be revived in a vicarious fame as the father of Eugene O'Neill, was playing in the nineties "The Count of

Monte Cristo." John Drew played "The Squire of Dames" and "The Liars"; Ethel Barrymore in "Trelawney of the Wells." Denman Thompson appeared year after year in "The Old Homestead"; Chauncey Olcott

Madame Sarah Bernhardt, on the occasion of one of her "farewell tours" to America.

in "The Minstrel of Clare"; Andrew Mack in "Myles Aroon." It was the period of the best fame of Nat Goodwin, whose nervousness on first nights expressed itself in literal seasickness, and who said: "A first night is a hoss-race that lasts three hours"; who had got his start "as

From the Albert Davis Collection.

John Drew in his youth.

From the Albert Davis Collection.

Ada Rehan.

From the Albert Davis Collection.

James A. Herne as Captain Marble in "Sag Harbor."

the hind legs of the heifer in the famous production of 'Evangeline' in Boston." Before that, Goodwin had been with Emerson's Minstrels. So had Francis Wilson. Many others, subsequently to be known as stars of the drama, got part of their apprenticeship in minstrelsy. Joseph Jefferson, in his youth, had danced Jim Crow in black-face; William H. Crane had been on the tambourine end of Pell's Minstrels. Minstrelsy, which began about 1840, was still popular in the nineties, with Primrose and West and McIntyre and Heath among its stars. Lew Dockstader, who used to imitate Roosevelt, outlived the vogue of minstrelsy, which had begun to pass by 1910. In 1891, at the age of thirteen, George M. Cohan played with his family in "Peck's Bad Boy." Mr. Cohan played the part of "Henry Peck" — "that incorrigible lad with a heart of gold," as the programme said.

In the nineties Sarah Bernhardt was beginning that series of tours in which she added the sentiment of farewell to the other graces of her performance — and generously repeated the combination in some four or five subsequent farewell tours.

There was a vogue of the "Prisoner of Zenda" type of romance. Edward H. Sothern was making love over sundials in castle gardens, and fighting duels with his cloak held over his left arm. So was the tall, dark, slender, romantic-looking James K. Hackett. As Walter Eaton put it, after doing me the kindness of reading the first draft of this chapter: "Just as the new realism was edging in, the old romance was going out in a blaze of glory. It was a superb theatre to be young in; in fact, it was a great world to be young in."

During the winter nights, in those days before the movie and the radio supplied a different form of entertainment; in that period, when the flesh-and-blood drama

— the more flesh-and-blood the better — still continued its age-long monopoly — during those winter nights of the nineties, in hundreds of little American towns, and also in big cities where not everybody as yet had become oversophisticated, Eliza crossed the ice, the bloodhounds

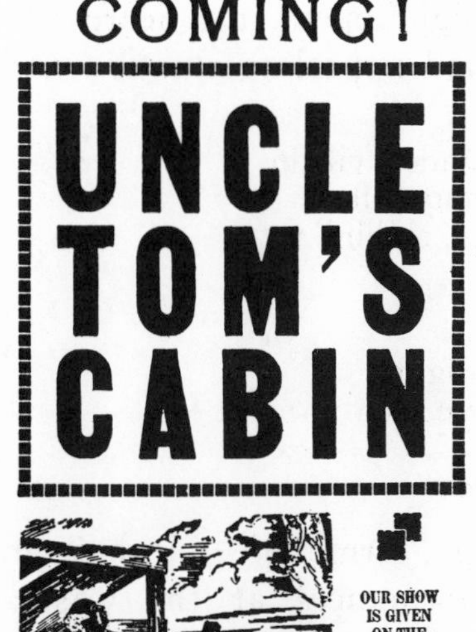

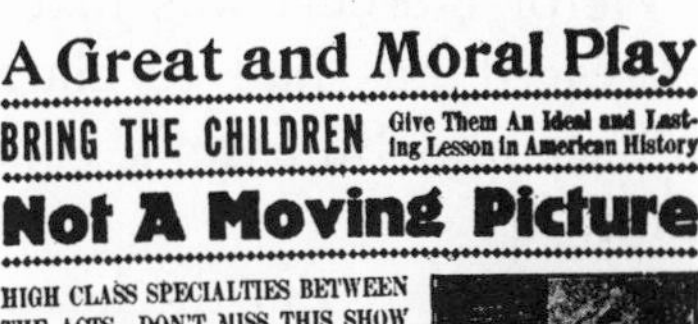

"Uncle Tom's Cabin."
These old-time pictures were still being used by the travelling "Tommers" in 1925.

bayed the runaway slave, Topsy just grew, Simon Legree cracked his whip, Little Eva drew tears, Uncle Tom went his burdened way. "Uncle Tom's Cabin" not only still held its sway; actually, it was a whole department of the drama, and there was a class of roving players who called themselves "Tommers." As late as March 21, 1901, *Life* recorded: ". . . 'Uncle Tom's Cabin,' from which no dramatist collects royalties, is to-day the greatest money-maker of any attraction on the stage of New York City."

In the same year, *Puck* said: "It is predicted that the most important dramatic event of the present century will be the permanent withdrawal[1] from the stage of 'Uncle Tom's Cabin.'"

Victor Herbert was just beginning to give America the nearest it has had to classic light opera, the nearest to Gilbert and Sullivan's combined appeal to emotion and mind, in

I'm the heavy-handed villain,
Who is anxious and willin'
To turn an honest shillin'
When I can.

And

Star light, star bright,
Very first star I've seen to-night —
Tell me, tell me,
All I want to know.

Francis Wilson was playing "Erminie" — it had an extraordinary run, 1256 performances at the Casino Theatre, New York — and making popular two lovely bits of music. One, "Good Night":

Oh, 'tis growing late, 'tis growing late,
And time indeed to end the fête,
Or we shall see the morning's light
Before we say to you good night.

[1] In April, 1925, *Scribner's Magazine* printed an article about Uncle Tom shows and the Tommers, which spoke of them as wholly of the past. This turned out to be, like the report of Mark Twain's death, exaggerated. The week the article appeared there was an Uncle Tom show at Lockport, N. Y. A reporter of the Buffalo *Evening News*, having called on the manager to investigate *Scribner's* premature report of the death of the institution, quoted him as saying: "Yes, sir, yes, sir, the old show's going good. We been standin' 'em up wherever we go. Open up galleries that ain't been open for years. Big cities and medium towns, we make 'em all—" There was evidence of decay, however, in his statement that the appearance of his show in Louisville, Ky., had been the first that had played Tom there in twenty-five years. In Evanston, Ills., "the show filled the gallery which had not been opened for twenty-nine years." He knew of only one other Tom show playing in theatres. There were half a dozen or more tent shows. One was owned by a man named Tom Finn, of Hoosick Falls, N. Y., who "made a lotta money out of it. He hits the one-store towns but he packs 'em in."

The other a lullaby, of which the chorus was:

Bye, bye, drowsiness o'ertaking,
Pretty little eyelids sleep,
Bye, bye, watching till thou'rt waking,
Darling, be thy slumber deep.

The nineties was the period of Reginald De Koven's "Robin Hood" and its popular "Brown October Ale":

And it's will ye quaff with me, my lads, and it's will ye quaff with me?
It is a draught of nut-brown ale I offer unto ye;
All foaming in the tankard, lads, it cheers the heart forlorn,
Oh, here's a friend to ev'ry one, 'tis stout John Barleycorn.

So laugh, lads, and quaff, lads, 'twill make you stout and hale,
Through all my days I'll sing the praise of brown October ale.

America's taste for humor included appreciation of a type that went with the times, and largely passed with them. Charles Hoyt's[1] score of farces were good-humored, witty, frank, vulgar — not in the sense, necessarily, of something to disapprove, but of something common to many and agreeable to share. "He tells his jokes," said Hapgood, "as healthy men do in a smoking-room, offhand, bringing out the humor rather than anything behind it; nobody could be more American." In "A Trip to Chinatown" a stock-raiser said: "I hate to talk about myself, but I bet I know more about art than any man as raises hogs in these United States." Another of Hoyt's farces gave currency to "Do I look as bad as I feel? I'd hate to feel as bad as you look."

May Irwin in one of her plays introduced a couple so poor "they hired a room over a restaurant and inhaled their meals." In another, as a mother whose little daughter admitted having had ten glasses of lemonade, Miss Irwin, with the seriousness she could summon to her broad features, asked: "And honestly, under the surface,

[1] Hoyt's creations included "A Brass Monkey," "A Bunch of Keys," ' A Milk White Flag," "A Texas Steer."

are you happy?" In another of Miss Irwin's burlesques this was new:

"Your life-line shows you are going to die of starvation among strangers."
"Shipwreck?"
"No; boarding-house."

Jokes, sayings, phrases, now utterly trite, were, in the farces of the nineties, pristine with joyous surprise, received with boisterous laughter, for weeks afterward providing the materials for glad conversations that began "Have you heard the latest?" One of Miss Irwin's plays included the last example, I think, of a brand of witticism that had served the stage and the story-teller for more than fifty years — its passing reflected a change in the very composition of the American people. The point of one of the commonest variations lay in an Irishman using the seat of his trousers as part of the mechanism of illumination, and rejecting with suspicion all the more modern ways then being introduced for lighting a match. The other most common variation, as Miss Irwin told it, pictured an Irishman refusing a job as a diver because the occupation, though more than usually remunerative and otherwise appealing to his zest for danger, precluded what was indispensable to good workmanship, the opportunity to spit on his hands. That joke in the nineties was passing rapidly. The "Once there were two Irishmen" story was beginning to give way to the "two Jews" one — Pat and Mike retiring before Abe and Sol.

Weber and Fields were climbing to the heights of popular favor with a company that included, in the beginning, David Warfield, later an assured and deserved success in legitimate drama. In one of the Weber and Fields farces, Warfield was Sigmund Cohenski, a millionaire Jew, whose daughter Uneeda was in love with a captain of the United States navy.

"The captain is my ideal of a hero," Uneeda told her father.

"A hero! Is dot a business? A tailor is a business, a shoemaker is a business, but a hero? Better you should marry a bookkeeper," Warfield exclaimed.

"A bookkeeper? I suppose you think the pen is mightier than the sword," the girl sneered.

"You bet you my life," said Papa Cohenski. "Could you sign checks with a sword?" [1]

From the Albert Davis Collection.

An early performance of Weber and Fields.

A noise being heard outside, it was announced a soldier had been shot. Weber asked: "Where?" Fields replied: "In the excitement." Another that originated in a Weber and Fields show in 1900 must have been, I suppose, one of the earliest uses of a terminology now safely sanctified in the dictionary. It was one of the most successful "gags" of 1900:

First Chorus Girl: "I got a pearl out of an oyster at Shanley's."

Second Chorus Girl: "That's nothing. I got a whole diamond necklace out of a lobster."

The nineties were the birth-time of many more that in 1925 seemed even older than a quarter-century. It was in the fall of 1900, in a burlesque called "Fiddle-de-dee,"

[1] Reproduced in "Weber and Fields," by Felix Isman, an exceptionally attractive book about a portion of the field of the stage. Another book, of quite different character, useful to those who would recall and understand what was best on the stage of the nineties, is Norman Hapgood's "The Stage in America, 1897–1900." In those years Hapgood was dramatic critic for the New York *Commercial Advertiser.* No other critic, and few actors or playwrights, did more to encourage taste and intelligence on the American stage.

that De Wolf Hopper, explaining to the audience that he had come back to the New York stage to escape one-night stands and sleeping-cars, added: "When I finally reached Washington and a stationary bed, I had to hire

From the Albert Davis Collection.

Weber and Fields chorus of the nineties, with Peter Dailey.

two men to shake the bed all night and pour cinders down my neck."

VIII

In the nineties Mr. Hopper was reciting up and down the land that greatest,[1] that most frequently declaimed epic of American sport, "Casey at the Bat":

It looked extremely rocky for the Mudville nine that day;
The score stood two to four, with but an inning left to play.
So, when Cooney died at second, and Burrows did the same,
A pallor wreathed the features of the patrons of the game.

[1] At least, so it seemed to us then. But when, in September, 1924, I tried to get an authentic copy for the purposes of this book, I was chilled by a sentence in a letter from M. Witmark & Sons, Publishers of Beautiful Ballads, Sacred—Secular: "Regret to advise you that 'Casey at the Bat' is out of print." They could not even give me the author's address.

A straggling few got up to go, leaving there the rest,
With that hope that springs eternal within the human breast,
For they thought, "If only Casey could get a whack at that,"
They'd put up even money now, with Casey at the bat.

But Flynn preceded Casey, and likewise so did Blake,
And the former was a puddin', and the latter was a fake,
So on that stricken multitude a deathlike silence sat,
For there seemed but little chance of Casey's getting to the bat.

But Flynn let drive a "single," to the wonderment of all,
And the much-despised Blakey "tore the cover off the ball."
And when the dust had lifted and they saw what had occurred,
There was Blakey safe at second, and Flynn ahuggin' third.

Then from the gladdening multitude went up a joyous yell,
It rumbled in the mountain-tops, it rattled in the dell;
It struck upon the hillside and rebounded on the flat;
For Casey, mighty Casey, was advancing to the bat.

There was ease in Casey's manner as he stepped into his place;
There was pride in Casey's bearing, and a smile on Casey's face.
And when, responding to the cheers, he lightly doffed his hat,
No stranger in the crowd could doubt 'twas Casey at the bat.

Ten thousand eyes were on him as he rubbed his hands with dirt,
Five thousand tongues applauded when he wiped them on his shirt;
Then while the New York pitcher ground the ball into his hip,
Defiance gleamed in Casey's eye, a sneer curled Casey's lip.

And now the leather-covered sphere came whirling through the air,
And Casey stood awatching it in haughty grandeur there.
Close by the sturdy batsman the ball unheeded sped —
"That ain't my style," said Casey. "Strike one!" the umpire said.

From the benches, black with people, there went up a muffled roar,
Like the beating of storm waves on a stern and distant shore.
"Kill him! Kill the umpire!" shouted some one on the stand.
And it's likely they'd have killed him had not Casey raised a hand.

With a smile of Christian charity great Casey's visage shone;
He stilled the rising tumult; he bade the game go on;

He signalled to Sir Timothy, once more the spheroid flew;
But Casey still ignored it, and the umpire said: "Strike two!"

"Fraud!" cried the maddened thousands, and echo answered "Fraud!"
But one scornful look from Casey and the audience was awed.
They saw his face grow stern and cold, they saw his muscles strain,
And they knew that Casey wouldn't let that ball go by again.

The sneer is gone from Casey's lip, his teeth are clinched in hate;
He pounds with cruel violence his bat upon the plate.
And now the pitcher holds the ball, and now he lets it go,
And now the air is shattered by the force of Casey's blow.

Ah, somewhere in this favored land the sun is shining bright;
The band is playing somewhere, and somewhere hearts are light.
And somewhere men are laughing, and somewhere children shout:
But there is no joy in Mudville — mighty Casey has struck out.[1]

IX

The nineties was the day of the bicycle, of which, at that time, much was said in the same words that, in 1925, were used of the automobile. Youths and maidens rode on tandems — who has heard that word as a recent experience? And yet in the nineties it was in as common use as, later, roadster or sedan. It was during, and of, the nineties that E. Benjamin Andrews wrote: "A species of clumsy bicycle obtained considerable pop-

[1] This version is the result of some pains to be authentic. In September, 1924, De Wolf Hopper, still kicking nimble legs at the age of sixty-six, still giving fresh pleasures to a younger generation and recalling old pleasures to a passing one, with revivals of "The Mikado," "Pinafore," and "The Prince of Pilsen"—Mr. Hopper wrote me while on tour, from the Adams House in Boston:

"As to the number of times I have recited it, it is beyond the realm of human imaginings to compass. I did it first in May, 1888, at Wallack's Theatre, New York City. How many times I've done it since can best be numbered by the stars in the Milky Way. The author of 'Casey' is Mr. Ernest L. Thayer. Millions have claimed that honor, but HE IS THE ONE."

ularity in the United States in 1868. The fad proved temporary, but was the forerunner of an abiding[1] national habit. The first bicycle proper was brought to this country in 1876, being exhibited at the Centennial. Two years later 'wheels' began to be manufactured here. Each instrument consisted of one large wheel, to which were attached cranks and pedals, and one small one connected with the first by a curved 'backbone,' this being surmounted by a saddle. The danger of riding the high wheel led to many variations of its design, none of which were successful; and bicycling continued to be experts' work until 1889, when the 'safety' became prominent. In this machine the two wheels were made of the same size, the saddle placed above and between them. The popularity of this form of bicycle[2] was amazingly enhanced by the adoption of inflated or pneumatic tires, an invention half a century old but now finding its first successful application. Bicycle-makers[3] multiplied and

This bicycle, now preserved in the National Museum at Washington, was the style common in the eighties and early nineties, until displaced by the safety.

[1] By reading other historians, one learns to be cautious about using such words as "abiding" or "permanent."

[2] There were bicycle clubs that used to have "Century runs" on Sundays and holidays. The Pullman road race for bicyclists from Chicago to Pullman, Ills., was a sporting event. There were as many as a thousand riders, many in black tights. The bicycle was attended by a "parking" problem, miniature of the automobile parking problem. Bicycles were parked, not on the street, but in the office-buildings. At the Chicago Athletic Club there was a big room for bicycles. Some women bicyclers wore bloomers.

[3] Some of the popular makes, names as familiar in the nineties as Ford and Buick and Packard were in 1925, were: Columbia, Imperial, Stormer, Sterling,

prospered despite the panic of 1893. Sewing-machine and arms companies turned to the manufacture of bicycles. Agitation and legislation for good roads became a phenomenon of the times. Railroads were in some States compelled to take bicycles as baggage. The

From a photograph by New York "World."

Riding a tandem bicycle at Coney Island, 1896.

'safety' pattern was so modified as to enable ladies to ride it with little change in their attire, and the exercise was welcomed by many. While makers and sellers of wheels and wheel equipment throve, liverymen and horse-dealers did less business. Clothiers complained[1] that only cycling suits could be sold. Liquor-dealers in some sections could not vend their wares in intoxicating quantities even among young men who had formerly indulged

("Built like a watch"), Crawford, Spalding, Cleveland, Monarch, Stearns, Syracuse, Barnes ("Like a trusted steed"), Featherstone, Pierce ("A study in vibration"), Tribune, and Victor.

[1] Precisely the things that were said about the automobile twenty years later.

freely. People in the most moderate circumstances would rigidly economize in other directions for the sake of purchasing cycles. When comfortable and hygienic saddles came into use, physicians indorsed the exercise. One prominent New York practitioner believed that no other invention for 200 years had, from a physical point of view, done so much for the human family."[1]

X

The vogue of the bicycle was reflected in one of the most popular songs of the nineties, "Daisy Bell":

> Daisy, Daisy, give me your answer true.
> I'm half crazy, all for the love of you!
> It won't be a stylish marriage,
> I can't afford a carriage,
> But you'll look sweet
> Upon the seat
> Of a bicycle built for two!

In setting down here, and elsewhere in these volumes, stanzas and choruses of the popular songs from year to year, I had thought to arm myself against the superiority of the critical[2] by quoting from Plato, whose judgment on

[1] W. L. Whittlesey, of Princeton University, makes the point that riding a bicycle meant exercise; the automobile does not. He thinks many successful men of the period of 1910–25 won on the energy built up on the bicycle. Also he thinks the growth of college and club athletics arose out of bicycle clubs.

[2] "I shall cheerfully bear the reproach of having descended below the dignity of history if I can succeed in placing before the English of the nineteenth century a true picture of the life. . . ."—From Macaulay's Introduction to his "History of England."

"I know histhry isn't thrue, Hinnissy, because it ain't like what I see ivry day in Halsted Sthreet. If any wan comes along with a histhry iv Greece or Rome that'll show me th' people fightin', gettin' dhrunk, makin' love, gettin' married, owin' th' groceryman an' bein' without hard coal, I'll believe they was a Greece or Rome, but not befure. Historyans is like doctors. They are always lookin' f'r symptoms. Those iv them that writes about their own times examines th' tongue an' feels th' pulse an' makes a wrong diagnosis. Th' other kind iv histhry is a post-mortem examination. It tells ye what a counthry died iv. But I'd like to know what it lived iv."—Finley Peter Dunne, "Observations by Mr. Dooley."

Copyright, MDCCCXCII, by T. B. Harms & Co.

"Daisy Bell."

the relation between music and national manners and institutions, as set down in "The Republic," was:

The introduction of a new kind of music must be shunned as imperilling the whole state, since styles of music are never disturbed without affecting the most important political institutions. The new style, gradually gaining a lodgment, quietly insinuates itself into manners and customs; and from these it issues in greater force . . . goes on to attack laws and constitutions, displaying the utmost impudence, until it ends by overturning everything, both in public and in private.

To try to trace an application of this theory of Plato to anything happening in America would be intricate and full of pitfalls, yet there are some facts that seem like fragments of significance.

The most characteristic — indeed, almost the only, indigenous American music is the Negro melody. The father of true Negro music, as it was known prior to 1900, was Stephen Collins Foster, composer of "Old Folks at Home" ("Suwanee River"), "Old Black Joe," "Massa's in the Cold, Cold Ground," and more than a hundred other similar songs. Foster, born in a western Pennsylvania village, spent his mature life in Kentucky and elsewhere in the South. He was "old-timey folks," as the Southern phrase has it — American to the core of his heart, and his songs equally so.

Beginning about 1900 and continuing through the quarter-century following, this older indigenous Negro music began to be jostled by variations not genuinely indigenous, first "ragtime" and "coon songs," and later "mammy songs." These were tinpanny, staccato, lacking in the plaintive sentiment of the older Negro music, which was a true expression of the Negro soul. They were distant in inspiration, mood, geographic origin — in almost every respect — from Foster's faithful and sympathetic interpretation of the true South. The divergence of the new from the old, in inspiration and in view-point, is aptly shown by an article in *Vanity Fair*, April, 1925, written by Mr. Al Jolson of the New York stage, one of the most successful popularizers of so-called "mammy songs."

The title read: "M a a a a a m-m y ! M a a a a a m-m y !" and the article began:

> Having spent the greater part of my life singing about my mammy in the Sunny South, I had begun to believe that such a person really existed. Vocalizing so often, so vehemently, about "the charms of my mammy's arms" and "climbing tenderlee upon her knee," I longed to visit the Paradise that the song-writers tell us lies below the line on which Mr. Mason collaborated with Mr. Dixon. . . . The Shubert brothers, who are my managers, were willing that I should sing of the South but unwilling that I should go there. "Why should you," they argued, "when in the North there are so many more profitable one-night stands?" . . . I was a trifle disappointed to learn that the trains left for Dixie at six-thirty. It was Irving Berlin who had led me to believe that I would take a Midnight Choo-Choo. . . .

After reciting some disillusionments that his New York anticipations found in the South, Mr. Jolson concluded:

> But after all, maybe I am too caustic in my remarks about the South. When all is said and done, there's only one South! —Thank God!

One read that, one recognized the unsympathetic point of view, one realized how far it was from the spirit in which Stephen Foster had written the earlier melodies. Then one recalled that the vogue of the fabricated "mammy song" of New York origin was contemporaneous with certain other phenomena happening in America, including some fundamental and definite changes in American "manners and customs," "political institutions," "laws and constitutions." One recalled that, and was reminded, with rather startling force, of Plato's theory.

At the very least, one can assume that the South may have found something in the artificiality of Mr. Jolson's songs as disillusioning to them as the South was to him; that the South, and the West as well, may have had some subtle, subconscious sense of this supercilious attitude of the New Yorkers who were writing and singing the "mammy songs" of 1925 — a vague resentment of the manhandling of a thing so indigenous as Negro melody; may have felt a subtle spiritual sense of jangling discord between the genuine Negro music with which they had long been familiar at home and as it was fabricated by New York.

One can be certain the feeling went that far at least. But it is a worth-while speculation about our American national psychology whether the instinctive emotions of the simpler old-fashioned Americans of the South and West may have gone deeper and may have accounted for, or at least been associated with, some of the social and political phenomena of the time. May it be possible that the old-time American of the rural South and West felt in his own way, vaguely but poignantly, the menace that Plato was able to put in warning words? Felt instinctively that "styles of music are never disturbed without affecting the most important political institutions"; that "the new style gradually gaining a lodgment, [would] quietly insinuate itself into manners and customs . . . attack laws and constitutions, displaying the utmost impudence, until it ends by overturning everything"?

In any event, this was precisely the period, in the rural parts of the country especially, of a passionately defensive native Americanism that found expression in the immigration restriction law; in insistence upon political isolation for America; in susceptibility to suspicion against institutions charged with having foreign origins or affiliations; in such phrases as "hundred-per-cent American"; in readiness to join a secret society based on intolerance of aliens (including, paradoxically, intolerance toward the Negro); and, as a minor but real manifestation, in suspicion against New York City and ideas emanating from it, on the theory that New York, in its attitude upon some matters, was more nearly alien than representative American.[1]

[1] In November, 1925, the president of the Metropolitan Opera Company of New York, Mr. Otto Kahn, felt called upon to issue a statement defending the

To be sure, one would be obliged at this point to find a consistent explanation for the fact that some of the music regarded as most typically American was written by a son of foreign parents, John Philip Sousa. Also, as respects classical music, America would have been rather poverty-stricken but for foreign composers and artists. When they brought Russian, Polish, and other European music to America, the contributions were recognized as having beauty and taste. No one thought of objecting to that — on the contrary, all welcomed it as an enrichment. It was the manhandling of our native American music that offended. All of which entails some difficulty in finding deductions from Plato's theory.

Addison attributes importance to popular songs on other grounds. In *The Spectator* (No. 70) he declared:

> An ordinary song or ballad, that is the delight of the common people, cannot fail to please all such readers as are not unqualified for the entertainment by their affectation or ignorance. . . . For it is impossible that anything should be universally tasted and approved by the multitude, though they are only the rabble of the nation, which hath not in it some peculiar aptness to please and gratify the mind of man.

I am obliged to say, however, that I suspect Addison was thinking of the traditional songs of the country people of the England of his time; and I am not certain how much identity there is, in their relation to the indigenous culture of the people, between, on the one hand, those old folk-songs of eighteenth-century England, which were handed down from father to son by word of mouth, and, on the other hand, the ordinary American popular song that lasts for a year or a summer and is forgotten. The songs and ballads Addison had in mind were such

company against charges and demands that the company "discriminates against American art and artists"; that it fails to give adequate opportunities to American composers and American operas; that it should have operas in foreign languages translated into English for production in New York.

as "Country Gardens," "Blue-Eyed Stranger," "Haste to the Wedding," the Morris dances, "Old Woman Tossed Up in a Blanket," "The Gallant Hussar," "The Girl I Left Behind Me," "We Won't Go Home Until Morning." I should hesitate decidedly to say there is much in common between these fine old folk-songs and such ephemeral popular songs as "Good-Night, Nurse," "Waltz Me Around Again, Willie," "A Lemon in the Garden of Love."

Some of the songs quoted elsewhere in this work, like "O Susanna, Don't You Cry for Me,"[1] and "O'er the Mountains Westward Ho," and such songs as "Old Black Joe" and "Suwanee River," are probably true indigenous American equivalents for the English folk-songs. The ordinary, ephemeral popular songs, sometimes written for commercial motives and often circulated by commercial methods, decidedly have not the status of folk-songs.

However, I leave further elucidation on this general topic, of the relation of popular songs to national characteristics, to the more learned in this particular field. For the present purpose I do no more than set down some stanzas and choruses from a few of the songs that were sung in the nineties. They belong in this book, if on no greater basis than that they were widely sung. The number of persons who sang, whistled, hummed, played, or otherwise expressed their souls vicariously through these songs was millions. As for those who heard them, the number can be stated with fair exactness: take the census for 1890 and add 1 per cent for each year to that particular year in the nineties that was the time of any one of these songs. Which is the same as saying that everybody heard these tunes; wherefore, if for no other

[1] "O Susanna, Don't You Cry for Me," and "O'er the Mountains Westward Ho" are quoted in Chapter 8.

reason, they have a place in the history of the time. In addition, some of these songs have allusions to vogues of the time, like "Daisy Bell," or were associated with particular events, as "There'll Be a Hot Time in the Old Town To-Night," a "coon song" which was the most popular air for the bands during the Spanish-American War.

"There'll Be a Hot Time in the Old Town To-Night."

Among the song-writers themselves, Paul Dresser[1] was frequenty appraised as being, in the nineties, nearest to Stephen Foster as the father of the American ballad. The two most famous successes of Dresser were: "On the Banks of the Wabash" and "Just Tell Them That You

[1] That was an adaptation of his real name; he was a brother of Theodore Dreiser, the novelist.

Saw Me." "On the Banks of the Wabash" brought to Indiana a distinction in popular music it already had in popular poetry through James Whitcomb Riley. Eventually Indiana adopted it as its State song, and, in the region of the Wabash, streets and a town were named after Dresser. The inspiration of "On the Banks of the Wabash" has been charmingly described by the composer's brother, Theodore Dreiser. The two were together on

one of those delightful summer Sunday mornings (1896, I believe). . . . "What do you suppose would make a good song these days?" he asked in an idle, meditative mood, sitting at the piano and thrumming while I at a near-by table was looking over my papers. . . . "Me?" I queried, almost contemptuously, I suppose. I could be very lofty at times in regard to his work, much as I admired him. . . . "I can't write those things. Why don't you write something about a State or a river? Look at 'My Old Kentucky Home,' 'Dixie,' 'Old Black Joe' — why don't you do something like that, something that suggests a part of America? People like that. Take Indiana — what's the matter with it? — the Wabash River? It's as good as any other river, and you were 'raised' beside it."

I have to smile even now as I recall the apparent zest or feeling with which all at once he seized on this. It seemed to appeal to him immensely. "That's not a bad idea," he agreed, "but how would you go about it? Why don't you write the words and let me put the music to them? We'll do it together!"

"But I can't," I replied. "I don't know how to do these things. You write it. I'll help — maybe."

After a little urging — I think the fineness of the morning had as much to do with it as anything — I took a piece of paper and after meditating a while scribbled in the most tentative manner imaginable the first verse and chorus of that song almost as it was published. I think one or two lines were too long or didn't rhyme, but eventually either he or I hammered them into shape:

Oh, the moonlight's fair to-night along the Wabash,
From the fields there comes the breath of new-mown hay
Through the sycamores the candlelights are gleaming,
On the banks of the Wabash, far away.

"On the Banks of the Wabash, Far Away."

Theodore Dreiser has also described the beginning of his brother's other great success, "Just Tell Them That You Saw Me." It

must have followed an actual encounter with some woman or girl whose life had seemingly if not actually gone to wreck on the shore of love or passion. At any rate he came into the office . . . one gray November Sunday afternoon . . . and going into a small room which was fitted up with a piano . . . he began improvising or rather repeating over and over a certain strain which was evidently in his mind. A little while later he came out and said: "Listen to this, will you, Thee?" He played and sang the first verse and chorus. In the middle of the latter, so moved was he by the sentiment of it, his voice broke and he had to stop. . . . Later on (the following spring) I was literally astonished to see how . . . it suddenly began to sell, thousands upon thousands of copies being wrapped in great bundles under my very eyes and shipped by express or freight to various parts of the country. Letters and telegrams, even, from all parts of the nation began to pour in. . . . Some enterprising button firm got out a button on which the phrase was printed. Comedians on the stage, newspaper paragraphers, his bank teller or his tailor, even staid business men wishing to appear up to date, used it as a parting salute. The hand-organs, the bands, and the theatre orchestras everywhere were using it. . . . One could scarcely turn a corner or go into a cheap music-hall or variety house without hearing a parody of it.[1]

"Just Tell Them That You Saw Me."

A ballad of the same sort of homesickness and longing for the past as "On the Banks of the Wabash" — but a past with a very different setting — was "The Sidewalks of New York." It was revived a generation later, when Governor Smith of New York became a national political figure, by bands which at Democratic conven-

[1] The inevitable parodies accompanied it. One was:

"Just tell them that you saw me
But you didn't see me saw."

tions[1] played songs of the governor's youth on the East Side of New York.

Down in front of Casey's old brown wooden stoop,
On a summer's evening, we formed a merry group,
Boys and girls together, we would sing and waltz,
While the "ginnie" played the organ on the sidewalks of New York.

"The Sidewalks of New York."

[1] Alexander Woollcott in "The Story of Irving Berlin" describes how, at the Democratic convention in New York in 1924, various attempts were made to arouse the audience to sing patriotic songs, including "The Star-Spangled Banner" and "The Battle Hymn of the Republic." The delegates did not respond. These songs, as Mr. Woollcott puts it, were "not homely enough for so ornery and so shirt-sleeved an assemblage." But when some one started "East side, West side,

"Little Annie Rooney" was also of New York life:

She's my sweetheart, I'm her beau,
She's my Annie, I'm her Joe,
Soon we'll marry, nev-er to part
Little Annie Rooney is my sweetheart!

"The Bowery" was of the very heart of city life. It abounds with the up-to-date slang of the nineties, in lines and allusions such as "Folks who are 'onto' the city say," "pulling his leg," "bouncers," "held up," and "new coon in town." The verses describe a series of adventures of a country "yap" coming to the city for a good time. "There was the Bow'ry ablaze with lights; I had one of the devil's own nights!":

I had walk'd but a block or two,
When up came a fellow and me he knew;
Then a policeman came walking by,
Chased him away, and I ask'd him why?
"Wasn't he pulling your leg?" said he;
Said I, "He never laid hands on me!"
"Get off the Bow'ry, you Yap!" said he,
I'll never go there any more!

I went into an auction store,
I never saw any thieves before;
First he sold me a pair of socks,
Then said he, "how much for the box?"

all around the town," it "spread as flames catching in dry grass. It moved across the acres of hot, coatless delegates. It agitated even the pretentious people in the boxes. It swept the galleries. The listening streets heard it and carried it across the city. One had the illusion that an old song had come down out of the garret, lifted Al Smith to its shoulders and borne him triumphantly through his town. And while this song was making this unheralded return to the streets it celebrated, it occurred to some intuitive city editor to look about for the man who wrote it. Charles Lawler was the name given on the original copy. Was he still living? Did anybody know? A reporter went forth and found him. He was over in Brooklyn, a buck-and-wing dancer, a hoofer of the five-a-day, waiting for his turn to go on in an out-of-the-way music-hall. In the dressing-room, as he bent to fit on his clogging shoes, the reporter told him all about his triumph. It was news to him, for he had no associations with any such new-fangled contraption as the radio and he had not read the newspaper accounts of his second blooming at the convention across the river. In fact he could not read them. He was blind."

Some one said "two dollars!" I said three!
He emptied the box and gave it to me,
"I sold you the box, not the socks," said he.
I'll never go there any more!

"The Bowery."

[1] "Big Tim" Sullivan, a New York politician, said "The Bowery" killed that street, reduced the value of real estate by upward of 25 per cent.

Of small-town life there was "I Don't Want to Play in Your Yard," of which the chorus went:

I don't want to play in your yard,
I don't like you any more;
You'll be sorry when you see me
Sliding down our cellar door;
You can't holler down our rain-barrel;
You can't climb our apple-tree;
I don't want to play in your yard,
If you won't be good to me.

One of the most popular songs of the early nineties recited the misadventures of Dan McGinty,[1] who having "dressed in his best suit of clothes, Sunday morning just at nine," set out upon a holiday excursion, in the course of which he fell, first from a twenty-five-foot wall, and then into a coal-hole; thereafter he encountered the prejudiced attentions of two policemen; and finally, in the adventure that completed his unhappy day:

Down went McGinty to the bottom of the sea,
He must be very wet,
For they haven't found him yet. . . .
Dressed in his best suit of clothes.
There is nothing but a bubble where McGinty ought to be.

"Grandfather's Clock" expressed a domestic sentiment:

My grandfather's clock was too large for the shelf,
So it stood ninety years on the floor;
It was taller by half than the old man himself,
Tho' it weighed not a pennyweight more.

[1] Some of the songs widely sung in the early nineties had been written in the eighties, or even before. McGinty held over from the eighties. Most of the songs quoted here were written, as well as sung, in the nineties: "Daisy Bell," 1892; "There'll Be a Hot Time in the Old Town To-Night," 1896; "On the Banks of the Wabash," 1897; "Just Tell Them That You Saw Me," 1895; "The Sidewalks of New York," 1894; "The Bowery," 1892; "I Don't Want to Play in Your Yard," 1894; "Down Went McGinty," 1889; "Grandfather's Clock," 1876; "Sweet Marie," 1893; "When You and I Were Young, Maggie," 1866; "After the Ball," 1892; "I Had Fifteen Dollars in My Inside Pocket," 1885; "Where Did You Get That Hat?" 1888; "Little Annie Rooney," 1890. The years given here are the years of the copyrights.

It was bought on the morn of the day that he was born,
And was always his treasure and pride;
But it stopped short — never to go again —
When the old man died. . . .

Of the broadest appeal to youthful love was "Sweet Marie":

I've a secret in my heart, Sweet Marie;
A tale I would impart, love for thee.
Every daisy in the dell
Knows my secret, knows it well,
And yet I dare not tell
Sweet Marie!

"Sweet Marie."

A very appealing song of youth and love and old associations was "When You and I Were Young, Maggie." President Harding and Mrs. Harding were of the generation that learned this as young persons; thirty years later they used to sing it with intimate gatherings in the White House:

> I wandered to-day to the hill, Maggie,
> To watch the scene below;
> The creek and the creaking old mill, Maggie,
> As we used to long ago.
> The green grove is gone from the hill, Maggie,
> Where first the daisies sprang,
> The creaking old mill is still, Maggie,
> Since you and I were young. . . .

The common avenue for the introduction of popular songs, or at least for trying them out on the public, was, during the nineties, through the Negro minstrels, which were at that time still a popular institution; later it was done through cabaret and concert singers, sometimes paid for their services in popularization. Some of the songs came into favor through musical comedies in which they were sung. One writer of popular songs, Charles K. Harris, said that he had the device of guessing at the popular taste in songs through following the same taste as shown in plays[1] that take hold. Harris's most popular song was "After the Ball," written in 1892 and very popular during World's Fair year, 1893. It was first sung by May Irwin, and later introduced in Hoyt's "Trip to Chinatown." Harris's profits from this song were over $100,000. It was the earliest example of what the song-

[1] Harris gave illustrations of this device of his art. In the "History of American Music," by W. L. Hubbard, Mr. Harris is quoted as saying: "Such plays as 'The Second Mrs. Tanqueray' and 'The Crust of Society' were in vogue. I then wrote 'Cast Aside,' 'Fallen by the Wayside,' and 'There'll Come a Time Some Day.' Over 300,000 copies were sold of each. Then came the era of society drama, such as 'Charity Ball' and 'The Wife.' I wrote and published 'While the Dance Goes On,' 'Hearts,' 'You'll Never Know,' and 'Can Hearts So Soon Forget?'—which had enormous sales."

"After the Ball."

writing fraternity calls "a big smashing hit." Previous to the nineties, song-writing had been less commercial, both in its remuneration and its inspiration.

A bit of doggerel[1] of the nineties that contained a humorous allusion to the serious, even the acrimonious, history of the day was:

The mick that threw the brick —
He will never throw another.
For calling me an A. P. A.
He now lies under cover.
And above his head, these words are read,
You can see them if you rubber:
"Here lies the mick that threw the brick,
He'll never throw another."

Also, the etymologist of the future may be helped to identify the date when a new word qualified for the dictionary by the use, in this ditty, of the word "rubber" as a verb, intransitive — see also "rubberneck," noun.

Another topical ditty, having reference to events of the day, was sung during the 1892[2] campaign:

Harrison is a wise man
Cleveland is a fool,
Harrison rides a white horse,
Old Grover rides a mule.

A song that was popular in the eighties but hung over into the early nineties was "I Had Fifteen Dollars in My Inside Pocket." The chorus and one stanza — reminiscent of a day when Tammany Hall had the name of

[1] Mr. Rollin Lynde Hartt gave me this from his memory.

[2] Another Harrison-Cleveland campaign ditty, adapted from a popular song, was:

"The train is coming around the bend;
Good-bye, old Grover, good-bye.
It's loaded down with Harrison men;
Good-bye, old Grover, good-bye."

This was sung in the campaign of 1888. These two Harrison-Cleveland campaigns, 1888 and 1892, were the last in which songs, marching clubs, and torchlight processions played much part.

being more sinful than now — and reminiscent, also, of means and ways of extreme, if temporary and ultimately regrettable, exaltation, now not recognized as conventional or even legal — ran:

Oh, the gang they hung around the bar,
Like a swarm of educated mice,
Oh, they made me drink a "clarinette" punch
And a whiskey "sangaree" on ice.

I had fifteen dollars in my inside pocket,
Don't you see? To me it is a warning.
Saturday night I made a call on a friend of Tam'ny Hall,
And the divil a cent I had on Sunday morning.

The nineties was the period also of:

Where did you get that hat,
Where did you get that tile?
Isn't it a nobby one
And just the proper style?
I should like to have one
Just the same as that!
Where'er I go they'd shout "Hello!
Where did you get that hat?"

Some other songs popular in the nineties[1] were "Sunshine of Paradise Alley," 1895; "The Picture That Is Turned to the Wall," 1891; "Sucking Cider Through a Straw," 1891; "The Moth and the Flame," 1898; "She Was Bred in Old Kentucky," 1898; "Only a Bird in a Gilded Cage," 1899; "Ta-ra-ra-ra Boom de-ay," 1892; "Whistling Rufus," 1899; "The Cat Came Back," 1892; "Put Me Off at Buffalo," 1895; "And Her Golden Hair Was Hanging Down Her Back," 1894. "The Rosary" was sung for the first time in Boston by Francis Rogers in February, 1898. Other songs popular in the nineties were: "Rastus on Parade," 1896; "Two Little Girls in Blue," 1893; "Comrades," 1891; "White Wings That

[1] The years given here are the years of the copyrights.

Never Grow Weary — They Carry Me Over the Sea"; "My Sweetheart's the Man in the Moon," 1892.

Classical music was stimulated, as all art in America was, by the larger outlook that came from the World's Fair, the foreign exhibits there, the distinguished foreigners who visited America in connection with it, and the good music that was provided lavishly as an organized part of the fair. During the nineties large orchestras were established in some of the principal cities. Many European musicians toured the country: Busoni, De Pachmann, Monteau, Ysaye, and Paderewski. The fact that Paderewski was passing through a town was sufficient to draw hundreds of people to the railroad-station. Nellie Melba and Emma Calvé came in 1893. Madame Schumann-Heink made her first appearance in this country in Chicago in 1896. It was in 1896 that Columbia University made Edward MacDowell head of its department of music. MacDowell made an experiment in the direction of American national song-writing by the use of Indian melodies, "Indian Suite," Op. 48. Three American singers made reputations abroad — Emma Eames, Lillian Nordica, and Marie van Zandt.

The interest in music and the sale of sheet music were greatly stimulated by the increase of wealth that enabled larger numbers of people to have musical instruments in their homes. Music teachers began to appear in greater numbers. The upright piano was crowding the organ into the wings.[1]

Of one of the composers of instrumental music at this

[1] The old cottage-type organ, very ornate, with a mirror as well as drawers and shelves for holding small articles and bric-à-brac, was for many years the leading seller of the Sears, Roebuck Co., and continued so until 1914, when their piano sales went ahead of the organ business. The first pianos they sold were very ornate in design, embellished with carvings and mouldings. An attempt was made in 1910 to furnish a plainer design of more massive character. The massive design continued to be made plainer and smaller until the bungalow or apartment size instruments were introduced.

time, John Philip Sousa,[1] who for twelve years was the leader of the United States Marine Band, and whom we called, after a characteristic national bent, the "March King" — of Sousa, W. L. Hubbard[2] says:

> Sousa's marches never have been surpassed and rarely equalled. They are without doubt the most typical music which this country has yet produced, for they are deeply imbued with the American spirit. Sousa, above all others, has got the true martial swing. . . . No other composer, not even Johann Strauss, has attained as world-wide popularity as has Sousa. His music has been sold to thousands of bands in the United States alone, and has been heard in all parts of the civilized world. It has been very aptly stated that Sousa's marches contain all the nuances of military psychology, the long unisonal stride, the grip on the musket, the pride in the regiment, and the esprit de corps. They also have served as dance music, and the two-step was directly borne into vogue by them.

Some of the better known of Sousa's marches were: "The Washington Post," "Liberty Bell," "High School Cadets," "King Cotton," "El Capitan," and "Stars and Stripes Forever."

XI

Rudyard Kipling's poems were giving thrill after thrill; and youths on front porches were rolling out in rich barytones on the summer air the best song of homesick-

[1] "Sousa wrote march after march for a publisher who paid him only the nominal fee due him for making the band arrangement." He received "$90 for all his rights to the incomparable 'Stars and Stripes Forever,' to which two generations have marched." Sousa wrote: "I remember the first piece I ever tried to sell. I tramped with it from one dealer to another, until I was about desperate. Finally, I went into the offices of a Washington firm, determined to sell it there or give it up entirely. The manager was a kindly sort, but not in the least interested in my composition. First I offered it for $25. He thought 25 cents was exorbitant. Sadly I took it up to go. Near the door I saw a whole lot of dictionaries. 'Will you give me a dictionary for it?' I suggested. 'Yes,' he said, and so I sold my first song."

[2] "History of American Music."

ness, love, and romantic adventure in the English language,[1] "On the Road to Mandalay":

By the old Moulmein Pagoda, lookin' eastward to the sea,
There's a Burma girl asettin', and I know she thinks o' me;
For the wind is in the palm-trees, and the temple-bells they say:
"Come you back, you British soldier; come you back to
Mandalay!"

Large numbers of young people learned poems of Kipling by heart; he was about the last poet so honored. Another poet, some of whose verses became widely familiar as songs, was Richard Hovey, professor of literature at Barnard College, New York, and author (with Bliss Carman) of "Songs from Vagabondia," published in 1896:

Oh, we're all frank and twenty
When the spring is in the air;
And we've faith and hope aplenty,
And we've life and love to spare;
And its birds of a feather
When good fellows get together,
With a stein on the table and a heart without a care. . . .

XII

In the nineties there was a most famous evangelist, Dwight L. Moody, who was the predecessor of "Billy" Sunday. If one could make the comparison without violating taste, one might say Moody was to Sunday what the organ was to the saxophone, or the waltz to jazz. The impression Moody made on his time, on the thoughtful as well as on the crowd, was not ephemeral.

[1] Comparable to it as a love-song is Bayard Taylor's now comparatively little-known "Bedouin Love-Song," of which the correct version, from Stevenson's "Home Book of Verse," is:

"Till the sun grows cold,
And the stars are old,
And the leaves of the Judgment Book unfold."

James Keeley, formerly managing editor of the Chicago *Tribune*, wrote me: "Moody did more than flash across the sky; they're building a Moody tabernacle in Chicago to-day, May 25, 1925." Moody's death occurred December 22, 1899. He was not a theological scholar nor an expounder of dogma. He was a preacher of religion. When a boy working in a shoe store in Boston, he had been turned to what he made later his life-work by a devoted Sunday-school teacher. At first he carried on his evangelistic work during hours free from his duties as a salesman and "drummer." Finally he gave up business, and for forty years devoted himself to Christian work. At a Y. M. C. A. convention he met Ira D. Sankey, a song leader. Thereafter the two worked together. At Moody's death, *The Outlook* said: "It would be difficult to name any man in the present half-century who has done so much [as Mr. Moody] to give the power of spiritual vision to men who having eyes saw not. . . . He was the last of that school of evangelists."

At the Moody meetings, the hymns commonly sung were from the Moody and Sankey hymn-book, "Gospel Hymns." One of the most appealing was "The Ninety-and-Nine," by Ira D. Sankey and Elizabeth C. Clephane, of which two stanzas ran:

There were ninety-and-nine that safely lay in the shelter of the fold,
But one was out on the hills away, far from the gates of gold —
Away on the mountains wild and bare, away from the tender Shepherd's care
Away from the tender Shepherd's care.

"Lord, Thou hast here Thy ninety-and-nine; are they not enough for Thee?"
But the Shepherd made answer: "This lamb of mine has wandered away from me,
And although the road be rough and steep, I go to the desert to find my sheep,
I go to the desert to find my sheep."

Other Moody and Sankey hymns well known were "Rescue the Perishing," "Take Me as I Am," "Hiding in Thee," "Where Is My Wand'ring Boy?" "When the Mists Have Rolled Away," and "Saved by Grace."

Dwight L. Moody.

Ira D. Sankey.

A popular hymn of the nineties, written by James M. Black, was "When the Roll Is Called Up Yonder":

When the trumpet of the Lord shall sound, and time shall be no more,
And the morning breaks, eternal, bright, and fair;
When the saved of earth shall gather over on the other shore
And the roll is called up yonder, I'll be there.

CHORUS

When the roll is called up yonder,
When the roll is called up yonder,
When the roll is called up yonder,
When the roll is called up yonder, I'll be there.

XIII

That the American of the nineties had the capacity for being entertained by sheer fun, which is an expression of high spirits and a wholesome relation to life, is proved by the vogue of "The Purple Cow." Superficially, there did not seem to be much in it. It was sheer nonsense. But as merely that, its vogue was practically universal:

> I never saw a Purple Cow;
> I never hope to see one,
> But I can tell you anyhow;
> I'd rather see than be one.

Of this, Mr. Gelett Burgess wrote me, in 1924:

> "The Purple Cow" appeared in the first number of *The Lark* in May, 1895, virtually my first published writing. It immediately caught on, and was quoted in nearly every paper in the United States, sooner or later; and, years afterward, I read it in the column of jokes in an Edinburgh newspaper. It never seemed to die at all, and was parodied innumerable times. I have two big scrap-books, most of the items relating to it in one way or another. The curious thing about it has always been that my name[1] has invariably been connected with the quatrain. The humor is pretty hard to analyze. It is, in fact, sheer nonsense. And as nonsense is the hardest thing to write, and harder still to get itself printed, perhaps the fact that this *was* printed is why it made the inconsequent appeal[2] it did.

The little periodical *The Lark*, in which "The Purple Cow" appeared, was itself characteristic of the nineties, one of a vogue of little "Brownie" magazines, all amateur, started by the *Chap Book*. *The Lark* was the second; Elbert Hubbard's *Philistine* was an important successor. *The Lark* was unique in that it was spon-

[1] Of the innumerable parodies, one ascribed to the author of "The Purple Cow" a sentiment which there is no reason to suppose he ever felt—certainly there was no reason for him to feel it.

> "Ah, yes! I wrote 'The Purple Cow'—
> I'm Sorry, now, I Wrote it!
> But I can Tell you, Anyhow,
> I'll Kill you if you Quote it!"

[2] Arthur Ruhl writes: "I always supposed, and certainly most of us who read it at the time supposed—that 'The Purple Cow' was not merely nonsense but satirized in a way the 'impressionistic' painting of the time—the trick (no longer new) of giving things the colors they seemed in certain lights to have instead of painting them with what we usually assume are their 'real' colors."

taneous. Its policies included exclusion of comment on contemporary art or current events — it was as "timely" in 1925 as in 1895. Its humor was intended to be as comprehensible to one's grandfather as to one's grandchild. It was devoted to enthusiasm and *joie de vivre.* It was printed on Japanese bamboo paper, stencil-stained

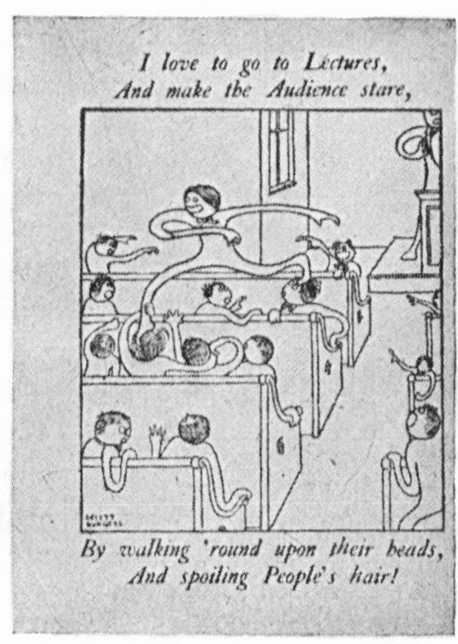

The cover, drawn by Ernest Peixotto, and one of the inside pages, drawn by Gelett Burgess, of two issues of *The Lark.*

on the edges in red and blue. It ran only two years. "When it began to make money," Mr. Burgess said, "it was stopped."

Mr. Burgess wrote much else in which the humor conformed to the usual models, including a series of books, "The Goops — A Manual of Manners for Polite Infants," which have been standard entertainment and instruction for several generations of children:

> The goops, they lick their fingers;
> The goops, they lick their knives.

They spill their broth on the table-cloth —
They lead untidy[1] lives.

Another bit of verse that had a unique vogue, written in 1897, by Strickland Gillilan, described one of the earliest skirmishes between the ordinary expansiveness of human nature and the beginning insistence of corporations on economy (in words and otherwise):

Superintindint wuz Flannigan;
Boss av the siction wuz Finnigin;
Whiniver the kyars got offen the thrack
An' muddled up things t' th' divil an' back,
Finnigin writ it to Flannigan,
Afther the wrick wuz all on agin.
That is, this Finnigin
Repoorted to Flannigan.

In his early reports Finnigin erred on the side of explicitness, permitted his Celtic gift for narrative to include many details interesting from a human point of view but not acceptable to the standards of conciseness and efficiency in the railroad office. So that Flannigan wrote back to him:

"Make 'em brief, Finnigin!"

To Finnigin this seemed, coming from one Celt to another, a trifle curt, and he made a resolution:

"From Finnigin to Flannigan,
Repoorts won't be long agin."

Thereafter:

Wan da-ay on the siction av Finnigin,
On the road sup'rintinded by Flannigan,
A rail give way on a bit av a curve
An' some kyars went off as they made the swerve.

[1] I wrote it that way from memory. Upon verification, I discovered the original version has "disgusting" instead of "untidy."

"There's nobody hurted," sez Finnigin,
"But repoorts must be made to Flannigan."
And he winked at McGorrigan,
As married a Finnigin.

Finnigin now discovered the law of literary composition which says it is condensation, not amplification, that takes pains; that the time consumed is in indirect ratio to the length:

He wuz shantyin' thin, wuz Finnigin,
As minny a railroader's been agin,
An' the shmoky ol' lamp wuz burnin' bright
In Finnigin's shanty all that night.
Bilin' down his repoort, was Finnigin!
An' he writed this here: "Muster Flannigan:
Off agin, on agin,
Gone agin.—Finnigin."[1]

XIV

The newspapers of the 1890's were more given to wit and deliberately high-spirited writing. In politics they were at once ruthless and interesting. They were strongly partisan. The later standard, adopted by some papers, of confining political views to the editorial page, was hardly thought of. Every column was frankly partisan. Republican papers fought Bryan with subtle arts of be-

[1] Mr. Gillilan, twenty-eight years later, recalled the inspiration, in a letter written me October 21, 1925, which I condense: "I was city editor and the rest of the staff of the Richmond, Indiana, *Palladium*. One day there was no news. One could stand at Eighth and Main and look four ways without seeing a moving object. I had already gone over the exchanges and clipped every interesting-looking story. . . . But the printers were still yelling 'Cope-e-e-e-e!' From an incident picked up about the office—the town was full of railroad Irish, and our foreman who told me the anecdote was named Fitzgibbons—I had evolved the rhyme and the rugged measure in my head as I walked back and forth from and to work. . . . That rhymed narrative was knocking around inside my head ALONE. Unless I got it out there would never be anything else in there. I didn't need the verse, but I needed the space, so that morning before breakfast I had emptied my head on a piece of laundry wrapping-paper. The printers were sore when I handed it in. It was pen-and-ink copy and only for the man who had the nonpareil case. It was verse, and dialect verse at that. . . . When the paper came out that night a lot of old local fossils who had never been known to smile, called across the street to me, 'Hello, Finnigin!' and laughed *out loud!*"

littlement, ridicule. On January 1, 1900, the Chicago *Times-Herald* printed, and the Indianapolis *Journal* reprinted, a long despatch from Austin, Texas, of which the nature and presumable intent is sufficiently to be inferred from this extract. The head-line was "Happy Days for Bryan":

> As has been set forth in previous despatches, ex-Governor Hogg is getting up many unique forms of entertainment for his guest, that peerless leader, W. J. Bryan. The two statesmen have shot ducks and caught panthers, and learned to ride ostriches. The people of this city have, in fact, come to look for something new every day. It seems that Mr. Bryan's friends have privately informed Governor Hogg that the peerless leader must in some way be made to forget how much Lincoln reminds him of himself. They were becoming alarmed at his condition. He would, according to these zealous guardians, awake at night, sit up in bed, and exclaim: "Ah, I have had a beautiful dream in which I saw Lincoln and heard his voice, and I could not believe that it wasn't me. Lincoln in 1860. Me in 1900!"
>
> Governor Hogg has, therefore, been asked to try to make the peerless leader think of something else, and he is doing his best in this direction. On Monday last the ex-Governor and the peerless leader played leap-frog for three hours in the former's back yard, but after the game the great Nebraskan arose and said: "This is fine sport. It reminds me of when Lincoln was a young man and was the champion wrestler of his township. Lincoln in 1860. Me in 1900."

And so on and on — the theme was reiterated with Bryan hanging by his toes, "skinning the cat," teaching Governor Hogg's[1] gander to walk on stilts; and always, according to the papers, reminding himself of Lincoln.

It is certainly not wholly amiss to assume that this

[1] Mr. Tom Finty, Jr., of the Dallas, Texas, *News*, tells me Governor Hogg, a man of big and richly flavored personality and gargantuan humor, was "in on" these jokes on his guest. When Bryan would complain indignantly to the newspaper men of the preposterous positions they were putting him in, Hogg would sit by and appear to be as indignantly and even more solemnly shocked than Bryan. A few hours later, Hogg would foregather privately with the newspaper men and contribute with his richly inventive wit to another instalment of the grotesque rôles in which Bryan was being put.

sort of thing had among its motives a malevolent one, a wish on the part of some of the larger newspapers to belittle Bryan. At the same time, it is true that the newspapers of that time were given to elaborate examples of this kind of humorous inveracity, deliberate and yet so farcical that few could be deceived, a kind of newspaper writing that later became almost wholly unknown. Probably because the same sort of thing was familiar, the reader at that time did not see as much malice in this example as does the reader of to-day. Yet some malice there certainly was, and the intention to make Bryan look ridiculous. Possibly this method of disparagement, practised by the great newspapers which were under suspicion of control by the financial interests Bryan fought, may have helped Bryan to keep his hold on the people.

XV

In 1898 the discovery of gold in the Klondike stirred men's imagination to an extravagance second only to the discovery in California fifty years before. Until that year, Alaska, which had been purchased from Russia in 1867 for half a cent an acre, was looked upon as a remote hinterland. It was called, when referred to at all, the "back yard of the United States." In the newspapers and in the talk of the day it was mentioned less often than Heligoland or Armenia. Then:[1]

On the 16th of June, 1897, the steamer *Excelsior*, of the Alaska Commercial Company, steamed into the harbor of San Francisco. She had on board a number of prospectors who had wintered on the Yukon River. As they walked down the gangplank, they staggered under a weight of valises, boxes, and bundles. That night the news went East over the wires that the richest strike in all American mining history had been made the fall of the year before on Bonanza Creek, a tributary of the Klondike. . . . On the 17th the *Portland* . . . arrived at

[1] I quote from Mr. Tappan Adney's "The Klondike Stampede."

Seattle with some sixty or more miners and some $800,000 in gold-dust, confirming the report that the new find surpassed anything ever before found in the world. The Seattle papers, alive to the interest of their own city, as the outfitting-point for Alaska, plunged into the story with sensational fury. . . . The inhabitants of the coast cities were beside themselves with

Packers on the Chilcoot Pass Trail—the Klondike.

excitement. "Coast Again Gold Crazy" was the Eastern comment. A stampede unequalled in history was on. . . . Within a week the excitement reached the East. Every source of information about Alaska, or the route to be traversed in getting there, was besieged by thousands. . . . Companies were formed and stock offered to the public merely on the strength of starting for the Klondike. Men threw up good positions. Others, with homes and families, mortgaged their property and started; while thousands who could not command the one to two thousand dollars considered as the very least necessary to success, were grub-staked by friends equally affected by the excitement, but unable to go in person. The newspapers were filled with advice, information, stories of hardship and of good fortune; but not one person in ten, or a hundred, knew what the journey meant nor heeded the voice of warning.

"There are but few sane men," said one newspaper, wishing to caution its readers, "who would deliberately set out to make an Arctic trip in the fall of the year, yet this is exactly what those who now start for the Klondike are doing."[1] Another paper put its warning in heavy head-lines:

WINTER WILL SOON SET IN.

SUFFERING SEEMS INEVITABLE.

WHAT GOLD-SEEKERS MUST ENDURE — THEIR CHIEF FOOD IN WINTER IS BEAR FAT, AND A BATH OR A CHANGE OF CLOTHING IS DEATH.

In Dawson 6000 people spent the winter who did not know whether their stock of provisions would last until

[1] Another voyage to the Klondike, made a generation later, by a route that was not open to the gold-hunters of '97, was described by Mrs. Mary Lee Davis in *Scribner's Magazine* for June, 1924: "When the army aviators [in 1921] made their first flight to Nome and return they reached Fairbanks on the outward-bound journey one day at noon, after a late breakfast in Dawson. We were notified by wire when they took off from Dawson, and the entire population of Fairbanks, with many old-timers from adjoining camps and creeks, was gathered to welcome these new pioneers of the North. As the three planes in a beautiful arrow-head sweep lifted above the horizon and settled lightly as birds upon a near-by field I happened to notice an old prospector, a man who had been in Dawson country in '98 and who had in midwinter followed the gruelling unbroken overland trail when word had come of the Fairbanks strike, a trip which meant day upon day of the most bitter, patient, almost superhuman labor. This man was running now toward the landing-field, his face uplifted to the men in the air. Angry at his weakness and stumbling, he dashed the tears from his eyes with the back of a hard old hand and cried out as he ran: 'Broken trail, O God, broken trail!' It was not a curse, but a prayer, rather. Time and space, those hoary and primeval enemies of man, those fearsome dragons upon the Old Trail, these he was seeing routed, conquered, and utterly annihilated here before his dim old wondering eyes. And only those who had known the Old Trail in all its dangerous toil could know too the full true glory of that summer noonday's revelation."

spring. The usual fare was what they called the "three B's" — bread, beans, and bacon. "The meagre stock was doled out a few pounds at a time. . . . It was reported that a turkey reached Dawson at Christmas. That was a mistake. On April 10, however, a turkey, ready cooked and dressed, was brought by a Dutchman over the ice from Skagway, and was exhibited for several days to the wistful gaze of the public in the Pioneer Saloon, where it was finally raffled off, netting the owner $174; but the owner said he would not go through the hardship of the trip in for the same price again. Gold-dust was the medium of exchange. Money commanded five to ten per cent a month. The commercial companies and the saloons were custodians of dust. A miner would hand his sack, containing perhaps thousands of dollars, to a saloon-keeper, who put it in an unlocked drawer, where it was as safe as in a bank outside."

The Klondike gave rise to a vogue of adventure. It furnished both the inspiration and the materials for the first of the "red-blooded" novels, those of Jack London and Rex Beach. To the newspapers and magazines the Klondike provided a group of extravagantly picturesque characters in actual life, such as "Sweetwater Bill" Gates, who with an offhand gesture of careless generosity, characteristic of the place and of the time, made his sweetheart a present of her weight in gold. "Bill's" mother-in-law wrote a book[1] which described him, after his affluence, standing "in front of the lobby of the Baldwin Hotel in San Francisco every evening, smoothly shaved, his mustaches nicely brushed and curled, and wearing his favorite black Prince Albert and silk hat."

[1] "The True Life-Story of Sweetwater Bill Gates," by his mother-in-law, Mrs. Iola Bebbe.

XVI

In the nineties the blurred beginnings of the movie were appearing here and there under such names, then current, as the kineopticon, the animatograph, the cinematograph, the nickelodeon,[1] the biograph.

The egg of the comic supplement and the comic strip[2] was hatching in New York in the shape of Richard Outcault's "Yellow Kid," [3] chiefly under the auspices of Mr. Hearst's racy newspapers, then also beginners. The fact that Mr. Hearst's newspapers were the forum of the Yellow Kid's antics resulted, in some of the political controversies of the time, in Hearst being himself called the Yellow Kid. Without attempting to assign too carefully the relative degrees of paternity and affinity within this humorous and numerous tribe, it is probably not seriously distant from historical accuracy to say it was the popularity of the Yellow Kid that led later to the creation of "Happy Hooligan," the "Katzenjammer Kids,"

[1] This was the name—it had reference to the price of admission—that became fixed in the popular mind for a few years, until the crude beginning evolved into the more gorgeous butterfly of "the movies."

[2] The origin of the characters who later grew into the comic strip and multiplied themselves into the hilarious tribe they later became is credited by Mr. Gilbert Seldes in the "Seven Lively Arts" to Jimmie Swinnerton's little bears and tigers in the San Francisco *Examiner* in 1892.

[3] The birth of the Yellow Kid was described by Don C. Seitz in his biography of Joseph Pulitzer of the New York *World:* "A clever young illustrator, R. F. Outcault, brought in several half-page drawings showing scenes in the tenements, which were christened 'Hogan's Alley.' The pressman in charge, William J. Kelly, owed most of his experience with colors to printing block samples for George Mather's Sons, the ink-makers. When his efforts were criticised he replied that no one could print the wishy-washy color schemes that came to him in plate form; give him something solid and he would show results. Charles W. Saalberg, the colorist at the time, happened to be painting up one of Outcault's drawings; with his customary quickness, he replied: 'All right, I'll make this kid's dress solid yellow.' He did, and a one-tooth infant in the group of ragamuffins stood out like a sunrise. Kelly was good as his word. The 'Yellow Kid' became enormously popular. Outcault was bought by Hearst, but the *World* continued to use 'Hogan's Alley,' drawn and colored, however, by George B. Luks, since famous as a painter of the first rank. The two kids ran against each other in the rival comics, lent their 'yellow' to the extravagant competition, and added a new designation to newspaper vernacular."

"Foxy Grandpa," "Mutt and Jeff," the "Hall-Room Boys," and still later "Barney Google" and the "Honorable Andy Gump."

Palmer Cox's "Brownies" were delighting a generation of children who, as mature men and women, were to be turned back to reminiscence by Cox's death in 1924. "Little Lord Fauntleroy" was current literature and current drama, his clothes and his ways a current vogue. The book was dramatized by the author, Mrs. Frances Hodgson Burnett. Wallace Eddinger, later a star of many plays of grown-ups, was one of three children who originated the title rôle. In an interview at the time of Mrs. Burnett's death (November, 1924), Mr. Eddinger said:

> The rôle was originated by three of us. . . . We all rehearsed it about the same time and we all played it at the Broadway Theatre in New York. I was only seven when I began the Little Lord Fauntleroy part. I played it all over the United States, from Maine to California, and received as high as $250 a week. . . . To play the part, I had to have long golden curls. In addition I had to wear white cuffs and be, oh, so sweet, on the stage. As a result, the other boys used to call me "Sissy." After a while a boy seldom got beyond the first part of the word before I slammed him in the nose. There were other kids who were glad when the "Fauntleroy" vogue died, too. Their mothers were dressing them as counterparts of me in the rôle, and they were always getting into fights.

"Gentleman Jim" Corbett was at the zenith of the career which ended with his defeat in a fourteen-round fight[1] by "Bob" Fitzsimmons; and which gave to a pugilist the unique distinction of a place among dictionary-makers for having introduced into popular usage a technical and recondite term, "the solar plexus."

It was the time of Buffalo Bill in his prime . . . Mark Twain and his cream-white dress suit . . . Li Hung-Chang of the amazing queue and the gorgeous robes,

[1] On St. Patrick's Day, 1897.

cap and button, of which we shall never see the like again — when his successors, official Chinamen of the republic era, came to Washington to attend the Limitation of Armaments Conference in 1922, they wore the same black suits and "tombstone" shirt-fronts as Secre-

"Gentleman Jim" Corbett on the left; John L. Sullivan on the right, at "Jim" Jeffries's training headquarters. It was Corbett who added "solar plexus" to the vocabulary of prize-fighting.

tary Hughes . . . Carry Nation . . . Boss Croker . . . Mark Hanna . . . Doctor Parkhurst . . . Tom Johnson of Cleveland . . . Doctor Mary Walker . . . Ella Wheeler Wilcox and the widely quoted verse she wrote:

> Laugh and the world laughs with you;
> Weep and you weep alone.
> For this grim old earth
> Must borrow its mirth;
> It has troubles enough of its own. . . .

The Infanta Eulalie and her gown of soft spun glass, 2,500,000 threads weighing only one pound, and her beauty and vivacity, and her cigarettes, very shocking to America of the nineties . . . The Princess Chimay . . . "Chuck" Connors . . . Elbert Hubbard and the "Message to Garcia" . . . Captain Hobson sinking the *Merrimac* and being kissed for it . . . "Remember the *Maine*" . . . "Don't cheer, boys, the poor fellows are dying" . . . "Dewey did it" buttons . . . "Boys in Blue," a stirring alliteration not possible after khaki came in . . . The Rough Riders . . . The "White Squadron" . . . battleships painted white with funnels buff . . . "embalmed beef" . . . the Dingley tariff . . . "sound money" parades . . . the "full dinner-pail" . . . "infant industries."

Virginia Harned playing "Trilby" . . . "Ben Hur" . . . Madame Modjeska . . . Marie Dressler . . . Lillian Russell singing "Twickenham Ferry" and "The Kerry Dance" . . . The Florodora Sextette . . . Maggie Cline singing "Throw Him Down, McCloskey," and "Slide, Kelly, Slide" . . . living pictures . . . John L. Stoddard's "travel talks" illustrated with lantern-slides — he was the predecessor of Burton Holmes . . . Brink Thorne's run at the Yale-Princeton game of 1895 and Arthur Poe's in 1898 . . . "Big Bill" Edwards of the Princeton team of 1899 . . . "Pop" Anson . . . "red devils" and young Mr. Vanderbilt's "White Ghost," pioneers of the automobile . . . Maud S., whose record was 2.08¾ . . . hansoms, victorias, four-in-hands . . . buggies, sulkies, phaetons . . . coach-dogs, pug dogs . . . "two-fors," meaning two cigars for a nickel . . . big gold watch-chains . . . detachable cuffs . . . cuff-buttons without links . . . Sunday best and second best. . . .

What an attic tangle of jumbled memories.[1]

[1] "I consider that history should be a resurrection."—Michelet.

Stereoscopic views . . . the family photograph album on the marble-topped table in the parlor . . . mission furniture displacing plush . . . plaster casts, "Venus de

By courtesy of "Life."

"Introducing John L. Sullivan," a drawing by George Bellows of the old fighter after he had given up the prize-ring and become a national institution.

Milo," "the Winged Victory" . . . bisque statuary . . . wax flowers . . . cattails . . . peacock-feathers . . . mutton-leg sleeves . . . "straight-front" corsets . . . the "new woman" — how old she had become by 1925 . . . such phrases as "female seminary" dying out; "woman's sphere" coming in.

Paul Leicester Ford's "Story of an Untold Love" . . . James Lane Allen's "Choir Invisible" . . . "Tess of the D'Urbervilles" . . . The novels of Archibald Clavering Gunter and of Captain Charles King . . . Anthony Hope's "Prisoner of Zenda" and "The Dolly Dialogues" . . . Edward W. Townsend's "Chimmie Fadden," who talked

The "Ginny" played the organ on "The Sidewalks of New York."

the slang of "Say," "You know me," and "See?" . . . The vogue of young Stephen Crane and his "Red Badge of Courage" . . . John Kendrick Bangs's "House-boat on the Styx" . . . "M. Quad" and his quaint characters, "Mr. and Mrs. Bowser," "Brother Gardener" of "the Lime-Kiln Club," "The Arizona Kicker" . . . Edward Bok in *The Ladies' Home Journal* starting the "heart-to-heart" note in journalism . . . Frank Munsey and Samuel S. McClure starting the ten-cent magazine . . . Charles A. Dana editing the New York *Sun* . . . *The Youth's Companion* in its heyday . . . *The Family Story Paper* . . . *The Argosy* . . . Edward Penfield . . . A. B. Wenzell . . . the X-ray . . . the Keely motor . . . policemen wearing helmets . . . fire-engines drawn by galloping horses . . .

Steel frames for buildings were just coming in . . . hootchy-cootchy dancers . . . hoboes, tramps . . . bunco-steerers, confidence-men, green-goods men . . . hand-organs . . . mustache-cups . . . paper collars giving way to celluloid. . . souvenir spoons . . . candy hearts with "I love you truly" on them . . . cigarettes with pictures of actresses or baseball players . . . Cigar-stores had wooden Indians in front as commonly as barber-shops had striped poles . . . trolley-rides . . . Everybody of any consequence had railroad passes, half-fare for clergymen . . . You could order liquor on the train except when it was passing through a prohibition State, in which case the porter would look at his watch and tell you you could have your drink in fifty-one minutes, or as the distance might be . . . One could go to Europe first-class for fifty dollars . . . Ward McAllister . . . the "Four Hundred" [1] . . . James Whitcomb Riley writing "Neighborly Poems" . . . Eugene Field, "With Trumpet and Drum." . . .

No tobacco-shop of the nineties, and even later, was complete without its wooden Indian. In 1925 they were to be found only as museum pieces. Mr. H. R. Day, of Conesus, N. Y., is the owner of the one in the photograph.

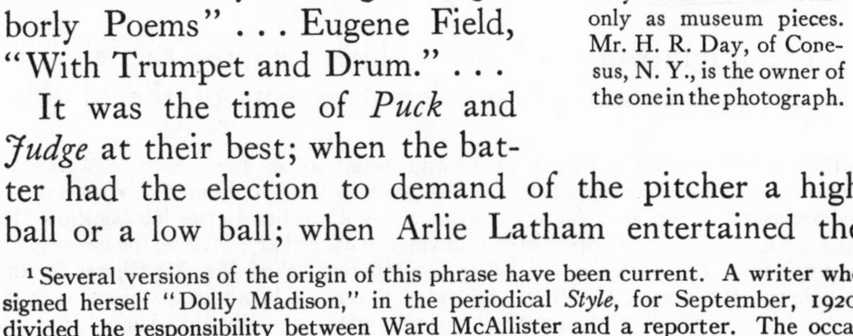

It was the time of *Puck* and *Judge* at their best; when the batter had the election to demand of the pitcher a high ball or a low ball; when Arlie Latham entertained the

[1] Several versions of the origin of this phrase have been current. A writer who signed herself "Dolly Madison," in the periodical *Style*, for September, 1920, divided the responsibility between Ward McAllister and a reporter. The occasion was the annual ball of Mrs. Astor. A reporter, under pressure from his city

bleachers with the sheer exuberance of his animal spirits; when Penelope embroidered sofa-pillows with the initials or the profiles of her young men friends; of pyrography, when other Penelopes made picture-frames and handkerchief-boxes by drawing designs upon wood with a red-hot iron, producing effects like those of dark-brown paint; the blacksmith-shop just beginning to give way to the pumping-station; the anvil to the vulcanizing machine; the livery-stable to the garage.

It was a time of inexpensive living, when Augustus Thomas bought in New York a five-pound shad with roe for thirty-five cents, for one of those meals at which he and Maurice Barrymore held wassail of wit; of promoters, captains of industry; of, first, the waltz, the polka, and the schottische, and, later, the two-step, the cake-walk, and ragtime.

It was a picturesque time, a time of gorgeous colors. A time, also — in fields other than politics and money-making — of greater leisure, of more amenity among men. As Augustus Thomas put it: "Life itself had a gentle pace, social intercourse a more genial temperature. Friends, meeting, stopped to exchange a word; men in groups told stories, laughed." "The time of peace, wherein we trusted."

XVII

The fragmentary allusions which compose this chapter on the lighter and more colorful aspects of the nineties

editor, gained entrance to the house and asked to see Mrs. Astor. A servant took refuge in the formula that Mrs. Astor was "not at home." When the reporter asked to see Mrs. Astor's secretary, the disturbed butler fell back on Mr. Ward McAllister. Mr. McAllister told the reporter that "Mrs. Astor never gives out the names of her guests." When the reporter asked Mr. McAllister for the number of the guests, McAllister replied: "There will be about 400 persons present. There are only that number of people who are really 'in society' in New York, you know." Thus the phrase was born, the newspapers did the rest.

MISCELLANEOUS

White Mountain Freezer

"Excellent Cream!"

Improved for 1895.

With which the finest quality of cream can be produced

IN 4 MINUTES.

Ice Cream at Home

Easily and quickly prepared, and at less than one half the cost at confectioner's, by using the

Improved "White Mountain."

Frozen Dainties—Fifty Choice Receipts by Mrs. LINCOLN—Mailed Free.

THE WHITE MOUNTAIN FREEZER CO.
NASHUA, N. H.

The Best Playing Cards

are those offered by the Burlington Route. We will send you on receipt of price, a dozen packs for $1.75, or lots of one gross and over for $17.50 per gross. Express charges prepaid. These are manufacturers' prices.

P. G. EUSTIS,
General Passenger Agent, C. B. & Q. R.R.,
CHICAGO, ILL.

WE PAY POST-AGE All you have guessed about life insurance may be wrong. If you wish to know the truth, send for "How and Why," issued by the PENN MUTUAL LIFE, 921-3-5 Chestnut Street, Philadelphia.

A CHAUTAUQUA OIL HEATER OR A CHAUTAUQUA DESK FREE WITH A COMBINATION BOX OF "SWEET HOME" SOAP FOR $10.00· THE LARKIN SOAP MFG. CO. BUFFALO, N.Y.

For Health and Recreation go to the Battery Park Hotel, Asheville, N. C.

BE BRILLIANT AND EMINENT! Brainworkers Everybody.
The new physiological discovery—**Memory Restorative Tablets** quickly and permanently increase the memory two to ten fold and greatly augment intellectual power; difficult studies, etc., easily mastered; truly marvelous, highly endorsed. Price, $1.00, post-paid. Send for Circular.
MEMORY TABLET CO., 114 Fifth Ave., New York.

USE COSMO BUTTERMILK SOAP.

A MODEL COMMUNITY in Southern **FLORIDA** amidst 25 clear lakes; high, rolling pine lands, free from malaria, swamps, and freezing.

NO Race Problem, because no Negroes. } "Start Right,
NO Temperance Question – No Liquor. } Keep Right."

500 Northern people; Church, School, P. O., Stores, etc., 80 homes and families located the past year; 600 acres planted in PINE-APPLES, LEMONS, ORANGES, GRAPES, ETC. 1000 tracts already sold, many resold at 100 to 400 per ct. advance. $2 and upwards per month accepted. **Cheap Hotel Board**, cheap lumber, cheap transportation. Full information in our **Florida Homeseeker** monthly, 50 cts. a year. Sample Free. **The Florida Development Co., Avon Park, Fla., or 99 Franklin St., N.Y.**

COLUMBIAN INKSTAND.

Best in the World. Inks the pen Just Right. No inky fingers, blots, or muddy ink. A boon to busy scribblers. Over 20 styles; $1.00 to $6.00 each. Sent prepaid. Catalogue free.
BOYD & ABBOT CO., 257 Broadway, New York.

Gautschi's Orphea **MUSIC BOXES** Highest Recommended
GAUTSCHI & SONS, Manufacturers, Importers, 1030 Chestnut St., Philadelphia.
SPECIALTY: Old Music Boxes Carefully Repaired, Improved, and Guaranteed.

Florence Home Needlework for 1894 is now ready. Send 6 cents mentioning year, and we will mail you the book 96 pages, 90 illustrations. NONOTUCK SILK CO., Florence, Mass.

ACME FOLDING BOAT CO., MIAMISBURG, O.

63

A page of advertisements taken from *Scribner's Magazine* for March, 1895.

aim at no more than to point out that there were other sides of life than the political and social movements of the time, upon which we have been obliged to lay much emphasis because they were the beginnings of the political movements and political figures of the 1900's.

Professor Charles R. Lingley, of Dartmouth College, in his "History of the United States Since the Civil War," says:

> Some day somebody will delineate the spiritual history of America since the Civil War — the compound of tradition, discontent, aspiration, idealism, materialism, selfishness, and hope that mark the floundering progress of these United States through the last half-century. He will read widely, ponder deeply, and tune his spirit with care to the task which he undertakes. I have not attempted this phase of our history, yet I believe that no account is complete without it.

Such a completeness of portrayal would show that American life in the nineties was various; that it had aspects other than either politics, on the one hand, or books, songs, and the stage, on the other. If one should venture so daring an effort as a condensed summary of the forces in American life, one would probably say that at this particular time many of them had to do with money, wealth. Some of the forces tugged toward money, some away from it; nearly all whirled around it. One large class was making money and finding various uses for it, some enjoyable and some not, some wholesome and some not. Whereas another large group was failing to make money, failing tc achieve economic or social parity with the other class, according to what were the standards of the day. With both classes, money was a chief concern. It was undoubtedly an age where money-making was the most prized career. The atmosphere of that infected even so fine an artist as Mark Twain and caused him, for a period at least, to set above his artistic ambition that of getting rich and living in the style of his millionaire friends.[1] That was a tragic aberration while it lasted.

After the Civil War, those who were put at a disadvantage by the government's action in cutting the amount of currency in half, grew, as a class, steadily poorer. They, plus those who had not the talent for money-making or the temperament for money-saving, came to compose one end of Carlyle's famous contrast, the "have-nots." As against these, the money-lenders who were advantaged by the government's deflation of currency, and those who had a talent for money-making, or were otherwise favorably situated — these composed the "haves." Between the two ran those currents of injustice, suspicion, and envy which composed the politics of the time.

The "haves" were far from being necessarily or uniformly happier than the "have-nots." With them there was a spiritual discontent that was often as carking as the economic discontent of the "have-nots." They had built up their great fortunes through the economic, political, and other advantages they had enjoyed since the Civil War. What to do with these fortunes was, during the nineties, not only a problem to the public but also a problem to the makers of them; and especially was it a problem to the inheritors of them. America, as yet, had no place for the idle rich, chiefly because there had been, as yet, no idle rich. Henry Adams described the average American of New York or Chicago during this period as "a pushing, energetic, ingenious person, always awake and trying to get ahead of his neighbors." Adams wrote: "That the American by temperament worked to excess was true; work and whiskey were his stimulants;

[1] This point is made by Stuart P. Sherman, who, among men of letters within the limits of my own reading, has a most penetrating insight into the America of his time.

work was a form of vice; but he never cared much for money or power after he earned them. The amusement of the pursuit was all the amusement he got from it; he had no use for wealth."

There were existing side by side, in the East especially, a first generation of the rich; and a second generation, the sons and daughters of the rich. The second generation was, in many cases, too attenuated for the sweaty business of making more money; and American life did not provide, to a sufficient degree, other careers. Some inheritors of money, looking for ways to spend both it and time, turned to European models of manners, diversion, and display; tried to imitate European aristocracy; and this gave rise to some of the more lurid social phenomena of the time.

If a man were not given to money-making, had not the knack of it, or the wish or incentive for it, and if he had no other strong bent, toward the arts or the like, there was not much in America at this time for him to do. It was this condition (with some other causes) that gave rise, in a college attended by many of the sons of the rich, to a phrase: "Harvard indifference."[1] Jacob Riis told a story of a Harvard teacher asking a recent graduate what was to be his work in the world. "Oh," said the latter, with a little yawn, "really, do you know, Professor, it does not seem to me that there is anything that is much worth while."

Riis told this story to Roosevelt, and describes the scorn with which Roosevelt regarded the sentiment. It was one of Roosevelt's definite contributions to his time

[1] Arthur Ruhl writes me: "Your explanation of 'Harvard indifference' is interesting and doubtless sound. But there was something more to it; there was a definite cult of cleverness, exquisiteness, and boredom at that time, as exemplified by Whistler, Wilde, 'The Green Carnation,' etc., and the 'indifference' at Cambridge was partly, at least, an attempt to get into the mode."

Mr. Ruhl is right. The vogue he mentions took strong hold in England. In America, it did not go far. With us, the satirizing of it was a more definite thread that he, being a Harvard man, and of inherited wealth, showed to others of his class ways to spend their lives with satisfaction to themselves and advantage to their country.

An epitome, in a way, of the America of the nineties, as the nineties were seen by one of the shrewdest Amer-

in the life of the time than the practice of it. The classic American satire on it, the most widely read, heard, and quoted, was Edmund Vance Cooke's "Fin de Siècle":

This life's a hollow bubble,
Don't you know?
Just a painted piece of twoubble,
Don't you know?
We come to earth to cwy,
We gwow oldeh and we sigh,
Oldeh still and then we die,
Don't you know?

It is all a howwid mix,
Don't you know?
Business, love and politics,
Don't you know? . . .

Business, oh, that's beastly twade,
Don't you know?
Something's lost or something's made,
Don't you know?
And you wowwy, and you mope,
And you hang youah highest hope
On the pwice, pe'haps of soap,
Don't you know?

Politics! oh, just a lawk,
Don't you know?
Just a nightmaeh in the dawk,
Don't you know?
You pe'spiah all day and night,
And afteh all the fight,
Why pe'haps the w'ong man's wight,
Don't you know?

That was printed and reprinted numberless times. Charles Hoyt had music written for it and introduced it in "A Night in New York." It was so popular Hoyt retained it in "A Day and a Night." Still later it was interpolated in "The Belle of New York."

Returning to "Harvard indifference," still other elements entered into it. One was an honest pose of restraint, calm, understatement, a distaste for exaggeration, expansiveness. Another was a kind of passive resistance to the cult of money.

ican humorists, is to be found in "Mr. Dooley." Mr. Dooley is writing in 1897, on the occasion of Queen Victoria's Diamond Jubilee. After reviewing what he conceives to have been her recollections about England, he turns to his own review of America:

> While she was lookin' on in England, I was lookin' on in this counthry. I have seen America spread out from th' Atlantic to th' Pacific, with a branch office iv th' Standard Ile Comp'ny in ivry hamlet. I've seen th' shackles dropped fr'm th' slave, so's he cud be lynched in Ohio . . . an' Corbett beat Sullivan, an' Fitz beat Corbett. . . . An' th' invintions . . . th' cotton-gin an' th' gin sour an' th' bicycle an' th' flyin'-machine an' th' nickel-in-th'-slot machine an' th' Croker machine an' th' sody-fountain an' — crownin' wurruk iv our civilization — th' cash raygister.

11

NEW TIMES, NEW EVENTS, NEW ISSUES

Radical Issues Associated with Currency Are Overcome, and Bryan with Them, by Two Metallurgists. The Spanish War Turns the Thoughts of Americans to a New Interest, and Provides a New Political Issue. Debate on Expansion.

In American political history, 1896 was a dividing point. It marked the climax and the ending of radicalism arising out of issues associated with currency. For a few years after 1896 there was no political discontent to speak of. It largely evaporated under the warming influence of generous emotions aroused by watching Cuba's struggle for freedom, the still warmer feelings that attended our taking part in that struggle, and the exaltation that accompanied our brief adventure in territorial annexation. It was assuaged by larger supplies of gold from the mines of the world, rising wages and prices, and the accelerated activity of business that came with the war. The political discontent that arose again about 1902 was from different causes, had different issues, and was led by a new spokesman.

Eighteen ninety-six was the zenith of Bryan's career. The day of his emergence, his "Cross of Gold" speech, was also to be the day of his highest reach. This is easy to see now; it was not seen at the time. During that 1896 campaign in which Bryan, after grasping the nomination with his "Cross of Gold" speech, threw his immense vitality into the effort to win the presidency, it was said that "probably no man in civil life had succeeded in inspiring so much terror, without taking life, as Bryan." [1] A New

[1] *The Nation*, New York.

York clergyman, Reverend Thomas Dixon,[1] spoke of Bryan as "a mouthing, slobbering demagogue, whose patriotism is all in his jaw-bone," at which, according to the New York *World*, "the audience howled." Reverend Charles Parkhurst, of New York, spoke of the silver movement as inimical to credit and an attempt, "deliberate and hot-blooded," to destroy what little of it remained, and declared: "I dare, in God's pulpit, to brand such attempts as accursed and treasonable." Roosevelt, then comparatively unknown, said of Bryan and his associates, that they were, "as regards the essential principles of government, in hearty sympathy with their remote skin-clad ancestors who lived in caves and fought one another with stone-headed axes and ate the mammoth woolly rhinoceros."

The New York *Tribune* referred to Bryan as "the wretched, rattle-pated boy, posing in vapid vanity and mouthing resounding rottenness . . . apt . . . at lies and forgeries and blasphemies and all the nameless iniquities of that campaign against the Ten Commandments." The New York *Sun* shrewdly tempered violence with wit:

> He was born eloquent and attracted much attention by repeating "Casabianca" when he was only eleven months old. He is not very much older now, but much more eloquent; and his eloquence is of the inspired sort, like that of a phonograph or telephone or speaking-tube. Whenever he opens his lips words of fire fly out, roman candles, cannon crackers, rockets, pin-wheels. A very beautiful show, but as the Honorable Tobias Castor says: "What it's all about, the Lord only knows."

Henry Watterson's Louisville *Courier-Journal* trumpeted:

> He is a boy orator. He is a dishonest dodger. He is a daring adventurer. He is a political faker. He is not of the material

[1] Later Mr. Dixon left the ministry and became an author of rather lurid novels and motion-pictures. "The Clansman" is the one best known, and is typical.

of which the people of the United States have ever made a President, nor is he even of the material of which any party has ever before made a candidate.[1]

Epithets devised by friends, and used by enemies in sarcasm, were: The Boy Orator of the Platte,[2] Bryan the Brave, the Great Commoner, The Peerless One, the Magnet of the Platte.

Bryan used to repeat what his enemies said with a smile and manner that was subtly designed as half-way between Christ forgiving his persecutors and John L. Sullivan showing himself a good sport.

The gold section of Bryan's own party deserted. Some went openly and organized a Gold Democratic party with a separate ticket. Others, aiming to keep their party regularity, merely knifed Bryan. David B. Hill, the Democratic leader of New York State, returning from the convention, on being asked: "Are you still a Democrat?" replied: "Yes, I am a Democrat still, very still."

While Bryan was "whirlwinding" 18,000 miles up and down the country McKinley stuck, though with occasional fits of trepidation, to his "front-porch" campaign; but in September he decided, if matters became more threatening, to take the stump in Illinois, Indiana, Michigan, Iowa, and Kansas. Hanna, who had planned a vacation after bringing to success, in June, 1896, his eighteen months' work to get the Republican nomination for McKinley, wrote to a friend that "the Chicago

[1] "It was fortunate that nearly all of the large daily papers, whether Democratic or Republican, were ardent advocates of the cause of sound money; copies of these were industriously circulated [by the Republican campaign managers]. . . . Hanna had a high opinion of the influence of the Fourth Estate, and knew the hold the weekly country journals had on their readers. He sent them specially prepared matter, plates, and ready-prints."—James Ford Rhodes, "The McKinley and Roosevelt Administrations."

[2] About this designation of Bryan, Senator Foraker had a brutal but witty comment on the Platte River: "Six inches deep and six miles wide at the mouth."

Convention [which nominated Bryan] has changed everything," and that the campaign "will be work and hard work from the start."[1] He abandoned his holiday cruise along the New England coast and — I quote from the historian Rhodes, who was his brother-in-law — "exerted his wonderful talent for organization and raised the necessary funds.[2] Soon gaining the confidence of New

Bryan's oratorical canvass for the presidency, 1896.
Every dot represents a town or city at which Bryan delivered one or more speeches. This pre-election tour holds the record for political "stumping."

York City financial men, he obtained from them important contributions. . . . Some concerns were assessed by Hanna according to what he conceived to be their financial interest in the canvass, a uniform assessment of one-fourth of one per cent being levied on the banks.[3] He systematized the expenditure and had the books kept on true business principles. The Republican National Committee spent between three and three and a half millions,

[1] Rhodes, "The McKinley and Roosevelt Administrations."

[2] Hanna was called "the fat-fryer." Henry L. Stoddard writes me: "Hanna was *a* fat-fryer, but not *the* fat-fryer. *The* fat-fryer was John P. Forster, president of the League of Young Republican Clubs. It was in 1888 that he wrote a letter suggesting 'to fry the fat out of the manufacturers.'"

[3] This was later forbidden by law.

and had also in reserve a guaranty fund which was not called upon."

II

While the gold raised by Hanna from the corporations may have been instrumental in preventing Bryan from

"I am sure the workingmen are with us." (Davenport, in the New York *Journal.*) During the 1896 campaign the Hearst papers mercilessly caricatured Mark Hanna, the friend and political manager of the Republican candidate, William McKinley.

winning the 1896 campaign, it was gold from a different source that really submerged his issue and himself.[1]

Bryan had staked everything on a single issue, the free

[1] While increase in the gold supply was the fundamental cause of Bryan's downfall, it is true, of course, that incidental causes contributed to his 1896 defeat. Mr. William Guggenheim, who is familiar with this broad subject as one of the family that is the largest owner of metal-mines in the world, and as a metallurgist and scholar, writes: "In 1896, India, a seller of wheat and buyer of silver, experienced a crop failure, while the United States that year produced wheat in abundance. The result was that as wheat rose in price the price of silver fell, and the pet props of Bryan's theory were pulled from under it. Had the reverse conditions existed—that is, had India produced wheat in abundance in 1896 and had the United States experienced a short crop . . . it is my belief Bryan would have been elected President of the United States. But fate willed differently." Mr. B. M. Baruch, who has read these chapters, has also called my attention to the effect on Bryan's fortunes of the price of wheat at the height of the 1896 campaign.

coinage of silver in the ratio of 16 to 1. In his "Cross of Gold" speech he had said:

If they ask us why it is that we say more on the money question than we say upon the tariff question, I reply that if protection has slain its thousands, the gold standard has slain its tens of thousands.[1] If they ask us why we do not embody in our platform all the things that we believe in, we reply that when we have restored the money of the Constitution, all other necessary reforms will be possible; but that until this is done there is no other reform that can be accomplished.

How the East regarded Bryan in the Free Silver campaign of 1896.
This cartoon in the New York *Press* was entitled: "A suggestion for the 53-cent dollar."

Focussing everything on the one issue of free silver was good political and forensic art in that it made the campaign simple for the ordinary man to understand; but it had the defect that if the issue should become obsolete, Bryan, being so completely identified with it, would fall. Not only would he fail in this campaign; he would imperil his whole future. "16 to 1" was Bryan's whole bag of tricks.

During the period while Bryan was riding high on the issue of the scarcity of gold and currency, two obscure metallurgists unconsciously set a snare for him — two

[1] One of Bryan's most effective oratorical devices was the habitual use of phrases and figures of speech which, while short of literal quotation from the Bible, had the even more effective quality of stirring Bible memories in the hearer.

men from the world of science, who had nothing to do with politics, who were not even Americans, but Scotchmen, living in South Africa; who, at the time they did the thing that ultimately checked Bryan's political career, had never heard of him.

"The man who pulls the string—the mine owner." (The New York *Press*.) The cartoonist here depicts Bryan as the puppet of the rich Western silver-mine owners who wanted a market for their silver.

Bryan rose on the scarcity of gold.[1] For twenty-five years preceding the year, 1890, that Bryan first got himself elected to Congress, there had been no increase in the annual production of gold. Actually, the annual increment had grown smaller. The supply of gold failed

[1] Scarcity, that is, relative to growth of population in the United States and the increased demand for gold for currency in the United States, Germany, India, and elsewhere.

to keep pace with the increase of population. This falling trend of gold is shown in the following figures of the world's gold production for typical years:

1866	$129,614,000	1883	$95,392,000
1871	115,577,000	1887	105,778,900
1874	90,750,000	1890	118,848,700
1880	108,778,800		

"Statistical Abstract," 1922.

Out of that diminishing trend in the annual production of gold and its economic consequences to the farmer and debtor classes, Bryan made his political issue, the free coinage of silver as currency. If that scarcity of gold had not occurred, Bryan might have lived all his years a relatively inconspicuous lawyer in Lincoln, Nebraska.

Then, in the very year when Bryan got his first election to Congress, that lagging trend of the gold-mines, upon which his career rested, turned and went against him. The economic effects of changes in the gold supply do not spread out over the world until some time after the changes; and the political effects must wait until after the economic effects have shown themselves. Gold production was working steadily against Bryan; ultimately it caught up with him.

How rapidly the world's annual gold production increased from 1890 on is shown by the figures for each year:

1890	$118,848,700	1895	$198,763,600
1891	130,650,000	1896	202,251,600
1892	146,651,500	1897	236,073,700
1893	157,494,800	1898	286,879,700
1894	181,175,600		

"Statistical Abstract," 1922.

Bryan as a leader resting his whole political existence on the issue of the free coinage of silver in the proportion of 16 to 1, could no more oppose those rising figures of gold than King Canute could make the tides stand still. By 1898 the gold production was more than twice what it had been in 1890. After eight years of the changed trend, the political effects were beginning to show; and by 1898 Bryan had reached his zenith and begun his decline.

Told not in terms of politics, but in the austere technical phrases of a standard encyclopædia, the following is the story of Bryan's fall:

CYANIDE PROCESS. — In 1890 the cyanide process, invented by MacArthur and Forrest, was introduced on the Rand, and has almost entirely superseded other methods of recovering finely divided gold. In it the finely crushed ores, concentrates, or slimes are leached in vats, with a very dilute solution of potassium cyanide, containing 0.05 to 0.3 per cent of potassium cyanide, or its equivalent in sodium cyanide, which is allowed to remain for twelve to twenty-four hours to dissolve the gold. The cyanide solution is then run off into zinc precipitating boxes, and the gold precipitated by clean zinc shavings or by electrolysis, about 1½ grains of gold being left in each ton of solution.

The essential quality of this new process was that it extracted more gold from the same amount of ore. This increase of gold, disastrous to Bryan, was further accelerated by new discoveries in Australia, South Africa, and later the Klondike. By 1908, when Bryan made his last hopeless fight for the presidency, the annual production of gold was $442,837,000. That is, in the last year that Bryan bid unsuccessfully for favor, the annual increment of gold was nearly four times what it had been in 1890, when he made his first and successful appeal as a candidate for Congress.

Silver also was taking a course disastrous to Bryan. In the first period, when gold was actually diminishing, from $122,989,000 in 1865, down to $118,848,700 in 1890 — in that period of gold's decline, silver mounted very fast, more than trebled itself, from $45,772,000 in 1865 to $163,032,000 in 1890. Then, when gold made the turn and more than doubled in eight years, from $118,848,-700 in 1890 to $286,879,700 in 1898 — in that period silver hung back, going only from $163,032,000 in 1890 to $218,576,000 in 1898. It was as if silver, ungrateful to its great champion, treacherously co-operated with mounting gold to destroy him.

Greater abundance of gold made it easier for the debtor to get currency to pay his debts. The issues associated with currency died down. By the early 1900's, those particular causes of discontent, and the demand for a currency cure, ebbed.[1] Thereafter the discontent concerned itself more with the other conditions, the trusts, abuses in railroad management, monopolies, corrupt relations between business and government. Of these causes of discontent, Roosevelt became the spokesman. Bryan tried to get aboard the new set of forces, but was handicapped by his earlier identity with issues that had gone over the dam. In the competition between Roosevelt and Bryan, Roosevelt was steadily in the lead and steadily successful — Bryan steadily unsuccessful. During the remainder of Bryan's career, he presented the picture of seizing new issues from the current of events: in 1900, imperialism; in 1908, opposition to the trusts; in other years, government ownership of the railroads; after 1915, prohibition. On none of these issues was he destined to become President. That ecstatic prophecy of John Clark Ridpath: "We intend that the patriot and statesman, William Jennings Bryan, shall be, as he deserves to be, President of the United States . . . and that under his wholesome and patriotic administration a

[1] On March 14, 1900, Congress, in the hands of the Republicans, passed, without any great excitement, the act making gold the single standard of currency, thus ending an issue that had dominated American politics for almost a generation.

new century of peace shall be ushered in"[1] — that ecstatic prophecy, that determined purpose, was destined never to come true. Bryan's star had begun to wane with the rise of gold; the new star was Roosevelt's.

III

Before Bryan had had time to rest from his 1896 campaign, before McKinley took office, the momentum of a course of events happening outside the United States turned the eyes and thoughts of America away from its domestic concerns, led it to look abroad, changed for the time the current of American history, involved us in adventure overseas; and for a period of more than three years caused us to be preoccupied with the unfamiliar and difficult business of administering distant dependencies, and with the issues, novel to us, of expansion and imperialism.

For decades the American people had watched with sympathetic interest the struggles of Cuba for liberation from Spanish rule. Sympathy was deepened to an emotion of outrage when the Spanish Governor-General Weyler took a step that became notorious as the "reconcentrado" proclamation:

> I order and command that all the inhabitants of the country now outside . . . the towns, shall, within . . . eight days, concentrate themselves in the towns. . . . Any individual who after the expiration of this period is found in the unhabited parts will be considered a rebel and tried as such.

The cruelty of this measure, which President McKinley characterized as "not civilized warfare but extermination," had a profound effect on Americans. From all sides came the demand that we intervene. McKinley, however, was not to be hurried. He detested the thought of war.

[1] This prophecy is printed more fully in Chapter 6.

In a conversation with Cleveland at the White House the night before his first inauguration, he said:

> If I can only go out of office at the end of my term with the knowledge that I have done what lay in my power to avert this terrible calamity with the success that has crowned your patience and persistence, I shall be the happiest man in the world.

Business and conservative interests did not want intervention. Newspapers[1] and the people demanded it.

McKinley steadily resisted the pressure, tried to find some solution other than war. He asked Whitelaw Reid to ascertain through Spanish friends of the latter whether Spain would sell Cuba to the United States, and was informed that "Spain would never sell the brightest jewel in her crown." He did his best to prevent the filibustering from our shores which gave offense to Spain, and during the first nine months of his administration "successfully prevented the departure of a single military expedition or armed vessel." As late as January 27, 1898, at a White House diplomatic dinner, he took pains to show particular attention to the Spanish minister. But American sympathy with Cuba grew, and with it, Spanish resentment.

On February 15, 1898, the American battleship *Maine*, while in the harbor of Havana, was blown up with the loss of 266 American seamen. That made war inevitable. For forty days American indignation and American martial spirit grew, while a court of inquiry examined the wreck. It reported that the disaster had been caused by the application of an external force from below upward, unquestionably a mine.

[1] Whitelaw Reid wrote to McKinley, March 8, 1898: "The impression I got on crossing the Continent was that the more intelligent classes are not greatly affected by the sensational press; but that, on a conviction that the *Maine* was blown up by Spanish agency, with or without the active connivance of the present Spanish authorities, there would be no restraining them. Meantime I have never seen a more profound or touching readiness to trust the President, and await his word."

On April 11, President McKinley sent a message to Congress which said nothing of the *Maine*, but asked authorization to use the armed forces of the nation to compel Spain to evacuate Cuba. Congress, however, believed that the sinking of the *Maine* was itself sufficient

"Notice of funeral hereafter." (Detroit *News*.)
At the start of the Spanish-American War the Spanish people believed that the "Yankee pigs" would soon be beaten to their knees.

justification for war. A joint resolution of the House and Senate was promulgated, enumerating Spain's misdeeds in Cuba, which had culminated "in the destruction of a United States battleship, with 266 of its officers and crew, while on a friendly visit to the harbor of Havana." The resolution declared "that the people of Cuba are and of right ought to be free and independent," that the United States disclaimed "any disposition or intention to exercise sovereignty, jurisdiction, or control over said island, except for the pacification thereof," and, lastly, that once pacification were accomplished, the United States would "leave the government and control of the island to its people."

This joint resolution was communicated to the representative of Spain at Washington, together with notice that Spain would be given three days in which to accede to the American demands. Spain declined, the ministers of the two countries were given their passports, and a state of war began on April 23.

On May 1, Admiral Dewey sank the Spanish fleet in Manila Bay. On July 3, Sampson and Schley destroyed the other Spanish fleet at Santiago, and shortly thereafter the Spanish land-forces in Cuba surrendered. On August 12, the war ended with a protocol in which Spain ceded Porto Rico and the Island of Guam to the United States. In October, peace commissioners met in Paris, where, on December 10, 1898, the peace treaty was signed. On February 9, 1899, the treaty was ratified by the United States Senate with but one vote to spare. By this treaty Spain formally ceded to the United States the Philippine Islands for a consideration of $20,000,000, together with the other Spanish possessions mentioned in the protocol.

Out of the discussion of this treaty in the Senate and through the country, Bryan snatched political resurrection.

IV

Bryan, defeated by McKinley in 1896, surveyed his private and political concerns. Politically he had the leadership, contested but nevertheless secure, of one of the two great parties. Personally he was a poor young man out of a job and with a family. His source of income immediately preceding his nomination, the editorship of the Omaha *World-Herald*, had been limited both as to remuneration and scope. For a return to his earlier career in the law he had little taste. But he had one asset. As an orator he was literally peerless. Audiences all over the country were beseeching him to speak, the invitations carrying promises of appropriate remuneration.[1] He

[1] Also, at this time, he wrote "The First Battle"—from the point of view of orthodox book construction a weird hodge-podge of autobiography, Bryanesque

made prolonged lecture tours, North, South, East, and West. His magic with audiences was undiminished. Everywhere, enthusiasm attended him. The uncompromisingly Republican *Times-Herald* of Chicago in July, 1899, said of him: "He has found in several States that the Democratic party leaders consider the silver issue a

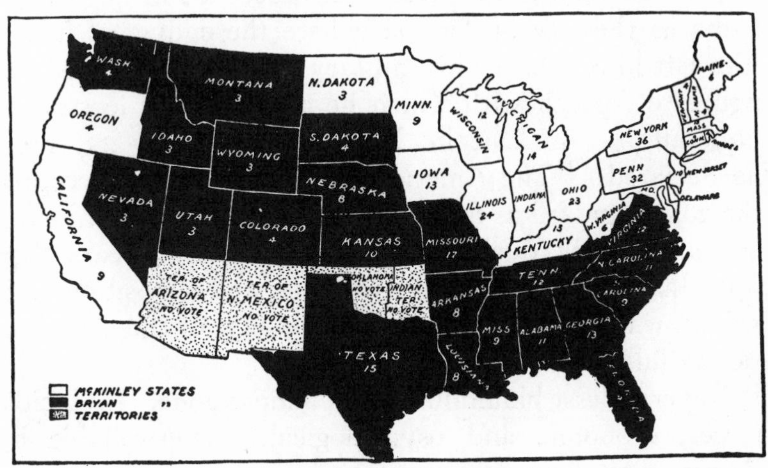

The election results in 1896.
Bryan came nearest to reaching the presidency. With 50,000 more votes, properly distributed, he would have won.

disastrous one, and in those States the popular vote would certainly be hostile to his silver policy; but wherever he goes he meets with manifestations of an almost fanatical personal loyalty. Very few American politicians have been the objects of such general or intense devotion."

But however popular Bryan personally might be, his old issue was waning. When in one of his speeches he said, "I stand just where I stood three years ago," the Republican editor of the New York *Press* emitted one of those peculiarly effective bits of wit of which the point

philosophy, and propaganda; but nevertheless with attraction for those who can see reality in unconventional forms. The book ran into many editions, for there were tens of thousands of people who were fanatic about Bryan personally.

lies in that entrancing subtlety of the last word, after the comma: "Sit down, Mr. Bryan. You must be awfully tired, too."

When America declared war on Spain, Bryan aligned himself in support of President McKinley, helped organize the Third Nebraska Volunteers, was made colonel, and at the head of that regiment proceeded as far toward Cuba as the city of Tampa, where the ending of hostilities left him. Out of his military service he enriched the figures of speech with which he continued to lecture on bimetallism. In Lincoln, Neb., on December 23, 1898, he declared: "The American people have not accepted the gold standard as final.[1] It has wrought more injustice in our country during the last twenty-five years than Spain has wrought in all her colonies, and opposition to it will grow until the gold and silver coinage of the Constitution is fully restored."

Nevertheless, bimetallism was almost gone. Invincible forces, economic and psychological, uncontrollable by Bryan or anybody else, were working against it.

By 1899 Bryan was looking to the nomination once more. This project was of a nature to call for Bryan's serious and perhaps agile concern. By this time he realized that silver as an issue was running against the current. With the silver issue he could get the Democratic nomination, but with it alone his chances of being elected President would be slighter than they had been four years before. It was necessary to have new issues in addition to silver or as a substitute for it.

When the next nomination was less than a year ahead, September 12, 1899, Bryan, at a conference in Chicago on the trust question, proposed that trusts and monop-

[1] All the same, they had. Less than two years later, March 14, 1900, Congress recorded the end of the bimetallism issue in a statute making gold the single standard.

olies should be subjected to control by requiring that all corporations be licensed by the Federal Government; that no stock-watering should be permitted; that the amount of capital for any one corporation should be limited; that there should be certified public statements of earnings, expenses, profits, and other details; and that penitentiary sentences should be imposed for violation of these regulations.

Even more directly than the current agitation about trusts, the ending of the Spanish War provided Bryan with yet another issue, imperialism. The treaty of peace, as written at Paris, had given the United States unlimited control over Porto Rico and the Philippines and a limited relation to Cuba. Because of this, the treaty gave rise in the Senate and throughout the country to an opposition much like that which later attended the treaty of peace at the end of the Great War. Both from Democrats and from a group of Republicans led by the venerable Senator Hoar of Massachusetts, there was stubborn opposition to ratification of the treaty by the Senate. Bryan won some commendation by taking a course which included, as one of its principles, refusal to embarrass the administration in a matter within the field of foreign affairs. He took the stand that the treaty should be ratified in order to establish peace promptly; but that as soon thereafter as possible, the dependencies handed over to us should be set free. The treaty was ratified. Immediately there arose the issue of imperialism, with Bryan as one of the conspicuous leaders of the anti-expansionists. It became apparent that this would be the leading issue at the approaching election of 1900.

Bryan's adroit seizing of these new issues, coupled with the absence of any formidable rival for the leadership of the party, reduced those Democrats who did not like him to a state of fulminating resignation. In such a mood the editor of the Brooklyn *Eagle* wrote: "Bryan is a candidate for renomination, with the manner of a despot and the desperation of an anarch. Possibly he may lose a renomination. Probably he will gain it. He will, if he can, make it not worth having. In that case, it might go to him unanimously."

For a time it seemed the nomination would go to Bryan without opposition. The fitful search[1] of the anti-Bryan elements of the party for another candidate had, so far, found no one venturesome enough to make the fight against the Commoner.

[1] One of the most persistent searchers for a new candidate to offset Bryan was Joseph Pulitzer, of the New York *World;* it was out of Pulitzer's efforts, chiefly, that arose the episode described in the next chapter.

12

DEWEY

The Most Remarkable Announcement, Probably, of a Serious Presidential Candidacy, Ever Made in America. An Almost Equally Unique Newspaper Beat and How It Came About. Dewey's Elevation to Command of the American Asiatic Squadron Preceding the Spanish War. A Spanish Official's Description of America, its People, its Soldiers and Sailors. "You May Fire when Ready, Gridley." The Victory of Manila Bay. Popular Reception of the News in America. "Hoch der Kaiser." The Extraordinary Adulation Heaped on Dewey when He Arrived in America. He Is Given a House. He Marries. The Dewey Arch, One of the Most Beautiful Examples of Monumental Statuary Ever Devised in America, Meant to Be Perpetuated in Marble and Granite, but Actually Carried Off by the Garbage Men to the City Dump. Together with Various Reflections About Popular Heroes and Public Fickleness.

THEN, one morning in early April, with the Democratic National Convention of 1900 only three months away, Bryan's leisurely march toward nomination by acclamation was interrupted by one of the most curious announcements of a presidential candidacy ever made, one of the most naïve declarations ever given out by any man who had even the briefest part in American politics. It came from a figure whose contact with important American history was brief, lasting in all barely three years, but who, while his importance endured, engaged the attention of the people in several different ways, all of them engrossing and some spectacular.

At six o'clock in the evening of April 3, 1900, Admiral George Dewey, at his home in Washington, gave to a correspondent of the New York *World*[1] an interview which, in the outcome that attended it, composed the closing phase of Dewey as a serious figure in contemporary American life. The interview read:

Yes; I realize that the time has arrived when I must definitely define my position.

When I arrived in this country last September, I said then that nothing would induce me to be a candidate for the Presidency. Since then, however, I have had the leisure and inclination to study the matter, and have reached a different

[1] This episode was no less outstanding as a journalistic beat than unique as an announcement of presidential ambition. Mr. Samuel G. Blythe, who at the time was in charge of *The World* bureau at Washington, has told me the circumstances. From his account I paraphrase and condense the following: Many newspapers, wanting some one to contest against Bryan for the Democratic nomination, kept suggesting that Dewey should run. Shoals of newspaper correspondents called on Dewey. Most of them he would not see, and to those he did see he would not talk. From time to time, the thing flared up and died down, each flare-up of newspaper interest being accompanied by more newspaper visitations on Dewey, all increasingly fruitless. One night, the home office of *The World* in New York sent a telegram to Mr. Blythe, asking him to make another try at Dewey. Mr. Blythe says: "I stuck it on the spike. It seemed just one of those telegraphic things that in those days used to come in from editors of all grades, dozens of them a day, suggesting, ordering, and so on. However, after the boys who worked in the bureau with me had turned in their afternoon copy and were getting out for dinner, I called in my state, war, and navy man, Horace J. Mock, and said: 'Mock, the office wants us to make another try for Dewey. I have no idea you can get anything, but you live up that way, so drop in and ask for the old man and see if he has decided anything yet.'"

Mock took the telegram to Dewey's house about 6.30, rang the bell, and was shown in. He handed Dewey the telegram, which read: "Please make another effort to find out whether Admiral Dewey is a candidate for President."

"Yes," said the admiral, "I have decided to become a candidate."

The two then discussed the form of the interview. Presently Mrs. Dewey came in. Among them they drafted the statement as it appeared. By the time it was in the form the Deweys wanted, it was nine o'clock in the evening. Mock made a fair copy, and, realizing the importance of it, asked Dewey to sign it, saying he would like to keep the notes for a souvenir. Dewey signed. Mock, being a good newspaper man of the day when exclusive stories were more sought than now, impressed on the admiral the necessity of not saying a word to any other person until the interview should be published the following morning. The admiral agreed. Mr. Blythe continues:

"About half-past nine o'clock, when I was wondering what had become of Mock, he burst into my office waving a statement, and said he had the exclusive announcement that Dewey would run. I went to the wire, told *The World* what we had, and cautioned the greatest secrecy and care that not a word should leak out. Then I locked up *The World* bureau, and not a person went in or out of the place until we had word from New York that *The World* with the statement in was on the streets."

conclusion, inasmuch as so many assurances have come to me from my countrymen that I would be acceptable as a candidate for this great office.

If the American people want me for this high office, I shall be only too willing to serve them.

It is the highest honor in the gift of this nation; what citizen would refuse it?

Since studying this subject I am convinced that the office of the President is not such a very difficult one to fill, his duties being mainly to execute the laws of Congress. Should I be chosen for this exalted position I would execute the laws of Congress as faithfully as I have always executed the orders of my superiors.

"Is there any political significance in your trips West?" *The World* correspondent asked.

"No; I am simply filling the engagements made months ago — long before I ever thought seriously of the Presidency."

"On what platform will you stand?"

"I think I have said enough at this time, and possibly too much."

From a photograph by Clinedinst.

Admiral George Dewey, commander of the Asiatic squadron during the Spanish-American War, whose victory over the Spanish fleet at Manila in 1898 opened a new vista of American history.

After the reader has taken in the various qualities of that announcement, including what inevitably seems its complacency, let us go back and follow the beginning, the rise, the decline, and the fall, which compose one of the most picturesque careers in late American history. As seen twenty-five years later, it is but an episode, an incident where the gods of history seem to step aside for a moment from the march of serious events to amuse themselves with a little ironic dance by the side of the road. But at the moment it seemed like history itself; and the historians of the day so treated it.

II

Admiral Dewey — at the beginning of this episode it was Commodore Dewey — had served under Farragut in the Civil War, had remained in the navy, and by his fifties[1] was one of those many naval officers who went along from day to day doing their duty well and looking to no future more exciting than the placid rounding out of their naval service in routine ways. To him, as to many others, there came the engaging hint of adventurous change in this quiet prospect, through the growing imminence of the Spanish War. In the fall of 1897 he learned from Theodore Roosevelt, then assistant secretary of the navy, that choice of a commander for the Asiatic squadron rested between himself and Commodore John A. Howell, and that strong political influence had been brought to bear on the secretary of the navy to name the latter.[2] Dewey, although he was one of those naval officers whose high traditions included distaste for political influence within the service, felt he was justified under the circumstances in soliciting the aid of Senator Proctor, of his native State, Vermont, who, delighted at the opportunity of serving Dewey, immediately called

[1] Dewey was born December 26, 1837.

[2] "Roosevelt was a stanch supporter of Dewey. He stood solidly for his retention when high naval officials and politicians were urging the selection of another leader for the Pacific fleet. San Francisco and a few other Western cities objected to the selection of Dewey. They had in mind a 'favorite son.' But Roosevelt stood to his guns. One day a delegation called upon him to protest against the Dewey appointment. Roosevelt heard them through and then answered them rather vehemently:

"'Gentlemen, I can't agree with you. We have looked up his record. We have looked him straight in the eyes. He is a fighter. We'll not change now. Pleased to have met you. Good day, gentlemen.'"—From "The Life of Theodore Roosevelt," Wm. Draper Lewis.

on President McKinley and received the promise of the appointment before he left the White House. On October 21, 1897, the order was issued directing Dewey to sail from San Francisco on December 7 to relieve acting Rear-Admiral McNair as commander of the Asiatic squadron.

On the eve of Dewey's departure for the Orient he was given a banquet by some friends at the Metropolitan Club in Washington. One of the features was a toast in verse recited by Archibald Hopkins. In the words of the toast was something illustrative of the certainty with which war with Spain had come to be regarded by army and navy men; something prophetic of a grandiose quality that was destined to attend Dewey's next few years; something prophetic of the extravagance of emotion on the part of the American people which was to attend our war against Spain. One stanza read:

> We know our honor'll be sustained
> Where'er our pennant flies,
> Our rights respected and maintained,
> Whatever power defies.

Another stanza included, among other things that make it worth reprinting, a closing line which, read after the passing of twenty-seven years, suggests a change in popular customs and taste:

> And when he takes the homeward tack,
> Beneath an admiral's flag,
> We'll hail that day that brings him back,
> And have another jag.[1]

Dewey, with these words ringing in his ears — one

[1] "Jag," Mr. Hopkins informs me, suggested itself to him more because it rhymed with "flag" than because of his anticipation of any definite degree or form of exaltation. In the difficult balance between propriety and the requirements of poetry, he experimented with another version, in which the second line was changed to

"His admiral's flag on high";

but that, too, led no farther than a compromise in which the last line read:

"We'll drink the cellar dry."

wonders a little about their propriety, considering that our tension with Spain was yet four months short of the stage where war was actually proclaimed — Dewey left for Nagasaki, Japan, to take command of the fleet.

III

Dewey's management of affairs justified the spirit of the song, and justified the confidence his fellow naval officers had in him. After an enforced wait of six weeks for the arrival of the *Concord* bringing ammunition, he changed his base from Japanese waters to the harbor of Hong Kong, the latter being a more advantageous port than Nagasaki or Yokohama from which to proceed to the attack on Admiral Montojo's fleet at Manila. When Dewey reached Hong Kong he learned of the destruction the previous day, February 15, in Havana harbor, of the battleship *Maine*, with the loss of 266 of her crew.

This news convinced Dewey the war would come. He held daily drills. He bought provisions and coal in adequate quantities. He ordered fresh ammunition from America. He bought a merchant ship, the *Zafiro*, and kept her under private registry to act as a supply-boat for the fleet. He made arrangements with a Chinese comprador for the future purchase of supplies, and did it so discreetly and circumspectly as not to give cause for Spanish protests about violations of neutrality. As soon as the declaration of war made it necessary for Great Britain to proclaim neutrality — Hong Kong thereby becoming a closed port to belligerent ships — Dewey steamed out of the British harbor. (To the cheers, incidentally, of British tars, and martial American music played by the bands of the British men-of-war.) He went thirty miles away, and anchored in the Chinese harbor of Mirs, China being impotent to enforce her neutrality. There Dewey awaited the arrival of the

American consul, Williams, from Manila, who was expected to bring late information about the defenses of that city.

On the arrival of Williams, Dewey set sail.

Among the items of information brought by Williams was a copy of a bombastic proclamation issued on the 23d of April by the Spanish general, Basilio Augustin, military governor of the Philippines. Dewey recognized the psychological value of it for his own uses. As soon as the fleet reached open sea, he caused the crew of each ship to be mustered, and had read to them the proclamation that had been designed to stir the martial spirit of the Spanish soldiers. It began:

> Spaniards! Between Spain and the United States of North America hostilities have broken out.
>
> The North American people, constituted of all the social excrescences, have exhausted our patience, and provoked war by their perfidious machinations. . . . The struggle will be short and decisive. The God of victories will give us one as brilliant and complete as the righteousness and justice of our cause demand. Spain . . . will emerge triumphantly from this new test, humiliating and blasting the adventurers from those States which, without cohesion and without a history, offer to humanity only infamous traditions and the ungrateful spectacle of a Congress in which appear united insolence and defamation, cowardice and cynicism.
>
> A squadron manned by foreigners, possessing neither instruction nor discipline, is preparing to come to this archipelago with the ruffianly intention of robbing us of all that means life, honor, and liberty.

The proclamation included charges that the Americans would try to substitute Protestantism for the Catholic faith, would plunder the Philippines, and would compel inhabitants of the islands to man ships and to labor. The concluding sentences ran:

> Vain designs! Ridiculous boastings! Your indomitable bravery will suffice to frustrate the attempt to carry them into

realization. . . . The aggressors shall not profane the tombs of your fathers; they shall not gratify their lustful passions at the cost of our wives' and daughters' honor, or appropriate the property your industry has accumulated as a provision for your old age.

Filipinos! Prepare for the struggle; and, united under the glorious Spanish flag, which is ever covered with laurels, let us fight with the belief that victory will crown our efforts; and to the calls of our enemies let us oppose with the decision of the Christian and the patriot the cry of "Viva España!"

IV

Midnight of April 30, 1898, found Dewey off the harbor of Manila, twenty-six miles out from the city. With lights darkened and at reduced speed the squadron slowly steamed through the entrance[1] to the harbor, past the three sentinel islands — Corregidor, Caballo, and El Fraile. On passing El Fraile, three shots fired by the Spanish shore batteries were answered by the American ships. No further opposition was offered by the Spaniards. Once safely past these island defenses and inside the harbor, quiet reigned, and Dewey's ships slowly milled about, waiting for dawn.

With the first coming of light, firing was commenced by the Luneta and two other Manila batteries and later by the Spanish fleet anchored under the batteries of Cavité.

The only reply made by Dewey was the order from the flag-ship *Olympia* to close in on the Spanish fleet. The manœuvre was executed perfectly. The American fleet, with the *Olympia* in the lead, approached to within

[1] Practically all the histories say the entrance was strewn with mines; but Admiral Bradley A. Fiske, who has read this proof and who was with Dewey, says there were none. He writes: "I had requested Dewey before we left Hong Kong to give me the job of pulling up the mines in Manila Bay, but was told there were none. Subsequently I found this to be true. I found mines and electric apparatus under construction in the Cavité Arsenal, but none had even been finished."

two and one-half miles of the Spaniards. This range being satisfactory, Dewey imperturbably gave his famous order — an order of which both the terseness and the imperturbability had a large part in shaping the particular kind of fame that America later heaped on him:

"You may fire when ready, Gridley." [1]

Five times Dewey manœuvred his fleet, as in a review, before the Spanish ships. At the end of the fifth series of broadsides, Dewey gave that other of his famous orders which also contributed to his subsequent reputation for laconic imperturbability, the order to "draw off for breakfast." In his autobiography Dewey says that breakfast was a secondary consideration, the primary reason for the order being that he had received an erroneous report that but fifteen rounds of ammunition for the five-inch battery remained on the flag-ship. Also he was influenced by the fact that the air was so filled with smoke as to make accurate firing impossible.

When roll was called on the American ships, it developed that not one man had been killed and only eight injured, although for several hours the fleet had been subjected at close quarters to a fire of which the volume was exceeded, as it now appeared, only by its inaccuracy.

After breakfast, the air having cleared of smoke, it was seen that the Spanish fleet had suffered heavily; several ships had been sunk and others were in flames. But as the Spaniards had not yet run up the white flag, the slaughter was recommenced. In a short while it culminated in the silencing of the land-batteries[2] and the absolute destruction of the armada which, so valorously

[1] The order is sometimes reported in the less compact form: "You may fire when you are ready, Gridley." It was the shorter form that was generally circulated in the American newspapers; the very terseness of it helped to stimulate the enthusiasm that later arose.

[2] Although the Cavité land-batteries were silenced, the city of Manila continued to be held by the Spaniards until the arrival of American land-forces months later.

but futilely, had attempted to protect Spain's greatest remaining colony and to live up to the spirit of proud traditions more than 400 years old, traditions of such national heroes as Columbus and Magellan, Cortez and Hernando de Soto.

V

All this was on May 1. For a full week, America, 7000 miles away, had only garbled fragments of news, none authentic and much of it disturbing. The Spaniards still held the city of Manila and controlled the only cable. During the interval when Dewey had withdrawn "for breakfast," the Spanish governor-general really thought he had beaten, or at least repelled, the American vessels, and sent a triumphant message to the Spanish court at Madrid. Versions of this message trickled out to America. Later, when there was no longer any question that Dewey had been victorious, the Spanish commander sent other accounts designed to provide the soporific of euphemism to the Spanish people. These also found their way to America and were correspondingly disturbing and suspense-provoking. Dewey proposed to the Spanish governor-general at Manila that the cable be neutralized and used by both, but the latter, having no notion of giving up his monopoly of the mechanism for face-saving, declined. Thereupon Dewey fished up the cable and cut it.

For its true information America had to wait until Dewey could send a despatch-boat, which was not until May 5, four days after the battle. It took two more days for the despatch-boat to reach Hong Kong.

The first direct despatch to America about the battle of Manila was an historic newspaper beat. The author of it was Edward W. Harden, who was serving the Chicago *Tribune* and the New York *World*. Harden's presence at the battle was wholly a stroke of fortune. He was a brother-in-law of Frank Vanderlip, then assistant secretary of the treasury. The Treasury, some months before, had put into commission a new revenue cutter, the *McCullough.* She was sent to the Far East, and Harden, with John T. McCutcheon, also a Chicago newspaper man, was invited to make the trip. When the *McCullough* reached Singapore, the captain received news of the war with Spain, and was instructed to place his vessel under the command of Commodore Dewey and accompany him to Manila. By that incident Harden and McCutcheon were transformed from sightseeing visitors on a Treasury revenue cutter to war correspondents on a naval vessel. Following the battle, after the Spanish governor-general had refused to share the cable with Dewey, and after Dewey had cut it, on Thursday, May 5, the *McCullough* was ordered to Hong Kong to file the admiral's despatches. By this time a third newspaper man had been added to the party, Joseph L. Stickney, of the New York *Herald*, who had been on Dewey's flag-ship the *Olympia.* A fourth man, Flag-Lieutenant Brumby, was sent by the admiral to file his official reports.

As the despatch-boat was leaving Manila, Admiral Dewey told the three correspondents they were free to send any stories they wished regarding the battle and events leading up to and following it, but he imposed two conditions: they should not speculate as to his probable future course (in other words, they were free to talk about what he had done but could give no intimation as to what they thought he might do in the future); and they should permit Dewey's messages to be filed before theirs. Mr. Harden wrote me, May 20, 1925:

When we arrived in Hong Kong we were met by Consul-General Rounseville Wildman, who came out in a steam-launch and took us ashore. As the launch came alongside the dock, I saw Stickney prepare to make a pier-head leap, which he did. But I was younger and a little spryer than he, and I beat him to the dock. We both jumped into rickshaws and started for the cable office. I went through an alley while he went around the street. I handed my despatches into the receiving-window, but Stickney, who followed me, went into the office of the manager. The Chinese clerk in charge of the window had never seen a three-thousand-word despatch and refused to accept it, saying I would have to talk to the manager. I left my despatch with him, refusing to have it returned to me, while I went into the manager's office. I told the manager that my despatch had been filed before Stickney's, and that mine had precedence. He denied this and said I should have brought it to him. I stood on my rights. On his continuing to refuse to take my point of view, I wrote and filed a despatch to the general manager of the cable lines in London, setting forth in brief the situation and demanding the immediate discharge of the manager. I sent a like message to the New York *World*. The manager refused to accept or transmit the messages, saying they were not press despatches. But when I offered to pay cash for them he had a change of heart and admitted that my contention was right and that my despatch should go first. . . . Stickney left the office as soon as I came in, under the impression that he was getting his message through first. McCutcheon came third. After both had left, I then filed a short message giving in brief the results of the battle, which I marked "Urgent," a rate which was then in effect and on which the charge was three times the commercial rate, or $9.90 a word as compared with $1.15, the charge for press matter. I was forced to pay cash for it, which fortunately I was able to do. I was careful to notify the manager that under the arrangement we had with Admiral Dewey my despatches as well as the others were to follow those sent by the Admiral. Flag-Lieutenant Brumby, in filing his despatch, which was in code, specified that it should be "repeated." The consequence was that at each station where it was taken off the cable for relay, it was repeated back to the sender for O. K. While my "urgent" despatch followed the Admiral's, at the first point where there were two cables, mine went on without interruption while the Admiral's was repeated, as I understand, about six times between Hong Kong and Washington. . . . As a result of the repeating of the Admiral's messages, I got a beat on his despatches by about six or seven hours.

Harden's despatch reached the New York *World* between three and four o'clock in the morning, and *The World* was able to print it in much of their edition.

The Chicago *Tribune* shared with the New York *World* the right to Harden's despatches. How it fared is told by James Keeley, then managing editor:

> Harden's despatch hit New York about three o'clock in the morning [Eastern time]. There was a poker game in *The World* office. Our correspondent, Murphy, was in it. When the cable operator called up to tell *The World* of this important message, all the others in the game had hands except Murphy. He answered the telephone. The operator read the message to him. He took it down, hopped to our leased wire, and we had it about five minutes later. I stopped the presses, yanked back about 30,000 copies of the city edition, locked the doors, and got out an extra which went to every subscriber. . . .

As soon as Keeley's newspaper function had been competently cared for, he called President McKinley and Secretary Long of the navy out of bed in Washington by telephone and gave them the first detailed news of the battle of Manila. It was noon before Dewey's official despatch had overcome the delays of repeating and been decoded.

VI

This was seven days after the battle. The mere duration of delay was one of the elements that contributed to just that dramatic quality which fed the fires of American emotion. Also the Spanish, in their early reports, which trickled to America by way of Madrid, had colored such news as they sent at all in such a way as to cause America to think Dewey's squadron had suffered heavily. The combination of these disturbing rumors, together with the seven days of suspense and the other dramatic factors focussing on the emotions of America, was as if some cosmic stage-manager were arranging things in just the

way best designed for this particular act in the whole drama of Dewey. The consequence was that when the definite news finally came through, a tremendous wave of enthusiasm swept over the country. Dewey became in America such a figure as only arises once in many decades. Margherita Arlina Hamm wrote a "Hymn to Dewey." A

"The Manila incident reflected in the faces of Europe."—New York *Bee*.

famous composer of the day, Victor Herbert, wrote "The Fight Is Made and Won." There were dozens of Dewey songs. The most popular was one printed in the Topeka *Capital*, which, sung to an air partly sentimental and partly triumphant, travelled the length and breadth of the land.[1]

Oh, dewy was the morning
Upon the first of May,
And Dewey was the Admiral,
Down in Manila Bay.
And dewy were the Regent's eyes
Them[2] orbs of royal blue,
And dew we feel discouraged?
I dew not think we dew!

[1] Written by Eugene Ware, a well-known Kansas lawyer and poet, whose pen name was "Ironquill." The original manuscript of this poem now hangs in the offices of the Kansas State Historical Society in Topeka. Mr. Ware wrote it at the request of the city editor of the *Capital*, J. F. Jarrell, who, as he says, "wanted to hook up Kansas in some manner with the battle of Manila Bay, so I asked Ware to write a poem that could be blurbed out on the first page."

[2] "Them" is correct. That is the way Ware wrote it. Ware was a scholar and a poet of distinction. He felt that "them" had a peculiar value, and insisted it be printed that way.

It seems odd, at the distance of twenty-seven years, to think that most of us got intoxicated over that bit of verse. But we did.

The newspapers were no less excited. Some characteristic head-lines read:

DIGNIFIED SENATORS FORGET
Their Dignity and Yell
"Hip, Hooray!"

And:

HERE IS HOW
IT WAS DONE
Story of the Greatest
Naval Engagement of
Modern Times.

Some public men, and even some professional navy men, were no less exalted than the newspaper head-line writers. One of them, Commodore Winfield Scott Schley, in an interview given on board the flag-ship *Brooklyn*, on May 11, 1898, four days after the news of the victory, said: "Admiral Dewey's victory at Manila must deservedly take its place side by side with the greatest naval victories of the world's history." [1]

[1] In one quarter, at least, this disposition toward adulation endured as late as 1901. Henry Cabot Lodge, in his "History of the Spanish War," published in that year, favorably compared Dewey's exploit with that of Nelson at Aboukir.

Admiral Bradley A. Fiske notes on the margin of my proof: "Yes, if Nelson's fame rested on the Nile alone, he and Dewey would be in the same class." In a subsequent letter Admiral Fiske writes: "You make the battle of Manila and Dewey's achievements in Manila Bay seem less important than they really were. There is an impression broadcast that battles are great or little according to the number of people who fought in them and the number killed, regardless of results. This is misleading. Many battles have caused great loss of life, yet were really unimportant; while many battles causing little loss of life were very important, because they decided questions and furnished new starting-points for the paths of history. The battle of Manila Bay was one of the most important ever fought. It decided that the United States should start in a direction in which it had never travelled before. It placed the United States in the family of great nations, and it put Spain into outer darkness. Before the battle, British Navy officers treated the United States Navy officers with condescension. In fact, Europeans as a

Congress conferred on Dewey the rank of admiral of the navy, a higher honor than had ever been given before in American history. Also it was provided that Dewey need not retire when he reached the statutory age, unless he so wished; and that if he did retire voluntarily, his emoluments should not be diminished. Princeton and the University of Pennsylvania gave Dewey LL.D.'s; and Norwich University, the college he had attended before entering Annapolis, made him "Master of Military Science." Colonel Watterson, of the Louisville *Courier-Journal*, started a Dewey-for-President boom, but gave it up on learning that — at that time, apparently — Dewey did not approve.[1]

Within the United States the high note of adulation was universal. Only outside the borders of the country

body treated all Americans so. They have never done so since. We left Hong-Kong to go to Manila on April 27th, and returned some time after the battle. It was as plain as day that the European residents of Hong-Kong, of all positions of society, regarded Americans in a very different way. Their whole manner and attitude toward us had suddenly become quite as toward equals. After the battle, and after Dewey's forceful and yet tactful handling of the difficult situation in Manila Bay for eighteen months, without a single mistake of any kind, Europeans realized that Americans had in them a strategic ability with which they had never been credited. The very perfection of Dewey's work has made the winning of the battle seem easy, as a fine gymnast's work makes his feat seem easy. If the Spaniards had put their fleet under the guns of Manila, not one American ship would ever have left the harbor. Dewey realized the situation at once and steamed directly at the Spanish fleet, ignoring the shore batteries. The Spaniards ought to have won the battle if they had fought it correctly. They had all the trumps."

[1] Dewey, at this time, across the world from contact with American politics, apparently entertaned no faintest degree of political ambition. On the contrary, shortly after the Cavité victory, in reply to a query if he would be a candidate for the presidency, Dewey cabled: "I would not accept a nomination for the Presidency of the United States. I have no desire for any political office. I am unfitted for it, having neither the education nor the training. I am deeply grateful for many expressions of kindly sentiment from the American people, but I desire to retire in peace to the enjoyment of my old age. The Navy is one profession, politics another. I am too old to learn a new profession now. I have no political associations and my health would never stand the strain of a canvass. I have been approached by politicians repeatedly, in one way or another, but I have refused absolutely to consider any proposition whatever. This is final."

Admiral Fiske writes me: "At a dinner given by Dewey to his captains the night before he left Manila for home, he asked their advice about the Presidency and was advised by each one not to consider it for a moment."

could one find less hot-blooded appraisal. Some foreign critics qualified their apportionment of credit to Dewey's skill by emphasizing the characteristic complacence of the Spaniards, their naval and military slovenliness, which qualities had caused their fleet to be inefficient, undisciplined, ill-cared-for. The Toronto (Canada) *Saturday Night*, on August 27, 1899, said:

> There is every reason to believe that he [Dewey] would give a creditable account of himself if he ever found it necessary to engage in a battle, but of course it is absurd to class him with the great sailors of history because of the Manila incident.[1]

Nothing of that sort, however, was heard in the United States. America's ecstasy of exaltation went on from height to height. It was fed by the news of other events at Manila, where, although Montojo's fleet had been destroyed, Spanish armies still held the city; and where Dewey, with a high sense of accountability and with admirable restraint against what must have been much temptation to any man's ego, remained until the day when he should see enough American troops actually landed in the archipelago to make victory complete and permanent.

VII

It was as if the same cosmic stage-manager, whose moment of whimsical irony had been so well satisfied by the results of the seven days of dramatic pause between

[1] The perspective lent by a quarter of a century shows that neither the fulsome nor the disparaging critics were entirely right. The generally recognized facts are that Dewey, with six fighting ships, operating 7000 miles from a home base, boldly entered an unfamiliar harbor, sailing past powerful, modern, Krupp-equipped shore batteries; and destroyed an enemy fleet of ten fighting ships and two torpedo-boats fighting from anchorage (which overbalanced the American fleet's advantage of superior speed) at a place in the bay selected by the Spanish admiral as presumably giving him an advantage over the attacking fleet. Dewey having been victorious, no disparagement of him has much weight, and the verdict must be accepted that his plan as conceived and carried out was flawless.

the battle of Manila Bay and the arrival of the news in America, now determined to provide some seventy times seven days of suspense between the arrival of the news and the arrival of the admiral himself; determined, in order to make Dewey's apotheosis the greater, to insert that prolonged pause before letting the American people have the opportunity they craved cumulatively, through increasing weeks of suspense, to intoxicate themselves with the actual presence of the hero. The cosmic spirit provided these nearly seventeen months of suspense, and supplied the period with just the sort of incident and byplay best adapted to lead to the ultimate dénouement.

Immediately after Dewey's victory at Manila, the American public was excited with rumors that a new Spanish fleet[1] was headed toward the Philippines. Such an expedition actually started, though it never got far enough to be threatening. But another embarrassing complication arose which Dewey handled in a manner that added to his personal and professional reputation. British, French, Japanese, and German men-of-war entered the harbor, ostensibly to observe operations and protect the interests of their nationals. All except the Germans observed the customary and well-understood naval etiquette. On May 6 the German cruiser *Irene* dropped anchor at a point selected by her commander, without observing the courtesy of consulting the wishes of the commander of the blockading squadron. This breach of established procedure was followed on May 9 by the German cruiser *Kormoran* entering the harbor, without prearrangement with Dewey, at three o'clock in the morning. When her lights were seen, Dewey de-

[1] America was seeing ghosts of Spanish fleets all through the early summer of 1898. Many persons refrained from taking their customary vacations at the seashore. Boston capitalists sent their securities inland to Worcester. Roosevelt wrote of it as "a fairly comic panic. . . . The state of nervousness along the seacoast was funny."

spatched a launch to board her, since although she flew the German flag, it was apprehended that she might be a Spaniard using the German flag as a ruse. When she paid no heed to the steam-launch's hail, a shot was sent across her bows. This warning was sufficient to impress on the commanders of visiting war-ships that Dewey would insist on his fleet being treated like a grown-up navy. Nevertheless, he was constantly subject to petty annoyances[1] at the hands of Rear-Admiral von Diederichs, who at one time had five German war-ships in the harbor, although the "interests" he was protecting consisted of but one German importing house.

Out of these annoyances from the Germans arose another of those wholly casual episodes that added to the flame of enthusiasm for Dewey. One of the captains who had been at Manila with Dewey was Joseph Bullock Coghlan, whose command, the *Raleigh*, had been the first ship to return the fire of the Spanish land-batteries. Captain Coghlan was the earliest of Dewey's officers to return home, and his arrival was made the occasion, on April 21, 1899, for a prelude to the reception that was later to be given Dewey himself. At a dinner at the Union League Club in New York, Captain Coghlan told some stirring stories about the passages between Dewey and the Germans, and then recited "Hoch! Der Kaiser!" [2]

HOCH! DER KAISER!

Der Kaiser of dis Faterland
Und Gott on high all dings command.
Ve two — ach! Don't you understand?
Myself — und Gott.

[1] "Petty annoyances" is hardly strong enough. Von Diederichs at his best was tactless and boorish; at his worst he was offensively truculent. At times both Admiral Dewey and the British commander, Chichester, felt there was reason to apprehend that the Germans might give armed aid to the Spanish.

[2] The verses, after Captain Coghlan made them famous, were variously attributed to Alexander Macgregor Rose and to Lieutenant Myers of the cruiser *Charleston*. The authentic author is Rose, a Scotch school-teacher and Presbyterian clergyman.

Vile some men sing der power divine,
Mine soldiers sing "Die Wacht am Rhine,"
Und drink der health in Rhenish wine
Of Me — und Gott.

Dere's France, she swaggers all aroundt;
She's ausgespield, of no account,
To much we dink she don't amount;
Myself — und Gott.

She will not dare to fight again,
But if she shouldt, I'll show her blain
Dot Elsass und (in French) Lorraine
Are mein — by Gott!

Dere's grandma[1] dinks she's nicht small beer,
Mit Boers und such she interfere;
She'll learn none owns dis hemisphere
But me — und Gott!

She dinks, good frau, fine ships she's got
Und soldiers mit der scarlet goat.
Ach! We could knock dem! Pouf! Like dot.
Myself — mit Gott.

In dimes of peace, brepare for wars.
I bear de spear und helm of Mars.
Und care not for a dousand Czars,
Myself — mit Gott!

In fact, I humor efery whim,
Mit aspect dark und visage grim;
Gott pulls mit me, und I mit him,
Myself — und Gott!

The next day the New York German-language paper, the *Staats-Zeitung*, had the following head-line:

OUR AMERICAN COUSINS

CAPTAIN COGHLAN SPEAKS OF THE OCCURRENCES AT MANILA. AND THE UNION LEAGUE CLUB SINGS JEERING SONGS ABOUT "OUR KAISER."

Captain Coghlan of the *Raleigh* Again Reflects the Hatred of the Germans in a Speech Before the Union League Club.

[1] Queen Victoria.

The German press characterized the poem as an "expression of wine humor," and attributed authorship to a "Bowery bard." The German ambassador, Herr von Holleben, protested to the State Department. He criticised the poem as "too nasty to be noticed." Secretary Hay deprecated the lack of good taste on the part of Coghlan, but said that the Navy Department had jurisdiction of the matter and that Captain Coghlan had made his speech in a private club. The Navy Department reprimanded Captain Coghlan. The country felt it was done with a solemn wink. Officially the incident was closed. But the verse and the stories Captain Coghlan had told about Dewey "calling down" the Germans went all over the country and increased the rapturous anticipation of the return of Dewey himself.

VIII

Finally, in September, 1899, Dewey felt he had seen enough American troops actually landed at Manila to preserve the newly won archipelago for his country. After seventeen months of dramatic suspense since the date of his victory, he started home. The anticipation of his return was the occasion for a new outburst of exultation in America. The newspaper poets and the amateurs of verse began again. One, Mr. Lue Vernon, poured out his exultant heart:

Admiral George Dewey
  Coming home, they say.
Bring out the pyrotechnics,
  Let's have a holiday.

Shoot up colored rockets,
  Turn the searchlights high;
See the name of Dewey
  Ablazing in the sky.

Sank the Spanish navy,
In a manner new,
Honored grand Old Glory;
Did it shipshape, too.

The newspaper clippings that had sung Dewey's praises during the months since his victory were gathered together and presented to him in a volume that weighed a hundred and fifty pounds and was bound in solid silver. *Life* had an "Admiral's number." The temper of the country at this time is illustrated by the head-line from the Cincinnati *Enquirer* of September 10, 1899, glorifying what was meant to be the permanent monument to Dewey's victory, a Dewey Memorial Arch, at Madison Square, New York City, of which we shall read more in a moment:

DEWEY'S
WHITE TRIUMPHAL ARCH
IS MODELLED AFTER THAT
OF TITUS.
Was a Labor of Love for the
Sculptors.
Best Talent of America Worked
Upon it.
Almost Ready for Our Hero to Ride
Under While New York Goes
Into a Frenzy.

For a description of the country's greeting to Dewey, let us turn to Dewey's own account as given in his autobiography — an account which not only paints the picture adequately but also reflects just that naïveté which made it possible for a hero himself to write an account of his own reception which should not be inadequate to the heights of the occasion:

From all parts of the United States had come requests for a journey across the country by rail. Our inland cities seemed to be vieing with one another in plans for magnificent receptions. Towns, children, and articles of commerce were named after me. I was assured that nothing like the enthusiasm for a man and a deed had ever been known. I knew what to do in command of the Asiatic squadron, but being of flesh and blood and not a superman, it seemed impossible to live up to all that was expected of me as a returning hero. . . . Dewey arches, Dewey flags, and "Welcome, Dewey" in electric lights on the span of the Brooklyn Bridge! The great city of New York made holiday. Its crowds banked the piers, the roofs, and Riverside Drive, when the *Olympia*, leading the North Atlantic squadron, which won Santiago, proceeded up the North River; and they packed the streets for the land parade in token of public emotion, while the gold loving-cup which came to me with the freedom of the city expressed the municipality's official tribute. . . . I was no less deeply affected when I stood on the steps of the State House at Montpelier, with the grounds filled with "home folks," and when on the steps of the east front of the Capitol I received from the hands of the President the sword of honor which Congress had voted me.

This was apotheosis.

IX

Within less than a month after his New York reception, and within a few days after his reception in Washington, Dewey, in a conference sought by a committee in charge of collecting funds for the house which was to be given him as one of the country's many marks of honor, was reported as having specified within narrow limits the district in which it would be satisfactory to him to have his residence; and as having indicated that he wished a small, modest house, with a small dining-room capable of seating, say, eighteen persons.

This episode had, among the people and in the newspapers, a reaction to be accounted for on the theory, let us assume, that seventeen months is a long time for a people to sustain a single emotion at high pitch. Some newspapers ventured to hint a slight wonder that the

Spartan idol should be concerned with such details as the dimensions of his dining-room; and there were allusions to a popular proverb about excessively minute inspection of a gift-horse.

Just a few weeks later, and less than two months after his arrival home, on November 9, 1899, in the presbytery of St. Paul's Catholic Church in Washington, Dewey took to himself a bride — and immediately learned that a public which has made a man a hero has, by the essential nature of that act, established with him a relation of watchful guardianship which regards itself as justified in frank discussion and admonition about matters which, as to men not heroes, have the sanctity and immunity of personal intimacy. Indeed, stronger than that, it was as if the American public had elected itself to be Admiral Dewey's bride; and as if the admiral had committed bigamy; or, at best, it was as if he had procured a divorce, abruptly and without just cause. There was newspaper and street talk of his age, sixty-two; and generalizations based thereon as to the limits of the maturity at which men may properly marry. It was recalled, as having some kind of bearing on this particular case, that the admiral had been twenty-six years a widower, his first wife, who bore him one son, having died in 1873. There was equally frank discussion of the age of the bride, her antecedents, her associations, and her previous station in life. She was the widow of General W. B. Hazen, U. S. A., and sister of John R. McLean, then owner of the Washington *Post* and the Cincinnati *Enquirer*. There was even discussion of the lady's religious affiliations. She was a Catholic; and the anti-Catholic prejudice which at all times exists among a large portion of the American public had for some time been actively eruptive under the name of the A. P. A.[1]

[1] American Protective Association, founded March 3, 1887, at Clinton, Iowa.

A few days after the wedding it became known that the admiral, as a token of devotion to his bride, had deeded to her the house in Washington which the people had given him. At that the public, which had made itself the admiral's godmother, felt it had something to talk about which passed the borders of mere academic discussion and became a material issue. In addition to the matter for argument about ethics, which the public saw in the transfer, there was a whisper, in circles susceptible to this sort of thing, that the house, now owned by the admiral's Catholic wife, would become the official seat of the papacy at the American capital.

There came to be gossip in Washington that there was friction between Dewey and President McKinley, on the ground that in the social circles of the capital not enough was being made of the admiral and Mrs. Dewey. There was talk of the magnificence of Mrs. Dewey's gowns and jewels, echoes of a fame she retained from the days when, as the wife of the military attaché of the American Embassy at the Austrian court, she vied with the nobility of Austria in the splendor of her apparel. Further impetus to this kind of gossip was given by rumors that she was going to change her religious faith. Reared a Presbyterian, she later became an Episcopalian, and it was while at the Catholic court of Austria that she had become a Catholic.[1]

[1] In *Current Literature*, June, 1900, under the heading "Contemporary Celebrities," there is the following quotation from a friendly article originally printed in the New York *Herald*: "In order to settle a question concerning her church affiliations, it is only necessary to say that her early married life was spent at the Austrian Court. An air of Catholicity (*sic*) pervades fashionable Vienna, and it was there that she acquired the custom of attending the Church of Rome. Nothing was more natural to a woman of a religious turn of mind than to follow the fashionable crowd to the fashionable church. . . . If, as it is now whispered, she is to leave Rome for the Protestant faith, she will be only going back to the teachings of her childhood."

X

Although all these things had happened to Dewey's popularity, he still had a vogue. He received invitations to visit all parts of the country; when he accepted he was received with interest and curiosity, even with cordiality. As there were many Democrats who would be glad of any means of keeping from Bryan that presidential nomination which was drifting toward him by default, doubtless it was frequently whispered into Dewey's ear that he ought to run. In any event, about six o'clock of the evening of April 3, 1900, Dewey gave to the Washington correspondent of the New York *World* the announcement printed at the beginning of this chapter.

The first reaction of the newspapers was the record of the reception of sensational news. The Atlanta *Constitution* on the following morning heralded Dewey's announcement with a three-column head-line, a degree of conspicuousness not as common then as now, and reflecting the importance, the extraordinariness, so to speak, of the event:

DEWEY'S MIND IS CHANGED
HE WILL RUN FOR PRESIDENT

THE ADMIRAL SAYS HE WILL OBEY
ORDERS AS USUAL

Manila Hero Yields to the
Persuasion of His Friends

Thinks the Office Easy to Fill

Declares He Will, if Elected, Obey
the Orders of Congress as he
Has Always Obeyed Those of his
Superiors in the Navy

That was the first reaction of the newspapers, a reaction that merely recorded the sensational quality of the news. But the succeeding reaction reflected the difference between the Dewey who, six months before, had been an unqualified hero, and the Dewey who had mar-

"I wouldn't care if he did sting me." (St. Paul *Pioneer Press.*)
A satirical cartoon that appeared about the time Dewey made his famous announcement that he was a candidate for the presidency.

ried and deeded to his wife the house that had been the people's gift to him. The Atlanta *Constitution* of the very next day, April 5, had this head-line:

LEADERS LAUGH AT POOR DEWEY

THE ADMIRAL IS A POLITICAL SENSATION FOR ONCE

The Entire Capital Is Laughing at the Former Hero

Throughout the country the news of Dewey's political aspirations was received with regret mingled with ridicule. Responsibility was laid at the door of the ambitions of Mrs. Dewey,[1] who found herself for a short time the cynosure of all eyes. The situation was to her liking, and she freely gave interviews in which she discussed the candidacy of her husband. This trait of hers was the subject of a queerly barbed paragraph in *Life:*

> The report that George Dewey, formerly known as the hero of Manila Bay, will stump the country for Bryan and Stevenson, is said to be a canard. Mrs. Dewey has denied that the report is not true.

Dewey's candidacy was generally characterized as the "climax to a series of unfortunate mistakes." Senator Bacon, of Georgia, said: "While Admiral Dewey was a hero, he was a dangerous presidential possibility, but since he became a human being and indulged his fancies as others have done, he has lost his hold upon the hero-worshippers." [2]

The following passage from *The Review of Reviews* was the effort of an editor who was a courteous gentleman to state the situation as urbanely as possible; to achieve, in the mildest available words, the effect of what, in other quarters and in a later time, would have been described as inviting the newly announced candidate to "take the air":

> When Congress revived for his benefit the rank of admiral of the navy, and he was designated to this great office as a life position, he had received honor and recognition that might

[1] This was the impression current at the time in the press and among the public. Inquiry made in 1925, of persons who had been close to Dewey, resulted in expressions of judgment agreeing with the popular impression.

[2] *Life*, coupling Dewey with another naval hero of the Spanish War, Captain Richmond Pearson Hobson, and with an ephemeral British hero of the Boer War, General Buller, put the instability of popular emotion into four compact lines:

> "These heroes—erst extolling—
> A fickle public drops;
> Folks chase a ball that's rolling,
> And kick it when it stops."

well have been regarded as filling his cup to overflowing. So unbounded was the confidence of the country in his good sense and knowledge of the questions at stake, that a great part of the public opinion of America reserved judgment upon the questions whether or not we were rightly in the Philippines, and whether or not we ought to stay there, until the admiral should speak. . . . The country has not ceased to entertain very loyal and devoted regard for the splendid sailor and commander who served his country so boldly in destroying the Spanish fleet at Manila, and so discreetly in the long and tedious months that followed. But ecstatic hero-worship is not a continuing mood. No American in his lifetime, not even Washington or Lincoln, ever experienced the sensation of being idolatrously worshipped by his fellow citizens with unflagging zest for more than a few days at a time. It is a practical world and there are many things demanding attention. And thus, while we do not mean to neglect our heroes, we cannot make it our business to think of them all the time. Last year the whole country was thinking of Dewey with such ardor that if the presidential election had occurred then, and his name had been before the people, nobody would have cared to run against him, and his election would have been practically unanimous. But enthusiasm has cooled down, and people are thinking more of business and less of glory. They have resumed their more or less sharp differences of political opinion, and are not in the mood for electing a hero regardless of his politics.

"Man overboard." (Minneapolis *Journal.*) Reflecting the feeling of the people toward Dewey's presidential candidacy.

Under the harsh glare of this public disapproval and ridicule, Dewey's political aspirations withered. Not being able to annihilate Spanish fleets every day, he was soon elbowed off the front page by the Boer War and the raging political struggle. In 1901 he became news again for a short time when he presided over the Schley Court of Inquiry; and again in 1903, through some pungent remarks he made, from an American point of view, about the German Kaiser's new fleet. Otherwise, he lapsed into desuetude, not to be resurrected until his death, on January 16, 1917. Even then, the crash of the volley fired over his grave by the Annapolis midshipmen on January 20 was drowned in the thunder of the guns along the Hindenburg Line.[1]

This cartoon, from the St. Paul *Pioneer Press*, was entitled: "Most everybody says this suit looks best on me."

XI

Meantime that arch which had been built by popular subscription at Madison Square, New York; the arch to which the best sculptors of the day had devoted their art; the arch under which the returning hero of Manila Bay had ridden at the head of a parade of soldiers, sailors, and civil dignitaries; that arch which symbolized

[1] On March 27, 1925, Dewey unexpectedly became front-page news again when his widow, then in her eightieth year, had his body removed from the National Cemetery at Arlington to the Mount St. Albans Cathedral, where reposes also the body of Woodrow Wilson.

"Naval Victory," which was designed partly after the Arch of Titus at Rome, and resembled the Arc de Triomphe at Paris in having its piers cut by lateral arches —

As it stood when Dewey marched under it, it was

The Dewey Arch, Fifth Avenue and 23d Street, New York City.

made of lath and wood and plaster painted white. As such, it was intended to be merely the model, to be made permanent later in marble and granite. For that purpose of permanence, a public subscription was under way. But as Dewey subsided in popular favor, the subscriptions lagged. In the course of months, passers up Fifth Avenue noticed its beauty — it really was a thing of glorious beauty[1] — marred by peeling patches

[1] The Chicago *Inter Ocean* of September 2, 1900, said: "All who have seen the monumental arches of the Old World agree that in originality, grace, animation, spontaneity, and symmetry the Dewey Arch is worthy of perpetuity, for it is one of the most splendid creations of imagination and skill the world has seen. . . . The arch itself, in its vivacity, dignity, and fascination would have

of plaster and paint. The dirt of the town stuck to it. It took on a sagging dilapidation. Finally it was adjudged a nuisance which might collapse upon pedestrians. The last sight the public had of it was the city workmen and garbage-collectors carrying it off to the city dump.

XII

All of which was summed up in a sentence from that popular humorist and philosopher, "Mr. Dooley," who, then and for several of the early years of this century, contributed succinct wisdom to the passing show:

> When a grateful raypublic, Mr. Hinnessy, builds an ar'rch to its conquering hero, it should be made of brick, so that we can have something convanyient to hurl after him when he has passed by.

That quotation is from memory. The following is literal. It appears in "Public Gratitude," by Finley Peter Dunne, as printed in "Mr. Dooley's Philosophy":

> Raypublics ar-re not always ongrateful. . . . On'y whin they give ye much gratichood ye want to freeze some iv it, or it won't keep.

XIII

In reading over what has been said about Dewey, the writer is beset by the reflection that must trouble every historian — doubts as to whether just the right selection has been made of episodes and quotations, and an uneasy disinclination to take the responsibility for being

been a perennial object-lesson in beauty and patriotism for the entire country. Alas for the fickleness of human worship! . . ."

The New York *Herald* asked: "Have the echoes of the guns that woke the morning silence in Manila Bay that May day two years ago died away? Has the memory of the gallant feat of arms faded?"

The Literary Digest for December 22, 1900, under the heading "The Passing of the Arch," said: "The final abandonment of the plan for the permanent naval arch in sculptured stone, to perpetuate the temporary but beautiful structure in Madison Square, New York, has called out many expressions of regret. The wooden and staff arch has now been removed, and the cash and pledges, amounting to about $200,000, are to be returned to the donors."

the author or the vehicle of a judgment which, whether the writer wishes it or not, is inherent in any narrative. In the present case, it is desirable to say some things in the nature of corrective.

If the net impression of what has been said so far about the drama of Dewey is that he cut an absurd figure, that is unfortunate. There were two parties to the series of episodes: one was Dewey; the other was the American people.[1] If one of the two must stand in history as being, so far as this series of episodes is concerned, a little absurd, it is the American people. Dewey did not change; the American people did. The Dewey who was jeered in April of 1900 was precisely the same Dewey who was idolized in May of 1898, and up until November of 1899. Change, indeed, was strongly unlikely to happen within Dewey's exceptionally solid personality. He was a sturdy, steadfast, dependable man. It was the American public, or a large portion of it, that went through this cycle of fickleness, and a portion of the American press that stimulated or reflected it.

And so, lest this narrative be overbalanced in recording the change in the public and press attitude toward Dewey, it is desirable to include some expressions from sources that deplored — stronger than deplored — felt disgust with this evidence of a surprising capacity for volatility in the American people. The New York *Times* said:

> For our own sake and for Dewey's sake, it is too bad, not merely because it makes us appear ridiculous in the eyes of foreigners, but because these alternating currents of emotion, this most abrupt substitution of the cold shoulder for the warm heart, argue a want of steadiness in our make-up.

The Chicago *Inter Ocean* said that to forget Dewey's services in making possible a new era in our national life

[1] It was not really quite so simple as that; there was also Mrs. Dewey.

"even overnight, for some petty mistake in his private life, is to shame the name of gratitude and to discredit the intelligence of the American people."

Some indignant persons who felt outraged at the about-face in the public attitude toward Dewey, and especially at the audience of a Washington biograph entertainment that hissed the admiral's photograph, wrote to the papers offering to refund from their private pockets the subscription of any dissatisfied contributor to the Dewey home fund. The Chicago *Tribune* recalled the gifts of palaces worth millions with which England expressed its gratitude to its military heroes, and described the outcry against Dewey in America as "humiliating and belittling." Other papers recalled that "General Grant and General Sherman sold outright houses that had been given them in recognition of their services, and no one thinks the less of them for it."

The most gallant defense of Dewey, the just and manly recalling of the ability and character that attended his services to his country, came from Mr. Hearst's New York *Journal:*

Admiral Dewey may undo the deed to the house presented him by a small portion of his fellow countrymen, but he can never undo the deed of May 1, last year. He asked no favors of his country or of his countrymen. He asked no favors of Montojo. He asked no favors of foreign fleets anchored at Manila. He asked for no demonstration in his honor, and, lastly, he did not ask for a house. But what he does ask at present is to be let alone. He has spent almost all his life at sea, and the least this country can do is to allow him to enjoy his "shore leave" to the end of his days. Suppose a war were to break out to-morrow. Ah! there is where the shoe pinches. It would be, "For God's sake, send Dewey to the front"; "By all means, hurry Dewey after them; let the country rely on Dewey." Wall Street would go down on its marrow-bones and perform rites to him. The persons who regret their miserable contributions would turn to Dewey with prayers. Then do you know what this grizzled old sailor would do? Newly married, and with almost the only domestic happiness he has ever known before him, he would buckle on his sword, hoist the four-starred flag of Farragut, and go to battle for the honor of his country and the welfare of his selfish countrymen.

As for the announcement of his candidacy for President, which brought the final outburst of jeers against Dewey, and marked his end as a national character, it was extraordinary; but its extraordinariness lay in its naïveté, in the simplicity of the direct and honest mind it came from. What it showed more than anything else was that Dewey was not a politician. He lacked understanding of the art that has to do with popular psychology, and therefore did not make the sort of announcement that a politician would have made. Dewey's announcement was a simple statement of a decision he had come to, and of his reflections about it. That caused it to have the quality, usually disturbing in political communications, of unfamiliarity. It was subjected to the not infrequent fate of the unfamiliar, the fate of being laughed at. A cynically succinct person might express all this by saying that poor Dewey was wholly lacking in experience or knowledge of the arts of political "bunk," and, therefore, when he ventured into politics, came to grief.

13

ROOSEVELT BECOMES PRESIDENT

DEWEY'S candidacy for the Democratic nomination having "blown up," Bryan's nomination was inevitable. He got it on July 4, 1900, at Kansas City. The platform made anti-imperialism the major issue, antimonopoly secondary, and free silver very minor. Bryan's address in response to the notification committee was devoted almost exclusively to anti-imperialism.

Bryan received little credit for his anti-imperialist position from the more thoughtful and important leaders of that policy. On the contrary, he was reviled for his line of thought, which had led him to advocate that we should, first, ratify the treaty with Spain in order to achieve a state of peace; and, second, immediately thereafter liberate the peoples we took over. Bryan may not have thought of this policy as compromise — he was not a man of compromise. But the policy, and Bryan's advocacy of it, had the muddying effect of compromise on popular thought, and a numbing effect on senatorial action. The real anti-imperialist leaders of the country believed they would have been able to defeat ratification of the treaty with Spain but for Bryan's persuasion of Democratic senators to adopt his confusing policy. The ablest of the anti-imperialist leaders, the outstanding man among them by far, was Senator George Frisbie Hoar, of Massachusetts, a Republican. Senator Hoar was markedly a man of serene scholarship and gentle urbanity. Probably he was more nearly angry, more nearly moved to irritated speech, than at any other time in his venerable life, when he said:

The war with Spain was over; we had no title to anything in the Philippines but the city of Manila. At that point in came Mr. Bryan and got all that were needed of his followers to force through the Senate a treaty which made lawful our ownership of the whole of the Philippines, and pledged the faith of the country that we should pay for them, and, accord-

Bryan accepts the nomination for President at a public meeting at Indianapolis, August 8, 1900.

ing to many high constitutional authorities, made it the duty of the President to reduce them to submission. That act was itself a declaration of war upon the people of the Philippines, and the strife which had been but an accidental outbreak became war. And for that war Mr. Bryan is more responsible than any other single person since the treaty left the hands of the President. Everything I tried to do was brought to naught by the action of Mr. Bryan.

In the 1900 campaign Bryan was less restrained than in 1896. He had the air of having become a little embittered. On his visit to Salem, his birthplace, in the campaign he told an audience: "They [the Republicans] will buy every vote that can be bought. They will coerce every vote that can be coerced. They will intimidate every laboring man who can be intimidated. They will bribe every election judge who can be bribed. They will corrupt every court that can be corrupted."

The Republican candidates were William McKinley running for re-election as President, and Theodore Roosevelt for Vice-President.[1] Roosevelt did the active campaigning, McKinley repeating his front-porch campaign of four years before. Roosevelt visited 24 States, travelled 21,000 miles, and made nearly 700 speeches. He was no less violent than Bryan. In the stronghold of the free-silver country, at Victor, Col., not far from Cripple Creek, he told an audience of miners: "In my State the men who were put on the committee on platform to draw up an antitrust plank at the Democratic National Convention at Kansas City had their pockets stuffed with ice-trust stock." Whereupon some one in the audience, recalling a scandal of the Republican administration's management of the Spanish-American War, shouted: "What about the rotten beef?"

"I ate it," Roosevelt responded, "and you'll never get near enough to be hit by a bullet or within five miles of it." This passage was followed by a near-riot, in which Roosevelt, on his way to his train, was protected from physical violence by a group of his former Rough Riders.

Bryan lost, by a popular vote of 7,219,530 for McKinley and Roosevelt, to 6,358,061 for Bryan and Stevenson. For the moment the country seemed to follow the imperialist course,[2] and actually elected the party of that policy. The country's action, however, was based not

[1] How Roosevelt was made Vice-President chiefly by his enemies, and how this promotion against his will turned out to be his opportunity, is told in Chapter 4.

[2] See Chapter 3.

wholly on the issue of imperialism, but on others, and even more markedly, on the personalities involved. Bryan lost, not more to McKinley, who was the Republican presidential candidate against him, than to the vice-presidential candidate, Theodore Roosevelt.

From a photograph by Pach Bros.

President McKinley and Vice-President Hobart in front of the latter's home at Norwood Park, New Jersey, in the summer of 1899.

II

Roosevelt, elected Vice-President, ended his term as governor of New York on New Year's Day, 1901, with a conviction that his political career was over. He took a hunting trip to Colorado, returned to Washington in time to be sworn in as Vice-President on March 4, and presided over a brief executive session of the Senate. He did not enjoy the duty nor perform it particularly well. He, like the enemies who had manœuvred him into the position, thought he had been shelved. Roosevelt shared their belief in the tradition, not wholly accurate except in more recent years, that the vice-presidency is normally the grave[1] of political ambition, and prepared to use the leisure attending that office for studying law. He wrote to John Proctor Clarke, then justice of the supreme court of New York:

> Just a line in reference to my studying law. I have been one year in the law school, and at that time was also in my cousin John's office. Now, could I go into an office in New York — say Evarts & Choate — or study in New York or here in Oyster Bay, so as to get admitted to the bar before the end of my term as Vice-President?

With the same intention he asked advice from Alton B. Parker, then chief judge of the court of appeals of New York, and destined to be, three years later, Roosevelt's Democratic opponent for the presidency. Judge Parker advised him to enroll in the Columbia Law School. Roosevelt replied: "As soon as I get back to Washington I shall begin to attend the law school there, and when I have completed my two years' course and feel myself fit I shall apply for the examination."

Before actually entering, he consulted his friend Justice White, later chief justice of the Supreme Court, as to whether it would be any infringement of propriety for him, while Vice-President, to enroll himself as a student in one of the law schools at Washington. Justice White thought this might be dubious, but advised Roosevelt what law-books to read and offered to quiz him every Saturday evening. With the expectation of making this use of his enforced leisure, in preparation for a new career, Roosevelt spent the summer writing, travelling, and speech-making.

[1] Since Martin Van Buren no Vice-President has been elevated later to the presidency, except through the accident of the death of the President. The tradition is to the effect that a Vice-President can only profit by the death of the President, and that all other chances run toward political desuetude. It is true of recent but not of the early years of our history. (See Chapter 4.)

Then, on the evening of September 6, Roosevelt, just finishing an address at Isle la Motte, near Burlington, Vt., received a message that President McKinley had been shot by the anarchist Czolgosz.[1] Roosevelt went at once to Buffalo. The President was still alive and seemed to improve. After two days the physicians gave Roosevelt such assurances that he, like the rest of the country, thought McKinley out of danger. Roosevelt went to join his family in the Adirondacks. On the afternoon of the 13th he with several members of his family climbed Mount Tahawus. As they were resting near the summit a guide came into view on the trail below. "I felt at once," wrote Roosevelt in his "Autobiography," "that he had bad news, and, sure enough, he handed me a telegram saying that the President's condition was much worse and that I must come to Buffalo immediately."

A famous Roosevelt cartoon by Davenport: "He's good enough for me."

Roosevelt was ten miles from the nearest horse. He reached the club-house after dark, procured with some difficulty a horse and wagon, and alone with the driver began the thirty-five-mile drive to the railroad-station. The road was not much more than a wilderness trail. The night was dark and foggy. Wherever they could they

[1] An account of the assassination of McKinley will be found in Chapter 20.

changed horses. It was dawn as Roosevelt stepped on the station platform at North Creek to find his secretary, William Loeb, waiting with a special train. From Loeb he learned that McKinley had died during the night. Late in the afternoon he reached Buffalo. Elihu Root, secretary of war, told him it was advisable that there should be no further delay in taking the oath of office. Roosevelt took the oath, in the house where McKinley was lying dead, on September 14.

That ceremony was the beginning of the Roosevelt era.

14

THE LARGER HISTORY

Matters Other than Political Which, It Is Ventured, May Be More Important. The Relation of Values in Human Affairs, and Therefore in History. The Increase in the Average Man's Tenure on Life. The Contributions to the Average Man's Welfare Made by the Men Who Discovered the Cause of Yellow Fever; by Those Who Perfected the Automobile; by Those Who Invented the Flying-Machine; Others Who Devised and Made Available Vacuum Cleaners, Window-Screens, Bathtubs; Yet Others Who Made Hens More Fruitful, Caused Cows to Give More Milk and Steers to Yield More Beef. And Yet Others Who Contributed to Man's Pleasure and Satisfaction in Literature and Song.

THIS narrative has now covered the beginnings of Roosevelt and Bryan, together with the origins of some of the conditions that gave rise to these leaders and to the political and social movements of the years following 1900. These movements, and the personalities associated with them, compose the substance of most of the formal histories of the time, as indeed such movements and such personalities comprise the substance of most of the conventional histories of all times. For example, Mr. James Ford Rhodes's narrative of "The McKinley and Roosevelt Administrations, 1896 to 1907," is, like the same historian's previous volumes, a standard history of the period it covers, and a most excellent one.[1] Being standard, it conforms to the almost universally accepted

[1] Mr. Rhodes's equipment of scholarship, his painstaking accuracy—all his admirable qualities—are supplemented, for the purposes of a history of this period, by the fact that he was the brother-in-law of Mark Hanna, and had that advantage of intimate access to the inner politics of the time. Moreover, Mr. Rhodes, before he was a historian, was a successful business man, and had that equipment for exceptional understanding of the economic life of the period.

practice, in that it is almost wholly political. The politicians of the time, McKinley, Roosevelt, Bryan, Hanna, Taft, and the others, together with their activities, are treated exhaustively. But the book contains no mention of the perfection of the internal-combustion engine and the other mechanical devices which, resulting in the automobile, had so marked an effect on American life. Neither does it contain any allusion to the invention by which Orville and Wilbur Wright enabled man to ascend into the air and control his movements there. The political aspects of the controversy between the advocates of gold and those of silver are covered with admirably painstaking thoroughness; but there is no mention whatever of the two metallurgists, MacArthur and Forrest, whose discovery of the cyanide process of extracting gold from low-grade ores had, by increasing the world's supply of gold, rather more to do with the outcome of that contest than all the millions of words uttered by Bryan and the other political participants in the controversy.

There is another concept of history. Among formal historians, it is most conspicuously followed by Macaulay, and the conception itself is eloquently expressed in a few sentences from his opening chapter, in which he felt obliged to explain his innovation, in words slightly suggesting the truculence of a man who knows he is going to encounter criticism:

> I should very imperfectly execute the task which I have undertaken if I were merely to treat of battles and sieges, of the rise and fall of administrations, . . . and of debates in Parliament. It will be my endeavour to relate the history of the people as well as the history of the government, to trace the progress of useful and ornamental arts, to describe the rise of religious sects and the changes of literary taste, to portray the manners of successive generations, and not to pass by with neglect even the revolutions which have taken place in dress, furniture, repasts, and public amusements.

Among American historians this conception is best illustrated by John Bach McMaster's "History of the American People." Mr. McMaster's statement of the conception is especially adapted to America, because his history makes more emphatic that aspect of events which Macaulay alluded to as "the progress of useful arts."

From a photograph by Brown Bros.

Orville, Catherine, and Wilbur Wright.

The subject of my narrative is the history of the people of the United States of America. . . . In the course of this narrative much, indeed, must be written of wars . . . of presidents, of congresses, of embassies, of treaties, of the ambition of political leaders in the senate-house, and of . . . parties. Yet the history of the people shall be the chief theme. At every stage of the splendid progress . . . it shall be my purpose to describe the dress, the occupations, the amusements, the literary canons of the times; to note the changes of manners and morals; to trace the growth of [the] humane spirit. . . . Nor shall it be less my aim to recount the manifold improvements which, in a thousand ways, have multiplied the conveniences of life and ministered to the happiness of our race; to describe the rise and progress of that long series of mechanical inventions and discoveries which is now the ad-

> miration of the world, and our just pride and boast; to tell how, under the benign influence of liberty and peace, there sprang up . . . a prosperity unparalleled in the annals of human affairs . . . how the ingenuity of her people became fruitful of wonders far more astonishing than any of which the alchemists had ever dreamed. Such a mingling of social with political history is necessary to a correct understanding. . . . The consequence has been such a moral and social advance as the world has never seen before. . . .

If Mr. McMaster, writing in 1883 of American history up to that year, found it necessary and appropriate to use words of exaltation, we shall have to try to find super-superlative ones to describe the period of the present history, 1900–25. For the advances and achievements which seemed to Mr. McMaster, in 1883, to justify such phrases as "unparalleled" and "wonders" and "admiration of the world" and "the world has never seen before" — those advances and achievements were so far outdone in the period from 1900 to 1925, that the former were to the latter as the bicycle to the automobile; as the mere balloon to the perfected flying-machine; as the tintype to the motion-picture. Far more than in the time and country Macaulay dealt with, and much more than in the period of American history Mr. McMaster covered — to a much more conspicuous degree was 1900 to 1925 in America a period when the history of the people was determined less by politicians than by leaders in other walks of life. The achievements of America from 1900 to 1925 were markedly more important in the fields of science, the invention and perfection of mechanical processes, and the extension of knowledge, than in the field of politics. The more formal historians would probably say that the most important event after 1900 was America's participation in the Great War. That would be a tenable assertion. Any attempt to set up another topic as of competing importance puts a heavy burden of proof on the proponent. Nevertheless, it is a reasonable query whether there is not equal importance in the fact that during this period the average man's tenure of life was

"Aladdin—I wish—I wish I had a—now—I wish I had sump'n to wish for!" Cartoonist Donald McKee in *Judge* for March, 1925, depicts the material enrichments of man during the first quarter of the twentieth century.

increased by about six years. In a history which aims to keep in mind the average man, it may be that the scientists who, by discoveries in the field of the prevention and cure of disease, increased by 12 per cent that average man's tenure of existence on this earth, multiplied his defenses against disease, increased his immunity from untimely death, should appropriately be given as

Cartoonist Kirby, of the New York *World*, pictures the politician resentfully yielding the front page to the scientist.

much mention as the politicians and military leaders who conducted us into and through the Great War.

One concrete illustration, chosen chiefly because of the coincidence in time and place that gives it vivid concreteness: On the Isthmus of Panama during the early years of this period, three things were done: one political — a revolution, and some further transactions having to do with the government of the United States; the second, in the field of engineering, the digging of a canal which reduces by 8000 miles, and by upward of twenty days, the transporting of goods and passengers by water between the Atlantic and Pacific coasts of the United States; the third, in the field of science, the proof that yellow fever[1] is caused by infection from mosquitoes, and the beginning of the wiping of that disease from the face of the earth. This discovery led to others equally important and beneficent through showing the way toward the prevention and cure of other diseases due to animal parasites.

Alexis Carrel, a leader in medical science.

The theory of the present history is that the latter two accomplishments, the engineering and medical[2] ones, are fully as important as the political one; that the individuals concerned are as deserving of emphasis, and that they and their deeds can be made as interesting to the reader.

[1] Actually, it was in the year 1900, in August and September, that Doctor Walter Reed and his associates proved that yellow fever is caused by a mosquito. In February of the following year, Doctor Gorgas began his work of exterminating the disease.

[2] Not only in these larger respects was Doctor Gorgas's work the more important. It was Doctor Gorgas's achievement, more than any one act of governments or engineers, that made possible the digging of the Canal. Disease had defeated past efforts to dig the Canal; it would have defeated future ones.

II

Any painstaking estimate of the interest the public had during this period in men and subjects — either the superficial interest that expressed itself in common discussion, or the fundamental interest that affected the

"Segis Pietertje Prospect," the champion milk producer, owned by the Carnation Stock Farm, Seattle, Wash.

people without their knowing much about it at the time — any such estimate would be compelled to recognize that — or at least to query whether[1] —

Henry Ford, as the manufacturer of inexpensive automobiles, may have had a more deep-reaching effect on the lives of average Americans than Warren G. Harding;

That the person[2] who invented the typewriter, and thereby was largely responsible for introducing women into business offices, for the passing of the dependent "old maid aunt" and the coming of the independent

[1] "No ordinary misfortune, no ordinary misgovernment, will do so much to make a nation wretched, as the constant progress of physical knowledge and the constant effort of every man to better himself will do to make a nation prosperous."—Macaulay, "History of England."

[2] C. Latham Sholes.

"bachelor girl" — that this inventor may have been of more fundamental consequence to a larger number of human beings than Joseph G. Cannon;

That the discovery of the remedy for diabetes may have done more for human happiness than the entire thirty-one years of Henry Cabot Lodge in the Senate;

Lady Jewel, champion egg-layer of the world, owned by H. M. Leathers, Woodland, Wash.

That the acquisition of the Philippine Islands may have been of less real consequence to the average American than the increase in the effectiveness and abundance of fly-paper and window-screens;

That the perfecting of the vacuum cleaner and the electric flat-iron may have meant as much to the average woman as the bringing of woman suffrage;

That the making of bathtubs, modern plumbing, running water, steam heat, and the like, accessible to the average man, may have meant more to that average man than, let us say, all the proceedings of the convention that nominated Alton B. Parker for the presidency;

That the raising of the maximum yield of milk given by one cow from 23,189 pounds per year in 1897 to 37,381 pounds per year in 1920;[1] and the raising of the maximum

[1] Belle Sarcastic is officially credited with having given 23,189 pounds of milk and 721 pounds of butter-fat in 1897. Segis Pietertje Prospect made the record for milk production of 37,381 pounds during the 365 days preceding the 19th of December, 1920. Another cow, Dekol Plus Segis Dixie, made the butter-fat record, her production for the year ending June 27, 1923, having been 1349 pounds. The achievements of these cows are told in the greater detail they deserve in a later volume. So likewise will the equally laudable pre-eminence of certain cattle and hogs and the men who bred them.

yield of eggs laid in a year by one hen from 254, which was the record in 1900, to 335 in 1922[1] — that these achievements may have been of greater consequence to average human beings than, let us say, the invention of the direct primary — regardless for the moment of how the credit should be distributed as between the cow and the hen that made these records, on the one hand, and, on the other, those men of patient art who devoted themselves to the practical science of breeding;

That the man who bred the "cat-ham" out of the early generations of Hereford cattle, and bred the big hindquarters in, may have been a more important person than the politician who put William Jennings Bryan in nomination for the presidency in 1908;

That the popular novels, from "David Harum" and "Eben Holden" in 1900 to "Main Street" and "Alice Adams" in the 1920's were as interesting to as many people and as important in their influence on popular thought as the same number of congressmen;

That the composers of "The Long, Long Trail" and "Over There," by their contribution of human sentiment to the morale of the soldiers, may possibly be entitled to rank with some names more formally associated with the winning of the war;

Whether there were not more Americans who took their political guidance from the philosophy of Mr. Dooley and the cartoons of Homer Davenport, of John McCutcheon, or Jay Darling, than from the more didactic political teachings of Champ Clark;

More who could name the tennis champion of the day than could name the man who ran for Vice-President with Taft in 1912;

More who could tell who were the five leading motion-

[1] "Lady Jewel" was the 1922 champion. She is the property of Mr. H. M. Leathers, of Woodland, Wash.

picture actors of the time than could name the five men who were Speakers of the House from 1900 to 1925;

That more people can name the five leading actors or singers of the day than can name the five American signers of the Versailles Treaty;

That such a poem as "The Man with the Hoe" may have had a larger relation, either as expression or as cause, to the American spirit as it was in 1900, than any speech made by any statesman in the same year.

Also, although there is high authority for the preference expressed in the saying "Let me write the ballads of a nation, and I care not who writes the laws" — nevertheless there are few historians, in the formal sense, who feel called upon to say much concerning the popular songs of the periods they write about.

Finally, I cannot recall any formal history that has recorded many jokes or provided much laughter; yet it is difficult to conceive that there were no jokes and no laughs, no Dooleys or George Ades or Will Rogerses during the periods those histories cover.

All this is merely meant to suggest that a history which aims to reflect the life of the people of the United States from 1900 to 1925, and to reflect that life in something like the actual proportions and relations in which it was lived, may properly go even farther than Doctor McMaster — audacious pioneer that he was — toward including aspects of life other than merely "presidents . . . congresses . . . embassies . . . treaties . . . political leaders . . . and parties."

15

1900: LOOKING BACKWARD AND LOOKING FORWARD

Self-Congratulation About the Past. Prophets Who Saw the Possibilities of the Automobile. Others Who Saw What They Deemed the Impossibility of the Flying-Machine. Some Who Saw Possibilities That Have Not Arrived. The Prophets of Pessimism. Mr. Wells's "Anticipations."

In 1900 and 1901, in the flood of newspaper and periodical literature evoked by the ending of one century and the beginning of another, there was much pointing with pride, much looking back a hundred years to the beginning of the preceding century, to 1800, to find data upon which could be set up a glorified contrast. Most of these contrasts emphasized material achievements.

There were compilations showing the advances in population, area, machinery, industry, invention, finance; reviews of the extension of the western boundary of settlement from the Appalachian Range to the Pacific Ocean, and of the number of States from fifteen to forty-five. There was much recalling of the time when Ohio, Indiana, Illinois, Michigan, and Wisconsin had been largely a wilderness unpeopled except by Indians and a few frontier settlements. There were grandiose recitals of the growth from the time when Philadelphia had been the largest city in America, with 66,000 people; New York second, with 60,000; Baltimore third, with 26,500; Boston fourth, with 25,000; and Charleston, S. C., fifth, with 19,000 — and Chicago had not been at all. There were detailed descriptions of the advances from the time when there had been no railroads, no telegraph, no telephone, no steamboat, no street-car, no electricity, no kerosene, no mower or reaper; when it had taken two days to go from New York to Philadelphia; when cooking-stoves, carpets, window-glass had been luxuries.

Elihu Root said the greatest achievement of the century had been the discovery of the process for making Bessemer steel. Henry George, Jr., declared it had been the commencement of the single-tax movement for the destruction of industrial slavery. Russell Sage, Doctor Cyrus Edson, Chauncey M. Depew, and Professor Langley united in the declaration that the application of electrical power marked the greatest achievement.

Some of those who, in 1900 and 1901, wrote of the changes during the century then closing, included in their reflections aspects of American life other than material. The Reverend Newell Dwight Hillis spoke of the century just passed as "one of the most fascinating chapters in the story of man's upward progress," because "for the first time government, invention, art, industry, and religion have served all the people rather than the patrician classes. . . . Now, fortunately, the millions join in the upward march."

This same note, the elevation of the common man, appeared in most of the discriminating discussions of what had been accomplished. The Indianapolis *Journal* for January 7, 1900, said: "No single feature of nineteenth-century progress has been more remarkable or more significant of advancing civilization than the improvement in the condition of the working classes"; and called attention to the fact that a hundred years before, "slavery existed in the whole of South America, all of the West Indies, and most of North America."

People generally, reviewing the century then just passed, were quite self-congratulatory, even self-laudatory. "Laws," recited Doctor Hillis, "are becoming more just, rulers humane; music is becoming sweeter and books wiser; homes are happier, and the individual heart becoming at once more just and more gentle. . . . For to-day, art, industry, invention, literature, learning, and government — all these are captives marching in Christ's triumphant procession up the hill of fame."

The writers who pointed out these contrasts for the delectation of the reader of 1900 had the air of regarding the country as having done marvellously; and not a little the manner of one who thinks not much else needs to be done.

II

Even more than recounting the marvels of the hundred years just ended, there was an outflow of prediction about the future. The newspapers and periodicals solicited it from persons whose eminence in various lines seemed to qualify them for visualizing the coming years. Inasmuch as it was chiefly persons of fairly luxuriant imagination who would be either inclined or qualified to forecast the future, the results were usually grandiose. Occasionally, however, the invitations to prophesy reached persons whose temperament led them to believe the world had done very well up to date, and that change was inadvisable and therefore improbable. One of these, dealing with transportation and communication, wrote confidently:

> Within the memory of this generation, the earth has been girdled with iron and steel, and the electric telegraph and the cable have practically annihilated terrestrial space; these modes of communication have come to stay, and they are ultimate.[1]

Another of those whose temperaments enabled them to speak with confident definiteness about finality, wrote in

[1] T. J. J. See, *Atlantic Monthly*, January, 1902.

The Literary Digest:[1] "The ordinary 'horseless carriage' is at present a luxury for the wealthy; and altho[2] its price will probably fall in the future, it will never, of course, come into as common use as the bicycle." In this

Life, in June, 1901, looked forward nine years and published this prophetic picture with the caption: "An intruder on the Speedway in 1910."

same field, the future trend of automobile development, an advertisement for the Mobile Company of America, in *The Cosmopolitan Magazine,*[3] declared with axiomatic

[1] October 14, 1899.

[2] This is the way the word was spelled. *The Literary Digest* was one of the very few organs of the English language that had consented to use that language in the manner devised by Andrew Carnegie's project for "simplified spelling."

[3] September, 1902.

confidence that "it may be laid down as a fact that the operation of a gasoline machine requires the employment of an expert of high intelligence and thorough training.[1] . . . The steam machine represents a power that is absolutely understood, and its reliability known beyond all question."[2]

There were even men of pre-eminent and unassailable position in science, whose temperament, or whose preoccupation with exactness, whose distrust of imagination, led them into scepticism about mechanical advances, and caused them to fix limits for the creative genius of man. Simon Newcomb, the astronomer, head of the Nautical Almanac Office of the United States Naval Observatory at Washington, wrote:[3]

> The example of the bird does not prove that man can fly. . . . There are many problems which have fascinated mankind since civilization began, which we have made little or no advance in solving. . . . May not our mechanicians . . . be ultimately forced to admit that aerial flight is one of that great class of problems with which man can never cope, and give up all attempts to grapple with it? . . . Imagine the proud possessor of the aeroplane darting through the air at a speed of several hundred feet per second! It is the speed alone that sustains him. How is he ever going to stop? . . . The construction of an aerial vehicle which could carry even a single man from place to place at pleasure requires the discovery of some new metal or some new force. Even with such a discovery we could not expect one to do more than carry its owner.

A scientist who ventured to be more imaginative than Doctor Newcomb was chided for his rashness. Doctor S. P. Langley, secretary of the Smithsonian Institution at Washington, had conducted some experiments look-

[1] In 1925 gasoline automobiles were driven by more than 17,000,000 people.

[2] In 1925 there was but one important make of American automobile using steam as its motive power.

[3] *The Independent*, October 22, 1903. Just two months later the Wright brothers made their initial flight at Kittyhawk, N. C. See Volume II.

ing toward aviation — they now rank as a milestone in that art — and had said that his experiments convinced him that "the great universal highway overhead is now soon to be opened," and that "airplanes may be

Passing of the horse.
An unusual example of accurate forecasting by a prophetic cartoonist, Homer Davenport. Published in the New York *Journal* in 1899, when hardly any one believed that the horse would really be supplanted.

built . . . to travel at speeds higher than any with which we are familiar."

Whereupon *The Popular Science Monthly* observed:

Doctor Langley seems to claim too much. . . . The secretary of the Smithsonian Institution should be the representative of

American science and should be extremely careful not to do anything that may lend itself to an interpretation that will bring injury on the scientific work of the government or of the country. . . . He could have placed his scientific knowledge at the disposal of army officers and expert mechanicians, and this would have been better than to attempt to become an inventor in a field where success is doubtful and where failure is likely to bring discredit, however undeserved, on scientific work.

The prophecy of limitation was much less in quantity, however, than the prophecy of expansiveness. Within the field of transportation, much of the forecasting dealt with subways for cities, a kind of prophecy that did not call for much boldness, because it was in 1900 that the earliest projects for underground transportation in New York began to take form. The builder of the first, John B. McDonald, wrote that "surface travel will be an oddity [in New York] twenty years from now";[1] and William Baldwin, president of the Long Island Railroad, predicted that "Philadelphia will be a suburb of New York in twenty years."[2] Charles M. Skinner wrote:

. . . much of local travel in the future will be over elevated roads — not in the public streets, where they have no place, but through yards, where they have bought a right of way — and through tunnels. Economy of facilities suggests the tunnel. . . . With good roads, and with trolley-cars to carry one to the shop, the prayer-meeting, the library, the school, the sewing-circle, the village improvement society, country industries will be made easier, touch with the markets more rapid, amusements more generous, and life will be broader, freer, more diverse.[3]

Thomas A. Edison, in an interview in the New York *Times*,[4] was quoted as saying:

Next year I will wager I can take a car of my own design fitted with my motor and battery, and go to Chicago and return in less time, and with more pleasure, than any other machine

[1] New York *World*, May 10, 1903.
[2] New York *World*, May 10, 1903.
[3] *Atlantic Monthly*, June, 1902.
[4] July 31, 1903.

in existence. There will be no breakdown, no explosion of gas or gasoline, and the trip will be made at an even twenty-five miles an hour.

The Providence *Journal* said: "The day is coming when practically every household will have a telephone, just as it has other modern facilities. This may seem a broad statement, but no one can read the figures of the last few years without seeing how general the use of the instrument is getting to be."

A prophecy that included two rather extraordinary details came from an odd figure of the time, John Jacob Astor, one of the three or four richest men in America, who combined with his custody of the largest amount of New York City real estate under one ownership, a really earnest, if occasionally naïve, preoccupation with some forms of art and science. Mr. Astor wrote that "as zoology shows us the amphibian metamorphosed into the land vertebrate, followed by the bird, so history reveals the aborigine's dugout, the Fifth Avenue omnibus, and the ox-cart, followed by the automobile, which is preparing the light and powerful engine that will soon propel the flying-machine. This will be a happy dawn for earth-dwellers, for war will become so destructive that it will probably bring its own end; and the human caterpillar, already mechanically converted into the grasshopper, will become a fairly beautiful butterfly. Street pavements will, of course, be smooth and easily cleaned — asphalt, bituminous macadam, or sheet steel; and keeping horses in large cities will doubtless be prohibited by the Board of Health, as stabling cows, pigs, or sheep is now. Second-story sidewalks, composed largely of translucent glass, leaving all the present street level to vehicles, are already badly needed, . . . and will doubtless have made their appearance in less than twenty years." [1]

[1] New York *World*, May 10, 1903.

There was widely read in America, and rather more sympathetically in America than in his own country, the really remarkable "Anticipations" of Mr. H. G. Wells. He exhorted his countrymen to "strip from their eyes the most blinding of all influences, acquiescence in the familiar." He was zealously interested in the "numerous experimental motors to-day." About these new vehicles the least pretentious of his predictions was that "their exasperating trail of stench will soon be fined away." He asked his sceptical readers to take his word for it that there would soon be "a light, powerful engine, smooth-running, not obnoxious to sensitive nostrils, and altogether suitable for high-road traffic. . . . It will be capable of a day's journey of 300 miles or more." As for the airplane, Mr. Wells believed it would come, but said: "I do not think it at all probable that aeronautics will ever come into play as a serious modification of transport and communication."

Even Mr. Wells, however, balked at the submarine: "I must confess that my imagination, in spite even of spurring, refuses to see any sort of submarine doing anything but suffocate its crew and founder at sea."

Aside from mechanics, within the field of social organization and control, one of the most striking of Mr. Wells's anticipations included an attitude toward persons afflicted with a craving for strong drink, markedly different from the attitude of those residents of the United States, who after the passage of the Eighteenth Amendment in 1918, felt that deprivation of access to the means for intoxication was the denial of a fundamental human right. Mr. Wells foresaw a New Republic, whose people

> will hold, I anticipate, that a certain portion of the population — the small minority, for example, afflicted with indisputably transmissible diseases, with transmissible mental disorders, with such hideous incurable habits of mind as the craving for

intoxication — exists only on sufferance, out of pity and patience, and on the understanding that they do not propagate; and I do not foresee any reason to suppose that they will hesitate to kill when that sufferance is abused. And I imagine also the plea and proof that a grave criminal is also insane will be regarded by them, not as a reason for mercy, but as an added reason for death.

Doctor Albert Shaw predicted in *The Review of Reviews* that "the twentieth century in future ages will be famous for the expanded and altered nature of international relations. It is not improbable that, when the events of the twentieth century fall into their true places in the perspectives of history, the work of the Hague Peace Conference will appear as the crowning achievement of the period and its best legacy to its successor." Andrew Carnegie was even more definite. He was hopeful "that ere the twentieth century closes, the earth will be purged of its foulest shame, the killing by men in battle under the name of war." [1]

There were not wanting the prophets of pessimism. The year 1900 was about the beginning of the importation of various literary missionaries from Russia, one of whom said:

> One fears for the future of mankind. The most ominous sign is not the fact that the cook, servant-girl, and lackey want the same pleasures which not long ago were the monopoly of the rich alone; but the fact that all, all without exception, rich and idle as well as poor and industrious, seek and demand daily amusements, gaiety, excitement, and keen impressions — demand it all as something without which life is impossible, which may not be denied them.[2]

The New York *World* gathered together a kind of symposuistic town meeting of the prophets of evil by inviting them to say what they believed to be the greatest menace of the new century. William Jennings Bryan

[1] *Literary Digest*, January 12, 1901.
[2] Eugene Markov, in the *Novoye Vremya.*

said: "The increasing influence of wealth will lead to increasing disregard of the inalienable rights of man." President Schurman, of Cornell, feared most the "exaltation, worship, and pursuit of money as the foremost good of life." Samuel Gompers was concerned about Oriental competition against American labor. Dean Farrar declared "the chief social danger is the dominance of drink." President Hadley, of Yale, thought it was "legislation based on the self-interest of individuals, or classes, instead of on public sentiment and public spirit." Ellen Terry, the growing artificiality in our social life. The Bishop of Gloucester, "self-advertising vanity." Sir Arthur Conan Doyle said "an ill-balanced, excitable, and sensation-mongering press." Max Beerbohm expressed the same apprehension in two words, "jumpy journals."

One man, the Archbishop of Canterbury, when asked what was the chief danger threatening the coming century, replied: "I have not the slightest idea."

16

SOME CONTRASTS AND CHANGES, 1900 TO 1925

Some Changes That Were Fundamental and Some Others on the Surface of Life. The Latter, Changes in Dress, Fashions, Manners, and the Like, Were Obvious. Others That Went on in the Make-Up of the Nation, and in Matters Most Vital to the People, Were Comparatively Unnoticed. A Change in the Racial Strains Entering into the American Stock. Another, in That Material Thing Which Man Prizes Most. Changes in Style of Hair-cutting, Dress, Dogs.

Of all changes, the most momentous to a country are, obviously, any that take place in the physical composition of the people, in their strains of blood and race. There were such changes in America: first, in a direction different from the past; and then, toward the end of the period, back to the old direction. The changes were slight, in proportion to the population as a whole; but at the time they were arrested they had a rapid momentum.

Always up to 1900 the largest strain by far in the racial composition of the American people had been that from northern and western Europe: from Great Britain, Germany, the Scandinavian countries. But in 1900, and for about twenty years preceding, the additions to the American stock from this strain, by immigration, were falling off. At the same time immigrants from the south and east of Europe, from Latin and Slavic countries, and from Hebrew centres, had begun to come in rapidly increasing numbers.

This tendency toward a change in the fundamental composition of the American stock was arrested by an act of Congress in 1921, followed by another in 1924. By that time the country had become uneasy, partly over the increase in immigration as a whole, and partly over the excessive proportion that was coming from sources different from the earlier sources of the American stock. These acts of Congress reflected a mood of doubt that came to the American people about the desirability of being "the melting-pot." [1] The act of 1924 limited the number of immigrants that could legally be admitted to 164,677[2] (as compared with 1,197,892 who had come during the last year of normal, unrestricted immigration). Within this total the number permitted to come from each country was 2 per cent of the natives of that country already in America in 1890. The aim was to keep the proportions of the different strains in America the same in the future as they had been in the past. This decision, made by the American people and put into effect through Congress, to exercise a deliberate control over the additions to their stock; and to keep those ad-

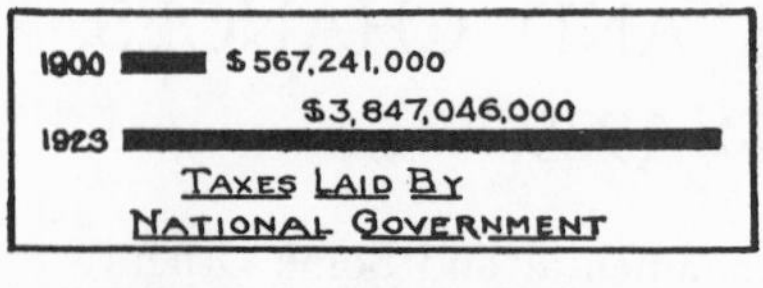

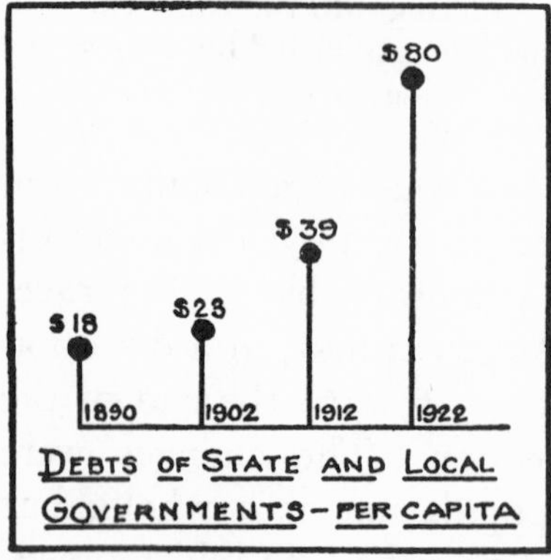

[1] "The melting-pot" was a phrase used by Israel Zangwill to describe America as it was about 1900. At the time, the implications of sentiment and altruism in the phrase rather pleased America.

[2] Plus some exemptions based chiefly on kinship to natives of the various countries who were already in America.

Courtesy of the U. S. Bureau of Public Roads.

Fifth Avenue in New York City as it was in 1900 and as it was in 1924. Examination will reveal one automobile among the horse-drawn vehicles of 1900, and one horse-drawn vehicle among the automobiles of 1924. Nothing in history is comparable to this rapid change in transportation.

ditions in conformity to the proportions already here, to maintain the degree of homogeneity already existing — this decision, because it went to the roots of the composition of the people, may reasonably be called the most far-reaching change that occurred in America during the course of this quarter-century. (The detailed history of the Immigration Restriction Acts of 1921 and 1924, the motives that led to restriction, and the results of the legislation, will appear in Volume IV.)

II

As changes in the composition of the stock are the most important to the nation as a whole; so, to the individual, changes in that material thing which he values most, namely, security of his tenure on life, may be classed as the most important.

In 1901 the average expectation of life in America, as determined for certain registered areas, was $49\frac{24}{100}$ years. In 1920 it was $54\frac{9}{100}$ years. These figures are from the official Bureau of Public Health at Washington. Another authority, Doctor Raymond Pearl of Johns Hopkins University, gives figures that differ slightly:

	1901	1920
Expectation of life, white males.........	48.23 years	54.05 years
Expectation of life, white females.......	51.08 years	56.41 years

In 1900, out of every 100,000 persons living in the then registered[1] area of the United States, 1755 died. In 1921 the death-rate per hundred thousand had been reduced to 1163.9, a decrease of 34 per cent.

The saving in human lives was at the rate of about 6

[1] By "registered" is meant States and districts where accurate vital statistics are recorded. These districts in 1900 represented 40 per cent of the population; in 1925 they covered 85 per cent.

By courtesy of Los Angeles Chamber of Commerce.

Los Angeles. Main Street and Temple Block, 1890 and 1925.

for each 1000 individuals. With a total population of approximately 110,000,000, this means that at the end of a single year, 1924 for example, a total of 660,000 Americans were alive who would have died during the year had the conditions affecting health and longevity

An institution that passed.
The livery-stable and the horse-drawn hearse. . . . This photograph was taken in York, Pennsylvania.

in 1900 remained unchanged. This addition to the security and length of tenure of human life, when worked out mathematically, turns out to be many times greater than the number of lives lost by America in the Great War. There are actuarial complexities in the working out of the figures, and refinements of actuarial point of view. But no method of computation will deny the broad result; namely, that the addition to the quantity of human life brought about during these twenty-five years was many times greater than the quantity of American human life destroyed by the Great War.

The agencies that have enriched man in this respect, that have increased his immunity to disease, the security of his life, his tenure on continued existence, have been, chiefly: advances in understanding of the causes of disease, advances in sanitation and other agencies for the

In 1900 there were not ten miles of concrete road in the United States; in 1925 approximately twenty thousand of them reached into remote mountain passes. This is the Ridge Route between Los Angeles and Bakersfield, Calif.

prevention of disease, the discovery of specific cures or specific preventives for some diseases, advances in surgery, professional nursing, greater watchfulness over water-supply, meat and milk inspection, better housing, better conditions of living and labor. Of all these the greatest single cause has been the discovery of means for safeguarding babies from the intestinal diseases that attack them up to the age of two years. In 1900 the death-rate from this cause was 108.8 per hundred thousand. By 1921 it had decreased to 41.9. The immense decrease of the death-rate from some other causes is shown in tables on these pages.

DEATH-RATES THAT HAVE DECREASED, 1900–22

(Per 100,000 of Population)

Cause	1900	1922
Typhoid and paratyphoid	35.9	7.5
Diphtheria	43.3	14.6
Influenza, pneumonia	181.5	88.3
Tuberculosis	201.9	97.0
Diarrhœa and enteritis (children under two years)	108.8	32.5

DEATH-RATES THAT HAVE INCREASED, 1900–22

(Per 100,000 of Population)

Cause	1900	1922
Cancer	63.0	86.8
Diabetes mellitus	9.7	18.4
Heart diseases	123.1	154.7

A few diseases, instead of declining in deadliness, increased. Some of these are shown in the accompanying tables. The least tolerable of all causes of death, the one which a civilized society ought to be able to control most surely, murder and the other forms of homicide, has increased to exactly four times what it was, from a rate of 2.1 in 1900 to 8.4 in 1922. Suicide has remained about stationary: 11.5 in 1900; 11.9 in 1922. The one appalling increase in the number of deaths, from a cause that is among the least excusable, has been in automobile accidents. The number of deaths from this cause was so small in 1900 as not to be reported. The automobile death-rate per 100,000 of population increased as follows:

1910	1.8
1915	5.9
1918	9.3
1920	10.4
1921	11.5
1922	12.5

In 1923 the number of deaths from automobiles reached the unforgivable total of 22,600.[1] At this rate, automobiles in the United States were killing almost as many Americans in two years as were killed in the Great War; and in three years as many as the number of Union soldiers killed in battle in the Civil War. As civilization

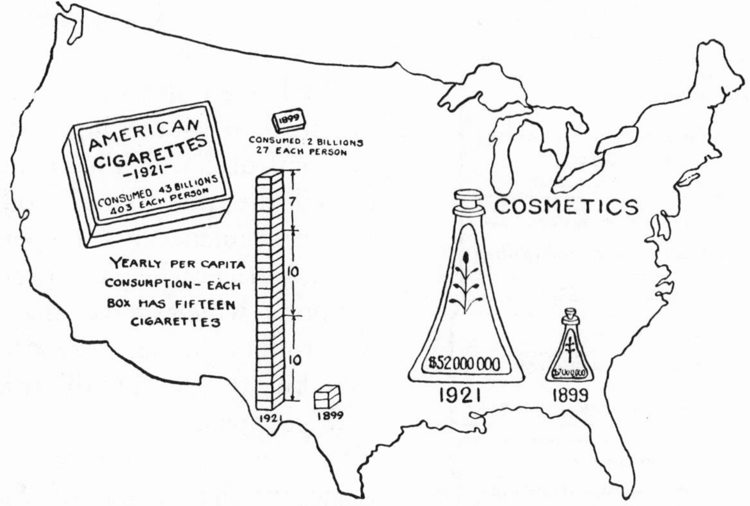

One of the signs of the lavish enrichment of the average American since 1900 was the increase in the consumption of luxuries.

expressed itself in the United States in the year 1925, the tolerance of this was probably its least lovely aspect.

III

One unqualified assertion that can be made about life in America during the period covered by this history is that no other epoch compares with it as respects the average man's access to material goods.

This has been brought about by many new inventions; by the adaptation of inventions and discoveries to com-

[1] Includes all street and highway fatalities.

mon uses; by the wide diffusion of newly invented machines, the extension of access to them to constantly increasing numbers of the people — such comforts, utilities, and luxuries as the automobile, electric heating and cooking devices and washing machines, the radio, aluminum, and scores of others. It has been achieved also by advances in stock-breeding and plant culture, which have increased the quantity of food; by improvements in transportation, refrigeration, and preservation, which have made the products of each section available to the inhabitants of all sections.

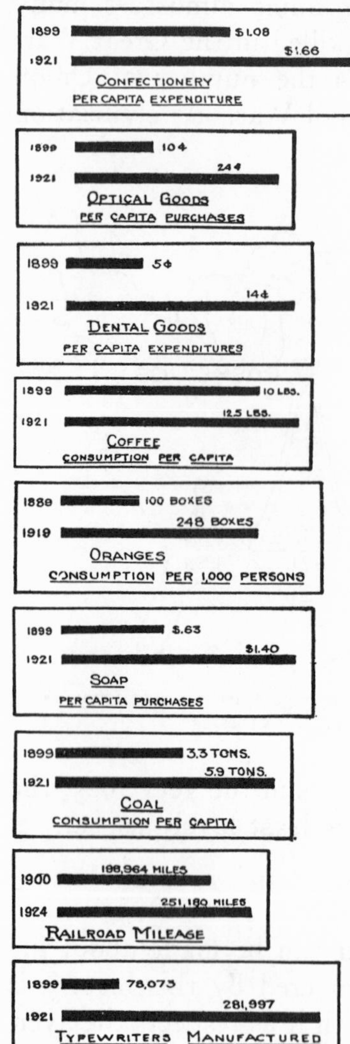

To express the immense increase in the access of the average man to goods, in terms of two familiar objects: The number of automobiles in the country increased from 13,824 in 1900 to about 17,000,000 in 1925, and the number of pairs of silk stockings sold, from 150,864 in 1899 to 217,066,092[1] in 1921. In both cases the percentage of increase is such as to be almost in the field of higher mathematics — in the first case

[1] Not all of these were natural silk. During this period means were perfected for making attractive "artificial silk," so called.

about 122,800 per cent; in the second about 98,550 per cent.

These are extreme examples, but it is hardly possible to exaggerate the speed and abundance in which goods that the average man wanted were made accessible to him. In 1900, the radio was not, nor for nearly twenty

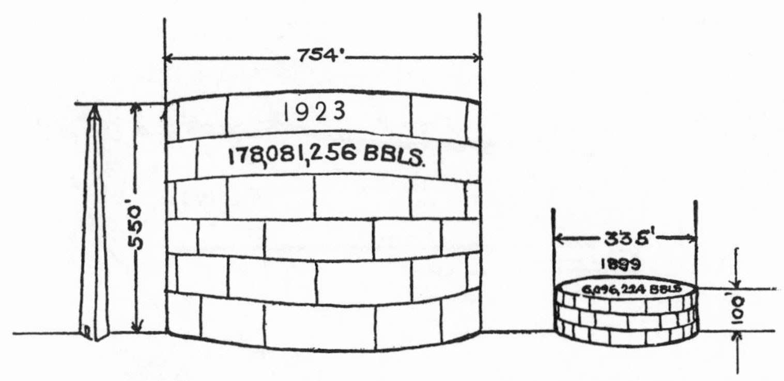

Gasoline.
A pictorial represe..tation of the quantity of gasoline produced in 1923 as compared with that of 1899.

years afterward. On January 1, 1920, it was estimated there were 5000 receiving sets in the United States, chiefly in the hands of persons having a technical interest in the new device. By January 1, 1924, approximately 2,500,000 sets had reached the public.[1]

It was as respects newly invented goods, of course, that the diffusion was most rapid, and the comparisons most striking. But the process was working as respects standard goods, ordinary necessities of life, everything. One measure is the quantity of goods carried on the railroads.

[1] Another set of figures showing the rapid diffusion of the radio is in the estimated sales during a period of five years:

1920	$2,000,000
1921	5,000,000
1922	60,000,000
1923	120,000,000
1924	325,000,000

In 1900 it was 1,101,680,238 tons; in 1922 it was 1,974,-618,324 tons.

Increases in goods for consumption, in the pleasure of communication or contact between relatives and friends

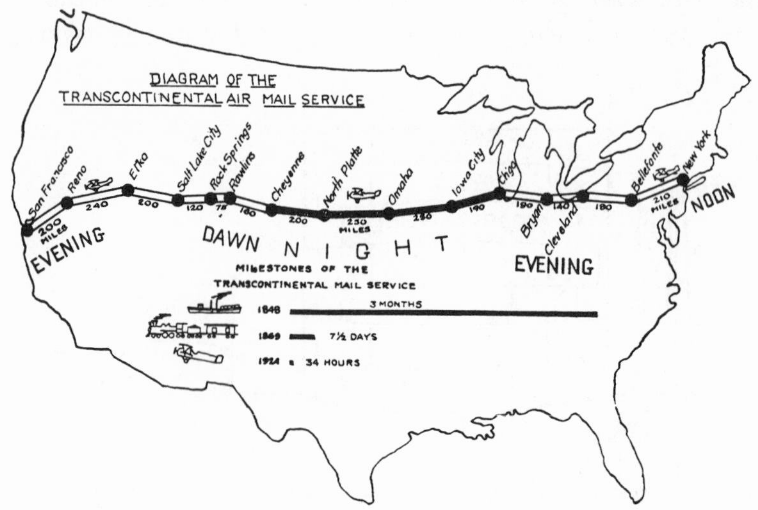

In 1924 mail was carried by airplanes from coast to coast in 34 hours.

and in entertainment, are measured by some comparative figures in the field of communication: In 1900 the number of postage-stamps used by the American people was 3,998,544,564; in 1922 it was 14,261,948,813. On July 1, 1900, the number of persons served by rural free delivery was 185,000; in 1924 it was 6,500,000. The total receipts of the post-offices of the United States increased from $102,354,579 in 1900 to $532,827,925 in 1923.

In 1900 the number of telegrams sent in the United States was 79,696,227; in 1917, 155,263,206. In 1900 the number of miles of wire in use was 1,159,618, and in 1917, 1,888,793. In 1900 the number of separate rides taken on American railroads was 576,865,230. By 1920 it had more than doubled, and was 1,269,912,881. This in spite of the growth in other methods of passenger transportation. In 1900 fast mail was carried from New York to San Francisco in 102 hours, by train. In 1924 on a test in about 27 hours, by airplane.

Some of these, and some other contrasts and changes

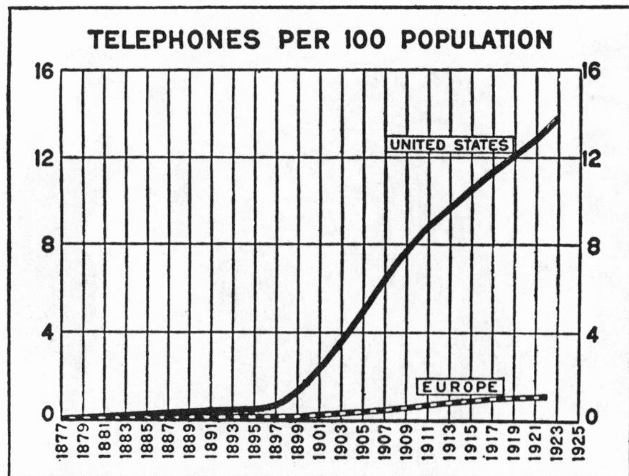

From "The Magazine of Wall Street."

Graph showing the phenomenal growth in the use of the telephone in the United States, as compared with Europe between 1900 and 1925. In the latter year, approximately two-thirds of all the world's telephones were in use within the borders of the United States.

are shown in diagrams and other graphic and pictorial efforts accompanying these pages.

IV

Of changes on the outward surface of American life, one of the most marked was in women's dress and adornment. Just before 1900, in the decade of the nineties, the vogue of the bicycle had begun a revolutionary innovation, which, after 1900, was carried further by a greater participation in athletics by women in colleges, by increased employment of women in business, and by certain curious consequences of the war.

The judgment of the authorities on this subject who

have been consulted by the writer agrees with common recollection, that the bicycle started the revolution. In the late eighties and early nineties, when the high wheel was supplanted by the "safety," women began timorously to ride. Previous to that, almost the only sport

1900 1925

Evolution in bathing costumes.
The illustration on the left is from *Vogue*, June 21, 1900.

freely permitted to women by old-fashioned convention had been croquet. Women had ridden horseback, but only on sedate side-saddles and in a costume, the "riding-habit," in which the amount of covering and cloth was even greater than in the long trains of ordinary dress.

Manufacturers began to make a safety bicycle adapted to women by nets to protect skirts from becoming tangled in the whirling wire spokes. Gradually and daringly a few women began to wear shorter skirts, weighting the hems down with little strips of lead.

The next insurgency against the stiff-laced conventionality of the Victorian period was lawn-tennis, accompanied by modification of stays and corsets. That met with

Upper row, from left to right, the illustrations are from *Vogue*, February 8, 1900; *Pictorial Review*, September, 1925; *Vogue*, January 11, 1900; *Scribner's Magazine*, September, 1925. *Lower row, left*, sport clothes, *Vogue*, for February 22, 1900, recommended this skirt: "There is nothing so sensible, comfortable, and clean. . . . The skirt just escapes the ground, or perhaps a little more." *Right*, from *Good Housekeeping*, August, 1925.

outraged criticism. "Ministers exhorted their congregations to eschew the ungraceful, unwomanly, and unrefined game which offended against all the canons of womanly dignity and delicacy." But sports for women began to be adopted in women's colleges, then beginning to expand. For various sports, including basket-ball, the more daring began to appear in bloomers, which were in reality trousers cut full and gathered at the knee to resemble a skirt. These garments were ridiculed in the press and denounced by the pulpit, and suffered once more the same reviling as had the bloomer[1] of 1851.

It took years for the changes in dress to pass from specialized costumes for sport into ordinary wear. A timorous start toward skirts ending at the ankles for street wear in bad weather was ridiculed, where not more gravely condemned, in the term, applied to dress and to wearers, "rainy-daisies."[2]

In 1900 the standards of style in appearance and dress ran to "smallness," and called for high, tight-laced corsets, tight kid gloves, and shoes usually a size or more too small. The standard of beauty in waists called for one that could be "easily clasped with two hands." Some

[1] Named for Mrs. Amelia Jenks Bloomer, an American dress-reformer and woman's rights advocate, who, having failed to win over the American women to her costume, went to England, where she was also unsuccessful. The garment consisted of a dress reaching to the knees, below which trousers cut full and gathered at the ankle were worn. Its adoption was advocated on the ground of "comfort, health, and unimpeded locomotion." Lectures were given in London and Dublin on and in the bloomer costume. Audiences did not take Mrs. Bloomer or her garment seriously, and the press jeered.

Another American woman, Doctor Mary Walker, who had been a nurse in the Civil War, where she had worn men's clothes for convenience and protection, insisted on continuing to wear the comfortable garments. Her attire caused a great deal of comment in the press, and she was arrested several times. It required a special act of Congress to grant her an exemption from the laws against women wearing men's clothing; and she continued to go her own way until her death, February 22, 1919

[2] In *Puck* for July 17, 1901, this witticism appeared:

"Aunt Priscilla, what is a centipede?

"It's a bug, with nearly as many feet as I thought I had the first time I wore a rainy-day skirt."

From the *Ladies' Home Journal*, September, 1925.
With this change disappeared hat-pins, hair-pins, hair-combs, false hair, and most of the natural hair.

women reduced their waists from a normal measurement of twenty to twenty-four inches, to eighteen or twenty. This was opposed by reformers and physicians, but they did not make much headway until years later. Kathleen Norris has described the conventionally dressed woman of 1900:

> She wore a wide-brimmed hat that caught the breezes, a high choking collar of satin or linen, and a flaring gored skirt that swept the street on all sides. Her full-sleeved shirt-waist had cuffs that were eternally getting dirty, her stock was always crushed and rumpled at the end of the day, and her skirt was a bitter trial. Its heavy "brush binding" had to be replaced every few weeks, for constant contact with the pavement reduced it to dirty fringe in no time at all. In wet weather the full skirt got soaked and icy. Even in fair weather its wearer had to bunch it in great folds and devote one hand to nothing else but the carrying of it.

A description of the dress of women in offices in 1900 is reflected by the following passage about suggestions for Christmas gifts in *The Ladies' Home Journal* for December, 1899: "If tempted to give a gown for office wear, let it be one of black, brown, or gray cravenetted serge. Of the three colors, black is to be preferred, on account of the unwritten law governing the style of dress adopted by the majority of self-supporting women. . . . To the self-supporting girl, the material for a frock of cloth or serge of an inconspicuous color would prove a useful gift, as would a tailored suit of cloth costing about fifteen dollars. A more dressy suit for church, concerts, etc., would also be appreciated."

By 1925 the "Sunday best" had passed away; woman tried to look her best at all times. Women in offices were as well dressed as women of leisure, and the Queen of Sheba was the model of both; while as regards cost, the economy of materials was in indirect proportion to the outlay of money. "Give feminine fashions time enough and they will starve all the moths to death," said the Detroit *Free Press* in June, 1925. There was much of that kind of satire in 1925. One widely quoted from "At 'Em, Arizona," ran: "The old sailor remarked that

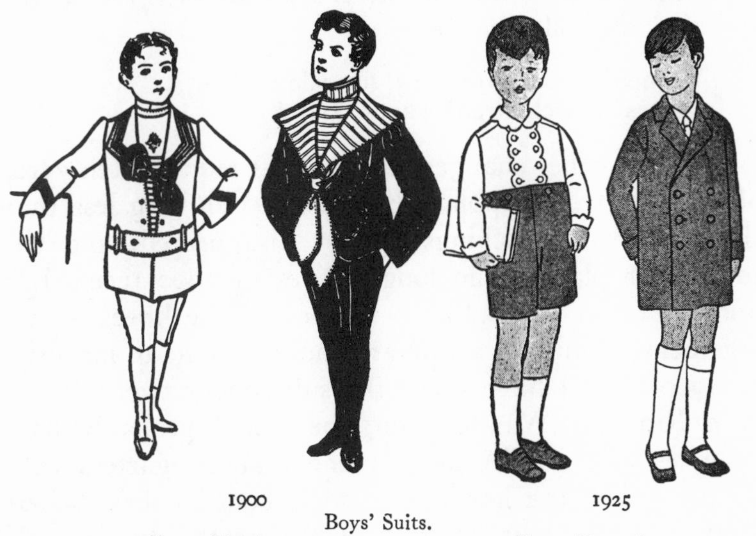

1900 1925
Boys' Suits.
Vogue, March 22, 1900. *Vogue*, December, 1925.

he supposed the girls wore their dresses at half-mast as a mark of respect to departed modesty."

The figure of fifteen dollars given as the cost of a woman's tailored suit, startling to read in the year 1925, is borne out by another passage in *The Ladies' Home Journal* for March, 1902, which lists a complete trousseau for a bride at a cost of seventy-five dollars. In the Chicago *Tribune* for January 1, 1900, an advertisement of Siegel, Cooper & Company included:

American Lady corsets....................	79c.
Ladies' muslin nightgowns, worth 39c......	19c.
Ladies' extra fine quality gowns...........	69c.
Ladies' good muslin corset-covers, trimmed in lace or embroidery..................	10c.
Black taffeta silk.........................	75c. yd.

> 50-inch all-wool, sponged and shrunk French cheviots, water and dust proof serges, all high-class fabrics, warranted for color and wear.................................. 79c.

In the same paper the advertisement of "The Fair included the following items:

> Women's shoes, worth $3, for sale at $1.97
> Misses' and children's shoes, $1.19

With the other changes, dresses that required ten yards of material were supplanted by some requiring less than three. Cotton stockings almost disappeared, and silk took their place. The long sleeves of 1900 receded to none at all in 1925. Skirts receded to the knees, stockings below them. If a woman who had come to maturity in 1900 should have spent the subsequent twenty years in a Rip Van Winkle sleep, she would probably have been less startled by an airplane than by garters worn visibly below the knee. The high boned collar passed. With it went tight-lacing, and almost the corset itself. In evening wear there was a change reflected in a Mutt and Jeff joke: Mutt had gone to a party and Jeff asked him what the ladies had on. Mutt replied: "I don't know; I didn't look under the table." Another newspaper picture of the change was compressed into four lines of verse in the Washington *Star* for July 4, 1925:

> I haven't anything to wear
> Friend Wife of yore would oft declare.
> And, as she dons her modern dress,
> Her argument is proved, I guess.

While many of the innovations in woman's appearance began with the bicycle and other sports as early as 1900, none made really rapid headway, and some did not start at all until after 1914. As late as May, 1909, *The Ladies' Home Journal* said:

A man has always been told that a woman's hair is her crowning glory. And he has believed it. In the eyes of many a man a woman's hair and the contour of her head have typified feminine beauty. But recently he has been puzzled to see the hair of his womankind increase amazingly in quantity until he has wondered why feminine hair should so suddenly have acquired the habit of growth. It has confused him. But simultaneously, with his wonderment he heard whisperings of "rats" and "puffs."

From a photograph by Paul Thompson.

Alice, daughter of Theodore Roosevelt, shortly after her marriage, in 1906, to Nicholas Longworth, later, in 1925, Speaker of the House of Representatives. The dress, typical of the early 1900's, presented difficulties in connection with the roads and the mode of conveyance of that period.

The World War brought a need and a demand for women at the front as nurses, stretcher-bearers, ambulance-drivers, workers in ammunition plants, factory-hands—occupations always before filled by men, and regarded as impossible for women. Women at the front discovered that under the limitations of time and otherwise, work and care for appearance, as well as defense against vermin, would be facilitated by short hair. Women in ammunition factories found that powder got into their hair and was dangerous.[1] The changes in dress and cus-

[1] About the same time a much emulated stage dancer, Mrs. Irene Castle, had a fever, which necessitated her hair being clipped. Her subsequent appearance on the stage stimulated the vogue in circles where considerations of utility would hardly have reached.

toms brought about by these and other conditions became one of the controverted subjects of the day; they were the occasion of sermons and furnished material for the comic sheet. The war-time newspapers carried photo-

A cartoon by Berryman, in the Washington, D. C., *Star*, for August 31, 1924.

graphs of women wearing overalls, knickers, and with hair bobbed. Other women, learning of the comfort and time-saving qualities of short hair, soon took up the practice. Finally it became a fad. At the end of the war it showed some signs of dying out, but was revived by moving-picture actresses. By the beginning of 1924, bobbed hair was practically universal. Nearly all the new spring hats were so small that only bobbed heads could get into them. Many women were forced to join the vogue. It was almost impossible to find a hat large enough for a woman with long hair. New and attractive styles of bobbing were invented. Flappers, middle-aged women, even gray-haired grandmothers, invaded man's last retreat, the barber-shop; men complained that

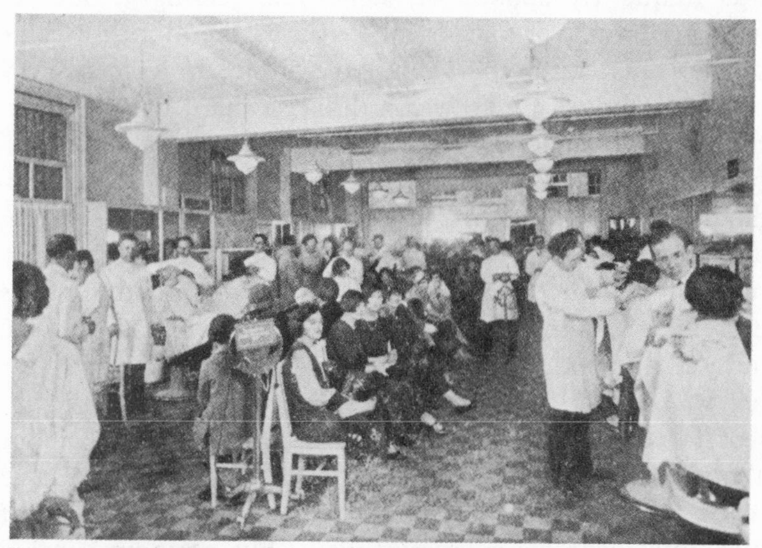

By courtesy of Franklin Simon.

Even the barber shops have changed. What prophet of 1900 would have dared predict that woman would elbow man from the barber's chair?

instead of finding *The Sporting Times* and *The Police Gazette* to pass the time while waiting for the call of "next," they were more likely to pick up *Vogue* or *The Ladies' Home Journal.* An ingenious barber in California put out a sign: "BARBER-SHOP FOR MEN ONLY."

V

Many changes that came in woman's world were associated with Edward Bok. For certain elevations in the taste of houses and house-furnishings he is more to be thanked than any other one man. Bok was editor of *The Ladies' Home Journal* from 1889 to 1919; from a circulation of 440,000 copies when he took hold of it to 2,000,000 when he retired. During most of that time, especially the early part of it, *The Ladies' Home Journal* was frequently spoken of, sometimes jeeringly, but yet with a measure of allegorical truth, as the monthly Bible of the American home. Bok gave advice to women, very positive advice, for he was a didactic man, with some of the crusader and much of the school-teacher in his temperament. Some of his counsel was in areas of extraordinary intimacy, affairs of the heart, proper decorum, and the like, such that the spectacle of this especially masculine man offering guidance to women in matters extremely feminine gave rise to astonishment, and to humor when the astonishment was not too great for levity. He and his periodical came to be a favorite subject for the newspaper comedians. In the period about 1900 there were as many Bok jokes as there came later to be Ford jokes. Bok smiled with those that smiled at him, and went his successful way. His periodical was a curious union of the highest literary quality with something that was a little more Laura-Jean-Libbey than Laura herself. He was the first to print some of the most important work of the best writers of the time, such as Kipling's "The Female of the Species." At the same time he carried such departments as "Side-Talks with Girls," and gave a heart-to-heart flavor to the whole periodical. The outstanding characteristic of his editing was intimate and personal service; he employed physicians and nurses of the highest standing, experts on cooking, and authorities in other lines,[1] for duties of which

[1] The employment by newspapers of physicians to write on health, and of others to conduct departments of "beauty hints" and the like, was in imitation of Bok.

their printed contributions were only a fraction; their chief function was to answer letters which the subscribers were solicited to send. Through the aggregate of all this, the best standards of cooking, nursing, and household management, as well as higher standards of taste in

This guide to "The right and wrong ways of holding skirts" was printed in the New York *Pictorial* as late as December 27, 1908.

houses, furniture, and decoration, were carried into homes throughout the length and breadth of the land.

Bok rendered an immense service to American women and American homes, though in some respects his leadership was rejected. He was conservative, and never took up the feminist movement, which became important on the intellectual side of the life of women. As to women's dress, also, he was unsuccessful. Some kind of tide, deeper than he knew, was running against him. His preaching about clothes was chiefly in the direction of austerity of appearance, and of the completeness of covering which, in the early 1900's, was supposed to be either a cause or an outward evidence of inner rectitude. His teaching about dress was in the opposite direction from the lip-sticks, the bobbed hair, the short stockings, and the other brevities that arose in spite of him. Once his crusading spirit led him to try really to revolutionize American dress. He started a formidable movement to get away from Paris as the source of styles and models, and to substitute New York and American designs, harking back to American themes, such as Indian costumes. He began his campaign with the slogan "American Fashions for American Women." He had three designers visit the Metropolitan Museum for new and artistic ideas. They worked for months; the designs were passed on by a board of New York women whose judgment in clothes was good, after which pages of them were published. The attempted innovation was widely advertised, and conventions of dressmakers were called to discuss American-made fashions. But in spite of all the formidable energy, the idea did not "take." Commercial forces and feminine nature were too much for Bok.

An effort he made to persuade women to cease, on grounds of humanity, from wearing aigrettes, was equally unsuccessful. He published photographs of the killing of the mother bird, and the starving young ones, convinced that they would make an appeal to the mother instinct in every woman, who would not seek personal adornment at such a cruel cost. After campaigning in four monthly issues of his periodical, he discovered that the sales of aigrettes, instead of diminishing, had more than quadrupled. His campaign had advertised the aigrette to thousands who had never before worn them, women who looked upon the aigrette as the badge of fashion. With characteristic zeal and tenacity, Bok turned to the legislatures, and succeeded in preventing, by the passage of laws, what he had been unable to prevent through reliance on the theory that the average woman, tender in the actual sight of cruelty, could be relied on to sacrifice ornament at the expense of suffering on the part of an impersonal bird some hundreds of miles away.

In many aspects of the life of women, Bok worked a revolution in the direction of simplicity and utility. His editorial genius lay largely in his realization of the superiority of the concrete and the visual, to mere abstractions. He knew that a picture can tell more than a page of text. Once he said that the way to lead women to appreciation of beauty was not to print an essay by Ruskin but to tell them how many packages of flower-seeds you can buy for fifteen cents, and print a diagram of how to plant them. He conducted competitions that brought in thousands of photographs of gardens in bloom, and printed many pages of them. By this, and a department entitled "Floral Hints and Helps," he stimulated the beautifying of lawns. In a department entitled "Beautiful America" he showed contrasting photographs of localities "before and after" the removal of offensive advertising signs and billboards. Another department, "How Much Can Be Done with Little," showed photographs of back yards before and after they were improved by planting vines, flowers, trees. He carried on campaigns against patent medicines, and printed photographs and plans showing how to get rid of mosquitoes. By these and similar methods in other fields he promoted simplicity and the other attributes of better taste. He used to print photographs side by side, labelling one "This chair is ugly," and the other "This chair is beautiful." Month after month he carried these comparisons through tables, beds, draperies, table decorations.

Bok had a large part in transforming the American house from the rather stark and box-like thing that was not uncommon in the nineties; and American interiors from standards of furniture and decoration which, so far as there were standards at all in the earlier period, were overbalanced on the side of tawdry ornateness. The American parlor of 1900 was furnished, usually, with "three-piece" sets, upholstered in red or green plush, gaudy successor to the horsehair, then just beginning to be looked on with disapproval. On the walls of typical American homes were large framed pictures in colors, landscapes, groups of idyllic children. For the bedroom and dining-room suites, golden oak was in vogue. On the floor was an ingrain carpet, with huge, highly colored floral designs, underlaid with padding and tacked down. In the banishing of these, Bok may have been helped by the fact that during and after the Spanish War, many thousands of American soldiers, tourists, business men, and school-teachers, visiting our newly acquired overseas dependencies, had the opportunity to be impressed with the æsthetic and hygienic qualities of bare floors.

By 1925 the once common box-like or L-shaped house had given way to a new and distinctly American type built on simpler and lovelier lines. Cupolas, balconies, fancy windows were discarded. Iron deer, dogs, and cupids ceased to adorn the lawns. Untidy back yards and old sheds gave way to sod lawns, walks of cement, and brick or metal garages. (Bok caused a good deal of commotion by printing a series of photographs of the more squalid parts of American cities in the spirit of a search to determine pre-eminence in municipal ugliness.) Interiors likewise became simpler and more attractive. Pantries gave way to built-in cupboards. Kitchens became more compact, were arranged to save labor and steps for the housewife. Kitchen sinks, which at first were made low, because they were the successor of wash-tubs into which the water had to be lifted and poured by hand, came to be built high when architects and contractors were compelled to realize that with water carried by pipes the need was to save back-bending. Cheerful colors were introduced on kitchen walls; linoleum in attractive designs on the floor. Part of the front porch was changed into a sun-room, heated in winter, screened in summer. The hat-rack gave way to the built-in closet. Other built-in features included buffets, bookcases, and beds. People began to buy and manufacturers to supply "period" furniture: styles of Adam, Louis XV, and Queen Anne periods. Colonial designs became popular. The old wooden folding-beds, which by day acted as desks and bookcases, disappeared. The brass bed arrived, and later the imitation-wood bed of steel.

VI

An interesting and accurate index to changes in clothes, ornaments, furnishings, tools, and ways of American life is supplied by the business records of the great mail-order houses. They had existed before 1900, but their great growth was made possible chiefly by two innovations, of which one, rural free delivery, came in 1896, and the other, the parcel-post, in 1913. These mail-order houses supplied customers in literally every hamlet and on almost every farm in America with a greater variety and volume of things in common use than any other merchants in the world. They sold by mail everything from a paper of pins to a nine-room house. They received as many as 200,000 letters a day, and sold upward of 100,000 different kinds of articles, including food, clothing, implements for farming, decorations for houses, tools for barns — even the houses and barns themselves. Their successive yearly catalogues from 1900 to 1925 constitute a social history of America. Through the helpfulness of the head of one of them, Mr. Julius Rosenwald, and his associates of Sears, Roebuck & Company, the writer was, in 1925, supplied with data about changes in popular taste and ways of life as revealed by the records of that company's contacts with upward of 6,000,000 customers, who, with their families, included over a quarter of the population of the country. How curiously close a touch the mail-order houses had with American

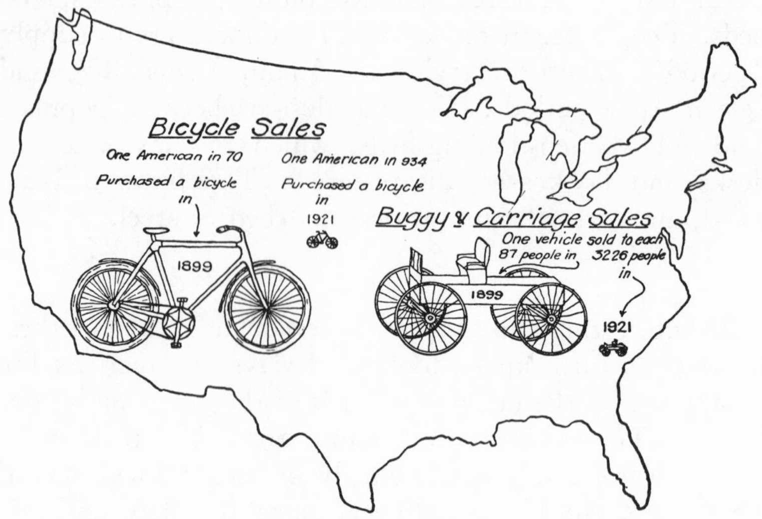

The eclipse of the bicycle and buggy.

life is illustrated by their ability to prophesy that almost twice as many babies would be born in 1920 as in 1919, their forecast being based on their sales of maternity corsets — an index that public statistics could not have supplied.

In the Sears, Roebuck catalogue of 1900 there was no mention of automobiles or automobile accessories. By 1925 this was one of the largest departments. The 1900 catalogue carried sixty-seven pages devoted to buggies, harness, saddles, and horse-blankets; the catalogue of 1925 had a scant eight. Stoves that the housewife used to take a pride in polishing with her own hands gave way to enamel surfaces. Wood-burning stoves and base-burners fed with hard coal gave way to a system of hot-air tubes from a furnace in the cellar, and these in turn to pipes carrying hot water or steam to radiators. The bathroom came to be an adjunct that every house could have,

Old and new types of factory buildings.
The first plant and the 1925 plant of the Victor Talking Machine Company.

and the daily bath a common institution.[1] The old-fashioned "rock-a-bye" cradle, theme of song and poem, was replaced by a crib with rubber-tired wheels, enclosed sides and top, with wire screens to protect the tiny occupant from flies and mosquitoes. By 1925 cradles were eagerly sought as antiques. New and indestructible toys made their appearance: gyroscope tops, educational toys. Teddy bears, "coon jiggers," Charlie Chaplin toys,

[1] It was about 1900 that a joke became current which recorded a small-town visitor to a city hotel writing home to his family: "The bathroom here is so nice I can hardly wait for Saturday night."

character dolls, able to say "Ma-ma," and made to withstand rough handling, replaced the dolls with china heads, which were often broken between Christmas and New Year's.

Pages of the mail-order catalogues record the early existence and later passing of a fad for a man to wear the emblem of his trade; the blacksmith hung a gold anvil or horseshoe from his watch-chain; the bartender a jewelled beer-keg; the sailor a miniature anchor or compass; the railroad engineer a small locomotive; the conductor a caboose. Gold-headed canes and umbrellas were a mark of solid affluence. Heavy, thick, gold watches — "turnips" they were sometimes called — were an indication of prosperity in the individual, and the common choice for a testimonial of esteem when a group of men wanted to honor one of their fellows.

The changes in men's clothing, though not as marked as in women's, were in the same direction, toward lighter weight and greater attention to appearance. In 1900 durability, wearableness, was the prized quality; by 1925 it was style and comfort. The 1900 man when "dressed up" wore a derby hat,[1] a woollen suit of dark color, the coat with padded shoulders, collar and cuffs stiffly laundered, and the shirt held together at the bosom with studs; toothpick shoes, fleece-lined underwear,[2] and heavy socks. Only the "dude" wore garters to hold his socks in place. There was no differentiation between summer suits and winter ones: the "second-best" did service on

[1] In 1900 Sears, Roebuck & Company did a large business in derby hats; in 1915 derbies disappeared from their catalogues; 98 per cent of the hats they sold in 1925 were of soft felt. The sale of caps increased in proportion to the spread of the automobile. Reports from hat manufacturers indicate that of all men's hats sold in 1900, 85 per cent were of felt and 15 per cent of straw; in 1925 the proportions were exactly reversed.

[2] In 1900 85 per cent of men's underwear consisted of shirts and drawers; in 1925, 85 per cent was union suits. Shirts that opened like coats were practically unknown in 1900; in 1925 they were the only kind made.

week-days the year round, and the Sunday suit was resurrected once a week, good weather or bad. Between 1900 and 1925 man adventured into grays, light shades of brown, powder blues; wore soft felt hats, soft collars

By courtesy of U. S. Signal Corps.

Left, An American soldier in the war with Spain. The uniform was poorly adapted to tropical wear. The blue woollen shirts, being dark, attracted mosquitoes, and being of wool multiplied the discomforts of campaigning in tropical swamps. The trousers were full-length, and when worn with leggings made the wearer appear uncouth.

Right, Uniform and equipment of American soldier during the Great War.

and cuffs, and socks of silk or lisle or other light-weight material. Plain dark-blue serge, which provided 50 per cent of men's wear in 1900, gave way to weaves and colors less simple. Substantial overcoats of heavy broadcloth, Merton, or Kersey, designed to last for years, were supplanted by lighter and flimsier materials designed to conform to rapidly changing styles, and to the expectation of not more than one season's use. There was a steady tendency to inconspicuousness in scarf-pins, cuff-links, and watch-chains.

Changes occurred in the types of literature ordered from mail-order houses. In 1900 the "best sellers" of the mail-order houses had to do with fortune-telling, palm-reading, dream-books,[1] after-dinner toasts. By 1925 books of this type had practically disappeared from stock. Bibles were steady sellers throughout the entire period, a marked increase taking place after the war.

Musical instruments changed. In 1900 the Sears-Roebuck catalogue displayed two full pages of mouth-organs, an instrument capable of giving forth inspiring melody when puffed by an expert, but in 1925 there were few mouth-organ virtuosos. With the mouth-organ into obscurity went the jew's-harp, an inexpensive mechanism whose simple note was drowned out by the saxophone that was popular in the 1920's. Something more happened in popular music than the crowding out of the mouth-organ and jew's-harp by the saxophone and the ukulele. The coming of "canned" music, the victrola, the phonograph and its variations was the true blight of the older and simpler instruments. Mechanical music brought versions of the clas-

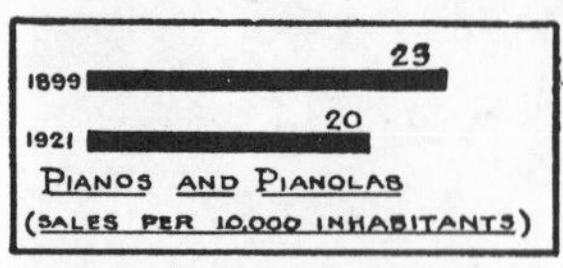

Piano and pianola production did not increase. They were overwhelmed first by the phonograph and then by the radio.

[1] The relative disappearance of such books reflected, fundamentally, a wider diffusion of knowledge of the laws of nature, of the acceptance of logic and the true relations of cause and effect. It is true that in 1925 dreams were looked upon as having significance by a type of person very different from those who in 1900 looked upon them as "signs." In 1925 there was a genuine effort to find significance in dreams, but this effort attempted to be consistent with science, with laws of psychology; there was a cult for the theory of dream psychology put out by Freud and other physicians. The relative disappearance of a primitive point of view about arbitrary relations between "signs" and coming events was an outstanding feature of the period. The disappearance, however, was far from complete. In the 1920's the wife of President Harding used to consult a Washington astrologer.

sics, and the reproduced voices of artists, to masses who otherwise would never have heard them. But the jew's-harp and the mouth-organ had the virtue that they required, and enabled, people to produce their own music.

A change in military uniforms and ornamentation.
Left, General Nelson A. Miles, between 1895 and 1903 commanding general of the United States Army, and, *right*, General John J. Pershing, head of the American troops in the Great War.

There was a greater quantity of music abroad in the America of 1925, but less making of music by the people.

The mail-order catalogues recorded much that passed and passed quickly, but recorded also the lingering fidelity of older persons to the familiar. As late as the 1920's, there were still customers for the type of footwear known as congress gaiters, that comfortable soft shoe with a rubber "gore" set in at the sides, worn during the eighties by both men and women. However, the old high-top boots, which took strength to pull on and a bootjack to pull off, passed out completely; they disappeared from the catalogues in 1920. The four-buckle "arctic," popular in 1900, went into obscurity, and emerged again in 1920, "flappers" making a fad of wearing them unbuckled. In a day of modern firearms, it is astonishing to learn that in 1920 Sears-Roebuck sold 500,000 percussion-caps for muzzle-loading rifles and shotguns. With so many labor-saving devices and improvements in the home, some women clung to the old-fashioned household utensils. As late as 1925, Sears-Roebuck continued to sell large quantities of flat-irons with handles attached, in spite of the fact that their catalogue carried illustrations of irons with detachable handles, and electric irons. The solid irons hold the heat longer, which probably accounts for their continued popularity. On the other hand, the old wooden tubs and pails were discarded for the more attractive, light-weight aluminum ones. The old oaken bucket lives now only in the song which was written about it, and in the memories of older persons. The old iron kettle, the iron skillet, the iron tea-kettle were in some eclipse in 1925, though there was still a demand for them in some parts of the country, principally in Pennsylvania, where the "Pennsylvania Dutch" supply, among all the strains that make up the American people, the one that is most tenacious of old ways, an exception to the whole national tendency.

One necessity forced upon the mail-order houses reflected a change that ran through American life. In 1900 they selected most of their fall lines a year before. In 1925 they were obliged to delay the selection so as to include every possible new idea, and sometimes, at the last moment, to add a bulletin of new styles. Farm customers came to be almost as close to the trend of styles as city customers.

In that experience of the mail-order houses was a

characteristic that ran all through American life. Increasing emphasis on style[1] was practically universal. Nearly everything was affected by it, nearly everybody succumbed to it. It was hard to resist, for once a style was established it flooded the retail shops, and the older models became difficult to be got by the few purchasers whose

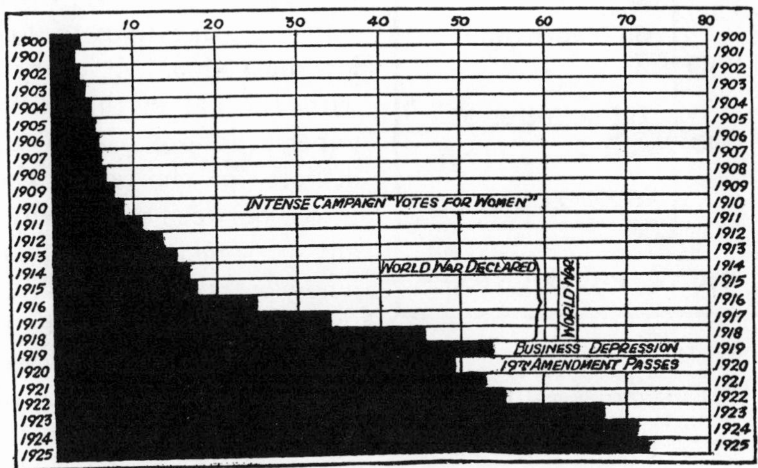

The growth of cigarette consumption for twenty-five years.

individualism, or loyalty to old ways, was superior to their servitude to vogue. It had deep-reaching effects on taste, even on character. Manufacturers and dealers ceased to strive for durability. Once they fell into the swing of making for style, they felt it was useless to produce goods that would wear well for more than a season. Consumers who were drummed and herded into fear of being out of style as to clothes and hats, came to fear to be out of

[1] Change of style is no new thing, however. Oliver Herford, in "The Story of the Skimpy Skirt," in *Harper's Weekly*, November 1, 1913, recalled from an Italian book printed in the sixteenth century the story of a fool "who went about the streets naked, carrying a piece of cloth upon his shoulders. He was asked by some one why he did not dress himself, since he had the materials. 'Because,' he replied, 'I wait to see in what manner the fashions will end. I do not like to use my cloth for a dress which in a little time will be of no use to me, on account of some new fashion.'"

style in thought. Individualism, strength of personality, came to be more rare. The advertising pages of the newspapers[1] and periodicals became dedicated to making people feel that to be out of the style was to be ridiculous.

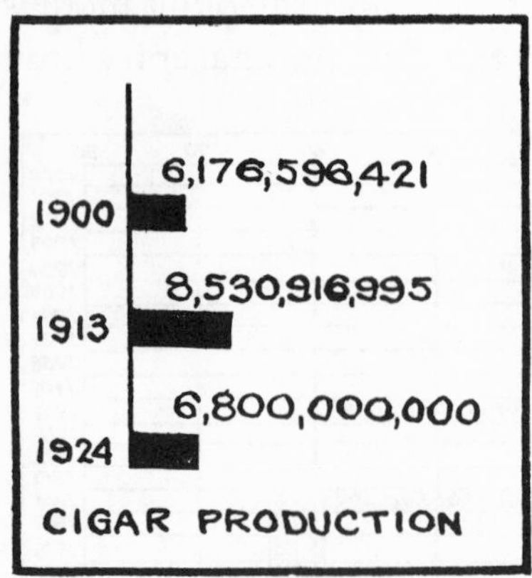

Cigar production started to increase in a normal proportion to population, but was overwhelmed by the cigarette, of which the production increased 1,500 per cent.

To the extent the reading matter reflected the spirit of the advertisements, there was the same urge to follow the vogue. Merchants, with the aid of the newspapers, adopted ingenious devices for shortening the period between styles; actually in some cities a man who wore a straw hat after October 1, or a felt one after May 1, was subjected to a jeering hardly short of rough handling.

It is little wonder if the spirit of quick change from style to style came to affect some of life's spiritual and æsthetic aspects, and practically every one of its material aspects. Who could have supposed that the owners[2] of dogs would yield to style, or that the dog himself could be made to conform to style? But he was.

[1] The Washington *Post*, Tuesday, May 13, 1924, printed a full-page advertisement reading: "YOU OWE YOUR HEAD THREE STRAW HATS. The Complete Hat Wardrobe of The Well-Dressed Man for Summer, 1924, consists of (1) A Sennit Straw (coarse-woven) for business and knockabout; (2) A Split Straw (fine-woven) to wear with the Tuxedo Jacket in the evening; (3) A Fancy Rough-Weave or Soft Straw for sports and country. Thus, you are ready for every occasion and obligation of Summer and you have the consciousness of being smartly, comfortably and appropriately hatted from get-up to go-to-bed."

[2] The most nearly universal of dog-owners and truest of dog-lovers never did yield to style or pay much attention to it. To the American boy, the mongrel of the neighborhood, all the better if a foundling or waif, was at all times the most satisfying of dogs.

VI

In the pages of this work there are many allusions to changes in taste. These records of the passing vogues will give rise to one kind of reflection or another, depending on whether the reader's years and temperament are those which think the age just past was the golden one, or think that every aspect of the world that is new is also good. There is one field of change as to which, for most persons, the reproduction of the vogues of an earlier day will recall sentiments associated with childhood, such that it will be difficult for any reader upward of twenty-one to admit that the dogs of to-day are the equal of those of yesterday.

From a photograph by Edmonston.

A pioneer of "bobbed hair," and an early advanced "feminist" in all respects, Dr. Mary Walker. She was authorized by Congress to wear male dress. Taken in 1914.

Fashion has passed through changes about dogs as it has about clothes, shoes, hats, hair-cuts, facial forestation, automobiles, drama, and fiction. I put it that way, "fashion has passed through changes"; but perhaps a diligent historian would be able to prove that most of these changes, which are described as arising in the taste of the people, really came about through the initiative and energy of commercial persons who had a shrewdly pecuniary realization that if the old could be made to seem passé (through propaganda, advertising, or what not) the new could be sold in profitable quantities. Certainly this motive has had a part in the changes in fashions in women's clothes, automobiles, and in some other fields. In the case of man's most loyal friend, some of the changes will take a good deal of proof to show they have been for the best — the change, for example, from the Newfoundland to the Pekinese. Many a fine breed of dog, whose worth had been known through generations, was elbowed gradually into the back corners and garrets of man's affection. Was there ever a finer animal than the Newfoundland, prized, among other reasons, for gentleness with children? In 1900, and during some years before, he guarded nearly every porch door, dozed on almost every hearthstone. By 1925 you might pass through the entire year, and travel far up and down the country, without seeing one, although a few professional breeders kept the strain alive, either out of sentiment — lest the Newfoundland join the passenger-pigeon and the bison — or in the vague hope that the agencies of vogue would spin the wheel and bring the old favorite back.

Almost as numerous as the Newfoundland in 1900 was the humorous, ludicrous, but intelligent pug. Readers of sufficient years will see in imagination that fat, familiar form with the upturned nose and the tail curled so absurdly in a circle, wheezing and puffing along, often towed by a youngster. The favor the pug enjoyed as a household dog was due largely to his gentleness and scrupulous cleanliness. By 1925 he was hardly to be found except occasionally in the possession of some ancient lady, loyal to youthful affection, sleepy, yawning, wheezing beside a footstool in front of a fireplace. Just why the honest, homely pug fell away in popularity is as inexplicable as a good many other changes in style. Possibly he was unable to reduce his waist-line to the fashionable slenderness of the Boston terrier or the sleek Borzoi of 1925. We could more easily have spared the noisy, yapping Pomeranian or the snuffling Pekinese.

John Drew (*top left*), when the Old English sheepdog was in vogue.

The dog that had the longest and greatest vogue of all, the mongrel; and the truest of dog-lovers, the American boy (*top centre*).

Rex Beach with English setter (*top right*).

Booth Tarkington and his French poodle. (*centre*).

Dachshund, popular in 1900 (*left lower*).

A Newfoundland, common in the 1890's. "Polaria" was imported from England by J. A. Graydon in an effort to re-establish the breed in America (*right lower*).

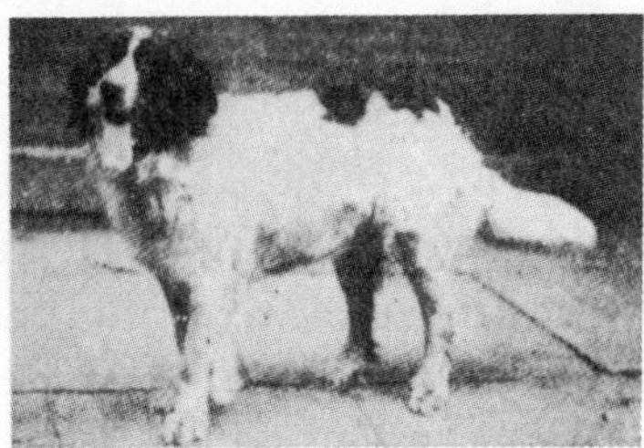

Of the dogs that succeeded the Newfoundland and the pug, many were aliens, exotics. They were introduced to America, as a rule, at the top of the world of fashion. Some became popular and familiar; others had a brief vogue in dog-shows, but never came in contact with the wider dog-world of collies, setters, pointers, beagles. The chow is one dog whose origin as an American fashion could probably be traced with fair accuracy. His vogue came after the American expedition to China at the time of the Boxer rebellion, in 1900. Among those who brought back chows as souvenirs of that then very strange land was Richard Harding Davis, the war correspondent and popular author. Descendants of Mr. Davis's importation were given to his friends and found their way into the New York Dog Show. Their oddity instantly attracted attention. They became the vogue of the élite for a few years and later were fairly common.

Appearance counts for much in popular taste. No doubt that same ludicrousness that had something to do with the eclipse of the pug accounted also for the brevity of the reign of the friendly, awkward dachshund. There can be nothing in the theory that the war brought his eclipse, for he had begun to lose ground long before the Kaiser brought misfortune to a good many things German.

If the dachshund suffered for his ancestry, the poodle should have come into high favor, for he was French from his blunt nose to the tip of his curling tail. On the contrary, the poodle, after the war, came to be rarely seen. The poodle, too, suffered from a touch of absurdity of appearance, for which the fault lay not with him, but with the style man adopted of clipping his coat. The King Charles spaniel and the Skye terrier, both of long-haired breeds, had a brief vogue and passed, as well as the Dalmatian and the sleek greyhound, the oldest dog man knows, dating back 7000 years. The smooth-haired fox-terrier, admirable dog, gave way to his cousin, the popular — for a brief while — wire-haired fox-terrier.

The breeds unknown in 1900 which by 1925 had passed through the stages of dog-show and fashion, and had begun to come into really popular favor, included the so-called police dog. One met them everywhere; in town, where one felt rather sympathetic to see them tugging at the leash, and in the country, where, as excellent watch-dogs, they rightfully belonged. They had a style, a presence, which seemed to be the quality that counted most in the 1920's.[1]

VII

In the year 1900 the writer of this history was twenty-five years old. In the year in which this is written, 1925, the writer, therefore, had lived through the last quarter of the nineteenth century and the first quarter of the twentieth. In the beginning of the earlier period, many of the oldest ways of life were still common. I did not see the crane[2] in actual use, but my older brothers did, and it

[1] Divers persons who have been kind enough to read the proofs of these pages as checks to accuracy have tempered their friendliness with pointed complaints about the failure to allude to certain favorites dear to individual memory: the Airedale, once the beneficiary of a vogue as great as that of the police dog in 1925; the setter, the pointer, and the beagle, at all times favorites on farms and among hunters; the spotted coach-dog, the St. Bernard; and—most popular dog of any age or clime—the mongrel. To all of which the shamed author's only plea is the rigidities of space.

[2] The associate who has helped in the preparation of this book returned the page of MS. containing this word, with the query: "What is a crane?"—convincing proof of how certainly this method of cooking has become an institution of the completely past. I referred him to Longfellow, "The Hanging of the Crane":

"The lights are out, and gone are all the guests
That thronging came with merriment and jests
To celebrate the hanging of the crane
In the new house—into the night are gone;
But still the fire upon the hearth burns on. . . ."

was still lying on the "old iron pile"[1] behind the corn-crib. The earliest lantern I carried as a boy was of a model as old, at least, as Shakespeare, a cylinder of tin with little jagged holes punched through it, large enough to let thin glimmers of light come through, and small enough not to let the wind blow out the candle which stood in a socket inside the cylinder. Candles were still in frequent use; the candle-mould, twelve long tubes of tin or zinc joined together, still a common household article. About that time, however, the coal-oil lamp was beginning to overcome the prejudice against novelty, and the fear, not infrequently justified, that it was dangerous, liable to explosion. The earliest ones were of plain glass with a wick of red flannel; later came ornate ones of painted china, wall-lamps with reflectors, and, finally, an exaltation of convenience and adornment, the hanging-lamp,

[1] The last mention of an "old iron pile" I have seen was an August, 1925, newspaper account of President Coolidge, when on a visit to his father's home in Plymouth, Vt., finding an old horseshoe, picking it up and carrying it to the old iron pile. Probably that was an example of the anachronism President Coolidge and his background were, a bit of early New England hanging over into a new generation. The old iron pile went out when new methods of extracting ore and handling iron in large quantities made it no longer economical to collect and transport the old horseshoes, worn-out ploughshares, and bits of broken iron that farm boys used to collect to await the junkman, who announced his coming with a droning, musical, "Any old iron, old bones, and old gum boots?"; or, in the cities, in a more lively air: "Any rags, any bones, any bottles to-day?" The passing of all this was more than a superficial detail of the surface of life. A modern school of political economists insists that President Coolidge's picking up that horseshoe was an economic mistake. They prove it, not only for a man of President Coolidge's income, but for a man of any income, however small. This is quite sound as a matter of figures. Something new came into the world with modern machinery. When nails were hand-made, a carpenter who dropped one and failed to pick it up was an undesirable workman. But when machine-made nails came, the efficiency experts worked it out that the time consumed in bending over to pick up a nail was greater than the cost of the new nail which the carpenter could pick out of his sack. Thereafter the carpenter who stopped to pick up a nail became the undesirable one. In figures, all this is perfectly sound. It is an incident of modern methods in industry, of machine-made goods produced in quantity, and of minute calculations into the cost of labor. But one wonders if something deteriorating in the personality of the individual did not come with the higher economy of machinery. The New England trait that hates to see anything go to waste is concerned no more with money than with an old-fashioned philosophy of life.

suspended from the ceiling at the middle of the room, and raised or lowered by a small chain on pulleys.

Many of the tools for farming were still the same as they had been for a thousand years. I have seen grain threshed from the straw by a flail,[1] two long sticks joined end to end by a leather thong six or eight inches long. The thresher used one as a handle and swung the other down on the straw spread on the barn floor. That steady drum-beat was a rainy-day sound on many a thrifty small farm.[2] In the 1880's, however, the large mechanical thresher had come into use as a community institution. It went the rounds from farm to farm with a professional threshing-crew. The earlier ones took their power from horses in a tread-mill; in the eighties the power came to be supplied by portable steam-engines. It was not until the nineties that these engines could move from farm to farm under their own power. In the early part of the period, the primitive hand-"cradle" for mowing wheat, oats, and rye was still to be found on every farm, though it was being displaced by the horse-drawn reaper. In the eighties there came a marvel, the "reaper-and-binder," which cut the grain, accumulated it in bundles, and tied them with twine, all in one process. The horse-drawn mowing-machine had already supplanted the scythe for everything except fence corners and small lots. It was during the eighties that the "hay-fork" became common, a mechanism of steel tines, rope, and pulleys, which lifted the hay from the wagon to the mow by horse-power.

Many of the changes during this period came from one

[1] I saw one in use in a New England barn as late as 1916.

[2] The experiences here recorded were on a small Eastern farm. On the large level farms of the West, men who in 1925 were fifty years old had never seen a flail. In all respects, modern machinery and modern methods came more rapidly in the West.

cause: the spread of the railroads. As late as the eighties and even into the nineties there survived a self-contained unit of society every few miles. On the little streams of the East there were grist-mills. The farmer hauled his wheat to the mill, saw it ground, and received in return

By courtesy of Armour and Company.

Before refrigeration and refrigerator-cars, packers stored their barrelled pork in mountainous piles adjacent to the slaughtering-houses. Hence the word "packer." Slaughtering was done only in the winter months.

flour which he used for his family, bran for the animals in the barn, and middlings for the poultry. Presently the railroads, and the rise of great flour-mills manufacturing on an immense scale, brought it about that the farmer sold his wheat outright at the railroad-station and then bought his flour from the local store as he needed it, both wheat and flour, meantime, having travelled hundreds or thousands of miles.

In the earlier period, butchering day, usually a cold day in late November or early December, was a universal institution on the farms. One or two hogs and a beef animal were killed. For pork, the operation began with the heating of stones in an outdoor fire. When sufficiently hot, the stones were thrown into a barrel of water into which, later, the slaughtered hog was sunk to soften his bristles for shaving. In due course the hams were salted and hung from hooks in the kitchen, together with one or two quarters of the slaughtered steer which for a year to follow provided food as dried beef. This institution, too, succumbed to the railroads and the rise of the great packing-houses. The farmer came to sell his hogs and cattle at the railroad-station for shipment to Chicago or the nearest packing-house elsewhere, and bought his meat from time to time as he needed it from the nearest meat-dealer. In lumber, the railroads brought the same transformation. As late as the eighties a farmer, about to build a barn, went into his wood-lot, chopped down the oaks and trimmed them with his broad-axe. When he had enough for the frame of the barn, there was a "raising" to which the neighbors came to help lift the heavy timbers and join them (often with a jollification afterward, that included hard cider). To a considerable extent even the boards were still sawed by local sawmills on the near-by streams. Presently that, too, gave way to the custom of buying lumber, ready-cut, brought from a distance; and to the specialized labor of the building contractor.

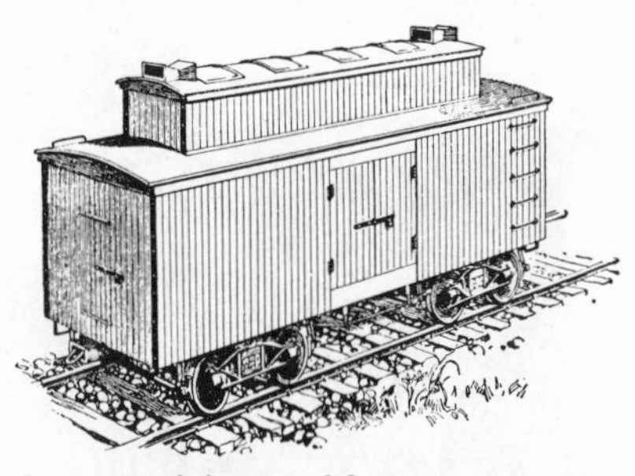

By courtesy of Armour and Company.

The first refrigerator-car.

The buggy, which to the youth of 1900 was the equivalent, not of the Ford, but of the two or three thousand dollar car of 1925, was, in the eighties, still largely a product of local makers who would build them to order at a hundred and fifty to two hundred dollars. The wheelwright-shop, often combined with the blacksmith-shop, still held sway with the local grist-mill as a community institution. On the timbers beneath the roof of every blacksmith-shop one could see the strips of hickory, curved ones for the wheels, drying in the slow warmth from the forge, a method of seasoning considered to be more desirable and durable than the quicker drying practised in factories.

By courtesy of Armour and Company.

The meat wagon of the 1890's. Everything is shown except the flies that accompanied it and were regarded as both unavoidable and harmless.

The farmer's wife, too, was still largely independent of the distant cannery. "Preserving" was a household rite that followed the season from strawberry-time through raspberries to blackberries and on to peaches and pears. In the fall, as one drove along the country roads, one sniffed the agreeable scent of drying fruit, and on lean-to roofs saw frames in which the sliced apples were drying in the autumn sun. In October or November apple-sauce making was an event like butchering day. Apple-butter making involved, for some of the household, or for relays of them, a romantic night in the open. The apples, pared and sliced, together with cider, were put into a large copper-lined pot that hung on a frame over an outdoor fire. The fire had to be kept going as much as forty-eight hours, and some one had steadily to keep the mixture moving with a long-handled wooden stirrer specially made for this work.

Every housewife had her own coffee-grinder, sausage-grinder, apple-parer. Ancient custom, and also a kind of pride, caused wife and husband as well to seek to produce and preserve as much of their food as possible — a workmanlike individualism destined to be overcome by the ease of railroad transportation, by the cheapness of quantity production in factories, by refrigerator-cars that lengthened the seasons for fresh fruit, and by cold-storage warehouses. In the earlier day the farmer depended on the local store for little more than sugar, usually the soft brown kind (much more delectable to children sent to carry it from the store than granulated sugar); molasses, drawn from a barrel into a jug; coffee, unground; tea and spices — all bought, often, not with cash, but through the barter of chickens, eggs, and butter. One may have a feeling for the greater economic independence of that day, even the romance of its greater simplicity and individuality; but one must admit that cleanliness, sanitation, and health had an advance in the transition from country-store, fly-smitten sugar-bins and molasses-barrels, from the dried cod and herring that hung like bronzed mummies from hooks or wires, and the pickle-barrel in the cellar, open alike to the storekeeper's hand and to adventurous insects — from these and other aspects of the old-time country store, to the cartons and bottles which, during the eighties and nineties, began to come on the railroads from distant factories, to be retailed by the local store, later by chain stores.

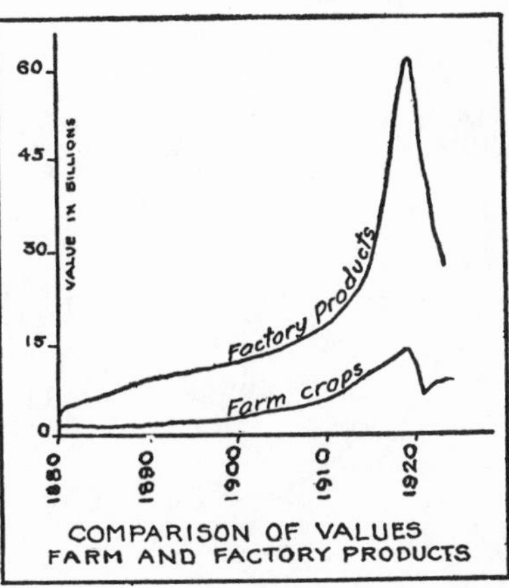

COMPARISON OF VALUES
FARM AND FACTORY PRODUCTS

Hand in hand with the changes brought by the railroads went others that reflected the universal trend toward specialization of labor. In the closing decades of the nineteenth century, on many farms, the milk was separated by the farmer's wife, through methods that had

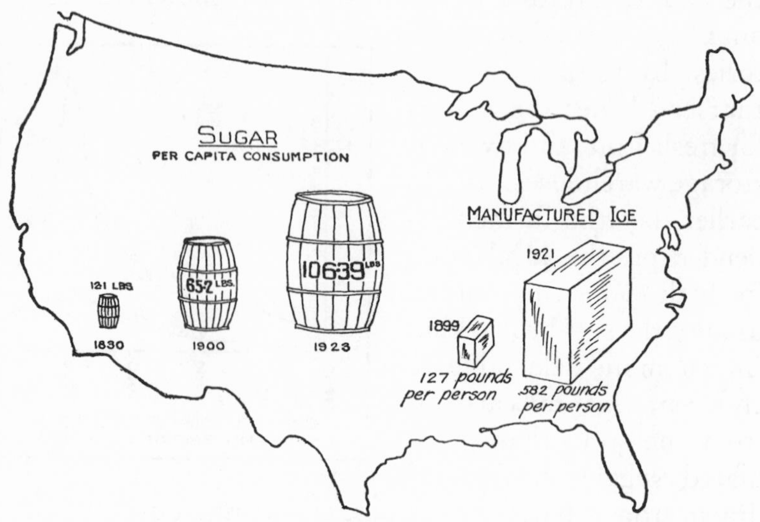

not changed much since the days of Jael. It was allowed to stand in pails in the cool water of the spring-house until the cream rose to the top, when it was removed with a "skimmer," a thin, saucer-shaped bit of metal, and put in crocks, large vessels of coarse gray earthenware, sometimes ornamented with blue. (The farmer's wife of 1880 bought them at the village store for five to twenty cents each; in 1925 they were on sale in antique shops at five to ten dollars each.) The week's accumulation of cream was turned to butter with an old-fashioned churn, the operation calling for several hours of hard work by wife or children. All this began to give way during the eighties to local "creameries" to which the farmer took his milk each morning and where the separation into cream and the residue of skim-milk or butter-milk was made by centrifugal separators operated by steam-power.

On any average farm of the nineties one could see, as articles of daily or seasonal use, knee-high leather boots —

By courtesy of U. S. Bureau of Public Roads.

Another institution that has passed. In 1925 one could search for months in the most backward districts before finding such an outfit as this.

the ones for boys frequently had copper reinforcement at the toes; ear-muffs, bits of velvet on a wire framework large enough to slip over the ear. Buffalo-robes in the early eighties could be bought for fifty cents or a dollar; by 1900 they, with the buffalo itself, had practically disappeared; by 1925 you counted it an adventure if you came across one at country "public sales" of the household goods of old farm families. There were sleighs, the bodies made sometimes of wood, sometimes of woven willow withes; those of unusual distinction of style were called "cutters." In winter the wheels of farm-wagons were replaced with sled-runners, and small bells were attached to the harness. The journey of such an equipage to the "crossroads store" or the village was attended with an agreeable glamour unknown to a generation inured to the automobile. Oxen were still common. "Buck" and "Berry" were as familiar as Mr. Ford's "Lizzie" later came to be; every boy knew what an ox or horse should do when ordered to "gee" or "haw." Speed was accelerated by a vocal cluck or "git ep," the 1890 equivalent of "step on the gas."

Among farmers and workers elsewhere, underwear made of bright-red flannel was in wide-spread favor, based on the presumed possession of a kind of superstitious virtue additional to its warmth. A harvest-field of the eighties or early nineties presented a picture almost like men in uniform — each harvester stripped to the waist except for the bright-red flannel undershirt. It was worn in winter for the sake of the warmth, and a popular idea that it was dangerous to change led to its retention throughout the summer, a prejudice with somewhat the same sanitary results as the one against night air. Fly-screens had not become general; there was a theory that the high, fringy bushes of the asparagus-plant would either repel flies or attract them — I forget which. In any event, such bushes were hung close to the ceiling over the dining-room table. Drains for reducing low land to cultivation were made as the earliest farmer must have made them: at the bottom of the ditch, two rows of flat stones set on edge and covered with other flat stones. During the eighties the railroads began to bring porous brick tile. Either on the old-time individual farms or in the communities were lime-kilns; they, together with the local bone-mill, and the product of the barn and chicken-yards, supplied the fertilizer.

Within the usual American home, Monday was always "wash-day," attended by a soapy, steamy scent of suds. Water frequently had to be carried in buckets from a well some distance from the house. The clothes were "put to

From a photograph by Underwood & Underwood.

A modern gasoline-motor fire-engine.

soak" the night before, and washing was begun as early as four in the morning. It was a matter of pride with housewives to have the washing hung before breakfast, and neighbors would vie with one another in seeing whose washing appeared earliest on the line. Tuesday was "ironing-day." The irons were heated on a hot stove. Men's "boiled" shirts, linen collars and cuffs, and women's and children's dresses and underwear with many yards of ruffles, starched to a wooden inflexibility, were "done up" at home. Wednesday was sewing and mending day. Women's and children's clothing was made at home, and usually the shirts of the men of the household. Darning huge piles of socks and stockings so perfectly that the darning could hardly be detected was a prized accomplishment of a good housewife. The best silk dress was often turned and remade to serve for a few more years. No man was ashamed to wear an honest patch. Thursday was a kind of mid-week rest-day; so far as it had fixed tasks, they were usually crocheting or embroidering, quilting, making rag carpets. Friday was cleaning-day. The thick carpets had to be swept with a broom; the housewife usually wore a dust-cap or towel wrapped around her head to protect her hair. After a thorough sweeping of rooms and stairs, furniture was dusted. Kitchen floors and porches were scrubbed, usually on hands and knees. The stoves were brightly polished. Saturday was "baking-day." All the bread and pastries were made in the home, large solid loaves, pies, cakes, doughnuts, and that delicacy most prized by the small boy — "cookies," usually made with a coating of white sugar and with a solitary raisin set like a jewel in the centre, and kept in a crock on an inaccessible shelf of the pantry to be doled out for good behavior or withheld for discipline. To use much "baker's bread" was an indictment, at once, of a housewife's industry and of her pride in her calling. Sunday was called the day of rest, but for the housewife it meant, often, the arrival of "company" and extra cooking. It was at this period that the old adage was most apt: "A man may work from sun to sun, but woman's work is never done."

To the relief of this routine of industry there came first the Chinese laundry, and later the community laundry as a business institution; the dry-cleaner, the electric washing-machine and wringer, the electric iron, the vacuum sweeper, the electric sewing-machine, the fireless cooker. Housework was completely revolutionized. The adaptations of electricity for housework began to arrive about 1900 in the cities. By 1925 the long antennæ of the power-stations had begun to reach out along country roads, and the conveniences that the city woman had been enjoying were now made available to the farmer's wife. For regions isolated from transmission lines compact generators driven by small gasoline or kerosene motors were devised, which furnished light for buildings, helped the housewife in her daily tasks, and pumped water for domestic uses. Electricity or gasoline began to milk the cows, curry the horses. In 1925 a list of devices sold by the New York Edison Company, with the cost per hour of current used by each, included:

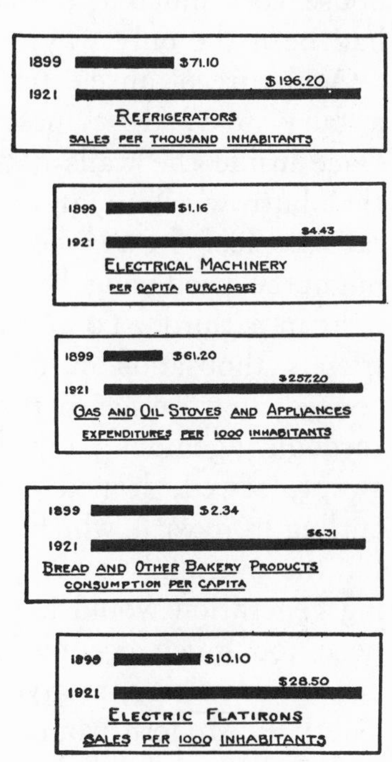

Dish-washer	2 c.	Waffle-iron	5 c.
Ironing-machine	7 c.	Toaster	3 c.
Sewing-machine	½ c.	Chafing-dish	7 c.
Vacuum sweeper	1 c.	Table-stove	5 c.
Washing-machine	2 c.	Fireless cooker	2½ c.

The installation of these electrical devices[1] cost, of course, much more than the primitive tools of the earlier day; but once installed, the labor that came from the power-house cost much less than the hand labor that before had been the only way.

A picture of an electric wire in a modern house excels a fairy-story. It comes through conduits or on poles. Once inside the walls it divides into a score of tentacles that burrow, climb, and reach, each ending in some separate service. In any house, at the same hour, electricity might be producing heat in one room, cold in another, light in a third. To yet another it brought the voices of friends thousands of miles away. It heated water, it cooked, it froze ice in the refrigerator, it carried healing through ingenious pads that curved on aching backs; it swept, sewed, ironed — and it provided heat for the curling-iron with which the housewife beautified herself for the evening's gaiety, a housewife who in the preceding generation would have accepted old age at forty and been too much occupied with the work, now done for her by electricity, to give much thought to adornment or gaiety. "Modern woman," said the Waco *News Tribune* in June, 1925, "may have faults, but she doesn't look as bent and worn as a 'dutiful wife' did in the old days."

By electricity and other sources of mechanical energy, life was made much less burdensome. In a sense, too, it was made more simple. To turn a switch was a long distance from the annual candle-dipping or the weekly task

[1] Light was practically the only common household use of electricity in 1900. Almost all the others, kitchen range, vacuum cleaner, refrigerator, dish-washing machine, floor-polisher, came after 1900.

of filling the kerosene-lamps. To turn a radiator valve was very different from the daily work of filling the woodbox. Doubtless something attractive, something possibly

By courtesy of the Edison Company.

An old-fashioned housewife's daily task, before the coming of electricity.

of essential value, was missed by the generation of children who thought of light as something you made with the pressure of a finger and thumb on a switch; of heat as something that came through pipes; of milk as something that appeared on the table by the agency of a milkman, whose visit was so early that many a child grew up without even seeing one. The vogue of the boy-scout movement, designed to recover, at much pains, the arts of chopping wood and making a fire, seemed to recognize that something had been lost with the disappearance of the household chores of earlier childhoods.

The coming of electricity and the gasoline motor might have given man and woman such a freedom from labor and constant care as would have seemed, to the earlier generation, an Arabian Night's dream. Release from much hard physical labor actually came, but life did not become more simple. New needs, new desires, were stimulated. Luxuries became necessities. Man, instead of regarding the new invention as releasing him from just that much labor, allowed it to add to the number of things he thought he must have, or his family thought they must have: radio, automobile, scores of articles that did not retain the status of novel luxuries but became familiar needs almost overnight. The average man conceded almost nothing to be beyond his wants or means.[1] Instead of comparing his state with the past, instead of reflecting that he was far richer in material comforts and conveniences than George Washington, who was the richest American of his generation — instead of that, the average man made his comparison with the richest of his own generation. He usually wanted as many conveniences, and through the beneficences of science, invention, and the social organization of America, was enabled to approximate what would otherwise have seemed

[1] The newspapers stimulated desire. An advertisement of the Crane Company in the New York *Times*, Sept. 10, 1925, began: "HAS YOUR FAMILY OUTGROWN ONE BATHROOM?" The Washington *Star* in 1924 printed the following in its reading matter: "Every motorist who plans the construction of a new home should figure on erecting a three-car garage. This message, offered by the Washington Automotive Trade Association, is viewed as being particularly valuable as a suggestion to the home-builder at this time, when many are finding the two-car garage inadequate."

his preposterous wishes. He got more goods, more things, but also he became more enmeshed in the anxieties of a complex and hurried way of life. He missed the chance of making a possibly more satisfying use of the release from physical labor that electricity brought, the chance for leisure, repose, simplicity of life, and the spiritual qualities that can go with simple living.

But the common generalization that compares the present unfavorably with the past, that pictures the earlier day as golden, is subject to a good deal of qualification. The anxiety to share the latest and highest standard of living may keep the modern man's nose to the grindstone of his family's presumed needs. But that is a fault of inner philosophy, of the individual's management of his personal existence. In any event, worry about meeting the instalments on the automobile is hardly to be compared with the anxiety that attended, as late as 1895, the presence, for example, of diphtheria in the family, or any of many other terrors that science banished.

17

A MODERN WARRIOR

THE history of this quarter-century in America, if written according to the model of older histories (that is, with emphasis on wars and military leaders), would begin by saying that about the opening of the twentieth century this nation was beset and infested by certain enemies, which continually made war upon it. They were of a peculiar malevolence and persistence, more ruthless and more dreaded than savages, and more successful in their assaults. They poisoned water and food, they launched their attacks through the invisible air, they recognized no laws of war or of humanity. It was impossible ever to have a truce with them; there was no such thing as compromise, or any kind of agreement or understanding. Some kept up their assault continuously, some renewed their attacks each year at fixed seasons, others at longer intervals. Some maintained at all times a foothold on our soil, were never completely dislodged; some went into furtive hiding-places to restore their strength, and returned to their attacks renewed in multitudes and malignity. Some of the most implacable had their strongholds just outside our borders, whence they invaded our shores with a deadliness that at times threw large American cities and great sections of the country into panic and flight. Flight was the sole escape, and that an uncertain one. Courage could only express itself in resignation. Acceptance of death from these enemies as something inevitable became a part of the national philosophy. They pursued methods of warfare so surely fatal, had weapons and arts of preparation and assault so secret and ingenious, that the people had no effective methods of defense, indeed practically no defense. The enemies took a toll of death so large as to have an appalling effect on the population; some with a malevolence like Herod's directed their attacks against the very young and destroyed a terrifying proportion of the infants and children.

These wars and invasions would form the principal substance of a history based on the older models; and such a history would recite, as a heroic climax, that beginning about 1900, there arose among the people thus beset certain leaders extraordinarily skilled in strategy, men of a persistence equal to the enemies' own, who invented and developed new means for defense. They gave their lives to study of the methods and equipment of the attackers, discovered facts never before known about the life of the enemies and their vulnerable points, and then, by infinitely painstaking experiments, built up ways not only of successful defense, but actually means to carry the war into the enemies' territory; with the result that some were extirpated utterly from the face of the earth, and others so crippled that they ceased to be a menace.

All this such a history would recite, and add that the people of the nation, in gratitude, set up monuments to the leaders of this successful war, exalted them above rulers and statesmen, and honored them as Vienna honored Sobieski, and Rome Scipio Africanus.

II

In the early months of 1900 there was in Havana, Cuba, an American army surgeon, Major William Crawford Gorgas, sent as an attaché of the American military government that occupied the city after the close of the Spanish-American War. Major Gorgas was of a serene, quiet-moving temperament, and at this time was in a state of mind composed mainly of confident satisfaction with his work and achievements, just a little disturbed by a recurring perplexity, a perplexity which he felt sure would presently disappear.

For his satisfaction, Major Gorgas had many and good reasons. He was in a career he had sought from childhood, and he had done well in it. As the son of an army officer[1] Gorgas had looked forward from boyhood to a military life. He achieved it, but only after many disappointments. After trying in vain to get into West Point, he attained the army by means of a medical education, procured at Bellevue Medical College, New York, under the adversity of a poverty so great that at one time he found himself wearing trousers patched with the remains of his old felt hat. Having secured his diploma he presented himself for the army medical examinations, against the steady advice of his soldier-father, whose final plea said:

> I have no objection to your passing the army examinations; nor would I object to a couple of years' service. But it would not be a life to look forward to as a permanent thing. It is not in the army that the sphere of a doctor is ennobling. I hope that something better will present itself before you graduate. Still I don't in the least object to preparation for the army examination. I think it confers a certain distinction to have passed it.

As an army doctor Gorgas served for twenty years at frontier posts, from the Dakotas to Texas. For several years, just before the Spanish-American War, he was at Fort Barrancas, Fla., where he had much experience with the yellow fever[2] that used to make incursions from

[1] Major Gorgas's father had served first in the Federal army, and later in the Confederate army (because of marriage to the daughter of the governor of Alabama). After the Civil War, the elder Gorgas was a teacher at Sewanee, Tenn., and later president of the University of Alabama.

[2] Nearly every year some part of the United States suffered a visitation of "Yellow Jack." The worst was in 1878, when an epidemic that went up the Mississippi River as far as Memphis carried off 16,000 lives.

Cuba. Earlier, at the army post near Brownsville, Texas, he had actually had yellow fever himself. This familiarity with tropical disease was one of the reasons for his being selected in January, 1899, to serve the American military government of Havana as chief surgeon.

III

Major Gorgas's job was to assist in the cleaning up of Havana. That was an Augean task. Havana was a pest-hole of filth, and the breeding-place of diseases of which the most terrifying was yellow fever. At this time the conditions were even worse than usual, for the city had suffered disruption and decay through the years of the Cuban insurrection and the Spanish effort to subdue it. The Spanish barracks in Havana were unsanitary, disease-ridden. The city had but one or two sewers, and these drained only a part of it. Garbage and other domestic wastes, together with the corpses of dead dogs and cats, were strewn about the narrow streets for the elements and the buzzards to dispose of. There were few sidewalks; the pedestrian was compelled to pick his way gingerly along among pools of stagnant water. By night it was impolitic for the uninitiated to stray very far from the bright lights of the centre of the city. Housewives, following the custom of disposing of slops after sunset, might appear momentarily

From a photograph by Underwood & Underwood.

General William Crawford Gorgas.

at an upper balcony, and, with a perfunctory "Look out, below!" cast into the night air the accumulated refuse of a day. The city was a miasma of odors, a hotbed of disease, not only yellow fever, but typhoid, malaria, dysentery, and other maladies usually associated with filth.

Yellow fever, at the time Gorgas went to Havana, in

An 1899 cartoon from the Minneapolis *Tribune* bearing the caption: "Governor Wood begins his duties."

December, 1898, had been less virulent than usual. It was, nevertheless, the most terrifying of Havana's diseases, and the job of cleaning up the city had yellow fever as its chief objective. Gorgas and the medical profession generally knew — that is the proper word at this point — that yellow fever was caused by filth. Among laymen, even well-informed laymen, there were all sorts of superstitions appropriate to its deadliness and to the sudden mystery of its invasions. Laymen surmised it was caused, or at least conveyed, by bananas, decaying coffee, noxious gases, "swamp miasma," putrefying animal and vegetable matter. The specifics used against it were varied, but mustard-seed, cigars, and whiskey were the favorites.

Cherrera, a typical town of the interior of the Republic of Panama.

Among doctors the theory was general that the cause or the means of infection was contact with the "black vomit" that was one of its incidents, or the bed-clothing or other articles that had been in contact with victims. Gorgas, as an expert with the best knowledge, regarded filth as its cause, and the cleaning up of filth as its certain preventive. He with Major William M. Black, U. S. Corps of Engineers, and Major Davis, of the Sanitary Department, acting under the authority of the governor-general, set about that work, not only as a means of checking the disease, but as an act indispensable to the success of the American military occupation of Cuba. During the fighting that had been going on a few months before between Spanish and American troops, both sides had been threatened with annihilation. They had been literally saturated with malaria, and to a less extent with yellow fever. Had the Spaniards been able to hold out a little longer, there is small doubt that the American troops — what might then have been left of them — would have been withdrawn, and the Cuban campaign would have been a failure. The same outlook faced the American military occupation that came after the peace, unless some effective means of curbing disease should be found.

But even more important than this consideration was the long and urgent wish of the United States to get at and stamp out yellow fever in the seat from which it made its periodic raids on the United States. So long as Cuba had remained a Spanish possession, the United States could do nothing apart from protesting fruitlessly, and establishing quarantines with their consequent blights on trade. But now, with the island under the control of the American army, America had the opportunity to attack yellow fever in its native stronghold, and free the American cities of the South from their constant menace. To accomplish this was the job of Major Gorgas and his colleagues.

IV

Within a few months after the Americans had taken over the government of Cuba, Major Gorgas and his associates seemed to have succeeded. They had wrought a spectacular change in the outward aspect of Havana. Gone were the puddles of stagnant water, the piles of rotting vegetables, the decaying carcasses, the unsightly rubbish. Gone, too, were the offensive odors. Havana blossomed forth as clean and wholesome as any city in the

A plaza in Panama, before and after being paved.

world — rather cleaner than American cities of the period. Of Havana during the summer of 1900, Gorgas wrote, in his book "Sanitation in Panama": "I believe that Havana was cleaner than any other city had ever been up to that time." How this transformation of an alien city was brought about by American army officers without rasping the sensibilities of the natives to the point of resistance is a story in itself. That it was done, and with a minimum of ill-feeling on the part of the Cubans, is a testimonial to the extraordinary executive capacity, combined with the tact and considerateness, of the American officers.

By courtesy of U. S. Signal Corps.

George M. Sternberg, surgeon-general at the head of the Army Medical Service at the time when physicians in the service discovered the cause of yellow fever and the means of its prevention.

The cleanliness of Havana following the occupation of the city by the American military authorities constituted the greatest of the reasons for the satisfaction of Gorgas and his fellow officers. They saw filth had gone; they felt sure that with filth, yellow fever also would depart.

Statistics seemed to justify their faith. During the first seven months of 1899 only seven deaths occurred from yellow fever.

V

But beginning in August of that year, 1899, immigrants from Spain began to come into Cuba. Between August and December, 1899, some 12,000 Spanish peasants arrived in Havana. With their presence yellow fever began to appear again. Whereas there had been but one death from this cause in January, 1899, there were eight in January, 1900. Throughout 1900 the epidemic grew. In all, fourteen hundred cases were reported, constituting, as it was put, with some exaggeration, by General Fitzhugh Lee, consul-general of the United States in Cuba, and a resident of many years in Havana, the worst outbreak the country had ever known.

Major-General Leonard Wood was Governor-General of Cuba, 1900. General Wood's presence as Governor-General of Cuba had historic importance in the fact that being a medical man he understood Colonel Gorgas's epoch-making effort to stamp out yellow fever, and gave him indispensable support.

It was clear that yellow fever had not been conquered, or even scotched. The presence of the new immigrants was the test. Necessarily they were non-immune, that is, they had not achieved immunity through having had the disease. The resident population of Havana was largely immune. It was to this fact, and not to the work of Major Gorgas and his associates, that the apparent success of 1899 had been due. It was now clear that sanitation, and such cleanliness as few cities anywhere had ever known, had not conquered yellow fever, nor affected it at all. The disease had not been destroyed, it had merely been quiescent for lack of material on which to feed. The satisfaction and confident hope which had been the mood of the American army physicians and sanitary officers in 1899, became, by the spring of 1900, baffled dismay.

From all sides hysteria clamored at the American officials. Nobody knew what should be done, but everybody demanded that something be done quickly. The pressure made itself felt in Washington; in June, 1900, Surgeon-General George M. Sternberg appointed a commission of four army surgeons — Walter Reed, James Carroll, Jesse W. Lazear, and Aristides Agramonte — to go to Havana and investigate.

VI

While Gorgas and his superior, Governor-General Leonard Wood, had been cleaning up Havana and preoccupied with the problem of yellow fever, they had come into frequent contact with an amiable old Cuban physician, Doctor Carlos J. Finlay. From the start Finlay used to throw friendly doubt on the theory that yellow fever was caused by filth. He was sceptical of Gorgas's expectation that the disease would vanish when the city was cleaned. Finlay had a theory, which he had clung to tenaciously for twenty years, that yellow fever was caused by the bite of a mosquito of the variety called Stegomyia. Being a man of cultivated mind and magnetic personality, Finlay, while expounding his theory, was always listened to politely; but as happens with many true prophets, few were converted to his belief. Mosquitoes of about 800 different species were known; how could it be possible that of these 800 Finlay had been able to fix on the one particular variety as the culprit? The idea bordered on the fantastic! Nor could Finlay bring forward evidence convincing to the scientific mind. On the contrary, the results of his own experiments with mosquitoes was destructive to the very theory he wanted

Doctor Walter Reed.

Doctor Aristides Agramonte.

Doctor Jesse W. Lazear.

Doctor James Carroll.

The Army Yellow Fever Commission.

to prove. Despite his more than one hundred attempts at inoculation by mosquitoes, he had scored not a single success.[1]

Still, Gorgas and the Americans could claim no greater success for their theory. The disproof of it was only too visible in the spectacle of Havana, although cleaner than it had ever been before, cleaner indeed than any other city in the world, nevertheless, being flagellated by a yellow-fever epidemic so severe as to be almost without precedent.

The Reed Commission, on arriving in Havana, listened to Finlay, but, like Gorgas, were not at first inclined to give his theory credence.

VII

Reed and his associates, surveying their problem, could follow one of two courses:[2] First, they could search for the bacillus of yellow fever, and after finding it seek a serum to counteract it. Second, they could determine the manner in which the infection was carried, whether by insects or by clothing, or bedding, or other articles coming in contact with the patient.

Before deciding which course to pursue, Reed made a

[1] The reason for Doctor Finlay's failure in all his experiments over a period of twenty years (in spite of the fact his hypothesis was correct) lay in his lack of familiarity with a certain factor of time entering into the passage of yellow fever from one victim to the next. This is explained on the following pages.

[2] A preliminary action of the Reed Commission consisted of some experiments designed to prove or to eliminate a theory that had come from Italy. Some years earlier, in 1897, Doctor Giuseppe Sanarelli had announced that he had discovered the specific yellow-fever bacillus, which he called *Bacillus icteroides*. Reed and Carroll, at the suggestion of Surgeon-General Sternberg, investigated the Italian's supposed discovery and found it to be no discovery at all. What Sanarelli had thought was a new germ was, they maintained, nothing else than the familiar bacillus of hog-cholera. Reed was confident that the bacillus isolated by the Italian had no direct connection with yellow fever, yet felt it his duty as a scientist to follow every lead. On reaching Havana he spent some time in taking the cultures of eighteen yellow-fever patients, and eleven cadavers, in not one of which could he find a trace of the germ that Sanarelli had claimed to be the cause of yellow fever. This eliminated once and for all the *Bacillus icteroides*, and cleared the way for positive work.

visit, on the last day of July, 1900, to the army barracks at Pinar del Rio, where a fair-sized epidemic was under way. Among the cases there Reed found exceptional significance in one. On June 6 one of the soldiers had been confined to a cell in the guard-house for some infraction of military discipline. Thirty-seven days later, on July 12, he had become suddenly ill, and on July 18 had died. Although eight other prisoners were in the cell with him, none of them had the disease. It was clear the dead soldier could not have caught the disease from his fellow prisoners, because none of them had it. It was equally clear that the victim's confinement in a cell had isolated him from most of the possible human sources of infection. If he had not caught it from another human being, how had he caught it? Reed conjectured that an insect, prob ably a mosquito, must have been the germ-carrier.

The birthplace (in 1925) of Doctor Walter Reed, "the army surgeon who planned and directed in Cuba the experiments which have given man control over that dreaded scourge, yellow fever."

This incident had a double effect. It caused Reed to follow the second of the two courses open to the commission; namely, to search not for the germ, but for the agency by which the germ was transmitted. And it caused him to recall and think again, this time more seriously, of the Cuban physician, Doctor Finlay, and his tenaciously held mosquito theory.

Reed and his associates had brought with them knowledge of a fact about yellow fever which had not been in

Finlay's possession. It was a fact not then associated with the mosquito theory, nor with any particular theory. It was merely an isolated fact, having to do with the time between attacks, the fact that a period of from twelve days to three weeks[1] elapses between the appearance of the first case of yellow fever in a community, and subsequent cases apparently derived from it. This phenomenon had been noticed by Doctor Henry R. Carter in 1898 while stationed in a small Mississippi town. Doctor Carter was in Havana during the period when the Reed Commission was making its investigations, and impressed on the commission the importance of this observation.

Doctor Carlos Finlay of Havana, Cuba. Patient and modest example of the true pioneer of science.

Reed, stimulated by what he had noticed at Pinar del Rio, and guided by his knowledge of the time-cycle in infection, began work in August, 1900, to determine what, if any, connection the Stegomyia had with yellow fever. Reed himself was obliged to return to the United States in connection with work he was doing on a typhoid-fever board, but before his departure he outlined to his associates, Doctors Lazear, Carroll, and Agramonte, the course they should follow.

On August 11 Doctor Lazear began experiments with

[1] In 1880 Doctor Stanford E. Chaillé had written: "Another curious property of the poison of yellow fever has been repeatedly noted. Very often the first set of cases has occurred one, two, or three weeks, sometimes longer, prior to the second set of cases, which begin, as it were, the resulting epidemic."—"Annual Report of the National Board of Health," 1880.

mosquitoes borrowed from Finlay. He allowed them to feed on yellow-fever patients and later on non-immunes—including himself. Results were negative, and almost convinced the experimenters they were on a false scent.

The reason for their failure was that while the time-factor was known to them in a broad way, it had not yet been refined to sufficient exactness. Much time and many more experiments were required to find the precise law; namely, that mosquitoes could not be infected by biting a patient except during the first three days of his illness, and that subsequently at least twelve days more must pass before the germ becomes virulent in the body of the mosquito.[1] The mosquitoes used in the early experiments of the Reed Commission had either not been applied to a yellow-fever patient within his first three days of illness, or, in case this first requirement was complied with, not enough time was given for the germ to reach the malignant stage within the body of the mosquito. It was autumn before positive results were secured.

[1] Finlay in all his twenty years of experimentation had not known of this time-factor. He did not know of the law, and he had not had the luck, in any of his experiments, to hit the element of time just right. In all his cases he had made the error of allowing his mosquitoes to bite patients after the initial three-day period was up, or of allowing them to bite volunteers for the experiments before the twelve days required for the parasite within the mosquito to reach the dangerous stage. This is a striking example of how scientific advances come, and of the difficulty of allocating credit for them. Finlay was indisputably the pioneer in evolving the mosquito theory. Only when Reed and his associates brought a fact that Finlay did not know (for which fact they in turn were indebted to yet other observers), and after they had made numerous experiments, did the Finlay theory reach the stage of exact proof, and become the basis of means of attacking the disease. Gorgas said that Finlay's work constituted the most striking example in history of "scientific clairvoyance."

Of the distribution of credit for scientific advances, the early contributions often made by men whose names remain obscure, Huber wrote: "In science at least, great names are landmarks; and the owners of these names have traversed and gleaned in fields where many a devoted laborer had delved and sown, and pathetically sweated blood in his altruistic zeal. . . . Nor does it in any wise detract from the gratitude due the great man that he has profited by the labors of others, adding what he can of his own, scrutinizing every detail, every datum, permeating and illuminating with his own genius, cementing the mass with his own deductions."

On August 27 a mosquito which happened to be in the virulent stage was applied to Doctor Carroll. A few days later Carroll fell ill. He recovered, but his health had been so impaired that he died a few years later. On September 13 Doctor Lazear was bitten by a mosquito of undetermined species. Five days afterward he took to his bed with yellow fever and died. (It was one of the most remunerative deaths, to humanity, in all history. His superior, Secretary of War Elihu Root, said: "The name of Doctor Jesse W. Lazear . . . should be written in the list of the martyrs who have died for humanity." Years later, in Johns Hopkins University, Baltimore, a tablet was set up reading: "Jesse W. Lazear. With more than courage and devotion of the soldier he risked and lost his life to show how a fearful pestilence is communicated and how its ravages may be prevented.")

The commission was now convinced of the truth of Finlay's theory. There still remained the task of bringing the proof of the relationship between yellow fever and the Stegomyia to a scientific basis, and also of determining if the disease could be transmitted in other ways. With funds furnished by Governor-General Leonard Wood,[1] who as a medical man had been sympathetically and understandingly watching the preliminary

[1] Doctor Aristides Agramonte, who was the only surviving member of the Reed Commission in the year this chapter was written, 1925, and who was kind enough to read the first draft, emphasized General Wood's contributions, both moral and material, in words concluding: "Without his [Wood's] unstinted support, neither Gorgas nor the Army Commission . . . would have been enabled to carry out their work."

Doctor Harvey Cushing, in his "Life of William Osler," listing the essential elements in the extermination of yellow fever, includes "a God-sent Governor-General [Wood] who had been a doctor," and elsewhere alludes to the latter as "an intelligent and courageous Military Governor . . . willing to take the responsibility for the carrying out of these experiments without getting the permission of Congress."

Yet another to whom Doctor Cushing and several others give some of the credit is Surgeon-General Sternberg. As head of the Army Medical Department work of the commission, the second set of experiments was inaugurated.

In an open, uncultivated field about a mile from Quemados, a suburb of Havana, an experimental sanitary station, named in honor of the first martyr, Doctor Lazear, was established on November 20, 1900. A strict quarantine was maintained to insure no intrusion of disease from outside. About half of those who subjected themselves to the commission's experiments were Spanish immigrants, who were attracted by the gratuity of $250 offered to those who volunteered for inoculation, and who believed that inoculation by mosquito would convert them, at slight risk, into immunes. The balance were young Americans. Seven tents were set up, each having two or three occupants, some immunes, others not. The first individual to subject himself to inoculation was John R. Kissinger, a private in the army. Kissinger was bitten

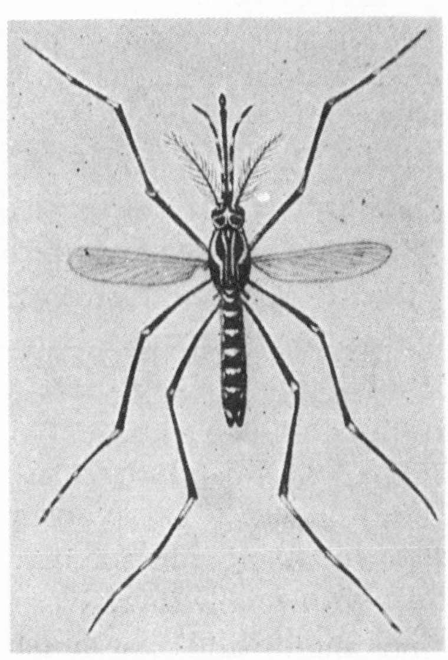

Male yellow-fever mosquito (Stegomyia Calopus).
Showing the feathery antennæ peculiar to the sex in most mosquitoes.

Sternberg had the ultimate responsibility, and took the risk that went with responsibility, a risk that involved experimenting on human beings. Doctor Cushing recites that at a subscription dinner given Doctor Sternberg on his retirement, June 13, 1902, "there had been some idle claims put forth, by partisans rather than principals, as to who deserved chief credit for the yellow-fever discoveries in Cuba. . . . It was Gorgas who put his finger on the point at issue, in his statement that had the work of the Commission been less fortunate in its outcome, General Sternberg would have received the entire blame, and consequently the success should be his also."

on November 20, and again on November 23 by a mosquito that had been allowed to suck the blood of a severe case of yellow fever on the fifth day of illness. From that, no ill effects followed. On December 5 he was bitten by five mosquitoes, all of which had bitten patients within the first three days. This time the inoculation "took," and Kissinger[1] became gravely ill. John J. Moran was next experimented upon, but without a positive result. Other inoculations, both of Americans and of Spaniards, followed, with such definite results that the commission was able to determine exactly the conditions whereby yellow fever is transmitted by the mosquito.

Lastly, the commission set to work on the other branch of their investigation, to determine if there were other possible methods of infection, or, by elimination, to reach convincing proof that the Stegomyia was the only way. For this purpose a small house was erected at Camp Lazear. On November 30, 1900, sheets, pillow-slips, blankets, and pajamas contaminated through contact with yellow-fever cases were placed in the building. That night and for nineteen nights thereafter, three courageous American non-immunes slept in the soiled

[1] A pitiful interest attaches to Kissinger, for the reason that later, after leaving the army, his health broke and he became a paralytic. He was cared for in his extremity by a faithful wife who filled the dual rôle of nurse and bread-winner. On March 2, 1907, Kissinger was placed on the pension roll, and for his services to his country and humanity was granted a monthly dole of $12. In 1906 Surgeon-General R. M. O'Reilly, in transmitting a report to the secretary of war, called attention to the niggardliness with which America rewards her public benefactors: "These total disbursements of this great nation in the way of rewards for those who made possible this discovery, and their families, amounts to $146 a month." In the year this was written, 1925, the total monthly disbursement of the government to the widows of Reed, Carroll, and Lazear, and to Kissinger, who was then still alive, was $475. Mrs. Reed's pension, amounting to $125 monthly, did not take effect until March 3, 1923, twenty-one years after Doctor Reed's death. Kissinger's pension continued at the rate of $12 monthly until December 16, 1922, when Congress increased it to $100. One year of yellow fever was estimated to have cost the State of Louisiana alone 4056 lives and $15,000,000. The Englishman Jenner, discoverer of vaccination, was granted £30,000 sterling by the British Government, and received £7383 sterling from a subscription taken in India.

pajamas, on beds reeking with the odors of black vomit and other excreta of yellow-fever patients. At the end of the twenty days they were released, their experience not having harmed them in the least. (Two other sets of volunteers went through the same ordeal with no ill effects.)

This experiment was concluded December 20, 1900. Eleven days later Doctor Reed wrote to his wife:

Columbia Barracks, Quemados, Cuba.
11:50 p.m., Dec. 31, 1900.

. . . Only ten minutes of the old century remain. Here have I been sitting, reading that most wonderful book, "La Roche on Yellow Fever," written in 1853. Forty-seven years later it has been permitted to me and my assistants to lift the impenetrable veil that has surrounded the causation of this most dreadful pest of humanity and to put it on a rational and scientific basis. I thank God that this has been accomplished during the latter days of the old century. May its cure be wrought in the early days of the new! The prayer that has been mine for twenty years, that I might be permitted in some way or at some time to do something to alleviate human suffering[1] has been granted! A thousand Happy New Years! . . . Hark, there go the twenty-four buglers in concert, all sounding "Taps" for the old year.

Less than two years later, on November 23, 1902, Reed died of appendicitis. He lies in Arlington Cemetery. His name is commemorated in the Walter Reed Hospital for soldiers, at Washington.

VIII

On February 4, 1901, the epochal report of the experiments of the Yellow Fever Commission, and the conclu-

[1] "[The physician] is the flower (such as it is) of our civilization; and when that stage of man is done with, and only remembered to be marvelled at in history, he will be thought to have shared as little as any in the defects of the period, and most notably exhibited the virtues of the race. Generosity he has, such as is possible to those who practise an art, never to those who drive a trade; discretion, tested by a hundred secrets; tact, tried in a thousand embarrassments; and what are more important, Heraclean cheerfulness and courage. So it is that he brings air and cheer into the sick-room, and often enough, though not so often as he wishes, brings healing."—Robert Louis Stevenson, "Underwoods."

sions drawn, were read before the Pan-American Medical Congress at Havana. On the same day Major Gorgas, now chief sanitary officer of Havana, announced as the programme of his department: "I am going to get rid of the mosquito."[1]

Mosquitoes had been so abundant in Havana for so long a time that they had come to be regarded as permanent in Nature's order. With the initiation of the campaign against them, housewives in Havana became subject to an official attention so painstaking and so thorough that at times they were driven almost to distraction. About all that was known of the Stegomyia was that it was a peculiarly domesticated insect. Whereas the seven hundred-odd other kinds of mosquitoes lived in swamps and deposited their eggs in stagnant water, the Stegomyia cared to live only in houses, and preferred to deposit its eggs only in clean sweet water, contained in a pitcher, a water-barrel, a cistern, or some domestic utensil. Gorgas prepared a card index in which every such receptacle was recorded. Inspectors, carrying sheafs of the index cards, visited periodically every house in Havana. In their presence housewives were compelled to produce all utensils capable of holding water. Woe unto the housewife attempting to "hold out" on the inspectors! If a single receptacle were missing, a search would be begun which would not end until it had been found. Water-barrels, cesspools, cisterns, and other fairly large deposits of water were screened, and a film of oil deposited

[1] Gorgas was not as certain he could "get rid of the mosquito" as the words of his announcement indicate. Something over a year later, in a report written on July 12, 1902, he gives a true picture of his real state of mind when he faced the task: "Yellow fever at the beginning of 1901 was about as bad as it had ever been in Havana at that time of the year. The city was infected in every part, and there was present probably the largest non-immune population that had ever before been in Havana. I had very little hope of accomplishing much; it seemed to me that even if the mosquito did convey yellow fever, he could not be gotten rid of."

on them which smothered the "wigglers" when they came to the top for air.

The effect of the new campaign was sensational. Reports of new cases dwindled from day to day. From the time when Gorgas started his warfare against the Stegomyia, but five deaths from yellow fever were recorded. The day came in 1901 when, for the first time in centuries, there was not a single case of yellow fever in Havana.[1]

IX

Estimates vary as to the relative importance of the contributions of Gorgas, Reed, and Finlay. Sanitarians are apt to stress the work of Gorgas. The Cubans, actuated by national pride, emphasize Doctor Finlay's theorizing and experimentation. Medical scientists generally feel that the work of Reed was paramount. It will serve if we consider the three coequal. Finlay developed the theory; Reed confirmed it; and Gorgas built his work upon it. There is abundant glory for all.

In bestowing an honorary degree upon Doctor Reed in 1902, President Eliot of Harvard with the terseness, the exquisiteness in the choice of words at once exact and resonant that made his bestowal of honorary degrees one of the high ceremonials of American life, summarized the task that Reed had performed so ably:

> Walter Reed, graduate in medicine of the University of Virginia, the Army surgeon who planned and directed in Cuba the experiments which have given man control over that fearful scourge, yellow fever.

[1] Mingled with the world-wide applause of scientists and laymen was a perceptible thread of jeering at the medical profession. In its issue of February 28, 1901, the humorous periodical *Life* remarked: "It looks as if the medical profession would be owing us an apology presently for the trouble the world has been put to for many years past to disinfect travellers and their effects and merchandise that have come from yellow-fever ports. The new theory about yellow fever, as developed by experiments of Doctor Walter Reed of the Army,

A few years later, in 1908, in awarding a similar degree to Gorgas, President Eliot said:

> William Crawford Gorgas, soldier; son of a Confederate soldier; first lieutenant, captain, major, and colonel in the Medical Corps of the United States Army; chief sanitary officer of the Isthmian Canal Zone; to-day the most successful administrator of the present efficiency and future promise of preventive medicine.

X

While Gorgas was fighting yellow fever in Havana, a conflict on a larger scale was just beginning something over a thousand miles away. Centuries before, in 1529, a Spanish explorer, Alvaro de Saavedra, had had the idea of cutting a canal through the Isthmus of Panama to facilitate the passage of ships between Europe and the Orient. By an air-line, the distance from the Atlantic to the Pacific at one point on the Isthmus is but forty miles. By opening a water lane here, ships could pass from one ocean to the other with a saving of distance and time, and with much greater safety than by passing around Cape Horn. But years grew into decades, and decades into centuries, and nothing was actually done until in the early 1880's, De Lesseps, constructor of the Suez Canal, formed a French corporation to dig a canal at Panama. At the beginning France was keyed up to a high pitch of hope, but misfortune attended the venture from the start, and soon hope turned to despair. Defects cropped up in the French organization. None of these defects, however, was comparable to the withering

is that it is carried nohow except by the agency of a certain female mosquito, who imparts it by her bite. If this theory turns out to be sound, it will be at once a triumph and a matter of mortification to the doctors, for, while it will be very clever and useful of them to have made such a discovery, think what they will be owing us on account of all the sulphur burned, and all the fuss and delay on yellow fever's account in the last century!"

effect of yellow fever, malaria, and other tropical diseases on the French workmen.

By the year 1900 little was left of the French attempt except a partly finished ditch, almost completely overgrown with jungle, with here and there a rusting, vine-

From a photograph by Underwood & Underwood.

"Monkey Hill" cemetery, which recorded the French failure at Panama.

grown junk-heap that had once been a costly excavating machine — that, and one of the saddest graveyards in the world, acres of little white crosses falling over and rotting under the jungle of tropical growth.

XI

Just as the French attempt was coming to acknowledged failure, in 1898, the United States determined to have an Isthmian canal of its own construction and ownership. The idea had been discussed in America for a century, and some desultory gestures had been made. But in 1898 the project was so far from crystallization that there was not even agreement upon a site. Then, on February 15 of that year, the battleship *Maine* was blown up in Havana harbor. That, with what had preceded, made war with Spain practically inevitable. There was immediate need for mobilization of American naval strength in the Gulf of Mexico. An indispensable battleship, the *Oregon*, was in the Pacific Ocean, at San Francisco. For seventy-one days, from March 19 to June 1, America, with strained suspense, through alternations of excited newspaper head-lines and intervals of menacing silence, followed the *Oregon's* slow progress from San Francisco all the way down the Pacific coast to South America, around Cape Horn, and up the Atlantic coast. By that experience[1] America's vague ambition for an Isthmian canal became an imperative decision.

President McKinley, in his message to the next Congress, December, 1898, made the recommendation. Con-

[1] The trip of the *Oregon* around Cape Horn was described by Admiral Chadwick, historian of the Spanish War, as "one unprecedented in battleship history and one which will long preserve its unique distinction." Secretary Long of the navy said it "has no parallel in history." Every American was stirred by it. Those who could express their emotion in verse did so. John James Meehan wrote "The Race of the *Oregon*":

"Lights out! And a prow turned toward the South,
And a canvas hiding each cannon's mouth,
And a ship like a silent ghost released
Is seeking her sister ships in the East. . . .

When your boys shall ask what the guns are for,
Then tell them the tale of the Spanish War,
And the breathless millions that looked upon
The matchless race of the *Oregon*."

Arthur Guiterman wrote "The Rush of the *Oregon*":

"They held her South to Magellan's mouth,
Then East they steered her, forth
Through the farther gate of the crafty strait,
And then they held her North.

Six thousand miles to the Indian Isles!
And the *Oregon* rushed home,
Her wake a swirl of jade and pearl,
Her bow a bend of foam."

That trip, and the emotions it aroused, had more to do with America determining to have a Panama Canal than any other cause.

gress, the following March, 1899, created an Isthmian Canal Commission. Secretary of State Hay negotiated with Great Britain the abrogation of an old treaty under which Great Britain had some embarrassing rights, and the substitution of the Hay-Pauncefote Treaty, which gave the United States unrestricted right to build the Canal. Senator Hanna in an epochal speech crystallized Senate opinion on the Panama route. The United States agreed to buy the property and franchise of the French company for $40,000,000. A treaty was negotiated with Colombia, owner of the Canal strip, for the purchase of the necessary rights. While the treaty was being held up in the Colombian congress, Panama revolted and set up an independent government. Within three days President Roosevelt recognized the new republic. Through Secretary of State Hay he negotiated a treaty with it, giving the United States the necessary land and rights.[1] In this driving sequence of more than five years, the preliminary obstacles to action by the United States were removed.

In May, 1904, Congress created a commission of seven men to dig the Canal. The personnel was prescribed by Congress on the theory that the Canal was a job of engineering; there were to be one army officer, one navy officer, and five engineers. The country as well as Congress thought of the Canal as merely a job of construction, engineering,[2] excavation — on an immense scale to be sure, but not otherwise formidable to a nation that had built 200,000 miles of railroad. All the public discussion during the past five years had been focussed on the political obstacles associated with Great Britain, Colombia,

[1] Each of the steps here compressed into a sentence was actually attended by volumes of debate. One, Roosevelt's relation to the Panama revolution, was and still is the most controverted incident of his career.

[2] History still assumes that, and treats the Canal as a triumph of engineering and steam-shovels.

and the Panama republic, and the commercial obstacle of the French company. With these out of the way it was thought nothing remained but to dig. The public fell into a mood of impatience. The newspapers carried a slogan: "Let the dirt fly!"

XII

But the doctors knew. They remembered yellow fever, and Gorgas. A delegation representing the American Medical Association, the New York Academy of Medicine, the Philadelphia College of Physicians, and other medical organizations, called on President Roosevelt. I quote from their spokesman, Doctor William H. Welch, of Johns Hopkins:

> We passed through a room crowded with persons waiting to see the President, and I felt that he must begrudge every minute we occupied, especially as what I had to say I had previously communicated to him by letter, and I knew that Leonard Wood had already urged upon him all that I could say, and more. I did not occupy more than ten minutes. . . . When we finished presenting our argument, which altogether could not have lasted more than fifteen minutes, President Roosevelt began talking to us, and continued for at least twenty minutes, in a very interesting, dramatic and amazingly outspoken fashion. He told us that he did not frame the law enacted by Congress, and it did not meet his ideas of what the situation demanded. He would have preferred a single director, who should select engineers, sanitarians, and other experts. Instead of that, he had to pick out seven members to make up a commission, and the law provided that no less than five of these should be engineers, without one word about a doctor or a sanitarian. "How can I, under these circumstances," he said, "put a doctor on the commission?" He said that he fully appreciated the importance of what we had told him, and he asked me to go at once to General Davis and tell him all about Gorgas, and the importance of the sanitary side of the work. He sat down and dictated the letter to Davis.

XIII

Gorgas became not a commissioner with authority, but a subordinate in charge of sanitation. With the mental attitude that went with his temperament and his army traditions, he accepted the handicap and began patiently to urge on the commission the fact he knew from his Havana experiences that disease, especially yellow fever and malaria, was the one insuperable difficulty, that the elimination of it was the indispensable step without which a Panama Canal could not be.[1] The entire forty-mile stretch along which the Canal was to be built was a sweltering miasma, in which disease and death stalked in a hundred forms.[2] Gorgas's thorough mind knew that if only the ordinary sanitary measures were adopted, not only would the Americans fail, they would never have a real chance. He constantly kept this point of view before his superiors, stressed the necessity of coping with disease in the new way he had evolved at Havana.

When one remembers the attention-arresting quality of Gorgas's achievement in Havana, how in a few months he had completely extirpated a malignant disease that had preyed upon man for centuries, it seems incredible that doubt of the mosquito theory of the propagation of yellow fever should continue to exist among men so supposedly well-informed and competent as the officials chosen to compose the first Isthmian Canal Commission. These men knew of the Reed experiments at Havana.

[1] Doctor Harvey Cushing, of Harvard University, in his "Life of William Osler," after summing up the discovery of the means of overcoming yellow fever, says that but for that ". . . well, the Panama Canal project would have been an impossibility." When history becomes more discriminating, it will be more general to view the Canal as chiefly a triumph of medical science.

[2] In 1885 James Anthony Froude wrote: "In all the world there is not perhaps now concentrated in any single spot so much . . . foul disease, such a hideous dung-heap of physical and moral abomination. The Isthmus is a damp, tropical jungle, intensely hot, swarming with mosquitoes . . . ; the home, even as Nature made it, of yellow fever, typhus, and dysentery."

They knew also that Gorgas had wiped out yellow fever in that city by screening the sick and by killing off the Stegomyia mosquito. They knew, further, or should have known, that a medical congress at Paris had canvassed the work of Reed and put its stamp of approval on the mosquito theory; that in different parts of the world the Reed experiments had been repeated, and that the results had completely corroborated everything the Reed Commission had asserted. Yet the commissioners intrusted with the building of the Panama Canal treated the whole theory of mosquito infection as balderdash.

Gorgas haunted the anteroom of Rear-Admiral John G. Walker, chairman of the Isthmian Canal Commission, pleading for adequate supplies of sulphur, pyrethrum powder, wire-screening, crude oil. During his interviews he frequently wasted the admiral's time by going over again and again the evidence in support of the mosquito theory. Never did he lose patience, but never did he make any impression. Gorgas was wrong, all wrong, maintained the admiral. The right way to drive disease from the Canal strip, he said, was to put into operation certain ideas of his own — eliminate filth, drain off stagnant water, bury the garbage and dead cats, paint the houses, and there would be no disease — this was, in its essentials, Admiral Walker's plan. In his zeal he even offered to draw up a minutely detailed set of rules to guide Gorgas in his work!

Discouraged, Gorgas turned from the commission to General George W. Davis, first governor of the Canal Zone. General Davis was a distinguished engineer — he had completed the Washington Monument — and Gorgas felt he might prove a powerful help, but Davis, too, disappointed him. "I'm your friend, Gorgas," Davis would tell him, "and I'm trying to set you right. On the mosquito you are simply wild. All who agree with you are wild. Get the idea out of your head. Yellow fever, as we all know, is caused by filth."

Gorgas did what he could, but he had no authority, and no sympathetic support from those who had authority; he had no materials and no funds to buy materials. The most he could do fell far short of adequacy.

XIV

In November, 1904, some members of an Italian opera troupe, playing in the cities and towns along the Canal, fell ill of yellow fever; within a few days two of them died. In the cruiser *Boston*, anchored off Colon, several of the crew caught the disease, and three died. In Panama and Colon, and in the temporary settlements along the route of the Canal, the disease caught hold. By the early months of 1905 a fair-sized epidemic was under way.

Now began the harvest of the bitter fruits of official stupidity and obstinacy. A panic seized upon the construction forces. The one thought uppermost in the minds of all was to get away. Even Chief Engineer John F. Wallace,[1] the one who in such an emergency should have heartened his followers by a brave show of intrepidity, intimated to Secretary of War Taft his intention of resigning. No explanation was given, but dread of yellow fever was the cause that received wide-spread credence. Desertion of the ship by the captain naturally did little to calm the crew. Workmen fled to the port cities, where they fought for passage on every outgoing ship. Cases were frequent where incoming employees refused to leave the ship at the Panaman ports, and continued on, anywhere, just to escape the death-trap that the Isthmus had now come to be.

[1] "That he lived in dread of yellow fever was no secret. . . . He was one of the officials who had taken the precaution of bringing his coffin with him."—William Crawford Gorgas, "His Life and Work," by Marie D. Gorgas and Burton J. Hendrick.

Stupidity clothed with authority is an odious bedfellow, and Gorgas was in bed with the Panama Canal Commission. He could not resign, or otherwise avoid the menace to his reputation — his army training and his temperament forbade that. He had warned his superiors the epidemic would come, had pleaded with them for the means to forestall it. But that, he knew, would not save him from the blame. When the epidemic arrived, the responsibility was on him, as he had known it would be. He was the sanitarian in charge, and therefore at fault. Gorgas came close to dismissal shortly after the epidemic started, but was saved by the fortunate visit to Panama of Doctor Charles A. L. Reed, of Cincinnati, a former president of the American Medical Association. Doctor Reed was a shrewd observer, and after a few weeks' inspection of the sanitary work on the Canal, returned to the United States, where he published his impressions. Writing of the red tape which hedged Gorgas in from all sides, he described an incident that later became a classic in Panama Canal administration:

> A woman in the insane department was delivered of a child; her condition was such that she could not nurse her offspring; the nurse applied to Major La Garde for a rubber nipple and a nursing-bottle; he had none—the requisition of last September had not yet been filled; he made out a requisition, took it to Colonel Gorgas for indorsement, then to Mr. Tobey, chief of the bureau of materials and supplies, for another indorsement, then to a clerk to have it copied and engrossed; then a messenger was permitted to go to a drug-store and buy a nursing-bottle and nipple, which finally reached the infant two days after the necessity for their use had arisen. The articles ought to have cost not more than thirty cents, but counting the money value of the time of the nurse, of Major La Garde, of his clerical help, of Colonel Gorgas, of Mr. Tobey, of Mr. Tobey's clerks, of the messenger, the cost to the Government of the United States was in the neighborhood of $6.75 — all due to the penny-wise and pound-foolish policy of the Commission.

Due in great part to this report of Doctor Reed, the first Isthmian Canal Commission was junked by President Roosevelt. The new commission was headed by Theodore P. Shonts, a contractor and railroad-builder from the Middle West. Shonts took up his duties in June, 1905, at the time when Gorgas was just getting the upper hand on the epidemic. Shonts was a "practical" man. He was frequently employed by bankers and managers of railroads as a "go-getter" driver of men. His education was of the scantiest; he knew little of science, and less of medicine; and could recognize a fact only when it hit him in the eye, painfully. He knew only the autocrat's ways of administration. Because an epidemic of yellow fever was raging on the Canal, he decided that Gorgas was not getting "results." Gorgas must go, he determined, and even went so far as to fix upon a successor to him, an old friend who was an osteopath. The new commission prepared a memorandum for Secretary Taft, recommending the dismissal of Gorgas, and all the other sanitarians in Panama who believed in the mosquito theory of disease transmission. Secretary Taft indorsed the recommendation as a matter of official routine, and passed it on to President Roosevelt, who was spending the summer at Oyster Bay. Roosevelt recognized that being a layman he was not competent to decide the merits of the case without consulting experts. Accordingly he wrote to Doctor Welch, dean of Johns Hopkins Medical School, who replied that in his opinion no one was as well qualified to conduct the sanitation of the Panama Canal as Colonel Gorgas. Still undecided, Roosevelt summoned his friend and personal physician, Doctor Alexander Lambert. Lambert spoke:

I am sorry for you, to-night, Mr. President. You are facing one of the greatest decisions in your career. Upon what you decide depends whether or not you are going to get your canal. If you fall back upon the old methods of sanitation, you will fail, just as the French failed. If you back up Gorgas and his ideas, and let him make his campaign against mosquitoes, then you get that canal. I can only give you my advice; you must decide for yourself. There is only one way of controlling yellow fever and malaria, and that is the eradication of the mosquitoes. But it is your canal; you must do the choosing, and you must choose to-night whether you are going to build that canal.

The President was convinced. Shonts was ordered to make peace with Gorgas.

Gorgas conducted a campaign of extermination of the Stegomyia mosquito, using the methods he had developed at Havana. At his request, the municipal governments of Panama and Colon passed ordinances fining householders five dollars for permitting mosquitoes in the larval stage on their premises. As in Havana, Gorgas's system gradually got the upper hand. Finally, on an afternoon in September, 1905, Gorgas, in a buoyant mood, entered the dissecting-room of the government hospital at Ancon, where a number of white-clad surgeons were at work on a cadaver.

"Take a good look at this man, boys," he told the surgeons, "for it's the last case of yellow fever you will ever see. There will never be any more deaths from this cause in Panama."

A confident assertion, this, to make about the spot that had for centuries been considered the world's incomparable hotbed of disease. Yet in the twenty years that have passed since that prediction was uttered, not a single death from yellow fever has been recorded.

XV

In 1907 another disruption of the administration of the Canal took place, precipitated by the resignation of Chief Engineer John F. Stevens. Profound discouragement with the project was now felt by the Administration at Washington and by the public generally. The construction was so vast an undertaking that it could not be carried on satisfactorily unless a settled policy were fixed upon and carried out resolutely. Such a course

Third Panama Canal Commission. Colonel George W. Goethals in centre; Gorgas at his left.

apparently could not be followed with civilians in the places of highest authority. President Roosevelt decided to form a new commission composed largely of army and navy officers. They at least could be relied upon not to resign, no matter how discouraged or disgruntled they might become. Lieutenant-Colonel George W. Goethals was named chief engineer and chairman of the new commission. Gorgas at last was made a commissioner[1]

[1] Others on the board were Major D. D. Gaillard, later to become famous as the genius of the Culebra Cut; Major William S. Sibert, creator of the Gatun Dam and Gatun Lake; J. S. C. Blackburn; H. F. Hodges; Jackson Smith; H. H. Rousseau, U. S. navy; and Joseph Bucklin Bishop, secretary.

in tardy recognition of his successful handling of the yellow-fever epidemic of three years before.

One of the first acts of the new chairman was to seek an interview with President Roosevelt. Goethals had analyzed the unsatisfactory records of his predecessors, and believed he knew what had been their main trouble. Red tape had done the mischief, he felt certain; red tape in crates, in bales, in ship-load lots—red tape in which former executives had become inextricably entangled, had stumbled, lost their way, and finally in desperation had given up. Building the Canal was a job of constant emergencies. Hourly, situations arose calling for instantaneous decision. It was really a war, a war on the jungle, on Nature herself. As such it could not effectively be carried on by swivel-chair strategists 2000 miles away, nor through hydra-headed decisions. This, at any rate, was Goethals's opinion, and in his interview with President Roosevelt he stressed the necessity of centralizing authority in the hands of one man. "I am willing to try it," he said in conclusion. The President acquiesced, and by executive order Goethals was made supreme authority in all matters connected with the Panama Canal.[1]

Gorgas, seeing a better system of administration in force, a fellow army officer at its head, and himself a member of the commission, hoped he would now be allowed to fight disease in his own way. Once more was

[1] Both Roosevelt and Colonel Goethals have told me of a scene that was repeated several times in Roosevelt's office. Roosevelt, after making Goethals chairman, sent one by one for others whom he intended to appoint as members. He introduced each to Colonel Goethals, bade them be seated, and then spoke to each substantially as follows: "Congress has ordered me to appoint a Panama Canal Commission of seven men. It ought to be one man, but Congress favors seven jobs rather than one. I am going to appoint you a member. It will be a position of ample remuneration and much honor. In appointing you I have only one qualification to make. Colonel Goethals here is to be chairman. He is to have complete authority. If at any time you do not agree with his policies, do not bother to tell me about it—your disagreement with him will constitute your resignation."

he disappointed. The trouble arose from Chairman Goethals's demands on his organization for greater economy and more efficiency. Goethals regarded no record as perfect. He spurred his men on to do more work at less cost. Gorgas in his sanitary work was spending about

A typical mosquito-proof building of the type erected by Americans at Panama.

$350,000 yearly,[1] a modest sum compared with the millions that were annually being poured into the project for other purposes than sanitation. The good health of the construction personnel, upon which the entire project rested, was being bought at a cost relatively trifling. Yet Goethals professed to consider this an extravagance. As he had done four years before with Admiral Walker, Gorgas argued with Goethals, always pleading to be allowed to do his own work unhampered and in the manner which experience had taught him was best.

[1] There are no exact figures. Gorgas himself estimated the cost of the sanitary work at about the equivalent of a bottle of beer a day for each workman.

One day, after a particularly trying discussion, Gorgas almost lost his temper. Goethals had said to him:

> Do you know, Gorgas, that every mosquito you kill costs the United States Government ten dollars?

With a smile just faintly tinged with malice, Gorgas replied:

> But just think, one of those ten-dollar mosquitoes might bite you, and what a loss that would be to the country.

Yellow fever was not the only disease to engage Gorgas's attention at the Canal. From the beginning he had also laid plans to eliminate malaria. Like yellow fever, this disease was propagated by a mosquito, the Anopheles, quite different in its habits from the Stegomyia. The warfare against the malaria mosquito consisted mainly in oiling or draining stagnant waters, cutting away all vegetable growths within a radius of 200 yards of every human habitation, and the breeding and dissemination of larvæ-eating minnows. The keeping of lizards, spiders, and other insects known to have a fondness for mosquitoes was encouraged. The effect on malaria of this bizarre campaign was almost as astounding as had been that on yellow fever following Gorgas's persecution of the Stegomyia mosquito at Havana. Between 1906 and 1913 the proportion of Canal workers admitted monthly to the malarial wards of the hospitals dropped from 40 to 10 per cent of the total. The reason why the decrease was not greater yet was given by Gorgas in a speech at St. Louis in 1915:

> I was much disappointed that we did not get rid of malaria on the Isthmus of Panama as we did at Havana. I had fully expected to do so, and when we went to the Isthmus we put into effect the same antimalarial measures that had been so successful at Havana. These measures were vigorously pushed for the first four years. At the end of our four years of work,

May, 1908, all power on the Isthmus was concentrated in the hands of a single man, the chairman of the Commission. This officer thought it advisable to make certain radical changes in the methods of sanitation. These changes, ordered by the chairman, took execution of the antimalarial work out of the hands of the sanitary authorities and placed them in the hands of men who had no special knowledge of antimalarial work. I argued against these changes as forcibly as I could, but to no avail. Looking back over my fifteen years of experience in tropical sanitation, I believe that if I could have continued at Panama the same methods that I had used previous to 1908, the results would have been the same as at Havana, and the canal workers would have been as entirely free from malaria as were the citizens of Havana.

The true monument to Gorgas's greatness will never be a thing of marble or granite. Undoubtedly in time a grateful humanity will fully comprehend the meaning of Gorgas and will erect monuments in his honor; but no sculptor's masterpiece can ever glorify Gorgas as do a simple set of figures:

The year the Canal was finished, 1914, the death-rate in the then registered area of the United States was 14.1 per thousand. In the Canal Zone it was 6 per thousand. In no part of the United States was man so immune to untimely death from disease as in the Panama Canal Zone. It might be stated even more broadly: Gorgas had, in ten years, converted the world's most pestilential wilderness into its most healthful spot.

XVI

After the completion of the Panama Canal, Gorgas was summoned to South Africa to fight pneumonia in the gold and diamond mines. He spent three months surveying the necessities, laid out a plan and appointed an administrator under whom, after four years, the death-rate from pneumonia went down from 350 per thousand to 3 per thousand, and the death-rate from all diseases to

6 per thousand. On his way back to the United States via Europe, Gorgas was given an ovation in London which, in the opinion of Sir William Osler, was the greatest ever given a medical man in England. In Gorgas's honor, Oxford University held a special convocation to confer on him the degree of Doctor of Science. "Preeminently distinguished," said the acting vice-chancellor, "sagacious, health-bringing, the modern Machaon of the American army, whom indeed I should wish to salute not only in Latin prose but also in Greek verse, thus:

Hail Router of the Plague of flies! Hail Isthmian Conqueror true!
Gorgas, to that wise Goddess dear, the Gorgon death who slew!

The reason for this and other honors[1] heaped upon Gorgas by England was expressed succinctly by the editor of *The Daily Mail:*

> Perhaps of all living Americans, Doctor Gorgas has conferred the greatest benefit on the human race. The whole world, particularly the British Empire, with its large tropical possessions, owes him a debt which Britons are proud to acknowledge.

While Gorgas was still in South Africa, word had reached him of his promotion by President Wilson to the surgeon-generalcy of the army. He took up his new duties on returning to Washington, but was not left long in official routine work. The International Health Board, formed a few years before by John D. Rockefeller, had decided on a world campaign for the elimination of yellow fever. Gorgas was asked to serve as the ambassador of the board to Latin-American countries, with the object of enlisting their active support. In June, 1916, accompanied by his friend Doctor Carter, Doctor Juan Guiteras,

[1] He was made an honorary major-general of the British army, and on a later trip was knighted by King George.

a colleague during the Havana days, and several other companions, he started on what eventually became a triumphal tour of all South America. All the countries of Latin America where yellow fever still existed agreed

S. S. *Kroonland* passing through the completed Panama Canal.

to co-operate with the International Health Board in a final campaign of extermination.

When the United States entered the Great War in April, 1917, Gorgas was the responsible head of the Medical Corps of the United States army. Three days after the signing of the Armistice he reached the retiring age, and laid down the duties of the surgeon-generalcy. He had no thought, however, of retiring to enjoy a comfortable old age. Although fond of intercourse with friends, of the theatre, and other attractions of the cities, Gorgas found his keenest pleasure in the war against disease.

At the age of sixty-four he again took up his suspended connection with the International Health Board, and directed a campaign against yellow fever at Guayaquil, Ecuador, with such success that within six months he broke the centuries-old hold of the disease on that city.

XVII

Gorgas now turned to the last stronghold of yellow fever, the west coast of Africa. With the Belgian Congo as his destination, he sailed, on May 8, 1920, for Europe, accompanied by his wife and a few intimate friends and associates. While in London preparing for his trip to the Congo, he suffered a paralytic stroke. A few weeks later he died. His funeral at St. Paul's Cathedral inspired this elegy by a London journalist:

> A riderless horse walked up Ludgate Hill the other day behind its sleeping master. . . . I looked down from the windows of the Little House with Green Shutters in the very shadow of the dome, and I thought that here indeed was a public opinion of which our London, and our country, and all the entire world, might well be proud. For here was no great Englishman, no great Briton, going to his rest; here was a ragged, barefoot boy being carried to St. Paul's after his life's work was done. He had done for the world one of the greatest things that an American brain has ever done; he had made the Panama Canal after thousands of people had died in the attempt. . . . The other day he rode up Ludgate Hill, sleeping his last sleep on earth, wrapped in the Stars and Stripes. There were thousands of men and women and children standing still, there were hundreds of men in khaki passing by, there were ambassadors and other great people, and the lonely woman who was on her way with her hero to conquer disease in Africa when death took him from her. And there was a riderless horse. All these came up Ludgate Hill, and as the sun poured down on this ancient way, our hearts and ears throbbing with the solemn music of the Dead March, we knew that we were looking on the passing of a man whose name would shine for ages in the history of our race. . . . He passed through the great door through which the sun streams into the nave

of St. Paul's, and there he lay with Nelson and Wellington and all that mighty host who came this way and passed into the universe. They will take him to his own land, but in truth he belongs to us all. He was one of Life's great helpers, for he cleaned up foul places and made them sweet, and now, as they said of Lincoln, "he belongs to the Ages."[1]

XVIII

We think of the discoverers in medical science as relieving man's body from disease. We fail to take account of what they do for man's spirit. The addition of some six years to the average man's life within a quarter-century is, in the aggregate, an immense enrichment of the world. Even greater is the enrichment that comes of relief from anxiety, the intellectual and spiritual release, the more abundant flowering of man's powers that follows rescue from the tyranny of fear.

History is crowded, literature is crowded, song is crowded, the drama is crowded, with military and political heroes who brought freedom to their peoples. Many have been sincere patriots; not a few have been merely following a personal ambition they happened to hold, and drumming up recruits by a familiar appeal to emotion. Grant them the best of motives and concede their achievements fully; still it may fairly be doubted if any political tyranny ever imposed on its people such a fear, such a longing for freedom, such a paralysis of the spirit, as disease. I doubt if the average Englishman felt himself as much oppressed by Charles I as by the plague; or if any colonial American was as much in dread of taxation without representation as of smallpox. And it may reasonably be contended that Walter Reed and William Crawford Gorgas brought to man freedom in a more

[1] This and some of the other quotations are taken from "William Crawford Gorgas, His Life and Work," written by his wife, Marie D. Gorgas, and Burton J. Hendrick.

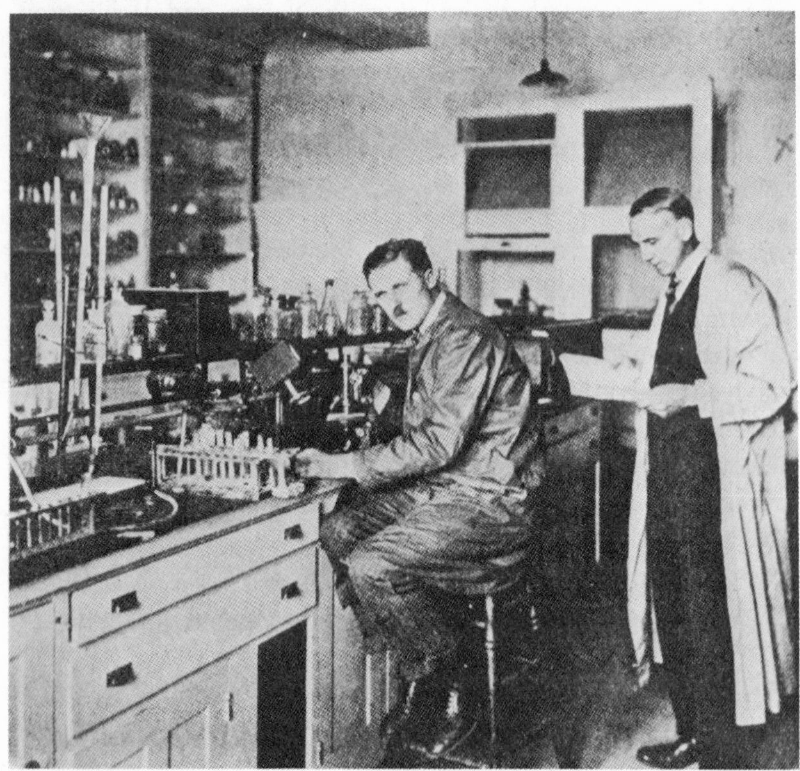

Dr. Charles H. Boissevain and Dr. Gerald B. Webb, in charge of the Research Laboratory at Colorado College maintained by the Colorado Tuberculosis Research Foundation.

happy sense and in a larger measure than any military or political leader.[1]

[1] For help in this chapter, the author is under obligation to many persons who were in contact with the events—some of whom supplied facts not easy to get, others who read the proofs at various stages—including:

General Leonard Wood, General R. E. Noble, General Walter D. McCaw, Colonel C. C. McCulloch, Jr., Doctor Juan Guiteras, Doctor Harvey Cushing, Doctor Theodore C. Lyster, Mrs. Marie D. Gorgas, Professor John H. Latane, Doctor Aristides Agramonte.

18

THE AUTOMOBILE EMERGES

A Popular Joke Which Marked a New Era. A Marvel of the Nineties. Some Early Automobile Rides. Some Pioneers of the "Horseless Vehicle." Steps in Its Development. America's Debt to Europe. An Achievement of Adaptation. Pioneers Who Survived. The Attitude of the Public and of Bankers. Racing. Advertising and Salesmanship. Erroneous Popular Assumptions. The Beginnings of "Quantity Production"; Its Social and Economic Effects.

Some ten years or so before the period of this history began, in the childhood of persons who in 1925 had reached the age of fifty or so, there was current one of those popular jokes, an example of the type of humorous stories which are in themselves landmarks of popular history, and by which the arrival of new institutions can be marked. This particular joke went about by word of mouth, at the time the horse-drawn street-car began to pass, when the cable-car and the trolley-car were a novelty. Probably the circulation of this jibe was confined to word of mouth; for there was in the telling of it a slightly impish ribaldry which in itself is a mark of the passage of time, of the change in manners and point of view, which permits to be put to-day, in the most staid and respectable of print, a kind of slightly daring joke, such that, if it had been printed at all a generation ago, would have been printed only with the cautious use of chastely euphemistic dashes for words which, in a later generation, are not banned. This joke represented a Chinaman standing on the sidewalk, watching with inscrutable intentness the passage of a trolley-car; and summing up the experience, from his point of view, in the remark: "No pushee, no pullee; but goee like hellee allee samee." For this and a world of similar jokes — most of them, doubtless, adaptations of the remark with which primitive Mark Twains had epitomized the arrival of the floating log and the animal's back as means by which bold spirits facilitated their motions on the surface of the waters and the earth — for this sort of popular humor there were several occasions during the decade or two preceding 1900 and since. A man who in 1925 was less than fifty years old had seen the invention of the trolley, its rise, and the beginning of its decline; had seen the rise of the bicycle, the peak of its use, and its decline; had seen the passing of the cable-car; had seen the passing of the horse-drawn street-car and bus; had seen the beginnings, the entire history so far of the automobile and of the airplane, as well.

On the streets of Chicago, in September, 1892, appeared a strange vehicle. "Ever since its arrival," said a contemporary account, "the sight of a well-loaded carriage moving along the streets at a spanking pace with no horses in front and apparently with nothing on board to give it motion, was a sight that has been too much, even for the wide-awake Chicagoan. It is most amusing to see the crowd gather whenever the vehicle appears. So great has been the curiosity that the owner when passing through the business section has had to appeal to the police to aid him in clearing the way."

The owner of this novelty of 1892, William Morrison, of Des Moines, Iowa, is credited with having been the first man in America to make an electric automobile — electric as distinguished from steam and gasoline. In the automobile industry the word "first" is perilous to use; for there is no one person, as there is in the field of older inventions, to whom can be ascribed the credit of being either the indisputable pioneer or, as yet, the popularly accepted one. If it were desired to set up a monument to the man primarily responsible for the presence, in the year 1925, of 17,000,000 automobiles in the United States, as there are monuments to inventors in other fields, it would be necessary, in this case, for the monument to be a composite figure, the features of which would need to be equitably distributed in the proportions of the claims made by many rivals and their partisans. If any schoolboy is asked who invented the steamboat, he replies "Fitch"; if asked about the cotton-gin, he replies "Whitney"; if about the sewing-machine, "Howe"; if about the reaper and binder, "McCormick"; if about the steam-locomotive, "Stephenson." But no schoolboy, and not even any authority within the automobile world, is able, with equally instant certainty, or within the compactness of a single name, to say that any one man is the inventor of the automobile. Or, if any name is set up as entitled to priority of time or credit, the claim is hotly disputed by the partisans of others. Not only as to the automobile as a whole, but even as to most of its fundamental parts, there is no accepted certainty in the allocation of credit for invention.[1]

Doubtless one reason for the greater glibness with which we name the inventors of older mechanisms, like the sewing-machine and the steamboat, is the distance in time since the older machines were perfected. Doubtless it is partly due also to the fact that at the times when these older machines were invented there was less setting down of things in print — history was more generally in the custody of word-of-mouth tradition, and tradition usually exalts personality. Probably a more discriminating truth would say that in the case of these older inventions there were there, too, contributions

[1] So far as any credit can be assigned, it must be to Europeans, not Americans.

from many different pioneers. And possibly, also, the schoolboy of a hundred years ahead of us, when asked who invented the automobile, may say "Henry Ford."

The best reason why no name is associated with invention of the automobile is that it was not an invention. Nobody invented it. Certainly nobody in America invented it. The automobile, in America especially, was an assembling, an adapting. Almost every adjunct to the automobile, as it was in 1900, had long been in use in other devices. The transmission, in one form or another, was an essential part of the lathes in every machine-shop and of the driving-wheel of most stationary engines. The frictionless bearing had been developed for the bicycle. The acetylene light was familiar to everybody. In short, the automobile was no more than a coordination and adaptation of old ideas and inventions, some of which, like the wheel, mingled their origins with the mists of antiquity. Possibly, in making such a comprehensive statement, we should except the electric spark used first by Benz in 1886 to ignite the explosive mixture in the cylinder of an engine, but even here it should be remembered that long before the human race had evolved intelligible speech, it was known that lightning could start fires: certainly Benjamin Franklin during a June thunder-storm in 1752 produced a real jump-spark with kite and key and his own good knuckles.

II

In the following table are a few of the mile-stones in the progress of what we know now as the automobile:

1678. The cannon. The modern gasoline-engine is mechanically and theoretically a development of the cannon, the chief difference being that in the automobile engine the place of the projectile is taken by a piston which returns on its path.

1760 to 1770. Construction of a steam road-carriage by Captain Nicholas Cugnot, a French artillery officer.

1804. Operation of a scow mounted on wheels and driven by a steam-engine by Oliver Evans, an American.[1]

1863. A Frenchman, Jean Joseph Etienne Lenoir, invented the hydrocarbon motor. Some authorities credit Lenoir with having driven a vehicle about Paris, using his internal-combustion engine for motive power. This year (1863) also witnessed the appearance of gasoline as a distillate of oil in the Pennsylvania oil-fields.

1874. Sir David Salomons, of London, completed the first vehicle to be driven by an electric battery.

1876. N. A. Otto, a German, invented the four-cycle internal-combustion engine, the type later universally used in gasoline-driven automobiles.

1879. George B. Selden, an American, applied for a patent on a vehicle driven by an internal-combustion engine. His application lingered in the Patent Office until 1895 before his patent (No. 549,160) was granted. Later this was the casus belli of the great Ford law-suit.

1883. Gottlieb Daimler, of Mannheim, Germany, perfected the "hot-tube" system of ignition, which soon ousted the previously used flame ignition.

1885. Gottlieb Daimler produced the first motorcycle.

1885. Carl Benz, a German, built the first successful gasoline-driven motor-car.

1892. An automobile was first equipped with pneu-

[1] In writing of Evans and his 1804 steam-automobile, James Rood Doolittle says: "When the people of Philadelphia saw the lumbering, creaking vehicle labor up Market Street, they concluded that—because the friction of wooden axle-trees supporting a body and engine which weighed, all told with fuel and everything else, something more than five tons, was hard to overcome—it must of necessity be condemned. They ridiculed the idea of driving such a weighty vehicle, because its rate of speed was not high. Evans shook his finger under the nose of his chief tormentor and pulled a bag of currency, containing his payment for the vehicle, from his pocket, offering to bet $3000 in cold cash that he could make a steam-carriage that would go faster over the Lancaster Turnpike than any horse the other fellow might select."

matic tires by Panhard & Levassor, French manufacturers.

1893. Several automobiles made in America functioned.

1897. The Renault Brothers, of Paris, perfected many refinements of the gasoline car, the most important being a three-speed transmission gear-set.

1898. Alexander Winton sold what is claimed to be the first American automobile driven by an internal-combustion motor to be marketed in the United States.

That selection of the main steps in the development of the automobile does not pretend to embrace more than a few. The first man who thought of gouging a hole through a round section of log, and thus made the transition from sledge to wheel, was a contributor to the twentieth-century automobile. So were the first men who melted metals from ore. So were all the discoverers in electricity. So were Goodyear and all his associates in the early rubber industry. So were the discoverers of processes for extracting gasoline out of crude oil. So, particularly, were the pioneers of the bicycle industry; ball bearings, pneumatic tires, and many other characteristics of the bicycle were incorporated into the automobile.

III

What really happened in America during the eighties and early nineties was that news and photographs trickled over from Europe of "horseless vehicles" that had been made there. Whereupon, in nearly every village and town in America, especially in the Middle West, the local mechanical genius devoted his whole being to this new device. This activity was typical also of what composed the first stage of the automobile industry in America, isolated persons making a single machine. Sometimes it was the local mechanical genius, sometimes the local crank.

In many respects this was the American spirit at its best, a feverish ferment of intellectual curiosity, mechanical ingenuity, and cleverness of adaptation. (It was precisely in one of these small-town bicycle-shops, and through this sort of process, by this sort of American, that the airplane emerged in Dayton, Ohio, a few years later.) Bicycle manufacturers, makers of baby-carriages, wagon-makers, toy-makers, mechanics, bicycle repair-men, perpetual-motion cranks, put their minds on the new idea from Europe. Of the Americans who later became manufacturers to any successful degree, Winton had been a bicycle repair-man, Franklin a die-caster, Ford a mechanic in an electric power-house, Pierce a manufacturer of bird-cages, bicycles, and refrigerators; Haynes had been field superintendent of a natural-gas company. The Studebaker car came out of a wagon factory, the Peerless from a clothes-wringer factory, the Stanley from a photographic dry-plate factory.

A suggestion by *Life* in the early nineteen hundreds.

All this American activity was adaptation, not invention. Such invention as there was, and most of the pioneering, was done in Europe. It is one of the commonest beliefs in America, and one of the most agreeable to national self-satisfaction, that we made the automobile. But we did not. An American historian of the industry, James Rood Doolittle, wrote: "We did not invent the first car that ran, we did not invent the internal-combustion hydrocarbon motor that is universally used to-day, we did not invent the first tires; but we have taught our teachers almost everything modern they know about such things." That is a frank admission, and there is even more truth in the admission than in the qualification at the close. In all respects — except salesmanship and quantity manufacture, which came later as American contributions — the automobile was a European product. Up to 1905 there were more motor vehicles in Great Britain than in America. Bearing in mind the difference in population and the difference in purchasing power of the people, the evidence of Europe's leadership is indisputable.[1] The American contribution was one of adaptation almost wholly. It is true that the process of adaptation to American conditions included a few advances that had the dignity of true originality. Because there were no good roads in America, the cars for use here had to be built so as to stand more strain. The American adaptors worked out new equations, new chemical com-

[1] So long as it was merely a matter of initiative in making and improving the automobile, Europe led. But the European machines were hand-made, therefore expensive. Only the rich could buy, and about 1908 Europe ran short of rich customers. Meantime, American manufacturers had developed manufacture by machinery. The American machine-made car was not so good as the European hand-made one; but being made by machinery could be sold cheaply. Thereafter, the immense number of possible customers in America for low-priced machines gave America the leadership. America's pre-eminence came rather from its great natural wealth, and its high standard of living, than from any genius on the part of American manufacturers. But the qualification must always be made that it was Americans who developed mass manufacture.

pounds, new tables of metal stress; also, springs which could at once insure ease on asphalt pavements, comparative comfort on cobblestones, and at the same time accommodate themselves to the very rough roads that were about the only kind America then had.[1]

IV

The second stage of the automobile in America was composed of the efforts of a comparatively small number, out of the many that tinkered at it, who had the wish to make a business of it, or whom circumstances permitted to get that far. In this stage, the ambition of the pioneers did not go beyond making one machine at a time, by hand, on order from such patrons as they could find.

Of the many scores of cranks and near-geniuses who in the late eighties and early nineties were experimenting with "horseless carriages," relatively few were successful

[1] On the allocation of credit between American and European manufacturers, I quote from a letter written me by Frederic L. Smith, of Detroit, himself one of the pioneers in the American industry: "It is undeniably true that in the infancy of the motor-car the American engineer and inventor discovered nothing new, applied nothing new, since all the elements were an old story. It is also true that in its later years most of the refinements in design and action came from Europe. The American attitude of mind toward the automobile was one of calm disregard of knowledge or experience to be gained from Europe, an attitude, in effect, of serving notice upon Europe that American brains were entirely sufficient. As a matter of fact, the automobile had a rather substantial historical background before any real development of the art occurred in the United States. The period from 1895 to 1900 may be safely put down as the truly experimental stage in America, the period during which American inventors and American automobile engineers, so called, were painfully and expensively proving that their English and French brethren were entirely correct in discarding the troublesome features which the American in turn would have to discard before a practical solution of his problem could be reached. The only factor with which England and the Continent did not have to reckon, as did America, was the double factor of extreme and splendid distance in this country, and the extreme and disreputable disrepair of most of the roads all the time and all the roads most of the time. For many years, imported cars, owing to their lesser road clearance, lesser distance between the bottom of the body of the car and the surface of the road, were at a distinct disadvantage on rough and muddy roads, compared with the American-made automobile in which the inequalities of the American country roads were reckoned with. To the metallurgists, chemists, and electricians in the United States must be handed the palm of successful achievement in overcoming mechanical difficulties and obstacles that were largely unknown abroad."

enough to impress their names and their creations on the public of their day. Only those who persevered year after year, undismayed by the jibes of their neighbors, are remembered at all.[1] In the newspapers of that period one saw references to builders of self-propelling vehicles who were utterly unknown in 1925. Of those who persevered and came to be regarded as indisputably connected with the beginning of the automobile in America, three names stand out.

Charles E. Duryea, of Chicopee, Mass., in the late eighties was engaged in the then booming bicycle business. By 1891 he had come to be such an expert that he did nothing but design bicycles which were built by the Ames Manufacturing Company. With the summer let-up in business in 1891, Duryea found time to design a gasoline motor, with the idea of using it to drive a vehicle. He was helped by his brother Frank, a toolmaker, whose advice proved invaluable. After many tribulations the first Duryea machine was finished in September, 1892. The brothers, fearing the ridicule they well knew would follow a breakdown on the public roads, decided to try out the machine indoors. The test was a success, but it was found that the engine was not quite strong enough. Encouraged, the brothers set to work to build a stronger engine. Almost a full year passed before they had finished. In the summer of 1893 everything was ready and the machine was tried out on the roads. This time

[1] Fifteen companies which started in the early days of the automobile were still in existence in 1925. Over a thousand that started had failed. The fifteen that lasted to 1925 are listed below, with the dates of their first cars:

Apperson	1901	Olds	1897
Buick	1903	Overland	1902
Cadillac	1902	Packard	1902
Ford	1903	Peerless	1900
Franklin	1900	Pierce-Arrow	1901
Haynes	1896	Stearns	1900
Locomobile	1899	Studebaker	1898
Maxwell	1904		

The Buggyaut of Charles Duryea, preserved in the Smithsonian Institution at Washington, is credited as being the second gasoline car made in America. It was built by Charles Duryea, of Chicopee Falls, Mass., in 1892–93, and made 7 to 8 miles an hour.

Courtesy of the Smithsonian Institution.

The first car built by Elwood Haynes. Equipped with pneumatic tires and a small one-cylinder gasoline engine, it ran at a speed of 8 to 10 miles per hour, on July 4, 1894, at Kokomo, Ind.

Courtesy of the Smithsonian Institution.

An early type of electric car, photographed by Harris and Ewing, at Washington, about 1909. The woman wearing the white hat is the wife of United States Senator William E. Borah.

From a photograph by Harris & Ewing.

the engine proved powerful enough and the weird hodge-podge of steel and wood and brass, after being cranked from the rear, started off at a good ten miles an hour — which speed it maintained until stopped, as there was no way for the driver to regulate the velocity by varying the quantity of gasoline fed to the motor. In the following year Duryea built another and better car. During 1894, 1895, and 1896 he won most of the races held in America, and was easily the outstanding figure in the automobile world. In 1896 his production rose to ten cars, each one better than the last. He was still designing automobiles in 1925, and threatening, with an idea for applying propelling force at the rim of a driving-wheel instead of at the shaft, to revolutionize the industry he did so much to start.

Another of the pioneers, one indeed who at his death in May, 1925, was termed by many the "Father of the automobile in America,"[1] was Elwood Haynes. Haynes, in 1890, was the field superintendent of a natural-gas company in Kokomo, Ind. His interest in the automobile was not merely that of a crank inventor. Rather it was due to dissatisfaction at losing so much time in his constant trips with a horse and buggy over the rough roads around Kokomo. As a substitute for the horse, he studied the possibilities of steam, electricity, and gasoline. In 1893 he purchased a small gasoline-engine, which he set up on blocks and started. The vibration was excessive, but Haynes figured it was no worse than the jars and jolts he was accustomed to in driving a buggy. He made rough sketches of the vehicle he had in mind, and with these went to see Elmer Apperson, who ran a small machine-shop in Kokomo. Apperson studied the sketches and listened to Haynes's explanations. The idea appealed to him, as it did to almost every American

[1] Haynes himself disavowed this title.

mechanic with a flair for "making things go." In the end he agreed to construct the "horseless carriage." Many of the parts that went into the first Haynes car could be bought in the open market and did not need to be studied out in detail and laboriously manufactured. Such were clutches, bicycle tires, wheels, and chains. Other parts, however, had to be built new. As the work went on, difficulties cropped up which necessitated varying the original plans. When such crises occurred, Apperson's brother Edgar, a bicycle repair-man, was called in. A good bicycle repair-man of those days could solve any mechanical tangle amenable to rule-of-thumb settlement, and Edgar Apperson was one of the best. With a bolt here, a shim there, and a bit of curved wire somewhere else, he nonchalantly overcame difficulties that had taxed the brains of his brother and Elwood Haynes. Finally the great day came when the vehicle was ready for trial. It is indicative of the moral fibre of the three builders and their confidence in their work that the trial was to be public, and that the date decided on was the Fourth of July, 1894, a day on which it was certain that the streets of Kokomo would be overflowing with holiday crowds predisposed and eager to jeer at failure. But no jeers were heard. The queer carriage, drawn by a horse through Kokomo to an outlying road, was followed by an avidly curious crowd. With the proud but nervous Haynes at the steering-rod, and the path cleared of onlookers, a crank was projected between the spokes of a rear wheel and the engine started. In a silence broken only by the puffing of the fretful motor, the car dashed away between the rows of awed watchers at a speed about twice as fast as a man's walk.

The third of the Americans who in the early nineties persisted in their attempts to build motor-driven vehicles was Henry Ford, of Detroit. Ford was regarded by his neighbors as a visionary who hadn't sense enough to work the forty acres of land given him by his father as a bribe to leave the city and return to the broader opportunities of farm life. As a boy, Ford had been interested in machinery, cheap watches, threshers and binders, mowing-machines. Before reaching his twenties he

Courtesy of Ford Motor Company.

Henry Ford at the wheel of his first car. It continues to occupy a place of honor in a special room of the Dearborn factory.

left the farm and went to Detroit to work in a powerhouse. In his spare time he tinkered at a gasoline-engine of his own contrivance, making a cylinder out of an old gas-pipe, a fly-wheel out of wood, and other parts out of odds and ends. Before this car was finished, Ford had married. Of the great moment in Ford's life, the day when his first automobile actually ran, there is a brief but vivid description in Doctor Samuel S. Marquis's book "Henry Ford":

I have heard from him and Mrs. Ford the story of the last forty-eight hours that he worked on that first car. Forty-eight hours without sleep. The second night Mrs. Ford sat up waiting the outcome of his efforts. The machine was nearing completion. Would it run? It was about 2 A. M. when he came in from the little shop that stood in the rear of the house. The car was finished and ready for a try-out. It was raining. Mrs. Ford threw a cloak over her shoulders and followed him to the shop. He rolled the little car out into the alley, started it, mounted the seat and drove off. The car went a short distance and stopped. The trouble was a minor one. The nut of a bolt had come off. It seems that there was some vibration in that first machine, which has been handed down to its millions of offspring.[1]

V

The gasoline automobile was not the first to get under way. In the first real automobile show ever held in America, in New York in 1900, more than one-third the space was taken up by displays of various electric cars; of the rest of the space, nearly all was consumed by steam-cars. Only a minor fraction was devoted to the type of car that later got the lead.

The electric car lost out largely because its power could only be renewed at electric charging-stations; and as these were only to be found in cities, its radius of motion was limited. The steam-car fell behind for a variety of reasons,[2] among which was the greater expert

[1] In 1895 Herman Kohlsaat, then owner of a Chicago newspaper, sponsored an endurance run in that city. It was set for Independence Day, but there was only one entry, the Haynes-Apperson buggy. The race was postponed to Labor Day, and then to Thanksgiving. On the night before, three inches of snow fell. There were six starters, four gasoline and two electric. The Haynes-Apperson machine on the way to Jackson Park had collided with a street-car and smashed a front wheel. The course was to be fifty-three and one-half miles. The electrics fell out early. Only two of the gasoline machines finished, the Duryea Wagon Motor Company of Springfield, Mass., winning, with the gas-wagon of H. Mueller & Co., of Decatur, Ills., a poor second. Franklin Duryea's time was ten hours and twenty-three minutes, an average speed of about five and a quarter miles an hour. "Old Dobbin Is Still in the Ring" was the caption of a three-inch story printed in the Chicago *Tribune*. Henry Ford had been unable to borrow enough money for car-fare to Chicago. "I never wanted anything so badly," he told Mr. Kohlsaat nineteen years later, "as to go to that race."

[2] Mr. E. M. Hallett, of the Stanley factory, writes me: "What has made the gas-engine possible in an automobile are the devices that have been invented that surround its operation, and, as you know, not hundreds but thousands of

knowledge required to operate it, the necessity the operator of a steam-car was under of securing a steam-engineer's license — a process not to be compared with the perfunctory examination of applicants for a driver's license as practised universally as late as 1925 — and the rather well-founded fear in the public mind of the dan-

Maxwell's car of the early 1900's arriving at Mt. Washington on one of the Glidden Tours.

gerous aspects of the steamer. (In the Glidden Tour of 1906, two steam-cars caught fire and burned.) The public was afraid of mishaps, in winter when undrained boilers and tanks were wrecked by the formation of ice, at all times because of the danger of explosions from leaking gasoline reservoirs. By 1925 these defects had been largely eliminated, but in that year only one company of any importance was producing

engineers have given their entire time to making the gas-car better. If a steam-car could have had one thousandth as much engineering ability at its disposal there would be no comparison in the two products, both in performance and reliability."

steam-cars in America, and the output of that company was in the neighborhood of only a thousand cars yearly.

The electric car that was the favorite in the early years of the century was, in many respects, more comfortable than its gasoline rival. It was smoother, less noisy, less smelly, easier to control. And as to the steam-car, which,

Testing an electric car in the Automobile Show of 1900, in Madison Square Garden, New York.

essentially, was a refinement of the railroad locomotive, many believe that if its development had not been restricted, it might have been more popular than the gasoline car. Possibly an additional reason for the gasoline machine leaving the others behind may have been some accident of personality, a greater aggregate of aggressive energy in those manufacturers who concentrated on gasoline.

VI

In 1895 there were 300 motor vehicles in more or less continuous operation in America. The qualification "more or less" is used advisedly. The occasional exhilarating periods, when the possessor of one of these 300 could dash along the cobbled thoroughfares of our cities at a continuing pace, were interspersed with hours of laborious "tinkering" and adjusting. Particularly exasperating was the process of starting the motor, which frequently entailed the draining of the victim's last reserve of strength, patience, and self-command. Nor, once the motor was started, did the autoist's lot become easy. Switches had to be pressed, and a complexity of pedals and levers had to be operated simultaneously by drivers wofully inexperienced. Frequently when the driver wished to go one way, the car went another. Not infrequently brakes or pedals refused to function, and terror-stricken drivers were carried helplessly along by iron steeds indifferent alike to prayers or curses from behind or obstacles in front. Even when the machines were not in use they were not out of mind of their harassed owners. As public garages had not yet appeared, the cars were kept, as a rule, in livery-stables, the personnel of which had scant sympathy for "man's new servant." Arousing in the breasts of the general public sentiments of curiosity and

Miss Maude Adams, in her curved-dash Oldsmobile.

derision, their delicate mechanisms were subjected to the pryings of small boys and stable hangers-on. Under such circumstances the great masses of the people were quite content to leave the automobile to the "bugs" who seemed to enjoy the struggle, and to the rich whose in-

By courtesy of U. S. Bureau of Public Roads.

A Tennessee village in 1909. The horse was still supreme in many parts of the South long after it had been driven from the roads in the North.

terest in the ownership of a horseless carriage outweighed the many inconveniences which possession entailed.

In spite of the not very encouraging position of the automobile at this period, there were not lacking those who foresaw its future. Among these optimistic prophets was a contributor to *The Eclectic Magazine* in 1895:

> I name ten years as the time within which we may see the railways given up to business traffic and persons in a hurry; the country dotted with airy vehicles flying along on roads that continental nations might be proud of; the "posting" system revived, with all its ancient glamour, only the 'ostler vanished, in whose place one summons the engineer. Electric trams and electric cabs shall have worked wonders in

our cities, which now will be clean and sweet instead of foul and muddy. As traffic becomes gentler, rates will diminish. Heads will no longer throb with disagreeable sights and sounds. The busy man will be able to think as he drifts along on wheels of softest motion; not agitated by thoughts of the wretched beast in front, nor distraught by noises round him. Modern life will have lost a few of its worst terrors.[1]

The ten years allowed by this prophet came and went without seeing much more than the beginning of the revolutionary changes in living conditions and transportation that he predicted. The "roads that continental nations might be proud of" had as yet hardly begun to emerge from the mud of 1900, and heads still throbbed from the smells and sounds produced by mankind's varied mediums of transportation. Nevertheless, progress was being made daily, and on an immense scale. The new industry called irresistibly to alert, adventurous young men. To them it mattered little that in its early period of development the automobile was a hapless thing, awkward, erratic, and ugly, compared with the trim rubber-tired carriages that sped along behind well-cared-for horses; or that it was destined, by almost unanimous popular opinion, to be relegated shortly to the oblivion from which it had emerged. These men — Pope, Winton, White, Whitney, Prescott, Gaeth, Lane, Farmer, Wilkinson, Moon, Pierce, Packard, Ford, Marmon, to mention but a few — took enthusiastic hold of the infant industry, with the result that by 1905 the number of cars under registry had grown to the impressive total of 77,988, compared with the 300 that had been in existence in America in 1895, ten years before.

This progress was doubly notable since it was made in the face of popular distrust of the automobile; and because important advances had to be made in the design

[1] He failed to predict that by 1925 one of the "worst terrors" of "modern life" was death by automobile.

By courtesy of U. S. Bureau of Public Roads.

The coming of good roads. The same car, the same man, and the same place.

and construction of cars to enable them to compete with the more advanced products of European factories. In the July, 1899, issue of *McClure's Magazine*, Ray Stannard Baker summed up the progress that had been made when the last century was coming to a close:

. . . Between the 1st of January and the 1st of May, 1899, companies with the enormous aggregate capitalization of

Allowing fifteen feet for each of the motor vehicles in use in the United States during 1924, and placing one behind another, a traffic line would be formed stretching twice around the globe.

more than $388,000,000 have been organized in New York, Boston, Chicago, and Philadelphia for the sole purpose of manufacturing and operating these new vehicles. At least eighty establishments are now actually engaged in building carriages, coaches, tricycles, delivery-wagons, and trucks, representing no fewer than 200 different types of vehicles, with nearly half as many methods of propulsion. Most of these concerns are far behind in their orders, and several of them are working day and night. A hundred electric cabs are plying familiarly on the streets of New York, and 200 more are being rushed to completion in order to supply the popular demand for horseless locomotion. At least twoscore of delivery-wagons, propelled chiefly by electricity, are in operation in American cities, and the private conveyances of various makes will number well into the hundreds. A motor-ambulance is in operation in Chicago; motor-trucks are at work in several different cities; a motor gun-carriage for use in the army will be ready in the summer. . . . At least two cities are using self-propelled fire-engines. A trip of 720 miles, from Cleveland to New York, over all kinds of country roads, has actually been made in a gasoline carriage, and an enthusiastic automobile traveller is now on his way from New England to San Francisco.

The sum Mr. Baker mentions, $388,000,000, was capitalization — not cash. Had the automotive industry been fed any such sum of real money early in 1899, the row subsequently hoed would have been easier. Until 1907 capital held aloof. Until 1905 or thereabouts the automobile was a toy of the mechanically inclined and a luxury of the well-to-do. On the streets of well-paved cities it was finding a limited employment by sharing with the horse the delivery service of department stores, and to an even more limited extent it vied with the now obsolete hansom and closed cab as a public conveyance. But it suffered from the odium of being an ostentatious luxury of the rich. The following stanzas of a parody appeared in *Life* as late as 1904 under the caption "The Charge of the Four Hundred":

Half a block, half a block,
  Half a block onward,
All in their motobiles
  Rode the Four Hundred.
"Forward!" the owners shout,
"Racing-car!" "Runabout!"
  Into Fifth Avenue
  Rode the Four Hundred.

"Forward!" the owners said.
Was there a man dismay'd?

Not, though the chauffeurs knew
  Some one had blundered.
Theirs not to make reply,
Theirs not to reason why,
Theirs but to kill or die.
  Into Fifth Avenue
  Rode the Four Hundred.[1]

Being a luxury, and so seductive a luxury as to tempt some people of moderate means to mortgage their homes and waste their substance in the purchase and maintenance of "devil wagons," as they were then facetiously called, it was but natural that they should be regarded askance by bankers and capitalists. Plenty of other reasons existed why capital should not flow into the industry. There was trouble over the early patents, and many suits about infringements; revolutionary changes were being made in the designs of cars at short intervals. What conservative custodian of capital would face his associates with the proposal that they invest heavily in an industry that was the butt of every jokesmith in the land? To readers accustomed to the ubiquity and the fool-proof quality of the automobile in 1925, a joke from *Life* in 1904 will suggest the earlier attitude toward the new invention:

"Yes, I enjoy my automobile immensely."
"But I never see you out."
"Oh, I haven't got that far yet. I am just learning to make my own repairs."

VII

In the days when no city could count on its streets more than a few score or at most a few hundred machines,

[1] The popular sentiment which at that time regarded the automobile as the exclusive prerogative of the rich was reflected in another bit of verse in *Life* for April 3, 1901, ending,

"A man who would now
Win the parvenu's bow,
Must belong to the automobility.

the custom was to treat automobilists with good-natured raillery. Even their occasional disruption of horse-traffic was overlooked in the amusement they afforded to common-sense individuals wedded to tried and true methods of locomotion. When, however, they began to crowd the streets and roads, a more severely critical attitude was

Early in the 1900's, the idea that the automobile would supplant the horse was satirized by this cartoon from *Life*, entitled "The Passing of the Horse."

noticeable. This was due to the accidents which began to occur with greater and greater frequency in which pedestrians were maimed or killed, while the autoists escaped unharmed. Such a case was treated editorially by the New York *Tribune* on December 27, 1900:

He Rang the Gong

A young woman was knocked down and fatally injured by an automobile vehicle while crossing Broadway on Christmas afternoon. She was a trained nurse, and therefore presumably intelligent, prudent, and active. The vehicle was moving rapidly, just how rapidly is not reported. The engineer in charge of it saw the young woman crossing the street and rang the gong in warning. Apparently, however, he did not abate the speed of the machine nor attempt to steer it out of the way. He considered his responsibility fully discharged by the ringing of the gong.

As accidents continued, the necessity was seen of finding some method for regulating the operation of the

As early as 1901, conditions were such as to inspire W. H. Walker in *Life* to ask: "Must we take the law in our own hands?"

vehicles; otherwise no one on the streets could call his life his own. Not a few people took the stand that the automobile was an unmitigated nuisance and should be ruled off the highways. In 1899 an ordinance was passed which barred Central Park, New York, to horseless vehicles. A sane course, well calculated to better conditions, was recommended by Cleveland Moffett in 1900:

The New York law requires that any person who would operate a steam-carriage in this city or State shall obtain an engineer's license, issued only to those who have passed a prescribed examination. Entirely proper is this law, and its application should extend to all motor-carriages; for it is absolute folly for any one to go forth on one of these powerful and rapid vehicles (as some too eager amateurs have done) without completely understanding its mechanism.

By 1904 the situation had grown so bad that New York State passed a law providing for a maximum rate of ten miles an hour in closely built-up districts; fifteen miles an hour in villages or cities outside the congested zones; and twenty miles an hour as the maximum elsewhere. The example set by New York was shortly thereafter followed by Kansas, Kentucky, and other States.

Naturally, this attempt to control automobiling met with strong opposition from the trade interests affected. Through organization and propaganda, they took up energetically, among other activities, resistance to regulation by local authorities.

VIII

As a stimulus to the business, racing was encouraged, in a sensational and rather tawdry way. Manufacturers made racing-cars, employed professional racers — Henry Ford raced once himself; Alexander Winton raced regularly. This brought the automobile to popular attention, but to the discriminating revealed the inferiority of American cars. A succession of defeats suffered by American-built machines was the basis of an editorial in the Louisville *Courier-Journal* for July 4, 1903:

The automobile-race for the Bennett Cup was by far the best of the series yet contested for that trophy. The speed made was more than sixty miles an hour. . . . To Americans the most impressive feature of the race was the miserable showing made by our representatives. None of them was really expected to win the race, unless through bad luck to the cars of France and Germany, . . . but it was thought they would do better than they did. Their failure must be attributed to two causes: the undoubted superiority of French and German cars and the inexperience of American drivers in long road races. France is at least five years ahead of the United States in the development of the automobile, while Germany is not far behind France. We have simply stolen the ideas of French and German manufacturers and adapted them to our own uses. . . . We do not deserve to win a trophy for international superiority.

This editorial was violent; but the fact was America was not the leader in the development of the automobile, except chiefly in two respects. One was quantity production in plants designed for immense mass manufacture; the other was marketing, salesmanship.

IX

While Americans did not invent the automobile, nor have any serious share in the improvement of it, they did make one immense contribution, and that constituted the third stage of the automobile in this country. It was Americans who made the automobile available to the average man. It is often assumed that the automobile industry was the pioneer of "quantity production," and that among automobile-makers Ford was the earliest to use this system. Neither assumption is correct. The automobile manufacturers merely took up an idea evolved a century earlier by Eli Whitney and elaborated on it to a stupendous, amazing degree. By 1925 "quantity production" had become an essential of American industry, and of importance far beyond its place in business, as being a long step in the enrichment of man, in making goods available to him at a price within his reach.

The early European manufacturers made automobiles "to order" and chiefly for the rich. So also did the early American manufacturers. In 1900[1] some American manu-

[1] This year may be fixed as the one in which experimentation ended and quantity production began. The next ten years of automobile history were the period of progressive standardization, progressive development of mass production.

facturers turned to the idea of making cars in quantities to be offered for sale as a standard article, and at a price that average men could pay. This necessitated abandonment of the fine hand-work of European machines. What these American pioneers of "quantity production" did was to select such parts of European models as were ca-

Onlookers parked in near-by fields to see the Vanderbilt Cup Race.

pable of being made in large quantities by machinery.[1] This involved the rejection of some of the best features of the European models. If the thing did not lend itself to machine manufacture, it was passed by. As a result, the Americans did not make the best machines, nor anything near the best; but they did make an acceptable machine that would start, go somewhere, and return, with a minimum of mechanical trouble, at small expense, and at a cost such that great numbers of people could buy.

In 1900 the Olds Motor Works erected in Detroit what was then the largest automobile factory in the country.

[1] To some extent, this innovation was forced on American manufacturers by the scarcity of labor, relative to Europe.

They concentrated their entire equipment and abilities on a single model — and that was a fundamental step in developing the theory and practice of quantity production. For the first time in automobile history, parts were ordered in thousand lots: 2000 sets of transmission-gears from Dodge Brothers; 2000 motors from Leland and Faulkner. They sold the car first for $600; then for $650. The first year, they made 400 machines; the second, 1600; the third, 4000. The capitalization of the firm was $350,000, but $200,000 was all the cash that ever went into the company. The first two years they paid out 105 per cent in cash dividends. That was the indisputable demonstration that the automobile could be more than a rich man's toy. This event, in the year 1900, was the birth of the automobile as a commercial reality.

The innovation of "mass production," "quantity production," "repetitive processes," as it is variously called, was the beginning of the second stage of the automobile, the stage of diffusion, which made it available to all. Mass production was accompanied by a new and enormously expanded development of advertising and marketing. Both mass production and advertising became fundamentally important American institutions, not only as respects the automobile but in the widest sense. They will be discussed in a future volume, as will also the later stages of the automobile, its progress from novelty to ubiquity, and the revolutionary material and social effects that accompanied it.

19

1900

A Fine American and a Fine Achievement. Beginning of the "Open-Door" Policy in China, Whereby John Hay Saves China from Dismemberment. First Civil Governments for Our New Dependencies. First Organized Automobile Race. Havana Has Its Last Epidemic of Yellow Fever. Beginnings of the Direct Election of Senators. First Use of the Direct Primary. Invention and First Use of the Commission Form of City Government. New York Starts Its First Subway. First Pacific Cable. Faint Beginning of the Radio. Beginning of the "B'gosh" School of Fiction, "David Harum," "Eben Holden." First Horseless Bus on Fifth Avenue, New York. Beginning of the "Hall of Fame." Death of Maud S. Congress Rejects a Polygamist. Gold Standard Adopted. Kentucky's Governor Assassinated. Confederate Veterans Meet at Louisville. Protest Against Continued Use of Word "Rebel." Chicago Drainage Canal Opened. New Records in North Polar Exploration, Steamships, Tall Buildings, Speed. Popular Books and Plays 1900.

In 1900 the foreign relations of the United States were in the hands of a man whose whole life had been a preparation, one of the finest American personalities of his generation. John Hay had been born in a Middle-West (then far-West) frontier one-story brick house, of pioneer but educated parents (his father was a physician and local editor, his mother the daughter of a graduate of Brown University), who supplied his early intellectual curiosity with opportunities to learn German, Latin, and Greek. The boy was sensitive to beauty in words, to the scenes of his home on the banks of the Mississippi, and to the racy Americanism that surrounded the village. When its name was changed from "Spunky Point" to Warsaw (as an incident of the vogue of Jane Porter's romantic novel "Thaddeus of Warsaw"), Hay railed at the stilted affectation, and hoped that "every man engaged in the outrage is called Smith in Heaven."[1] He went to Brown University, loved it, and not only got, but knew he was getting, and therefore appreciated, the wider horizons of life to which education introduced him. He wrote poems after the model of Poe (who to the 1850's was what Kipling was to the 1890's), and was made class poet; then, leaving a trail of bright affection behind him, returned to Illinois to study law and look forward to "corner-lots and tax-titles"; suffered the pains of an artist in an arid environment and wrote to literary friends he had made in New England about "a cool rest under the violets," but was shortly sending notes in French inviting the girls to picnics, dances, and church sociables. At Springfield, Illinois, he foregathered with a cultivated editor of Bavarian birth, John Nicolay, and worked in a law office next door to a long-legged, ungainly, homely character whom people had begun to call "Honest Abe." Lincoln, elected President, made Nicolay his secretary, and Nicolay asked if he couldn't take Hay along as assistant. Lincoln drawled something about not taking all Illinois to Washington, but consented. Both young men lived in hourly intimacy with Lincoln, listened to the wisdom of his dealing with public men, and to his humor when he would come into their bedroom in his nightshirt to read them something in Shakespeare, or the latest newspaper instalment of "Petroleum V. Nasby," the Civil War predecessor of "Mr. Dooley" and Will Rogers. Hay appreciated Lincoln, had the insight and

[1] This passage is from a letter written by Hay reproduced in William Roscoe Thayer's "Life of John Hay." Some of the other quotations in this chapter and much of the material are from the same source.

flexibility to get the full benefit of one of the greatest educational opportunities ever presented to any young man. By close association with immense responsibility he added something extremely important to his scholarship — grew to value deeds, as his instinct and training had taught him to value words. Lincoln came to trust him for tasks requiring tact, discretion, taste, human understanding.

After Lincoln's death, Hay served as secretary of legation at Paris, as chargé d'affaires at Vienna, as secretary at Madrid. He learned the good manners of diplomacy — and also how to avoid being fooled by its more devious ways; learned the varying equations between what men say and what they really think; learned to appraise kings, added shrewdness and common sense to his qualities of imagination. Between intervals of his diplomatic service he wrote short stories and articles for *Harper's*, *The Atlantic Monthly;* went back to the river slang of his boyhood for the Pike County ballads that gave him his literary fame, "Little Breeches," and the one about "Jim Bludso," who would

> Hold her nozzle agin the bank,
> 'Til the last galoot's ashore.

(Hay came later to feel about that poem as General Sherman felt about "Marching Through Georgia.") He increased his understanding of people by looking lecture audiences in the face, wrote "brevier" (that is, editorials) for the New York *Tribune* under Whitelaw Reid, married the daughter of a wealthy Cleveland banker, and settled down to literary work. His "Breadwinners," published anonymously in 1883, was the novel of the year — as a serial it was the largest success ever published in America up to that time. His biographer's epitome, "the first important polemic in American fiction in defense of property," is misleading, because Hay's imagination and sympathetic insight were for the common man, but his sense of taste loved order, and his mind was revolted by lack of intelligence — he was shocked by the stupid, reckless rioting in which some early labor movements expressed themselves. In the early nineties he ended ten years of collaboration on Nicolay and Hay's "Life of Lincoln," and went to live in Washington as a leisurely observer and as the companion of public men, American and foreign. Henry Cabot Lodge named Hay first in a very short list of the best talkers he ever met.

Hay's wide-ranging mind and gift of companionship carried him to acquaintance with everybody of importance in America, and most of those in Europe. The rarer spirits, men like William Dean Howells and Henry Adams, he more than knew; with them he had kinship. He became cosmopolitan without ceasing to prize America, versatile without ceasing to be scholarly. McKinley made him ambassador to England in 1897 and secretary of state in 1898.

On January 2, 1900, Hay announced to the Cabinet that he had completed negotiations for the "open door" in China. The negotiations consisted of securing assurances from the various Powers, Great Britain, France, Germany, Russia, Japan, and Italy, who then had or looked to acquiring interests in China, that in whatever influence they might exercise over China or any part of it, the treaty rights of the United States, and of all other nations, with China, would be respected; that neither our citizens and commerce, nor those of any other nation, would be placed at a disadvantage by any discriminating tariff laws or other conditions.

The "open-door" policy in China was an American idea. It was set up in contrast to the "spheres-of-influence" policy practised by other nations. "Spheres of influence" was really a euphemism for the "partition of China," which in 1900 was looked upon as well under way. Since her defeat by Japan in 1894, it had been realized that China was not a fighting nation, and could not defend herself against modern armies and navies. She lay like a stranded whale.

While Hay put his negotiations on the ground of maintaining the existing status of the interests of the United States in territory grabbed by other Powers (which was the only aspect he had a clear right to discuss), its effect was to take away some of the motive of the Powers for aggrandizement, and ultimately to save the territorial and national integrity of China.

John Hay (1838-1905)

The "open door" is one of the most creditable episodes in American diplomacy, an example of benevolent impulse accompanied by energy and shrewd skill in negotiation. Not one of the statesmen and nations that agreed to Hay's policy wanted to. It was like asking every man who believes in truth to stand up— the liars are obliged to be the first to rise. Hay saw through them perfectly; his insight into human nature was one of his strongest qualities. Doubtless he had his own moments of indignation, but he had learned something of patience and long-suffering self-restraint from Lincoln, although even in his mellow maturity he never quite ceased to be what his college mates described: "A fellow who would never do a mean act, nor tolerate one."

Every aspect of Hay's achievement excites enthusiasm. His vision and idealism were the more remarkable, since he was going against the current of the age, as only a scholar, a man who knew the world and history, would. The atmosphere of the time took the dismemberment of China for granted. The air was full of a hypocritical cant which put greed in words of benevolence — everybody not a White Man was regarded as a White Man's Burden. It was Europe, mainly, that was grabbing, but we were in it too, and there were plenty who would have counselled that our policy should be to join the scramble, take our share and take it in time. There was much talk about using the Philippines as a foothold for further expansion in the Orient. Hay took his course without any appearance of doing a daring thing; even in his own mind he did not seem to set it up as anything dramatic — it was just the natural expression of honesty and wisdom, the ordinary day's work of a gentleman in high office.

The "open-door" policy survived, and, despite some setbacks, grew so that in 1925 the integrity of China was far more secure than had seemed likely in 1900.[1]

Less than a month after the announcement of success in the "open-door" negotiations, Hay's altruistic course was made more difficult by the necessity of uniting with Great Britain, France, and Germany, in a joint note to the Chinese Government demanding protection for missionaries who, with other foreigners, were being subjected

[1] This was one occasion when the appraisement of the day was borne out by the subsequent facts. A writer in *The Review of Reviews* for January, 1900, said of Hay: "His great achievement will appear in history as the maintenance of the 'open door' in China, and the consequent postponement, if not prevention, of the threatened dismemberment of that empire, which will probably be considered one of the greatest achievements ever won by our diplomacy."

Up to 1925 it was certainly "postponement," and in that year seemed likely to be "prevention."

more and more to threats by the natives. This anti-foreign movement came to a head in June, 1900, when the foreign legations in Pekin were attacked. "The movement was a blind and misguided attempt to strike off foreign domination." (I quote from a letter sent me in 1925 by a Chinese authority.) Sir Robert Hart, an

American troops entering Tang-Chow during the Boxer Rebellion of 1900.

able Englishman, well equipped to know, "looked upon the Boxer movement as a national and patriotic one for freeing China of the foreigners to whom, rightly or wrongly, is attributed all the country's misfortunes during the last half-century." The Empress Dowager said that "the various powers cast upon us looks of tiger-like voracity, hustling each other in their endeavors to be the first to seize upon our . . . territories." While foreign encroachment was the mainspring of the movement, it was accelerated, among some fanatics, by antagonism toward Christian missionaries. (The word "Boxer" translated literally means "righteous harmony fists.") The immediate incentive to the outbreak was the seizing of portions of China by Russia, Great Britain, and France.

Troops of all the Great Powers were sent to relieve their legations, and to put down the uprising, for the Chinese Government was not only too feeble to resist foreign aggression, but even to put down internal conflict. The conditions seemed not only to tempt but almost to justify seizure of Chinese territory. The German Von Waldersee, as the highest in rank among the foreign commanders, was made commander-in-chief. Leaving Berlin, he wore the uniform presented to him by Emperor William, which the latter had worn on his voyage to Jerusalem. The German troops before leaving for China were harangued by the War Lord, who instructed them to so comport themselves in China that "no Chinese shall ever again dare even to look at a German askance." As it turned out, the Germans were no more ruthless than the troops of some other nations.

While the American Government participated energetically with troops and otherwise in rescuing foreigners and suppressing the outbreak, President McKinley and Secretary Hay maintained an attitude of sympathetic understanding of the cause, and controlled the situation in such a way as to avoid its being used as an occasion for the disruption of China's national and territorial entity. Hay persuaded the Powers to agree to joint occupation until the issues were settled, shrewdly assuming that in a joint occupation mutual jealousies would prevent any one Power from seizing any portion of the empire. He then persuaded England and Germany not to demand territory, and to oppose such a demand from the others. Thereafter it was agreed that the reparations should be in the form of money.

The amount was fixed, after some haggling, at $315,000,000. The Germans and some other Powers wished to demand more; the Americans less. About 7.3 per cent ($24,000,000) was allotted to America. This proved more than enough to meet the American claims. It occurred to an American missionary in China, Doctor Arthur H.

From "Le Cri de Paris," Paris.

A portrayal of the Kaiser's ruthlessness toward the Chinese in 1900 by a French artist.

Smith, that the United States should give back the unused portion to China for educational and cultural purposes, including the education of Chinese youths in American schools. Smith arranged through Doctor Lyman Abbott for an interview with President Roosevelt (Lawrence F. Abbott accompanied Doctor Smith at the interview). Roosevelt agreed, made the necessary recommendation to Congress, and in 1908 the unused portion, about $11,000,000, of the indemnity was restored. Prince Ch'ing wrote to the American minister in

Peking: "I was profoundly impressed with the justice and great friendliness of the American Government."

II

Other Events of 1900

January 2. "First Autostage in Fifth Avenue" was the caption over a New York *Herald* article describing an electric bus, with seats for eight persons inside and four outside. The fare was five cents.

January 2. Opening of the Chicago Drainage Canal. It was built to carry the sewage of Chicago, which previously had been deposited in Lake Michigan, through the Des Plaines and Illinois Rivers to the Mississippi. The canal is 40 miles long and 22 feet deep; its width varies between 160 and 300 feet. It cost $45,289,000.

January 9. Albert J. Beveridge, of Indiana, made his first speech as a United States senator. He had just returned from the scene of the American army's campaign to subdue the insurrection in the Philippines. His speech attacked the Democratic suggestion of letting the Philippines go, which he called a policy of "scuttle," and dealt with the Republican policy of expansion generally. (See Chapters 3 and 20.) At the conclusion Senator Beveridge presented the following resolution:

> That the Philippine Islands are territory belonging to the United States; and that it is the intention of the United States to retain them as such, and to establish and maintain such governmental control . . . as the situation may demand.

January 16. The contract for the first subway in New York City was awarded to John B. McDonald, whose bids for the several sections aggregated $35,000,000.

For almost twenty miles of its length the four-track tunnel was to be excavated through solid rock. By the successful completion of this enterprise, Contractor McDonald, and the banker who backed him, August Belmont, began a new era in urban transportation. The

A drawing made from one of the official plans of a local station in the New York subway, 1900.

courage required is suggested by the fact that only four years before, in 1896, the New York courts, Appellate Division, First Department, had refused to approve a subway project in a decision which to-day reads like a burlesque on judicial vision. The court began by quoting St. Luke, "for which of you, intending to build a tower, sitteth not down first and counteth the cost, whether he have sufficient to finish it?" From that the judges went on to say: "The probabilities indicate that after sinking $51,000,000 in it without being able to complete it, the enterprise would have to be abandoned. . . . All that beheld it would begin to mock, saying 'this city began to build and was not able to finish.'"

By 1925 upward of $600,000,000 had been spent for rapid-transit lines in New York, and subways had been adopted in Boston and Chicago.

January 25. The national House of Representatives, by a vote of 268 to 50, refused to allow Congressman-elect Brigham H. Roberts, of Utah, to occupy the seat in that body to which he had been elected. (The issue in the voting was almost wholly on procedure; whether Roberts should be denied a seat or whether he should be seated and immediately expelled.) The congressional committee that investigated the case reported:

That about 1878 he married —— ——, his first and lawful wife, with whom he has ever since lived as such and who, since their marriage, has borne him six children. That about 1885 he married as his plural wife —— ——, with whom he has ever since lived as such and who, since such marriage, has borne him six children, of whom the last were twins, born August 11, 1897. That some years after [his second plural marriage] he contracted another plural marriage with —— ——, with whom he has ever since lived in the habit and repute of marriage. Your committee is unable to fix the exact date of this marriage. . . . That these facts were generally known in Utah, publicly charged against him during his campaign for election, and were not denied by him. That the testimony bearing on these facts was taken in the presence of Mr. Roberts, and that he fully cross-questioned the witnesses, but declined to place himself on the witness-stand.

Roberts, speaking in Congress in his own defense, said:

I have lived with a good conscience until this day, and am sensible of no act of shame upon my part. You can brand me with shame and send me forth, but I shall leave with head erect and brow undaunted, and walk the earth as angels walk the clouds.

This was the last case involving the question of a member-elect proved to have practised polygamy. Some later ones were put on trial on the ground of being Mormons, but without being charged with polygamy. Congress took the ground that while the practice of polygamy was a bar, membership in the Mormon Church is not. The Mormon Church discontinued the sanction of polygamy in 1890. Most of the embarrassing cases that arose thereafter were of men who had married polygamously previous to 1890, and were faced with the question of what to do about their plural wives.

January 30. On entering the grounds of the State Capitol at Frankfort, William Goebel, Democratic contender for the governorship of Kentucky, was shot from ambush. He had the oath of office administered to him while in bed and died three days later. The shooting grew out of an election dispute between the Democratic and Republican candidates for governor. The Republican secretary of state, Caleb Powers, and others were arrested, tried, and convicted of complicity. Powers served in jail eight years, three months, and three days; he was then pardoned, and thereafter was elected to Congress four terms, 1911–19, by his mountain district.

January. The addition of 30,000 pages of new statute law by the legislatures of the forty-five States during the past two years was reported in the *Forum Magazine*.

February 6. President McKinley appointed William H. Taft, then a U. S. circuit judge, head of a new Philippine Commission to establish civil government in the islands. All five commissioners took after Taft in size — their average weight was 227 pounds — which gave rise to humorous comment about these men travelling in tropical lands in the hot season. It was said the Filipinos regarded them as "an imposing spectacle."

February 10. Seven thousand workmen on building construction in Chicago struck for an eight-hour day.

February 21. Leslie E. Keeley, promoter of a so-called "gold cure" for the liquor habit, died. The "Keeley cure" and "Keeley sanitariums" were widely advertised.

February 21. Miss Olga Nethersole and her managers were arrested in New York for producing "Sapho." The New York *Evening Post* said:

> It is not necessary to soil the columns of this paper with a particular account of the sickly sentimentality of Mr. Daudet's book or the reeking compost of filth and folly that the crude and frivolous Mr. Clyde Fitch has dug out of it, with which to mire the stage. It is enough to say that this heavy and foul rigmarole of lust, sap-headed sentiment, and putrid nonsense tells a vulgar, commonplace, and tiresome story about a harlot and a fool, showing how, in a carnal way, they fascinated each other, how the fool clove to his folly, and how the harlot, having bamboozled the fool, went away with a criminal rogue just out of prison. Into details of the relations between these cattle those commentators may enter who have a taste for muck and who can deliver expert opinions upon it.

The New York *Press* said:

> There is nothing shocking in it, and the rush to see it may stop when this fact is discovered, but it deserves some support for its own sake.

February 24. Richard Hovey died. Author (with Bliss Carman) of "Songs from Vagabondia" and "Last Songs from Vagabondia."

March 5. New York University received a gift of $100,000 to erect a "Hall of Fame for Great Americans."

In October twenty-nine names were chosen, of which those receiving most votes of the judges were: George Washington, 97; Abraham Lincoln, 96; Daniel Webster, 96; Benjamin Franklin, 94; Ulysses S. Grant, 92; John Marshall, 91; Thomas Jefferson, 90.

March 14. The end of a very long controversy. By the Gold Standard Act the gold dollar was declared to be the standard unit of value. "United States notes [greenbacks] and Treasury notes . . . shall be redeemed in gold coin." The gold standard papers referred to this bill as "a safeguard of the honor and credit of the United States"; the silver papers treated it as an "ill-omened currency bill intended to make the rich richer and the poor poorer." This action marked the death of "free silver" in the United States. So greatly had conditions changed, due to increases in the supply of gold from mines, that the passage of the bill excited nothing like the controversy that had attended, ten years before, minor skirmishes in this long battle. An account of the currency controversy will be found in Chapters 9 and 11.

March 18. Maud S. died, within one week of twenty-six years old. She had reigned as queen of the race-course longer than any other horse of her generation, and had a place in popular affection no race-horse since has had. Her record, a mile in 2.08¾, was made at Cleveland, Ohio, July 30, 1885, and stood until October 20, 1891, when it was lowered by one-half a second by Sunol, at Stockton, Calif. Maud S. was owned by Robert Bonner, who bought her from William H. Vanderbilt for $40,000.

March 24. The new Carnegie Steel Company was incorporated at Trenton, N. J., with the "enormous capitalization" of $160,000,000. (A little over a year later, the United States Steel Corporation was organized with a capitalization of $1,403,450,000.)

April 4. Admiral Dewey announced his willingness to be a candidate for the presidency. (See Chapter 12.)

April 11. The growing commercial importance of our dependencies in the Orient led the Senate to pass a bill appropriating $3,000,000 for a submarine cable from San Francisco to Hawaii. The bill, however, never became a law. The cable to Honolulu, the Commercial-Pacific, was laid by a private corporation in 1902.

April 12. President McKinley signed the Porto Rican tariff and civil government bill. This was the first legislation affecting the government of the dependencies we had acquired through the war. Its tariff provisions were the resultant of a sharp battle between the tendency to treat Porto Rico as on a parity with the States of the Union commercially; and, on the other hand, the protectionists, who saw a danger to home industries in allowing Porto Rican products to enter free of duty. The bill as passed laid upon all merchandise imported from Porto Rico into the United States a tariff equal to 15 per cent of the duties on imports from foreign countries into the United States. The arrangement was to work both ways. The government of the island was empowered to collect duties on imports from all countries at the same rates as those imposed by the tariff law of the United States; American exports enjoying, of course, the same reduction of 85 per cent as that granted by the United States to imports from Porto Rico. The sugar interests of Louisiana and California and the tobacco-growers of Connecticut were the strongest advocates of a tariff against Porto Rico. Opposition to a tariff, based on sentimental considerations, came from both Democrats and Republicans. The fact that Congress gave full territorial status, including free trade with the United States, to Hawaii, about the same time that it raised a tariff wall against Porto Rico, caused the San Juan (Porto Rico) *News* to sing:

> . . . My country, 'tis of thee
> That set Hawaii free,
> Of thee I sing! . . .
> Land of the brave and just,
> Land of the sugar trust,
> How sweet to be
> Held up outside the gate
> And made to pay the freight —
> I tell you what, it's great
> And tickles me!

April 13. A mile-stone in the innovation of electing United States senators by direct vote of the people, instead of through the legislatures. On this day, after years of agitation, the Lower House of Congress, by a vote of 240 to 15, adopted a resolution favoring a constitutional amendment for the election of United States senators by direct vote of the people. The action at this time was stimulated by two recent legislative scandals, one attending the selection of Matthew S. Quay by the Pennsylvania legislature, the other attending charges of bribery of the Montana legislature in connection with the election of William A. Clark.

The resolution was passed in the Lower House five times before the Senate concurred — in 1893, in 1894, in 1898 (by a vote of 185 to 11), in 1900 (240 to 15), and in 1902 practically unanimously, without a roll-call. Not until 1911, on June 12, did the Senate concur. Thereupon the amendment was submitted to the States, was ratified by the necessary number, and election of senators by State legislatures ceased on May 31, 1913.

April 15. The first well-organized automobile-race in America was held at Springfield, L. I. A. L. Riker, with an electric vehicle, won, covering fifty miles in the time, then considered remarkable, of two hours and three minutes. Electric, steam, and gasoline cars participated.

April 15. Workmen at Cornell Dam, Croton, New York, struck for an advance from $1.25 to $1.50 a day.

April 30. President McKinley signed the bill giving to the recently annexed Hawaiian Islands a territorial form of government, the same as Alaska, and, at that time, Oklahoma, New Mexico, and Arizona. Hawaii was the only one of our recently acquired overseas dependencies given this status. It was made subject to the same tariff and navigation laws as the United States, and the same laws against Chinese immigration. Monopolies were guarded against by limiting individual corporation landholdings to 1000 acres. The suffrage provision gave the vote to all speaking and writing "the American or Hawaiian language."

April. Dividend payments of the Standard Oil Company for the first quarter of 1900 amounted to $20,000,000, of which 15 per cent was an ordinary quarterly dividend, and the balance extra. This was the largest ever declared by any corporation up to that time for a like period. The prevalent prosperity manifested itself in other ways. During the late spring a seat on the New York Stock Exchange sold for $41,500.

May 21. Secretary Hay informed the Boer envoys that our country would not recede from its position of strict neutrality. We had previously offered to mediate, but Great Britain, having suffered reverses, felt she could not afford to jeopardize her prestige under the circumstances, and declined our offer. The visiting commission was greeted with enthusiasm wherever they went. At the White House they were courteously received by President McKinley, who was willing to chat with them on every subject except the one that most interested

Start of an early automobile race. John Jacob Astor was one of the entrants.

them. When they finally brought up the subject of an official protest by our government to Great Britain, President McKinley invited them to examine the view from the south side of the White House. It was commonly assumed that McKinley's disinclination to embarrass Great Britain was due partly to grateful recollection of Great Britain's attitude toward us when we were threatened with embarrassment by Germany during the Spanish War.

May 21. The eight-hour day received further official impetus by the passage of a bill by the House of Representatives making this the legal number of hours on government contracts.

May 30. A hundred thousand people went to Louisville, Ky., to witness the reunion of the veterans of the Confederate army, of whom 40,000 were still living, including 6 of the 19 lieutenants-general. Colonel Bushrod Washington of West Virginia protested against continuing to speak of Confederate soldiers as "rebels."

June 5. Stephen Crane died. A pioneer in realism, author of "The Red Badge of Courage."

June 19. Theodore Roosevelt got his formal start in national politics. The significance of the Republican National Convention assembled in Philadelphia seemed to lie in the renomination of William McKinley, of Ohio, for a second term; the real significance lay in the nomination for Vice-President, which went to Roosevelt, then governor of New York. (See Chapter 4.)

June 26. The U. S. Army Commission, headed by Doctor Walter Reed, appointed to investigate yellow fever, arrived at Havana and began the experiments which determined that the disease is spread solely by the female Stegomyia mosquito. (See Chapter 17.)

July 5. At the Democratic National Convention in Kansas City William J. Bryan was unanimously nominated for the presidency. His running-mate was Adlai Ewing Stevenson, who had been Vice-President during Cleveland's second term. The platform denounced the "colonial policy" of the Republican administration:

> The burning issue of imperialism growing out of the Spanish War involves the very existence of the Republic and the destruction of our free institutions. We regard it as the paramount issue of the campaign.

Although the gold standard had been formally adopted by Congress the preceding March, and there were many other evidences of the complete eclipse of the silver issue, the platform reaffirmed "the principles of the national Democratic platform adopted at Chicago in 1896," and once more demanded "the immediate restoration of the free and unlimited coinage of silver and gold at the present legal ratio of 16 to 1 without waiting for the aid or consent of any other nation."

July 15. W. K. Vanderbilt, Jr., drove his French automobile from Newport to Boston and back, 160 miles, in 3 hours, 57 minutes.

July 16. In the international athletic games at Paris America won sixteen out of twenty-one contests.

August 7. Eventual consolidation of the agricultural interests was forecast on this date by the formation at Topeka, Kan., of a farmers' trust to control the agricultural output of the Mississippi Valley. Farmers representing eight States and Oklahoma Territory took part.

August 8. Robert M. La Follette was nominated for governor of Wisconsin by the Republicans on a platform advocating nominations by direct popular vote and the abolition of party caucuses and conventions. This was one of the earliest steps in the direct primary. La Follette was elected, 264,420 to 160,764.

August 8. At Indianapolis, Bryan accepted the Democratic nomination for President in what he regarded as "one of the most important" of his political speeches. He gave it the title "Imperialism," and devoted it mainly to the Republican management of the Philippines.

August 13. Collis P. Huntington, the railroad-builder, died. Obituaries of him recounted that "he and his associates reduced the time from New York to San Francisco from six months to six days." [1]

August 14. The Hamburg-American steamer *Deutschland* completed a run from New York to Plymouth in 5 days, 11 hours, 45 minutes.

August 16. John James Ingalls died. He was a United States senator from Kansas and author of a famous poem "Opportunity," of which two often quoted lines were:

> Fame, love, and fortune on my footsteps wait . . .
> I knock unbidden once at every gate!

September 6. The Duke of Abruzzi's polar expedition returned to Tromsol, Norway, and announced it had reached 86 degrees 33 minutes north latitude, the highest point yet reached.

September 8. The almost complete destruction of Galveston, Texas, by a cyclonic hurricane. This catastrophe led to the devising of the "Commission Form of City Government," which subsequently was adopted by many cities, some adding to it the "City Manager" plan.

The storm was of unprecedented severity. Water from the Gulf of Mexico was driven in with such force that it piled up in the streets to a depth of from seven to seventeen feet. Six thousand lives were lost and property valued at $20,000,000 was destroyed. With extraordinary vigor Galveston prepared against a repetition of the disaster by pumping enough sand from the Gulf of Mexico to raise the level of the land on which Galveston

[1] In 1923, on June 23, Lieutenant Russell L. Maughan of the United State air service flew from New York to San Francisco in 21 hours, 44 minutes.

is built by seven feet, and by the construction of a massive sea-wall of concrete protected by granite rip-rap, which has successfully protected the city against severe storms in 1909 and 1915. Within five weeks of the disaster the city had so recuperated that business was going on in much the same volume as before.[1]

The Galveston Deep Water Committee, confronted by the emergency, took the lead in framing the proposed commission form of government. The charter was drafted by R. Waverly Smith, banker and lawyer; Walter Gresham, lawyer and former member of Congress; and Farrell D. Minor, lawyer. (For the germ of it they went back twenty-two years, to an act creating a taxing commission, which Memphis, Tenn., had devised after a similar emergency, the yellow-fever epidemic of 1878, had created a need in the latter city for a government with centralized authority, more compact, smaller, and more capable of quick and mobile action.) The charter as introduced in the Texas legislature in 1901 provided for a mayor-president and four commissioners to be appointed by the governor. Opposition in the legislature resulted in a compromise by which two of the commissioners were to be elected by the people. After the new government had been in force twenty months, the Texas court of appeals held the charter unconstitutional because of the appointive feature. A new charter was granted, making all members of the board elective. Excepting this change, the plan retained its original merits. The innovation caused many other cities to study the new plan and adopt it with various modifications.

[1] Mr. Tom Finty, Jr., who in 1900 was city editor of the Galveston *News*, and later was associated with the Dallas *News*, wrote me, July 27, 1925: "At the time of the storm the highest building in Galveston was six stories; since that time, three office-buildings of eight, ten and thirteen stories, respectively, have been erected. . . . The commerce of the port has steadily increased and with it the facilities have been augmented and modernized."

September 12. A first hint of the radio. *The Electrical Review* (English) recorded that at the session of the British Association for the Advancement of Science, at Bradford, England, the preceding Saturday, Sir William H. Preece announced that he had found it possible to convey audible speech six to eight miles without wires.

September 18. There was tried in Minneapolis, for the first time in America, a method of nominating candidates for office by direct primaries. The experiment had been authorized by the Minnesota legislature the previous year, and was restricted to the city of Minneapolis. The author of the idea was Oscar F. G. Day. Senator Washburn called it "the greatest political proposition ever introduced into American politics." A contemporary description said: "The public at once became deeply interested in the new power placed in their hands. . . . Nearly the entire vote of the city turned out." (A similar experiment, known as the "Crawford County system," had been tried locally in Pennsylvania several years before.)

September 18. One hundred and twelve thousand miners in the anthracite district went on strike. A result was a rise in the price of anthracite coal in New York of $1, to $6.50 a ton.

September 23. Despatches from Havana described the existence of a hundred cases of yellow fever. This was practically the last such news to leave Cuba. At this time Reed and Gorgas were well along in the work of wiping out yellow fever for all time from Cuba, and later from the rest of the world. (See Chapter 11.)

November 3. Repetition of the New York City "sound-money" parade of 1896. More than 100,000 Republicans marched in a heavy rain.

November 6. (Election Day.) McKinley and Roosevelt received 292 electoral votes to Bryan and Stevenson's 155. Bryan lost his own State, his own city, and his own precinct. Other than the South, Bryan carried only Idaho, Montana, Colorado, and Nevada.

Republican device in the 1900 campaign.
The dinner-pail, 14 feet high, was carried at the head of a parade in Youngstown, Ohio.

December 29. The State Department announced that negotiations for the purchase of the Danish West Indies were practically completed and awaited only the appropriation of money by Congress. More than twenty years passed before these negotiations came to fruit in the actual transfer of the islands to the United States.

December. The tallest building in New York in 1900 was of twenty-nine stories, at 13–21 Park Row. The height from the ground to top of the tower was 382 feet.

III

1900 was the year of the high vogue of novels about rural American life (known in the publishing fraternity as "b'gosh fiction"). The first was Edward Noyes Westcott's "David Harum" — everybody was quoting one of David's aphorisms: "Do unto the other feller the way he'd like to do unto you, an' do it fust." Before "David Harum" appeared, Irving Bacheller had written "Eben Holden" as a boy's book (a charming one, about life in the woods of northern New York), but the publishers, and the public, classified it with the "b'gosh" school.

Another definite field of popularity was early American history: Winston Churchill's "Richard Carvel," a story of the Revolution, which introduced Washington and John Paul Jones; Paul Leicester Ford's "Janice Meredith," and Maurice Thompson's "Alice of Old Vincennes." Mary Johnston's story of colonial Virginia, "To Have and to Hold," appeared this year, and reached a sale of more than 250,000 within six months.

A third group of novels popular this year were about knights and kings, remote in time or fancy: "When Knighthood Was in Flower," by Edward Caskoden (Charles Major); "The Cardinal's Snuff-box," by Henry Harland; "Via Crucis," a story of the Second Crusade, by F. Marion Crawford. Booth Tarkington's "Monsieur Beaucaire" appeared in 1900; by 1925 it had produced, so publishers said, in book, dramatic, and motion-picture royalties, a larger revenue than any other book ever published. Other novels of 1900 were "Eleanor," by Mrs. Humphry Ward; "Unleavened Bread," by Robert Grant; "The Master Christian," by Marie Corelli; the "Reign of Law," by James Lane Allen.

Among books not fiction, it was significant of something about to happen that the largest group included the word

"Trust" in their titles: Hopkins's "Coming Trust"; Jenks's "Trust Problem"; Apthorp's "Trusts and Their Relation to Industrial Problems"; Collier's "The Trusts"; Nettleton's "Trusts or Competition"; Ely's "Monopolies and Trusts."

1900 was the year of the dramatized novel. No successful fiction was permitted to escape. William H. Crane played in "David Harum"; John Drew in "Richard Carvel"; James K. Hackett in "The Pride of Jennico"; Mary Mannering in "Janice Meredith"; Viola Allen in "The Christian." Maude Adams played in "The Little Minister." Julia Marlowe played "Barbara Frietchie," and Weber and Fields burlesqued it as "Barbara Fidgety."

Several foreign players of the highest rank were in America: Madame Bernhardt and M. Coquelin presenting "Camille" and "La Tosca"; John Hare and Irene Van Brugh in "The Gay Lord Quex"; Henry Irving and Ellen Terry in a repertoire of exceptional distinction: "The Merchant of Venice," "Robespierre," "Waterloo," "The Bells," "Nance Oldfield."

E. H. Sothern and Virginia Harned played in "The Sunken Bell"; Henrietta Crosman in "Mistress Nell"; Annie Russell in "Miss Hobbs"; Blanche Bates in "Madame Butterfly"; Stuart Robson in "Oliver Goldsmith"; Nat Goodwin and Maxine Elliott in "When We Were Twenty-One." William Gillette continued "Sherlock Holmes"; James O'Neil, "Monte Cristo." Richard Mansfield's appearances during the year included "Dr. Jekyll and Mr. Hyde," "Cyrano de Bergerac," "The First Violin," "Beau Brummell," and "A Parisian Romance." Other productions of 1900, old and new, included "Ben Hur," "Quo Vadis," "Arizona," and "Florodora."

20

1901

Cleaning Up the Débris of the Spanish War. General Funston Captures Aguinaldo, Ending the Filipino Insurrection, and America Becomes Ecstatic Over an Ephemeral Hero. The Supreme Court Solves Several Riddles, in the "Insular Decisions," "a Judicial Drama of Truly Olympian Proportions." Cuba Is Accorded Freedom, Qualified by the Platt Amendment. Kaiser Wilhelm Becomes Indiscreet, Again—This Time a Little More So. The "Canteen" Abolished. McKinley Forswears a Third Term. The First Steam-Turbine Passenger-Ship. Around the World in Sixty Days. William Travers Jerome Elected District Attorney of New York. Marconi Sends the Letter S Across the Atlantic. McKinley Is Assassinated and Roosevelt Becomes President.

NINETEEN HUNDRED AND ONE saw the ending of the Filipino insurrection which came as a wholly unanticipated aftermath to the war with Spain.

When Dewey defeated the Spanish fleet at Manila, May 1, 1898, there was living in exile at Hong Kong a group of Filipino leaders, of whom the chief was Emilio Aguinaldo. Aguinaldo, two years before, had led an insurrection against the Spanish, and had quit on being paid 400,000 pesos. Eighteen days after Dewey's victory, Aguinaldo returned to Manila on board an American despatch-boat, to raise a Filipino army to co-operate in breaking the Spaniards' hold on the Philippines. As it turned out, the Americans needed no native assistance. The Spaniards in Manila were more than willing to surrender. Cut off from the possibility of help from Spain, their position had a curiously literal analogy to "between the devil and the deep sea." In front of them was the American fleet, whose prowess they had seen on May 1; behind them, the natives, excellent fighters, inspired with a semireligious zeal growing out of three hundred years of oppression. As between falling into the hands of the Americans and becoming a prey to the vengeful Filipinos, the Spaniards knew enough about both to prefer the former. In order to save their face with Madrid they arranged with Dewey for a demonstration of force on August 13, whereupon they surrendered, with a haste in proportion to their sense of relief. This was just one day after the peace protocol between Spain and the United States had been signed at Washington, news of which could not reach Manila because the cable from Hong Kong had been cut. The protocol left the status of the Philippines "in the air," merely providing, "The United States will occupy and hold the city, bay, and harbor of Manila, pending the conclusion of a treaty of peace, which shall determine the control, disposition, and government of the Philippines."

Emilio Aguinaldo, leader of the Filipino rebellion.

From the beginning of the war with Spain, some of the Filipino leaders had taken it for granted that with American victory we would abandon the Philippines, and permit the Filipinos to be independent.

That expectation was held by many Americans, who were puzzled about what to do with "what Dewey flung into our arms," as Whitelaw Reid put it. America had given no thought to this aspect of victory. On entering the war, Cuba was the Spanish possession on which our interest was focussed. The intention was not to take Cuba, but to free it — that intention had been made a pledge in a self-denying congressional resolution just before the declaration of war. When places like the Philippines, Porto Rico, and Guam came tumbling on us, we were rather dismayed. The Philippines worried us especially. The whole tradition of America was against having a distant Oriental possession. Our first feeling was one of unwelcome embarrassment, and the first impulse was to drop them and forget them just as quickly as the circumstances of the war would let us. The Cleveland *Leader* said: "The islands might all have sunk into the sea and few Americans would have known the difference." The New York *Press* said that to keep the Philippines would be "simply another 'Indian problem' multiplied by thirty." The Detroit *Journal* declared: "The best thought of the country is opposed to holding the Philippines."

As late as the Peace Conference, and even among the senators and other experienced public men who composed our Peace Commission, there were the haziest notions about what to do with the Philippines. When McKinley asked each commissioner for his private judgment, William R. Day, secretary of state, replied (I quote from Royal Cortissoz's "Life of Whitelaw Reid") that he "was strongly against retention of anything in the Philippines, unless possibly a coaling-station, and on even that he had some doubts." Justice Gray, of Delaware, "was even stronger than Day." Senator Cushman K. Davis, of Minnesota, thought we might retain "the northern part of the archipelago, giving away Mindanao and the whole southern part to Holland." Senator William P. Frye, of Maine, rather favored Davis's idea, and "dwelt on the fact that some opposition to our holding the islands had developed in New England and promised to grow." Whitelaw Reid alone among the commissioners favored unqualified retention, putting his position in the words:

> I don't see how we can honorably give them back to Spain. . . . Having broken down the power in control of them, we could not honorably desert them, and should be extremely unwise to turn over the task of controlling them to any other power.

That way of expressing it may sound unctuous, but actually it was a sincere and characteristic American point of view. The more thoughtful of those Americans who favored keeping the Philippines had comparatively little notion that any advantage could accrue to us; the real motive was embarrassment as to what else could be done with them, having regard to national honor and the fate of the inhabitants. There were others, it is true, whose advocacy of retention was put frankly on grounds of material advantage. Chambers of commerce on the Pacific coast passed resolutions in vaguely grandiose phrases about commercial expansion, Oriental trade. Some papers talked like adolescent boys about "the growing commercial importance of the United States." A certain amount of land lust was awakened in persons who, ignorant of conditions in the Philippines, thought of them as a source of free land for settlers, as our previous acquisitions from the Indians had been.

In the American Peace Commission, Whitelaw Reid converted the others to his view that the only way was for America to take possession of the Philippines and be responsible for them. That became the official American position, and on that basis the peace treaty was written.

Even after that, the Filipino leaders still hoped for independence, and had some reason to. The treaty had yet to be ratified by the Senate, and in that body, as well as throughout America, the school that opposed keeping the Philippines was strong. Outright rejection of the treaty was advocated by the venerable Senator Hoar, of Massachusetts, a Republican, on the fundamental argument of the Declaration of Independence: "Governments derive their just powers from the consent of the governed." He was supported by many senators and by a large section of American opinion. William J. Bryan took a position that, as respects the Filipinos, amounted to the same thing; he advocated that the treaty be ratified, in order to achieve a status of peace, but that thereafter the Filipinos be set free.

Aguinaldo and the Filipino leaders watched this long debate with increasing tension, keeping in touch with the Senate proceedings from day to day. By February 4, 1899, it was clear the Senate was going to ratify the treaty, and that the Philippines would be retained as an American possession. On that night the long strain broke with an exchange of shots between an American outpost and a band of Aguinaldo's followers. Two days later the Senate actually ratified the treaty. Thereupon the Filipino insurrection became general.

America now found itself involved in a war she did not anticipate, for which she had no wish. It was embarrassing and distressing. We had begun the Spanish War as a fight against a major European power, for the purpose of freeing the oppressed Cubans. We now found ourselves fighting a weak people, and in a rôle similar to what had been Spain's. There was no pride or other satisfaction to be got out of it. Yet it demanded increasing forces of American soldiers until the number reached 60,000; it lasted six times as long as the Spanish War, its cost was more than half as much,[1] and in every respect it was more vexatious.

The men on whom the unwelcome responsibility fell, President McKinley, Secretary of War Elihu Root, and the Administration, suppressed their distaste and put their shoulders to the wheel. The army went through with it. The public gave loyal support. Leaders of thought divided. Many gave support to the Administration easily; some had misgivings at heart but felt that helpfulness to the government was the paramount duty. These were irritated by others, equally high-minded, who put personal conviction above every other consideration. Rancor grew with debate. Dissension at home became only less disagreeable than fighting the Filipinos. The spirit of America became sour. Anger went to absurd lengths. A Republican periodical, *Judge*, went to great pains to make a cover in the form of a luridly colored picture of Aguinaldo standing with his foot on a slain American soldier. The title read "What Is Behind Aguinaldo, That Fiend Who Has Slain Many American Soldiers?" The reader, by raising a flap ingeniously cut, discovered the features of William J. Bryan.

The anti-Administration leaders were equally violent. Carl Schurz, formerly a Republican leader, turned savagely on the Administration, saying McKinley's actions were those of a "contemptible rascal." Those were utterly unfair words to use about McKinley, and unworthy from a man of Schurz's standing under any circumstances. Schurz was old, and like many Republicans who had fought with spiritual zeal to free the American slaves, he felt outraged at the position in which his country now found itself. A phrase used by McKinley, "benevolent

[1] James Ford Rhodes says the Spanish War cost $300,000,000; the Filipino insurrection an estimated $170,000,000.

assimilation," provided an easy mechanism for satire when put in juxtaposition with his request that the army be enlarged to 100,000. In Boston an anti-imperialist league worked energetically under leaders who commanded high respect. The New York *World* said, "Of course Aguinaldo's punishment should fit his crime, but what is his crime?" and demanded to know: "Is it not plain that the whole policy of pacification by force of arms is as impracticable as it is un-American?" The Baltimore *News* answered *The World's* rhetorical question, saying it was the "cruel and stupid ignoring" of Filipino ideals and aspirations that had plunged us "into the horrible mire in which we have now for nearly two years been floundering. Without a recognition of these national feelings and aspirations — which no people should be quicker to recognize than the Americans — we shall continue in that mire, to the disgrace of the American name and to the infinite damage of American ideals of justice and human rights."

Much of this opposition was on a high plane, argument about human liberty and the Constitution. But in the acrid rancor that descended upon the country, some of the criticism was carping and abusive. Some expressed itself in jeering ridicule of the army, which made its distasteful task longer and more difficult. Thomas B. Reed, one of the ablest Republican leaders of his generation, retired from his office of Speaker of the House, largely through disgust over the policy of expansion, and in private life poured sardonic irony on the Administration. One morning the newspapers printed a report that some captives taken by the American army included Aguinaldo's young son. Reed, that day, finding his law partner at work, affected surprise and said: "What, are you working to-day? I should think you would be celebrating; I see by the papers that the American army has captured the infant son of Aguinaldo, and at last accounts was in hot pursuit of the mother." In a letter to a friend about the cost of military operations in the Philippines, Reed spoke of trying "to find out how much each yellow man

Courtesy of U. S. Signal Corps.

An American army outpost near Manila at the time of the Filipino insurrection.

cost us in the bush. As I make it out, he has cost thirty dollars per Malay, and he is still in the bush. Why didn't you purchase him of Spain f.o.b., with definite freight-rate and insurance paid?" Andrew Carnegie wrote to a friend in the Administration: "You seem to have about finished your work of civilizing the Filipinos; it is thought that about 8000 of them have been completely civilized and sent to Heaven; I hope you like it."

The spirit of those who were determined to support the Administration's policy, even though they could not be very happy about it, was expressed by the Detroit *Journal:* "We shall not falter even though our new responsibilities confront us with problems to stagger a commencement orator." The sense of unwelcome responsibility was put in verse by a Boston *Transcript* poet:

O Dewey at Manila
  That fateful first of May,
When you sank the Spanish squadron
  In almost bloodless fray,
And gave your name to deathless fame;
  O glorious Dewey, say,
Why didn't you weigh anchor
  And softly sail away?

Meantime, for more than two years, the army kept at its disagreeable and difficult work. On the initial attack of the Filipinos on Manila, during the early days of February, 1899, the American forces were hard pressed. But after some months they had driven the insurgents from about Manila, captured many towns from them, dispersed many guerilla bands, and caught several of Aguinaldo's associates. Despite these successes, it was realized that the insurrection would drag on indefinitely so long as Aguinaldo remained at large.

Consequently, there was almost hysterical jubilance in America when, on March 27, 1901, news came that Aguinaldo had been captured, almost single-handed, by Brigadier-General Frederick Funston of the Volunteers. Funston, accompanied by three Americans, five ex-insurgent officers, and seventy-eight faithful Macabebe allies, hacked his way for three weeks through tropical jungles, aided from time to time by supplies from the insurgents, who had been deceived into believing the band was one of their own forces on their way to Aguinaldo with American prisoners. Once in Aguinaldo's camp, Funston and his followers quickly dispersed the native guard and seized Aguinaldo. Aguinaldo, after being taken to Manila, took an oath of loyalty to the American Government, and issued to his people, on April 19, 1901, a proclamation ending the rebellion.

Major-General Frederick Funston, capturer of Aguinaldo, described by William Allen White as "Explorer, Author, Planter, Captain, Colonel, Brigadier, and Major-General. The most talented, most useful, most ubiquitous Kansan the breezy, versatile old State has produced."

For a day Funston's spectacular feat was the talk of the world. In America the applause was more ecstatic than was warranted by its standing as a military operation. Judgments were more accurately proportioned to the sense of relief from a prolonged and disagreeable strain than to permanent values. Roosevelt wrote to Funston: "I take pride in this crowning exploit of a career filled with cool courage, iron endurance, and gallant daring, because you have added your name to the honor-roll of American worthies." Fulsome biographies of Funston were printed. There was even speculation about his chances for the presidency.[1]

[1] In Funston's native State, Kansas, the local editor-laureate several years later wrote this epic of the exploits of the local hero:

"He grew up on an Allen County farm. . . . He was educated in the Kansas State University, and worked on Kansas City newspapers, and later was train auditor on the Santa Fe, which is the Kansasest of all the Kansas railroads. He fought as captain of artillery in Cuba, and later commanded a Kansas regiment that has spread the glory of Kansas from the Yukon to the equator. He explored in Alaska, planted rubber and coffee in Yucatan, wrote books in New York, captured Aguinaldo, put down the Filipino rebellion, straddled an earthquake and rode it to fame in San Francisco, and was sent to Mexico to uphold the honor of

That was the climax of America's early adventure in expansion. The judgment of the world did not coincide with that of the London *Saturday Review*, for that periodical was usually critical of the United States. On this occasion it was unnecessarily harsh to America, unnecessarily belittling to Funston. Nevertheless its point of view was held by some Americans[1] as well:

> There have been more wicked wars than this on the liberties of the Filipinos, but never a more shabby war. It is nearly three years since the Americans, having gone to war with Spain for the liberties of Cuba, decided that it was their manifest destiny to deprive the Filipinos of their liberties. This was called "taking up the white man's burden." [2] For some time the Americans quite honestly believed that they were doing rather a noble, self-denying thing; but the cant phrases of three years ago are worn threadbare. . . . [The capture of Aguinaldo] was effected by a piece of sharp practice thoroughly in keeping with the rest of the war. Of all that curious mixture of sentiments, noble and ignoble, out of which the war with the Filipinos sprang, only the element of hypocrisy seems to have retained its original vigor.

Meantime the pacification of the Philippines pro-

the Stars and Stripes down there. He is a writer and a fighter with a punch. He is what might be called a 'diversified crop'; explorer, author, planter, captain, colonel, brigadier, and major-general—what's the matter with Funston, the most talented, most useful, most ubiquitous Kansan the breezy, versatile old State has produced? Jess Willard has his place in the Kansas hall of fame, all right. So has Walter Johnson, the baseball pitcher, and good Kansans they are, both of them. But the greatest of these is Funston. And now abideth these three: Funston first in war, Johnson first in sport, and Willard first in the jaw of the cinderman!"—William Allen White, in the Emporia *Gazette*, April 10, 1915.

[1] This verse appeared in *Life*, April 11, 1901:

"Sing a song of Funston:
How his treachery
Captured Aguinaldo;
Macabæus by.
Forgery and lying,
That's a modern thing. . . ."

[2] It was an English poet who had urged that course upon us as an imperious, one might say an imperial, call to duty. One of the "cant phrases," "Take Up the White Man's Burden," was Kipling's own—addressed both to the British in South Africa and to America in the Philippines. It should be said that the British generally felt more as Kipling did than as *The Saturday Review*.

ceeded. Governor-General William H. Taft had just the right personality to make an impression of justice and kindliness. The American Government sent hundreds of American school-teachers to serve in native schools.

Kipling's poem, "The White Man's Burden," inspired this American cartoon from the Denver *Post*. The title represented Uncle Sam as saying: "I don't like the job, Rudyard, my boy!"

Despite having to conduct classes in an idiom unknown at the start to the pupils, these modern crusaders achieved remarkable results. From the beginning they laid stress on soap and tooth-brushes. They taught American games, tennis, baseball, and football to Filipino children and to their elders. Stories began to trickle out of baseball games between teams clad in uniforms noteworthy for their scantiness. Argument and vituperation were as much a part of baseball there as here; and threats, happily never carried out, of correcting faulty decisions with bolos were an occasional Philippine version of "Kill the umpire!" Some tribal chiefs felt that they alone should be allowed to do the batting, leaving the base-running for the more menial of their followers.

During those early years progress was made in preparing the Filipinos for self-government. On February 27, 1901, an uncle of Aguinaldo, José Serapis, was appointed governor of the Province of Bulacan. Six weeks earlier municipal elections had been held in Baguio, Province of Benguet, Luzon — two of several steps that marked the close of one epoch in Philippine-American relations, and the beginning of another and happier one.

II

The "Insular Decisions"

The suppression of the Filipino insurrection was the conclusion of the military part of the Spanish War, But it did not end our problems. The central one, whether we should keep the Spanish possessions, had been decided affirmatively by the Senate's ratification of the Peace Treaty, February 6, 1899. That, in turn, had been confirmed in the popular election[1] of November 6, 1900, by the overwhelming triumph of McKinley, representing expansion, over Bryan, representing what he called anti-imperialism. But even after that many questions extremely interesting to everybody, and acutely

[1] A scholar of Democratic leanings to whom I submitted this proof makes a fine distinction here. He says the decision of the 1900 election was merely "not to let the dependencies go *at that time*."

embarrassing to the Republicans as a high-tariff party, were immediately forced on Congress and the Supreme Court. The very words "annexation" and "dependencies" suggest the embarrassment, for the question was, had we "annexed" them, and were they "dependencies"?

Sewing classes conducted by American teachers in the Philippines.

If not, what were they?[1] Had Porto Rico become a part of the United States in the same sense as California, for example, or Oklahoma? Were the people of Porto Rico and of the Philippines "citizens" in the same sense as persons living in Iowa or Arizona? In some Philippine Islands slavery was practised — could that go on under a Constitution which expressly forbade it in America?

The embarrassments reached into many fields: ethnological; voting rights; representation in Congress; the right of the dependencies to govern themselves; the propriety of letting these alien peoples have a voice in gov-

[1] The Philadelphia *Public Ledger*, in a satiric mood, asked about the status of one of the new dependencies: "Is it a nation, a State, a Territory, a republic, a colony, an annex, an ally, or a dependency?"

erning the United States, in selecting our Presidents. But the field in which the question came most quickly to the front was the one that touched commercial interests; namely, the tariff.

The Republican party, then in power, was for "expansion"; but also, and even more firmly, it was for tariff protection for American industries, meaning industries on the mainland of the United States. Hence their difficulty: If Porto Rico had become a part of the United States in the same sense as New York, or Oklahoma (then still a Territory), it followed that tobacco and sugar, for example, from our new dependencies, could come into the United States without paying duty. But if the other horn of the dilemma were accepted; namely, that Porto Rico had not become a part of the United States, but was still foreign territory, it followed that Germany could ship goods into Porto Rico or the Philippines without paying the American tariff duties — in which event, practically no American producer would be able to sell there. Unless we were careful, we should give to these dependencies precisely that grievance which George III gave the American colonies in 1774, through the Navigation Acts, and thereby brought on the Boston Tea-Party and the Revolutionary War.

President McKinley, although a Republican, and although in a peculiar sense the high priest of the Republican party's doctrine of a protective tariff, took the ground that "our plain duty is to abolish all customs tariffs between the United States and Porto Rico." Whereupon the American sugar-producers, and other protected interests, regarded McKinley as an apostate from the faith, an ingrate to those who had made him. In taking this position on the tariff, McKinley was at one with the Democrats. But he did not go the full length of the Democrats, who expressed their view in the slogan "The Constitution follows the flag" — not only as respects the tariff, but as respects civil rights, voting, and everything else in the Constitution. The Democrats thought we should not keep the distant dependencies at all. But they held that if we did take them in, we must take them all the way in. McKinley merely held that although the Constitution did not follow the flag, and although Congress had the right to impose a tariff on the dependencies, nevertheless, in common decency, Congress ought not to do so. In the tariff fight that followed in Congress, the regular Republicans outvoted the Democrats and the few Republican followers of McKinley who voted with the Democrats. The regular Republican majority treated Porto Rico as being neither a State nor a Territory, but a "possession" acquired through the treaty-making power, to which Congress could give or deny such rights and status as it might choose.

Ultimately, the puzzle was put up to the Supreme Court, which, in a group of test cases, handed down the Insular Decisions. They were regarded at the time, and even yet among lawyers and students, as immensely important, as "the most important since the Dred Scott decision,"[1] as a "judicial drama of truly Olympian proportions."[2] All but two of the cases were decided as a group on May 27, 1901, the remainder in the following December.

The court had to consider not only the tariff but all the aspects and implications of the whole situation, because its decision would be a precedent affecting civil liberties and all the other embarrassments involved in the novel relation, and affecting also any future annexations — at that time it looked as if America had em-

[1] Nelson's Encyclopædia.

[2] "The Supreme Court in United States History," by Charles Warren.

barked on a career of annexation. The situation called for some dexterity, and the court handled its difficult responsibility with what has turned out to be high wisdom. The justices recognized the practical difficulties in a theoretical consistency, and, although by a five-to-four decision, found a way out. Indeed, merely to say it was a five-to-four decision does not fully convey the tangle of intricacies within the court: the qualified assent and outright dissent; principle qualified by expediency and expediency restrained by principle; lesser minds bound by consistency, and bolder minds trying ingeniously to find ways of arriving at a conclusion which of necessity must be inconsistent, without being too glaringly inconsistent in logic.

It was Mr. Justice Brown who handed down the decision. Four of the other eight justices concurred, but declined to subscribe to the reasoning by which Justice Brown arrived at it. That is what gave point to the ironic description of the decision as being "by Brown, eight dissenting." In Justice Brown's logic, that is, his reasoning on the law of the case, not one of his colleagues concurred.

John W. Davis,[1] in describing these cases, said that Justice Brown "ploughed a lonely furrow." For a certain distance along the difficult path he was helped by Justices McKenna, Shiras, and White, who believed it was possible that a territory should have

> a relation to the United States between that of being a foreign country absolutely and that of being a domestic country absolutely.

That was precisely what had been denied by those who think in terms of language instead of in terms of fact.[2]

[1] Democratic candidate for President in 1924.
[2] For that type of mind there is an epithet, "wordsters."

Justice Brown, however, had the ingenuity to go on from there and devise the needed next step. He saved himself from being impaled on either horn of the dilemma by confidently and gracefully seizing one horn in one hand and the other in the other hand and swinging himself to a secure seat between. He invented a new phrase, adding one more to the terminology of state, territory, colony, dependency, and what-not. He said:

> We are . . . of opinion that . . . Porto Rico is a territory appurtenant—but not a part—of the United States.

In other words, Justice Brown and four others, making a majority, decided that Porto Rico and the Philippines are not part of the United States, and at the same time are not foreign.[1]

This ingenious defining of a middle ground gave rise to much misconception. Because expansion was an acutely partisan issue, there was partisan interpretation of the decisions. E. Benjamin Andrews, president of Brown University, who was a Bryan Democrat, said:

> Thus construed the Constitution did not *ex proprio vigore* follow our flag, nor could inhabitants of the acquired islands plead a single one of its guaranties unless Congress voted them such a right. They were subjects of the United States, not citizens. . . .

[1] As respects the tariff, which was the specific subject-matter, there is an adequate summary in Nelson's Encyclopædia: "The principles established by the decisions in these cases are as follows: (1) Before the ratification of the Treaty of Paris (1899) the military government in Porto Rico was an exercise of war power. Porto Rico was foreign territory, and the duties collected were valid (Dooley *vs.* United States). (2) On the ratification of the treaty, Porto Rico ceased to be foreign territory, and duties collected even under the same military government were invalid, and should be refunded (Dooley *vs.* United States; De Lima *vs.* Bidwell). (3) Porto Rico and the Philippines, while not foreign territory, are not part of the United States, but subject to the United States. Therefore the uniformity of duties, imposts, and excises demanded by the Constitution throughout the United States does not apply to the dependencies, for which Congress has the right to enact a separate tariff law. Congress has, in fact, complete power over ceded territory until such territory is made part of the United States."

That interpretation has persisted to this day. It is not quite correct. It is not true that inhabitants of our dependencies cannot "plead a single one" of the guaranties of the Constitution. They can plead some of them, and have pleaded some, and the Supreme Court has sustained them. The court's decision in the Insular Cases was, like the nature of the facts, "betwixt and between." There are some fundamental guaranties of which Congress cannot deprive the inhabitants of the dependencies; but there are some grants of power and limitations in the Constitution which, in the nature of things, do not apply in some of the possessions. For a correct statement of the effect of the Insular Decisions, let us turn to the best of authorities, Chief Justice Taft, speaking in 1922, in the case of Balzac *v.* Porto Rico:

> The Constitution of the United States is in force in Porto Rico, as it is wherever and whenever the sovereign power of that government is exerted. This has not only been admitted but emphasized by this court in all its authoritative expressions upon the issues arising in the Insular Cases. . . . The Constitution, however, contains grants of power, and limitations which, in the nature of things, are not always and everywhere applicable; and the real issue in the Insular Cases was not whether the Constitution extended to the Philippines or Porto Rico when we went there, but which ones of its provisions were applicable by way of limitation upon the exercise of executive and legislative power in dealing with new conditions and requirements. The guaranties of certain fundamental personal rights declared in the Constitution, as, for instance, that no person could be deprived of life, liberty, or property without due process of law, had, from the beginning, full application in the Philippines and Porto Rico.

Let us admit (and be grateful) that Justice Taft, in 1922, was more definite in thought, more clear in language, than his harassed predecessors of 1901.

Unsatisfactory as was this decision of a bizarrely divided court, it put the necessary O. K. on what had been done, and opened the way for appropriate legislation about the dependencies. The court could not well have done otherwise. They had to recognize the facts, and had to devise a way to seem to make the Constitution conform to the facts. We had the islands, we were determined to keep them — but we did not propose to give those alien peoples the same status, and an equal voice in governing us, as ourselves. Those were the facts, and the court had to find a way to save the face of the Constitution. That they did so is proof of their wisdom and sense of responsibility. The current of American history following the war was not determined by, and could not be checked by, the court. It was determined by whatever impulse it was in the people, or whatever leadership caused them, to embark on the war with Spain.

Mr. Dooley knew. His dissertation on the Supreme Court's decision in the Insular Cases was one of his most richly engaging. There was penetrating point in his picturing the decision as being handed down by "Justice Brown — Fuller, C. J., Gray, J., Harlan, J., Shiras, J., McKenna, J., White, J., Brewer, J., and Peckham, J., dissenting fr'm me an' each other."

As for himself, Mr. Dooley had doubts, based on personal no less than constitutional propriety, whether the "Constitution ought to shadow the flag to all th' tough resorts on th' Passyfic Coast." He said "the flag was so lively no constitution cud follow it an' survive." Out of the same concern for the Constitution's good health and decorous behavior, he said:

> Ye can't make me think th' constitution is goin' thrapezin' around ivrywhere a young leftinant in th' ar'rmy takes it into his head to stick a flagpole. It's too old. It's a home-stayin' constitution with a blue coat with brass buttons on to it, an' it walks with a goold-headed cane. It's old an' it's feeble an'

it prefers to set on the front stoop an' amuse the childer. It wudden't last a minyit in thim thropical climes.

But it was in the closing lines that Mr. Dooley showed himself not only the satirist with penetrating insight that he always was, but the philosopher he frequently was:

"Some say it laves the flag up in th' air an' some say that's where it laves the constitution. Annyhow, something's in the air. But there's wan thing I'm sure about."

"What's that?" asked Mr. Hennessy.

"That is," said Mr. Dooley, "no matter whether the constitution follows th' flag or not, th' Supreme Court follows th' illiction returns."

To say the Supreme Court follows the election returns is, of course, the conscious exaggeration of a humorist. We need not go so far. But the court does take account of election returns, and it necessarily follows the facts. It follows them; it does not lead them. A good deal of the incorrect thinking and muddled politics in the world is caused by a wrong assumption about the relative order of precedence as between facts, on the one hand, and statesmen and courts, on the other. We had the islands, the election of 1900 had showed we were determined to keep them, and everybody knew we were not going to grant them the same constitutional status as ourselves. Those were the facts the Supreme Court was obliged to take account of. The court, by means of a good deal of stretching, found a way to cover our new departure of taking on overseas dependencies, within the rigidities of a written constitution that did not foresee any such condition. As *The Review of Reviews* put it: "The decision of the Supreme Court means that we are not to be hampered in our serious policies by the ingenious use of logic in interpretation of an ancient document that was not intended to hamper posterity."

The whole episode, however, contributed, together with

the cooling down of the expansive emotions stirred up by the Spanish War, to a new mood, in which America was less headlong about acquiring overseas dependencies not readily assimilable.

III

Cuba and the Platt Amendment

A problem different from the rest was presented by Cuba. In making war on Spain, Congress had declared "that the people of the Island of Cuba are, and of right ought to be, free and independent." Later, to make our war aim even more clear to the world, and to answer the cynical suspicions of some European countries, as well as of some among our own people, Congress passed a "self-denying ordinance" in which we disclaimed any intention of exercising "sovereignty, jurisdiction, or control over said Island, except for the pacification thereof"; and pledged ourselves, so soon as pacification should be complete, "to leave the government and control of the Island to its people."

Following the Treaty of Paris, a provisional government was established over Cuba by the War Department, which undertook and successfully completed the task of making Cuba healthful. It built up an educational system. It organized the judiciary, and created governmental departments modelled on the American plan. By the end of 1900 the major part of its work was done.

On March 1, 1901, Congress approved an amendment presented by Senator Platt, of Connecticut, to the Army Appropriation bill, defining the relations between Cuba and the United States that should be in effect following the establishment of the Cuban republic. Condensed, the Platt Amendment provided:

That the Government of Cuba shall never enter into any treaty . . . with any foreign power . . . which will impair . . .

the independence of Cuba; nor in any manner . . . permit any foreign power . . . to obtain . . . lodgment in . . . any portion of said Island.

That said Government shall not assume nor contract any public debt . . . for the ultimate discharge of which the ordinary revenues of the Island . . . shall be inadequate.

That the Government of Cuba consents that the United States may exercise the right to intervene for the preservation of Cuban independence, the maintenance of a government adequate for the protection of life, property and individual liberty, and for discharging the obligations . . . imposed by the Treaty of Paris on the United States. . . .

That the Government of Cuba will execute, and as far as necessary extend, the plans already devised, or other plans to be mutually agreed upon, for the sanitation of the cities of the Island, to the end that a recurrence of epidemic and infectious diseases may be prevented. . . .

That the Isle of Pines shall be omitted from the proposed constitutional boundaries of Cuba and the title thereto left to future adjustment by treaty.

That . . . the Government of Cuba will sell or lease to the United States lands necessary for coaling or naval stations. . . .

That . . . the Government of Cuba will embody the foregoing provisions in a permanent treaty with the United States.

Whether these conditions violated the letter or the spirit, or both, of the self-denying declaration we had made to the world when we entered Cuba, was a much mooted question at the time and since. In the extreme nationalistic circles of Cuba the conditions were received with resentment. In the United States also, among the anti-imperialists, the belief was general that Congress had drifted away from the idealism of 1898, and even from our specific promises, in imposing conditions of any nature on Cuba in return for freeing her from Spain.

For several months during the spring of 1901 the Cuban Constitutional Convention, in session in Havana, debated whether or not to accept the Platt Amendment. Before final action, the convention sent a committee to Washington to supplicate the American Government not to insist on Cuba's adoption of the amendment. The Cuban visitors were invited to dine at the White House and were otherwise fêted; but McKinley was adamant in insisting on ratification. He called attention to the economic necessity of Cuba's securing a reciprocity trade agreement which would permit her to market her sugar-crops under advantageous conditions in the United States, and pointed out that the best way for Cuba to secure reciprocity was to accept the Platt Amendment promptly and cheerfully. With this rather vague promise of economic help, the committee returned to Havana. On June 12, 1901, the Platt Amendment was finally accepted by Cuba and incorporated in its constitution.

IV

Other Events of 1901

January 6. Philip D. Armour died. He started as a local butcher near his birthplace in Madison County, New York; spent six months following the gold rush to California, walking part way and riding a mule the rest; returned to Milwaukee and started a pork-packing business; moved its headquarters to Chicago in 1874 and, partly as a pork-packer, but more as a shrewd and daring speculator, became one of the country's wealthiest men.

January 9. The periodical *Electricity* recorded the failure of an attempt at telephoning over a submarine cable between Havana and Key West. This problem was not solved until 1920.

January 9. Congress abolished the officially authorized places for selling liquor on military reservations known as "canteens." The abolition was opposed by Secretary of War Root, who told a Senate committee that the opponents of the "canteen" were misguided people "doing

Satan's work in endeavoring to take these young fellows out from under the restraint and under the influences that surround them when they are in camp and drive them out into the horrible and demoralizing and damning surroundings that cluster around the outside of the camps."

January 10. The great Texas oil boom was started by the coming in of a well at Beaumont, which spouted 200 feet into the air. It took nine days to bring the well under control. Ex-Mayor Samuel M. Jones, of Toledo, who saw the well during this period, said:

> It is the greatest oil-well ever discovered in the United States. Its advent means that liquid fuel is to be the fuel of the twentieth century. Smoke, cinders, ashes, and soot will disappear along with war and other evidences of barbarism. During the next few years you will see locomotives passing through Corsicana using oil for fuel, and ocean steamers will be using it, too.

January 22. Queen Victoria died.

February 4. With funds from the Cuban Treasury granted by Governor-General Leonard Wood, Major William C. Gorgas began his campaign against yellow fever and mosquitoes in Havana. (See Chapter 17.)

February 9. Mrs. Carry A. Nation travelled from Topeka to Des Moines, Iowa, greeting great crowds.

March 3. An advertisement of J. P. Morgan & Co. announced the formation of the United States Steel Corporation, then and now the largest unit of business in all history. It was the climax, and most conspicuous example, of the evolution toward the large integrated unit form of organization in business; and marked also the climax of excited alarm against trusts in the world of public opinion.[1]

March 14. *Life* satirized mechanical music:

Freddie (who has been brought up with a pianola, rushing frantically up-stairs): "Oh, mama, mama! There's a man down-stairs playing the piano with his *hands!*"

March 28. Emperor William of Germany, dedicating an army barracks, enjoined his troops:

You . . . must be ready, day and night . . . to spill your blood, if need be, for your king and his house. . . . If ever . . . this town should rise . . . against its king in disobedience and insubordination, then the Alexander Grenadiers will hasten to the protection of their king, and, with their bayonets, soon teach the insolent a good lesson. . . . May valor, loyalty, and unquestioning obedience be the virtues which distinguish this regiment. Its deeds will then meet with the approval of me, its king and master. . . . Devotion to king and fatherland must be sealed with blood and life. . . . We shall always be the victors. . . . For there is a mighty Ally, that is the eternal God in Heaven. . . .

Friends of the Emperor explained the manifest fear of bodily harm that was the motif of the speech as being merely a "state of nerves" brought on by an attack on the Kaiser a short time before by a Bremen lunatic. Commentators less devoted to the Hohenzollerns hinted that only a serious mental derangement could explain the speech — if no revolt was brewing, what sane mind would fan one into flame by such utterances? The incident caused many Germans to question the pet tenets of Hohenzollern rule. In a cartoon in *Simplicissimus*, the humorous paper of the German capital, a lieutenant was depicted asking a private: "Tell me, Johann, why

[1] *Life*, on January 24, 1901, printed this witticism:
"Who made the world, Charles?"
"God made the world in 4004 B. C., but it was reorganized in 1901 by James J. Hill, J. Pierpont Morgan, and John D. Rockefeller."

should a soldier gladly give his life for the Emperor?" The reply was: "Yes indeed, Herr Lieutenant, *why should he?*" The New York *World* said:

> That 56,000,000 as intelligent, sensible, and self-respecting people as the Germans should acknowledge as their "sovereign" a person wild enough to give vent to such nonsense in the twentieth century would be melancholy were it not so ludicrous. And the culminating touch of humor is the formation of a committee of high officials of Berlin to wait upon this madman and assure him that "no one in Berlin entertains a thought of impudence or insubordination."

May 9. The Northern Pacific panic on the New York Stock Exchange in which the price of the shares rose from $110 to over a thousand dollars. It was the climax of a dramatic battle in which Edward H. Harriman fought against James J. Hill and J. Pierpont Morgan for control of the road.

June 2. James A. Herne, actor and playwright, died. He was to the drama what William Dean Howells was to fiction, the pioneer and teacher of absolute naturalism on the stage.[1] Herne's first successful play, "Hearts of Oak," ran twelve years.

June 6. The last of the volunteer troops left the Philippines en route to the United States, only regulars remaining in the islands.

June 7. Andrew Carnegie gave $10,000,000 in United States Steel Corporation bonds to Scotch universities. A Chicago *Times-Herald* poet satirized Carnegie's gifts in a "Psalm of the Strenuous Life":

> Let us then be up and doing,
> All becoming money kings;

[1] Walter Prichard Eaton wrote me in 1925: "It is almost true to say that Herne, with 'Margaret Fleming' and 'Griffith Davenport' was the only American playwright to anticipate Eugene O'Neill."

Some day we may be endowing
  Universities and things.
Lives of billionaires remind us
  That we've got to own the stock
If we want to leave behind us
  Libraries on every block.

June 10. President McKinley issued a statement:

I regret that the suggestion of a third term has been made. . . . There are now questions of the gravest importance before the Administration and the country, and their just consideration should not be prejudiced in the public mind by even the suspicion of the thought of a third term. . . . I will say now, once for all, expressing a long-settled conviction, that I not only am not and will not be a candidate for a third term, but would not accept a nomination for it, if it were tendered me. . . .

July 4. William Howard Taft became civil governor of the Philippines.

July 21. Charles Fitzmorris, a Chicago schoolboy sent by a Chicago paper, finished a record-breaking trip around the world in 60 days, 13 hours, 29 minutes, and $42\frac{4}{5}$ seconds. The previous record, made by Nellie Bly in 1889, was 72 days, 6 hours, 11 minutes. In 1903, Fitzmorris's record was broken by Henry Frederick, whose time was 54 days, 7 hours, 2 minutes. In 1911, Andre Jaeger-Schmidt made the journey in 39 days, 19 hours, 42 minutes, 38 seconds. John H. Mears in 1913 made a record of 35 days, 21 hours, 36 minutes, which still stood in 1925.

July 25. President McKinley, against the protests of American commercial interests, issued a proclamation establishing free trade between Porto Rico and the United States, and putting civil government for the island into effect, acting under a provision of the Foraker Act whereby the tariff might be dispensed with by presidential decree whenever the income from internal taxes of that dependency should be sufficient to defray the cost of government. Early in the summer of 1901, President McKinley's attention had been called to the fact that the island could now pay its way, by a resolution of the Porto Rican legislature, passed on July 4, asking that free trade should go into effect July 25, the third anniversary of the appearance of the American flag on Porto Rican soil.

July. *The Scientific American* described the trials on the Clyde of the *King Edward*, the first turbine passenger-steamer. A speed of more than twenty knots an hour was developed. It was predicted that the majority of ocean-going passenger-ships would be driven by turbines. This prediction has been fulfilled in the case of steamers where high speed is essential.

August 2. A trotting record of 2.02¼ was made by the stallion Cresceus at Columbus, Ohio.

August 15. Some verse in *Life*, by C. R. Bacon, described the summer styles in feminine dress:

> Now the Summer Girl, she packs her ducks,
> (It's beautiful weather for them!)
> And puts on a skirt with a thousand tucks,
> Three hundred ruffles and eighty pucks,
> Some darts and gores and a hem.

September 5. President McKinley made a plea for reciprocity which became a disputed point of Republican party doctrine for years:

> . . . Commercial competitors we are, commercial enemies we must not be. . . . Isolation is no longer possible. . . . We must not repose in fancied security that we can forever sell everything and buy little or nothing. . . . Reciprocity is the natural growth of our wonderful industrial development un-

der the domestic policy now firmly established. What we produce beyond our domestic consumption must have vent abroad. . . . The period of exclusiveness is past. Reciprocity treaties are in harmony with the spirit of the times; measures of retaliation are not. If perchance some of our tariffs are no longer needed for revenue, or to encourage and protect our industries at home, why should they not be employed to extend and promote our markets abroad?

Assassination of President McKinley

September 6. While attending a public reception at the Pan-American Exposition in Buffalo, President McKinley was shot by Leon F. Czolgosz. This eye-witness account was given by Secret Service Detective Ireland:

A few moments before Czolgosz, the assassin, approached, a man came along with three fingers of his right hand tied up in a bandage, and he had shaken hands with his left. When Czolgosz came up I noticed he was a boyish-looking fellow, with an innocent face, perfectly calm, and I also noticed that his right hand was wrapped in what appeared to be a bandage. I watched him closely, but was interrupted by the man in front of him, who held on to the President's hand an unusually long time. This man appeared to be an Italian, and wore a heavy black mustache. He was persistent, and it was necessary for me to push him along so that the others could reach the President. Just as he released the President's hand, and as the President was reaching for the hand of the assassin, there were two quick shots. Startled for a moment, I looked and saw the President draw his right hand up under his coat, straighten up, and, pressing his lips together, give Czolgosz the most scornful and contemptuous look possible to imagine. At the same time I reached for the young man and caught his left arm. The big negro standing just back of him, and who would have been next to take the President's hand, struck the young man in the neck with one hand, and with the other reached for the revolver, which had been discharged through the handkerchief, and the shots from which had set fire to the linen. Immediately a dozen men fell upon the assassin and bore him to the floor. While on the floor Czolgosz again tried to discharge the revolver, but before he could point it at the President it was knocked from his hand by the negro. . . . On the way down to the station Czolgosz would not say a word, but seemed greatly agitated.

The President's first thought, according to witnesses, was for his wife. "Be careful about her. Don't let her know," he said. Then, "Let no one hurt him," referring to the assassin. The early reports from the physicians were optimistic. One bullet had done little damage; the other had passed through both walls of the stomach. The wounds in the stomach were closed at once and it was believed that although serious they were not necessarily fatal. But gangrene set in, both in the stomach and the upper part of the kidney. Eight days after being wounded the President died. Czolgosz, of whom the common judgment was that he was a half-crazy anarchist, was tried and convicted, and on October 29 was electrocuted at the prison at Auburn, N. Y.

September. *The World's Work* described "The Biggest Ship," the newly built *Celtic*, 700 feet long, 37,700 tons displacement. In 1925 the biggest was the *Majestic*, 956 feet long, 64,000 tons displacement.

October 18. One of the most talked-of luncheons ever eaten in America, President Roosevelt's to Booker T. Washington.

October 19. Santos-Dumont in a dirigible airship flew from St. Cloud to the Eiffel Tower, circled it, and was back at his starting-point within thirty minutes. By this feat Santos-Dumont won the Deutsch Prize of 100,000 francs. A writer in *The Scientific American Supplement* was sceptical about the future of dirigibles:

It does not necessarily follow that he has accomplished anything of very great value. He has demonstrated the fact that with a very costly and delicate apparatus a skilful aeronaut may, under favorable conditions of wind and weather, rise from a given point, make a circle, and return to the spot from which he started without being killed, if he has good luck. The event, pleasant as it is, does not, however, mark a step in the direction of the practical realization of aerial navigation. It is probable that the solution of the problem of aerial navigation will never be reached in a way which will have any commercial value until the dirigible-balloon idea is abandoned and that of a mechanism built on a strictly mechanical basis substituted.

The dirigible-balloon idea had not been abandoned by 1925, although the history of this type of aircraft was more one of disaster and unfulfilled hopes than of sound achievement. Of two dirigibles of the Zeppelin type owned by the American Government in 1925, one, the *Shenandoah*, was wrecked while passing over Ohio on September 3, 1925, with a loss of fourteen lives.

October 24. Mrs. Anna Edson Taylor, in order to get money to pay the interest on her Texas ranch, went over Niagara Falls in a barrel — the first attempt ever accomplished without a fatal end. In the comment the news evoked, the Denver *Republican* thought Mrs. Taylor "seems to be taking a lot of credit that belongs to the barrel." The local Buffalo *Express*, taking the episode seriously, recited a number of sensational events of the year, including Santos-Dumont flying around the Eiffel Tower, and Alexander Winton "doing ten miles in his automobile at a rate so close to a mile a minute that we may as well let it go at that . . ." and concluded: "But we can't get over wishing that Niagara Falls were as high and mighty as they used to be before last Thursday."

November 1. The Charleston, S. C., Exposition was opened.

November 4. The Tammany organization in New York was beaten by the fusion ticket headed by Seth

Low, president of Columbia University. The election of the reform ticket was caused by the exposures of shocking corruption in the Police Department. William Travers Jerome, a fusionist, was elected district attorney.

November 8. The Isthmian Canal Treaty between Great Britain and the United States was signed.

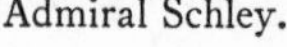

Admiral Schley.

Admiral Sampson.

December 10. A prolonged controversy between partisans of Admiral Winfield S. Schley and Admiral William T. Sampson, over the conduct of the former at the battle of Santiago, and the allocation of credit for victory, came to an end with the announcement of the findings of the Schley Court of Inquiry. The majority of the court held that Schley merited censure. Admiral George Dewey disagreed and presented a minority report in which he sustained Schley and assigned to him credit for the victory.

Public opinion, which first favored Schley, later swung around to Sampson. Sampson's death on May 6, 1902, was generally made the occasion for such eulogies as the following from the Buffalo *Express:*

. . . There is no question among . . . experts as to who earned the credit for the victory at Santiago. . . . The man who won the victory was the man whose tireless energy during thirty-nine days and nights . . . had kept the fleet in such a

Marconi in his wireless station at St. Johns, Newfoundland.

state of preparation that victory was assured at any hour, day or night, of that long period when the Spaniards cared to take the chances of battle; that no special orders were necessary when the critical moment came; that it was of no importance who the senior officer in actual command happened to be at the moment of the battle. Admiral Sampson did this, and those who fancy it was a trifling task have small knowledge of the history of naval warfare.

December 14. Guglielmo Marconi at his wireless station at St. John's, N. F., received signals from his transmitting-station at Cornwall, England, consisting of the letter S repeated over and over. Such advances had been made during the year in wireless communication over short distances that the American Naval Bureau of Equipment in May recommended:

1. That the use of homing pigeons be discontinued as soon as wireless telegraphy is introduced into the navy.

2. That, pending such action, no new pigeon-cotes be established.

December. During 1901 electrically driven street-cars were substituted for cable-cars on Broadway and several other New York streets. In the docks district, horse-cars were giving way to electric ones.

In 1901 the "best sellers" were led by another of Winston Churchill's historical novels, "The Crisis," in which Lincoln, Douglas, Sherman, and Grant were characters. Other popular novels were "The Eternal City," by Hall Caine; "The Right of Way," by Gilbert Parker, a Canadian novel; "Graustark," by George Barr McCutcheon; "Kim," by Rudyard Kipling; "The Cavalier," a novel of the South during the Civil War, by George W. Cable. This was the year of Frank Norris's "The Octopus," a story of a fight against the railroad trust. The trusts also appeared in fiction in "The Autocrats," by Charles K. Lush; in "The Warners," by Gertrude Potter; and in "By Bread Alone," by Isaac K. Friedman. Other novels of 1901 were: Mary E. Wilkins's "The Portion of Labor"; Mrs. Gertrude Atherton's "The Aristocrats"; Henry James's "The Sacred Fount"; Herbert G. (later H. G.) Wells's "The First Men in the Moon." Among books other than fiction there were two notable autobiographies which at once fitted the mood of the time and stimulated it: "The Making of an American," by Jacob A. Riis, a Danish immigrant who had become a leader in New York social welfare work, and Booker T. Washington's "Up from Slavery." Maeterlinck's "Life of the Bee" appeared this year.

Largely because American actors, playwrights, and managers had done hurried work to take advantage of the vogue of the dramatized popular novel the previous

"Gotham Court," one of the illustrations from "How the Other Half Lives" by Jacob A. Riis.
Mr. Riis's books did much to better living conditions in the tenements in New York City.

year, the best plays of 1901 were importations, and the best work was by foreign actors. From England, E. S. Willard played in "The Professor's Love Story"; Charles Hawtrey in "A Message from Mars"; John Hare in "The Gay Lord Quex." Other importations from England were "Mrs. Dane's Defense," with Margaret Anglin and William Faversham, and "Lady Huntworth's Experiment." From France came "L'Aiglon," in which Maude Adams's slender person, in the rôle of Napoleon's frail young son standing on the moonlit battle-field of Wagram, made one of her most engaging appeals.

Some of the vogue of the dramatized novel hung over. Julia Marlowe played in "When Knighthood Was in Flower"; Viola Allen in F. Marion Crawford's "In the Palace of the King," Miss Allen's second rôle after she became a star. On New Year's Eve Ada Rehan appeared in "Sweet Nell of Old Drury" before a New York audience in which "women tore bunches of violets from their bodices and threw them on the stage, and men waved their handkerchiefs to show their friendliness," to an actress for whom popular favor went hand in hand with the approval of the critical. Ethel Barrymore played 192 times in "Captain Jinks of the Horse Marines." Amelia Bingham appeared in Clyde Fitch's "The Climbers"; Annie Russell in "A Royal Family"; David Warfield played "The Auctioneer"; Mrs. Leslie Carter, "Du Barry"; Richard Mansfield, "Monsieur Beaucaire"; Mrs. Fiske in "The Unwelcome Mrs. Hatch"; Kyrle Bellew in "A Gentleman of France."

Among musical pieces "Florodora" took the palm for longevity; after 379 performances at one New York theatre it moved to another and kept on. Its record, completed the following year, was 547 performances. "Floradora's" success was made almost entirely by one of its numbers, the famous sextet, and by the personal attractiveness of the young women who sang it. "San Toy," in which James T. Powers played, immeasurably excelled "Florodora" in words, music, and taste. The "Favorite Family of Fun-makers," the "Four Cohans," played in "The Governor's Son," written by George M. Cohan.

21

1902

Nicaragua Gives Way to Panama as Canal Site. Carnegie Institute Founded. Industrializing of Niagara Falls Is Regulated. "Hell-Roarin' Jake" Smith Dropped from the Army. The Vogue of Ping-pong. Mont Pelée Erupts. J. P. Morgan Forms Shipping Combine. Cuba Becomes a Nation. The Beginning of Land Reclamation. General Amnesty in the Philippines. Flight and Suicide of Harry Tracy. Side-Saddle Discarded by Woman. President Roosevelt in Road Accident. "Pious Fund" Decision of the Hague Arbitration Court. Roosevelt Ends Coal Strike. Henry Ford Makes a Speed Record. Pennsylvania Railroad Starts Tunnelling into New York. America Lags in Rapid Transportation.

January 3. Up to this time the American project for an Isthmian canal contemplated crossing Nicaragua, because the narrower crossing in Panama was controlled by the French Panama Canal Company. On this day it was announced from Paris that the board of directors of the French company had decided to offer the canal property and franchises to the United States for $40,000,000. The fact that up to this time most of the activity looking to the Isthmian Canal had been in the field of agitation, diplomacy, and negotiation, led the Minneapolis *Times* to remark: "If pens were spades, the Isthmus would be all dug up by this time."

January 28. Andrew Carnegie, with a gift of $10,000,000, founded the Carnegie Institute of Washington, to "encourage in the broadest and most liberal manner investigation, research, and discovery, and the application of knowledge to the improvement of mankind."

February 23. The brigands in the Salonica district who on the 3d of September, 1901, had kidnapped Miss Ellen M. Stone, an American missionary, and her Bulgarian companion, Madame Tsilka, released their captives for a ransom of $72,500.

February 23. Prince Henry of Prussia, brother of the German Kaiser, arrived in New York, ostensibly to attend the launching of the Kaiser's American-built yacht *Meteor*, but more fundamentally to foster friendly relations between Germany and the United States. The *Meteor*, launched on the 25th, was christened by Miss Alice Roosevelt, eldest daughter of the President.

February. Agitation about diverting water from Niagara Falls for industrial purposes arrayed the public in two groups, one favoring increased use of the Falls for electrical power, the other advocating limitation, with the object of preserving the Falls in their natural beauty. A treaty was signed with Canada, limiting the amount of water that could be applied to industry to 56,000 cubic feet per second, of which 36,000 was apportioned to Canada and 20,000 to the United States.

March 8. President Roosevelt signed the Philippine tariff bill, providing that merchandise coming into the United States from the Philippines should pay less duty by 25 per cent than merchandise from other countries; and that all customs duties collected in American ports on imports from the Philippines should be turned over to the Philippine treasury.

April 4. The will of Cecil Rhodes was made public. It gave $10,000,000 to provide one hundred scholarships for American youths at Oxford University.

April 12. Reverend T. DeWitt Talmage died. He was a Presbyterian clergyman whose sermons were printed in hundreds of newspapers.

When Prince Henry of Prussia, brother of Kaiser Wilhelm, visited America, *Life*, February 27, 1902, pictured the arch of welcome it deemed appropriate.

April 20. Frank Stockton died. Author of "The Lady or the Tiger," "Rudder Grange," and other novels.

April 21. Brigadier-General Jacob H. Smith (known less formally as "Hell-Roarin' Jake") was put on trial at Manila on charges originating with newspaper reports that he had instructed a subordinate to "kill and burn and make Samar a howling wilderness." The court-martial recommended that General Smith be "admonished." Secretary of War Root found extenuating circumstances in the "conditions of the warfare with the cruel and barbarous savages." President Roosevelt also recognized "the cruelty, treachery, and total disregard of the rules and customs of civilized warfare" of the foes whom Smith had been fighting, but nevertheless ordered that he be immediately retired from active service.

April 28. The New York *World*, as part of a campaign against the "Beef Trust," printed some "Prices That Stagger Humanity." They were: sirloin steak, 24 c.; lamb chops, 18 c.; pork chops, 18 c.; ham, 18 c.

April. About this time ping-pong had the vogue that Mah Jong came to have in 1922 and the cross-word puzzle in 1924. In April, 1902, the Baltimore *American* described some aspects of the game:

"Where are you going, my pretty maid?" "I'm going ping-ponging, sir," she said. "May I go with you, my pretty maid?" "Yes, if you like, kind sir," she said. She led him away to the ping-pong net; and then came an hour he'll never forget; for his shoulders ache from the many stoops to pick up the balls, and his eyelid droops, where she smote him twice with her racket small, which left her hand as she struck the ball; and he'll never ping where she pongs again, for she heard him swear when she pinged him then.[1]

May 1. Immigration records were broken during 1902. In January, 18,000 arrived; in February, 30,000;

[1] In the same month a newspaper poet, writing in the Philadelphia *Bulletin*, acknowledged:

"I know I must be wrong,
But I cannot love ping-pong.
I cannot sing
In praise of ping;
I have no song
For pong."

in March, 57,000; and in April, 74,000. Most of the newcomers were from Italy, Austria-Hungary, or Russia.

May 6. Bret Harte died. He was the author of "Tales of the Argonauts," "A Protégé of Jack Hamlin's,"

Life for June 12, 1902, in a drawing by Otho Cushing, pictured even the gods as playing ping-pong.

and other novels; and of "Truthful James and Other Poems."

May 8. An eruption of Mont Pelée on the island of Martinique flooded the town and harbor of St. Pierre with molten lava. Loss of life was estimated at from 30,000 to 50,000. *Life* saw in this catastrophe a parallel to a cause of increasing deaths in the United States:

Attendant: Another large party has just arrived, sir.
St. Peter: Volcanoes or automobiles?

May 8. Announcement was made of a shipping combination, the International Mercantile Marine, sponsored by J. P. Morgan, which took in lines previously owned and controlled in Great Britain and lines previously owned and controlled in America. In America the feeling against "trusts," then at high tide, overcame the enthusiasm which otherwise might have been felt for the extension of American finance. In England public and official opinion was acutely alarmed over her shipping passing into foreign control.

May 9. Paul Leicester Ford died. He was the author of "Janice Meredith," "The Honorable Peter Stirling,' and other novels.

May 20. The American flag was lowered from the government buildings of Cuba and in its place was unfurled the lone-star banner of the new republic. Thus, four years after our entry into the Cuban War of Independence, America had the satisfaction of seeing Cuba launch her ship of state equipped with the best devices for safe navigation that American statesmanship could think of. John Kendrick Bangs wrote of the American work in preparing Cuba for self-government:

Uncle Sam . . . found Cuba unhealthy and he leaves her healthy; he found her without an adequate system of charities and hospitals and he leaves her a well-established one; he found her without schools and he leaves her with a . . . good school system established. . . . He found her without any knowledge of popular elections and without an electoral law; he has given her both. He found her prisons indescribably bad and leaves them as good as the average prisons of his own country. He has built up a good system of sanitary supervision throughout the island. . . . An immense amount of road and bridge building has been done. He has organized a system of civil service for the municipal police. He has enlisted, equipped, trained, and thoroughly established a rural guard which will compare favorably with any similar force. For the first time in history the carpetbagger in a situation of this kind has been held in subjection, and every penny of the trust has been administered for the benefit of the ward. It has been a wonderful showing.

June 15. Running time of trains on the Pennsylvania and New York Central Roads between New York and Chicago was reduced to twenty hours.

June 18. President Roosevelt signed the Federal Reclamation Act. Under its provisions a new bureau was added to the Department of the Interior, intrusted with constructing and operating irrigation works on the arid public lands in the West. Construction costs for the new works were to be met with funds realized by sales of public land. The reclaimed land was to be sold to settlers in lots of 160 acres or less, and the purchasers were to be given ten years in which to pay.

June. Governor-General Taft, on his way to Manila, stopped at Rome to negotiate with the Vatican for the ending of the tenure of Spanish friars to extensive landholdings in the Philippines. The lands were eventually purchased from the friars for about seven million dollars.

July 4. President Roosevelt granted amnesty to Filipino political prisoners, and established civil government throughout the archipelago. *The Review of Reviews* said:

> If the Filipinos behave themselves intelligently and sensibly, they will have a real legislative assembly of their own within five years, and will be several centuries nearer actual self-government than at any time previous to the arrival of Dewey in Manila Bay.

July 20. John W. Mackay died, the last of the "Bonanza kings" and almost the last of the early romantic millionaires whose fortunes were associated with pick and shovel in California. He was born in Dublin, Ireland, spent an immigrant boyhood in lower New York City, followed the 1849 rush of the Argonauts, made some money in California, grew rich from the Bonanza mine at Virginia City, Nev.; founded a bank; founded the Commercial Cable with James Gordon Bennett, and later founded the Postal Telegraph.

July. The increasing prevalence of divorce was reflected in the Philadelphia *Record:*

"This edition of the Bible is the very latest."
"But surely you can't improve on the Bible?"
"I refer especially to the 'Family Register.' Besides a page each for births, deaths, and marriages we give three pages for divorces."

July. Professor Brander Matthews, in *The International Monthly*, predicted that simplified spelling would make progress "like that of a glacier, as certain as it is irresistible." The National Educational Association had adopted for its official publications simplified spelling of twelve words: program, tho, altho, thoro, thorofare, thru, thruout, catalog, prolog, decalog, demagog, pedagog. The American Association for the Advancement of Science had adopted quinin, morphin, oxid, and some others.

August 6. Harry Tracy, a notorious outlaw, ended a fifty-nine-day flight through Oregon and Washington by committing suicide. The following account of his flight was printed in the New York *Times:*

The death of outlaw Tracy by his own hand ends perhaps the most remarkable man-hunt in the annals of crime. Since June 9 last Tracy, hunted by Indian trackers, bloodhounds, hundreds of authorized officers of the law, the State troops of Washington, and unnumbered volunteer bands of vigilantes, with a price on his head that amounted to a fortune, travelled over about fifteen hundred miles of wild country, and defied capture to the last. From the moment of his daring escape from the Oregon State Penitentiary to his last stand in the swamps of Lincoln County, near the eastern border of Washington, yesterday, he killed six officers of the law, slew his fellow fugitive, David Merrill, in a duel fought while men and hounds were on his heels, wounded nearly a dozen other officers of pursuing parties, and terrorized the people of two States. Living on the country he passed through, Tracy rode down stolen horses without number, robbed farmers of food, clothing, and money needed for his flight; crossed and recrossed rivers, hiding when he could and fighting when too hard pressed. Six times he shot his way through pursuing parties which surrounded him, and struggled on in his desperate race against death for liberty. The criminal exploits of Frank and Jesse James, the Younger brothers, Murel, and all the horde of desperate outlaws of the West pale beside the determined daring and reckless courage of the Oregon convict.

August 9. King Edward VII was crowned.

August 31. The San Francisco *Examiner* printed this, which reflected how far woman had got with her "new freedom" in 1902 — and reflected also a not uncommon tone and manner among newspapers at that time:[1]

. . . Saratoga the other day opened wide its eyes, and kept them wide open, too, when it saw Mrs. Adolph Ladenburg ride down past the hotels astride her Kentucky thoroughbred. There was no attempt on her part of concealing the fact that she was riding cross-saddle fashion. . . . Mrs. Ladenburg wears

[1] *Life* on May 23, 1901, printed this:

Oh, we might have heard serenely
Of the overthrow of kings,
Of the flight of mighty comets,
Or the fall of Saturn's rings; . . .
But the world seems sadly muddled,
Things have surely gone amiss

ly
bold- ride
women their
Boston nags
the like
Since this

skin-tight riding-breeches —, but, wait; she wears also a divided skirt. . . . Mrs. Ladenburg declares that it is the most comfortable riding-skirt ever devised, and that there is no suggestion of immodesty about it.

September 3. President Roosevelt narrowly escaped death when the carriage in which he was riding was struck by a trolley-car near Pittsfield, Mass. The President was injured in the leg and Secret Service Agent Craig, riding beside him, was killed.

September 4. A substitution of utilitarian adaptability in place of sentimental associations moved *Life* to say:

The blue suits in which we fought the Civil War have been condemned as too conspicuous, and after New Year's our soldiers are to go garbed in olive green that is guaranteed to blend with the landscape at a distance of eleven hundred yards. This is another result of the use of long-distance rifles, which have brought out unobtrusiveness as a leading military quality.

September. Cereal breakfast foods and the exploitation of them by advertising were new in the early 1900's. One of a series that passed the borders of advertising and became part of currently quoted humor, celebrated "Force," and made "Sunny Jim" a national character:

Jim Dumps' first-born—young Jim—a clerk,
Had wrecked his health by overwork.
His brain grew weak, his body thin,
Just as his father's once had been.
"Eat 'Force,'" Jim Senior begged of him.
He did. Now *he* is "Sunny Jim."

October 14. The Hague Arbitration Court rendered its first decision. The case was the United States (for the Roman Catholic archbishop of California) against the government of Mexico. By the decision, Mexico was to pay 1,420,682.67 pesos back annuities and thenceforth annually 43,050.99 pesos. The claim was for funds granted to the Catholic Church in Mexico (including

California) while the latter was a colony of Spain. After the Mexican independence and the cession of California to the United States, payment of California's share of the fund had lapsed.

October 21. Work was resumed in the anthracite-coal regions as a result of the unanimous vote taken at the mine-workers' convention two days before. The termination of this dispute, which had been dragging along since early May, and which threatened the users of anthracite coal with a serious famine at the beginning of winter, was effected by President Roosevelt, whose insistence that the rights of the public be respected, forced operators and miners into an agreement to settle the controversy by arbitration.

October 25. Frank Norris died. Author of "The Octopus," "The Pit," and other novels.

October 25. Woodrow Wilson was inaugurated president of Princeton University.

December 1. Henry Ford, at the wheel of his new seventy-horse-power racing-car, made an unofficial record of a mile in 1.01$\frac{1}{5}$ on the Grosse Point track, Detroit.

December 16. A franchise for tunnels under North and East Rivers, New York City, was granted to the Pennsylvania Railroad. Until these tunnels were built, all travellers going to New York from New Jersey and the South and West, and from Long Island, were compelled to leave the trains and cross on ferry-boats.

December. At the end of 1902, America lagged behind Europe in speed of rail transportation. At that time the

Paris-Calais Express ran on a schedule of three hours for the 184-mile trip, the average speed per hour being 61⅓ miles. The fastest train in America, the Twentieth Century Limited, made the 980-mile journey between New York and Chicago at an average of 49 miles per hour.

December. Doctor Adolf Lorenz, eminent Viennese surgeon, held open clinics in various cities of the United States, operating by "bloodless surgery" on hundreds of children suffering from clubfeet, dislocation of the hip, and similar ills.

In 1902 the vogue of the American historical novel was still on. Mary Johnston's "Audrey," the story of an orphan girl in Colonial Virginia, led the "best sellers." "Dorothy Vernon of Haddon Hall" revived the memories of Charles Major's "When Knighthood Was in Flower." Another "best seller" of 1902 was Owen Wister's "The Virginian," which with his previously published "Lin McLean" comprise the best picture of the then rapidly disappearing cowboy, whom Wister knew by personal contact. 1902 was the year of a bizarre sensation, "The Story of Mary MacLane," an autobiography written by a young Montana girl. Hamlin Garland published "The Captain of the Grey Horse Troop"; Stewart Edward White, "The Blazed Trail," a story of life in Michigan lumber-camps. Mrs. Edith Wharton published "The Valley of Decision"; Booth Tarkington, "The Two Vanrevels." Woodrow Wilson's "History of the American People" appeared in 1902. This was the year of George Horace Lorimer's "Letters of a Self-Made Merchant to His Son," which had a part in starting the vogue of the "go-getter" type of business man and salesman.

On the New York stage in 1902 the vogue of the dramatized novel continued. Daniel Frohman said its "tendency . . . is antagonistic to good dramatic art, but it keeps the theatres filled." One ingenious dramatist even experimented with a motif supplied by Ira D. Sankey's hymn, and made a melodrama of "The Ninety and Nine" The dramatized novels, either continued

Doctor Woodrow Wilson, *second from the left,* and Andrew Carnegie, *third from left,* at Princeton shortly after Wilson became President of Princeton.

from the previous year or staged in 1902 for the first time, included: Blanche Bates in "Under Two Flags"; Robert Edeson in "Soldiers of Fortune"; Virginia Harned in "Alice of Old Vincennes"; Richard Mansfield in "Monsieur Beaucaire" (in the fall of 1902 Mansfield played "Julius Cæsar"); "Tess of the D'Urbervilles"; "Eben Holden"; "The Helmet of Navarre." "Du Barry" with Mrs. Leslie Carter ran 163 times — Weber and Fields burlesqued it as "Du Hurry." Francis Wilson appeared in "The Toreador"; Maude Adams in "Quality Street"; Mrs. Fiske in "The Unwelcome Mrs. Hatch"; Ethel Barrymore in "The Country Mouse"; William

Faversham in "Imprudence"; John Drew in "The Mummy and the Humming-Bird"; Annie Russell in "The Girl and the Judge"; Henry Miller in "D'Arcy of the Guards"; Charles Hawtrey in "The Message from Mars." Mrs. Patrick Campbell appeared in "The Notorious Mrs. Ebbsmith" and "The Joy of Living." E. S. Willard appeared in "The Cardinal," "David Garrick," and "The Professor's Love Story." Madame Duse appeared in America after an absence of six years.

Other plays of 1902 included "A Gentleman of France"; a revival of "The Second Mrs. Tanqueray"; "Dolly Varden," which ran 156 times; a revival of "The Importance of Being Earnest"; a revival of "A Doll's House"; "The Sword of the King"; "The Stubbornness of Geraldine"; "Colorado." Ernest Seton-Thompson lectured on "Wild Animals I Have Known." Kellar was appearing in New York, the last of the older generation of magicians.

22

1903

The Supreme Court Sustains a "Grandfather Clause." Alaskan Boundary Tribunal. Rapid Action on the Isthmus of Panama. The "Lottery Decision" Opens the Way for Public Welfare Legislation. Doctor Wiley's "Poison Squad" and the "Pure Food" Law. First Flight of Man in an Airplane. First Pacific Cable. First Transcontinental Trip of an Automobile. Beginning of the Departments of Commerce and Labor. Beginning of the End of the Hookworm. End of the "Old-Fashioned Fourth." United States Steel Corporation Begins Profit-Sharing. A New "Longest Ship in the World." Women as Theatre Ushers. "Uncle Joe" Cannon Becomes Speaker. Reed Smoot Comes to the Senate, Accompanied by Some Excitement About the Mormon Church. The Iroquois Theatre Fire. New Hampshire Abandons Prohibition. "Undigested Securities." Union Labor Makes an Important Gain. Andrew Carnegie Gives, and Gives. Mark Twain Looks Forward, Inaccurately.

January 1. A plan for sharing profits with employees, one of the first in industrial history, was announced by the United States Steel Corporation.

January 11. Governor-General Taft was serenaded by 6000 Filipinos, who begged him not to accept an appointment to the United States Supreme Court, which it was reported President Roosevelt was about to tender him. Posters throughout Manila, printed in English, Spanish, and Tagalog, bore the slogan "We want Taft." This demonstration of good-will, following so soon after three years of armed resistance to the American Government, came as an agreeable shock. The New York *Commercial Advertiser* said: "If ever a man was animated by the true missionary spirit, he [Taft] is. . . . He is dominated by the wish and determination to make American control a help and a blessing."

January 20. The progress of wireless telegraphy was celebrated by an exchange of greetings between President Roosevelt and King Edward VII.

January 27. John D. Rockefeller gave $7,000,000, to be used in research for tuberculosis serum.

January 20. The election of Reed Smoot to the United States Senate by the Utah legislature led to the last outbreak of the public excitement which used to attend the Mormon Church and the institution formerly attached to it, polygamy. Against Smoot himself no charge of polygamy was made, but the investigation went far afield into the history of the Mormon Church and the practice of polygamy by some of its officers. President Joseph F. Smith testified that before the church edict of 1890 ending polygamy he had married six wives, that he continued to live with them after the edict, and that he had forty-two children, some born after the edict.[1] When asked what explanation he could give for practising polygamy in violation of the country's laws, Smith's rejoinder was the one to which Mormons similarly cir-

[1] During the time when the country was being diverted by the testimony about the Mormon Church and polygamy, it was said a monument was to be erected to Brigham Young. Thereupon John Kendrick Bangs wrote in *Life*, under the caption "To the Father of His Country," some verses whose point included witty allusions to some other topics of contemporary talk:

"Let his praises loud be sung!
Raise a shaft to Brigham Young . . .
Mortal who could faithful be
Not to one but sixty-three.
One who reckoned up his sons
Not by numbers but by tons,
For whatever might betide

cumstanced commonly attached virtue; namely, that he "would rather face the law than desert my family":

> The people of Utah have regarded the situation as an existing fact. These people, as a rule, are broad-minded and liberal in their views, and have condoned the offense — if offense it is — rather than interfere with my situation as they found it.

As to Smoot's membership and official relation with the Mormon Church, the Senate committee found no proof that it in any way or degree interfered with the conscientious fulfilling of his duties as United States senator, and he was allowed to retain his seat.

January. Mark Twain, in *The North American Review*, wrote with savage violence about Christian Science. He made a prediction — a little grotesque to read after the lapse of three-fourths of the period — that in thirty years Christian Science would become "the governing power of the Republic . . . the most insolent, unscrupulous, and tyrannical politico-religious master" since the Inquisition.

February 14. President Roosevelt signed the law creating the Department of Commerce and Labor, of which George B. Cortelyou became the first secretary. This, the ninth Cabinet office, was in 1913 broken into

To all racial suicide,
Rescue from oblivion's dust
Founder of the Nuptial Trust! . . .
Master hand of husbandry
At the altar ever be.
Sure preserver of the race,
Fountainhead of populace. . . .

JUVENTUS MAXIMUS,
SEMPER MATRIMONIUS!
PATER ET IMPERATOR!
FREQUENTISSIMUS UXOR!
MONUMENTUM RESPICE
HOC AD ARTEM BRIGAMY.'

two separate departments, one of Commerce, the other of Labor.

February 20. President Roosevelt signed the Elkins Anti-rebate bill, which had been passed by the House of Representatives by 241 to 6. This was a mile-stone in railroad regulation. Its purpose was to end rebates and discriminations by which the great shippers were enabled to cripple or destroy small competitors.

February 23. President Roosevelt signed an agreement by which the United States acquired sites for two naval stations in Cuba. On December 10 marines formally occupied the first, at Guantanamo.

February 23. The United States Supreme Court decided that Congress had the right to prohibit the carriage of lottery tickets from one State to another. This marked the effective ending, after a long contest, of the lottery business in the United States, whether in Louisiana or from foreign countries. The decision[1] had much more importance as a turning-point in American constitutional history. Its effect was to give to Congress large powers in a field formerly regarded as the exclusive jurisdiction of the States. In effect, it created a Federal police power, additional to that of the States. This decision opened the way for the Pure Food Act of 1906, the Meat Inspection Act of 1909, the Narcotics Acts of 1909 and 1914, and many other Federal laws which promoted the common welfare by attaching penalties to the transportation of forbidden articles from State to State.

February. A promise of better conditions for a large class of Americans was held out by Doctor Wardell Stiles, discoverer of the American species of hookworm, who

[1] Champion *v.* Ames.

said the "poor whites" of some parts of the South should not be condemned for their slovenly ways of life and distaste for work, because their lack of energy was due, not to any fault of their own, but to the hookworm parasite:

> If we were to place the strongest class of men and women in the country in the conditions of infection under which these poorer whites are living, they would within a generation or two deteriorate to the same poverty of mind, body, and worldly goods which is proverbial for the "poor white trash."

A campaign for the extermination of the hookworm was begun, and systematically carried on by the Rockefeller Foundation, with results that contributed to the growing energy of many parts of the South.

March 21. The report was made public of the Anthracite Coal Strike Commission created by President Roosevelt six months before, as an incident to the settlement of the great strike of 1902. Pending the investigation, the miners had gone to work in October, 1902. The report was favorable to the miners in most of the matters at issue. It provided for a retroactive increase of 10 per cent for the contract miners; for fewer hours and better working conditions; for a limitation of child labor; and, most important of all from the standpoint of the organized miners, it put the stamp of approval on the fundamental principles of union labor. Its dictum was that "no person shall be refused employment, or in any way discriminated against, on account of membership or non-membership in any labor organization; and there shall be no discrimination against or interference with any employee who is not a member of any labor organization by members of such organization."

March. The newspapers amused themselves and their readers with successive variations of a limerick:

There once was a man from Nantucket
Who kept all his cash in a bucket;
But his daughter, named Nan,
Ran away with a man,
And as for the bucket, Nantucket.
— Princeton *Tiger*

But he followed the pair to Pawtucket —
The man and the girl with the bucket;
And he said to the man
He was welcome to Nan,
But as for the bucket, Pawtucket.
— Chicago *Tribune*.

Then the pair followed Pa to Manhasset,
Where he still held the cash as an asset;
But Nan and the man
Stole the money and ran,
And as for the bucket, Manhasset.
— New York *Press*.

March 28. The Cuban Senate adopted the reciprocity treaty proposed by the United States. It provided that American goods exported to Cuba should pay 40 per cent less than the normal Cuban tariff, and that Cuban goods received at American ports should be granted a reduction of 20 per cent of the normal American tariff. On December 16 it was ratified by the United States Senate.

March 30. "Undigested securities" was added to America's vocabulary following an interview by a New York *Times* reporter with J. P. Morgan, who used the phrase to express his view of the cause of the prevailing economic uneasiness. The securities that had proved too much for the country's digestion were the mass that had been issued, largely by Morgan and his associates, as the inflated capitalization of trusts and combinations promoted, organized, and floated in 1901. Not the smallest item was the lot of 649,897 shares of Steel Common which they had taken as their profit in the organization of the United States Steel Corporation, and which a famous market manipulator, James R. Keene, had been employed to distribute in the boom stock-market of 1901.

April 20. Andrew Carnegie gave $1,500,000 to erect a temple of peace for the Hague Court of Arbitration.

April 21. The longest ship in the world, the *Kaiser Wilhelm II*, arrived in New York from Cherbourg on her maiden voyage. She displaced 26,500 tons, had a length of 706 feet 6 inches, and a beam of 72 feet.

April 27. The United States Supreme Court sustained the clause in the Alabama constitution by which Negroes could be disfranchised. After the Civil War, the North gave the Negroes the right to vote, tried to make the right secure by the Fourteenth and Fifteenth Amendments to the Federal Constitution, and for several years maintained troops in the South to enforce it. Later, the Southern States devised ways to prevent the Negro from voting, by ingenious clauses in their constitutions. The Alabama constitution, adopted in November, 1901, which was typical, was framed so as to restrict the privilege of voting to persons having education and a regular employment, or property worth $300, or having a war record, or having ancestors with a war record, or having good character and an understanding of the duties of citizenship. These State constitutions, although they evaded the Fourteenth and Fifteenth Amendments, were generally sustained by the Supreme Court of the United States. There was an increasing feeling in the North that it had been unwise judgment to try to force Negro suffrage on the South so quickly after the war, and also that suffrage was a local problem in which interference from outside could only have unhappy results. The justice who handed down the decision sustaining the Alabama constitution, Oliver Wendell Holmes, had himself fought in the Union army to free the Negro from slavery.

April. The French periodical *Correspondent* printed a collection of utterances by the German Kaiser. "I am your Emperor," ran one of them, made in a speech to a German audience, "by an immutable decree of God." Another was: "What I require of my people is a fidelity that never wavers." Another: "The assertion of an Emperor must not be disputed." On another occasion he enjoined a gathering of German bishops: "Regard me as the intermediary between you and Germany's ancient God."

May 1. New Hampshire, after forty-eight years of complete prohibition, substituted a system of licenses. In this same year New Hampshire rejected woman suffrage by a vote of 26,000 to 15,000.

May 20. The permanent treaty between Cuba and the United States embodying the provisions of the Platt Amendment was signed at Havana.

May 30. St. Gaudens's statue of General Sherman was unveiled in New York City.

May. Popular interest was excited by the "poison squad" organized by Doctor Harvey W. Wiley, head of the Bureau of Chemistry, in the Department of Agriculture at Washington, to determine the effects of preservatives and coloring-matter in food. A special kitchen and dining-room were set up in the Bureau, and volunteer "boarders" were drawn chiefly from Bureau employees. The public had already been aroused about preservatives in food four years before by charges made by General Nelson A. Miles concerning food furnished to the soldiers in the Spanish War, out of which arose the phrase "embalmed beef." Consequently there was much interest in Doctor Wiley's experiments, and much excitement over his conclusions, which were, as he wrote me in 1925, "that all these additions to food were deleterious." The experiments led to the enactment of the Federal Pure Food law, to many similar laws in the States, and to a stiffening up of food inspection everywhere. The crusade was stimulated by the publication, in 1906, of Upton Sinclair's "The Jungle," an exposure, in fiction form, of conditions portrayed by Sinclair as existing in some Chicago packing-houses. This book, and other events, caused President Roosevelt to order a Federal investigation. The reforms that resulted from all this were great, but Doctor Wiley in 1925, still a fighter at the age of eighty-one, felt strongly that much remained yet to be done.

Doctor Harvey W. Wiley. His pioneer work for pure food, in 1903, led to the National Pure Food Law, and to many reforms in the States.

June 3. Henry Romeike died. He was the originator of the business of supplying newspaper clippings.

June 26. The National Colored Immigration and Commercial Association petitioned President Roosevelt and Congress for $100,000,000 to transport American Negroes to Liberia.

July 1. The Ohio State auditor announced that for the first time in forty years the State was out of debt. Other debt-free States were: Illinois, Iowa, Nebraska, New Jersey, and West Virginia.

July 4. The first Pacific cable was opened. President Roosevelt and Governor Taft in the Philippines exchanged messages, and the President sent a round-the-world message which made the circuit in twelve minutes. The cable, 8000 miles long, was laid in four sections, three of which were longer than the cable from Europe to America. It stretched from San Francisco to Luzon, touching at Hawaii, Midway Islands, and Guam.

July 10. The Russian ambassador in London refused to forward to the Czar a protest of English Roman Catholics against the treatment of Negroes in the United States.

July 17. James A. McNeill Whistler died.

July 20. Pope Leo XIII died. The New Orleans *Times-Democrat* commented:

> It seems almost incredible that he should have looked on Napoleon at the zenith of his power, and should have held a high place in European affairs when Queen Victoria was a girl.

On August 4 the new Pope, former Cardinal Giuseppe Sarto, Patriarch of Venice, was elected, taking the name of Pius X.

July. Boston adopted the automobile as an adjunct to the policing of a scattered residence district.

August 4. St. Paul adopted an ordinance prohibiting the use of blank cartridges, bombs, pistols, and other noise-makers, as a means of celebrating July 4. This was the fruit of a nation-wide campaign, carried on for some years, which resulted in the general adoption of similar statutes. Much of the momentum for this campaign was supplied by the Chicago *Tribune*, through its managing editor, James Keeley.[1]

Courtesy of Keppel & Company.

James A. McNeill Whistler.

August 15. Joseph Pulitzer gave $2,000,000 for a school of journalism in Columbia University.

August 24. Lou Dillon, a chestnut mare, broke the world's record by trotting a mile in two minutes.

August 31. A Packard automobile, later called "Old Pacific," finished a fifty-two-day journey from San Francisco to New York. This was the first time an automobile crossed the continent under its own power.

[1] Mr. Keeley wrote me, in 1925: "My daughter Dorothy was sick, so sick it was touch and go whether she would live. The crisis came on July 3 and 4. The damnable din around my house wasn't doing her any good; in fact, we all thought it was the last straw that was pushing her over. I hadn't been to bed on the night of July 3, and about 11 o'clock in the morning of July 4 I called up my secretary to see if there was any news. He couldn't hear me, and I couldn't hear him because of the racket. The whole situation, I suppose, got on my nerves and I yelled: 'Frank, let's see how many people are being killed this year by this murderous travesty on patriotism.' The idea grew on me as I talked, and I told him to send messages to our correspondents in fifty of the largest cities in America, asking them to file the list of killed and injured. The list *The Tribune* printed next morning paralyzed every one. The next year I went at it systematically, sending out in advance prepared blanks for the use of correspondents all over the country."

October 7. The attempt at flight with a heavier-than-air flying-machine, designed by Samuel P. Langley of the Smithsonian Institution, resulted in failure, and gave rise to hilarious ridicule. The trial was made from a house-boat on the Potomac, and was inconclusive for

Lou Dillon, trotting mare, belonging to Mr. C. K. G. Billings, holder of the world's record of a mile in two minutes, made at the Readville Track, Mass., on August 24, 1903

the reason that in the take-off one of the wings impinged against a stanchion of the runway and was crippled. This was just three months and ten days before the Wright brothers made their historic first flight at Kitty Hawk, North Carolina. In 1914 Langley's machine was "reconditioned" and flown by Glenn Curtiss as an incident to a lawsuit over patents.

October 5. The year's champion batsman of the National Baseball League was Hans Wagner, of Pittsburgh, with an average of .355.

October 15. A humorist in *Life* wrote prophetically:

Mother to doctor, who is about to vaccinate little girl on the leg:

"Do it well above the knee, doctor. Since knickerbockers came, women wear legs, and bare legs may be in fashion before she grows up."

The first automobile to cross the continent (August 31, 1903).

October 16. In the column "On the Tip of the Tongue," in the New York *Press*, appeared the letter which started people sharpening pencils over the entire country, and for half a dozen years remained a subject of dispute and a means of pastime.

Brooklyn, October 12.

DEAR TIP:

Mary is 24 years old. She is twice as old as Anne was when she was as old as Anne is now. How old is Anne now? *A* says the answer is 16; *B* says 12. Which is correct?

JOHN MAHON.

October 17. The Alaskan Boundary Tribunal, sitting in London, voted 4 to 2 to sustain all but one of the American claims in the dispute with Canada over Alaskan boundaries. (Lord Alverstone, who with two Canadians represented British interests, voted with the three American members of the tribunal.) The dispute grew out of the interpretation of certain words in the Anglo-Russian treaty of 1825 defining the boundary-lines between Canada and Alaska. Part of the boundary was fixed in this treaty as a line parallel to the coast and ten marine leagues inland. Beginning in 1888 the Canadians advanced the claim that the ten leagues should be measured, not from the actual coast of the mainland, but from the outermost points of islands along the coast. This claim was not approved by the tribunal. The one point decided in Canada's favor was her claim to the main entrance to Portland Canal, at the southernmost point of continental Alaska.

October 22. Dan Patch broke the world's pacing record at Memphis, going a mile in 1:56½.

October 23. Members of an English educational commission, visiting the public schools of Washington, expressed amazement at learning that President Roosevelt's son Quentin was a regular pupil, and that he came and went unattended. The visitors asked what arrangements were made for the safety of the President's son, and how the school was kept "select" so that only the children of the "best families" could meet him. On being told that provisions for safety were unthought of, and that the son of the corner grocer was treated exactly as the son of the President, one of the commissioners remarked: "No better instance could have been offered of the real meaning of American democracy."

November 3. There began on the Isthmus of Panama a sequence of events of which the rapidity, unparalleled in the ordinarily slow processes of diplomacy, suggests part of the reason for the discussion that arose over them, and continued to the present day:

November 3. The Republic of Panama was proclaimed.

November 6. The United States recognized the Republic of Panama.

November 18. A treaty between the United States and Panama was signed by Secretary Hay and Mr. Bunau-Varilla, the minister of the new republic, giving the United States the right to build an Isthmian canal.

December 2. The treaty was ratified by Panama.

Professor Samuel Pierpont Langley, whose attempt at flight in the fall of 1903 ended in failure.

These events constituted the main steps by which, after long and vexatious delay, Roosevelt acquired for the United States the opportunity to build the Panama Canal. They composed one of the most spectacular events in his career, and the one out of which the most long-continued controversy arose.

November 10. Joseph G. Cannon became Speaker of the House of Representatives.

November 11. An event looked upon as having "social importance," the marriage of a New York heiress to an English duke, was attended by scenes described by the New York *Press:*

Roxburghe Wedding Made Scenes of Mad Confusion among Women in Street. . . . Police Clubbed Them from Church Where Duchess was Manufactured. . . . Whole Place Looted After the Ceremony. . . . Well Dressed but Indecently Curious Mob Made Nuptials of May Goelet Memorable. . . . The ceremony was simplicity itself, but the scene without and within the church where the wedding took place was one of the most amazing ever witnessed in the city of New York. Thousands of women, impelled by curiosity and forgetful of gentleness or of ordinary delicacy, pushed, hauled, surged and fought to get into the church; to get close to the carriage of the frightened bride; to carry off souvenirs; to touch the bridal robes; and to do a hundred and one other things, creating such an uproar and confusion that a platoon of police, armed with nightsticks, was actually compelled to charge upon them and, in many instances, to use force. . . . They fought, scratched, and screeched like a parcel of wildcats disputing a quarry.

November 14. Depressed business conditions following the "rich man's panic" in Wall Street was given as the cause for a 10 per cent reduction in the wages of 25,000 cotton-mill hands in Rhode Island. Two days previously, the United States Steel Corporation had announced a cut of $15,000,000 in its yearly pay-roll. Similar cuts were made in most of the industries throughout the country.

November 19. Carry A. Nation, the Kansas saloon-smasher, called at the White House, was refused an opportunity to see President Roosevelt, went to the Senate gallery, where she sold miniature hatchets, began a tirade, was arrested and fined $25.

December 16. Employment of women ushers by the Majestic Theatre in New York was described as "a brand-new job for the sex."

December 17. The first successful flight of an airplane in the history of the world was made by Orville and Wilbur Wright at Kitty Hawk, North Carolina.

December 30. The Iroquois Theatre at Chicago burned. "Mr. Bluebeard," with Eddie Foy as the principal comedian, was being presented before an audience made up largely of young people home from school or college for the Christmas vacation. Every one of the theatre's 1740 seats was occupied, and the aisles near the rear were filled solidly. The fire, starting from a defective electrical connection at the back of the stage, gained headway despite the efforts of stage-hands to beat it out. The audience suspected nothing until a large piece of burning muslin border fluttered to the stage, at sight of which the performers came to a pause, the orchestra faltered. Shouts of the stage-hands came clearly to the startled audience. Many left their seats but could make no progress through the clogged aisles. Others sought the emergency exits, but although the theatre was new and supposedly in excellent order, few of these doors could be opened. A general exodus was prevented by ushers and others who, believing the fire not serious, and fearing more a stampede in which many would be hurt, did all in their power to induce people to refrain from leaving the theatre. A momentary pause followed the appearance of Eddie Foy bearing his son in his arms. The comedian in his excitement had forgotten part of his costume, and his make-up was but half completed. Terror was not yet general, and many laughed at his grotesque appearance. Passing the boy to the conductor of the orchestra, he whispered: "For God's sake play, and keep on playing." The musicians responded bravely, but soon their efforts were smothered by the roar of flames fed by fresh air from opened doors. Men and women struggled to the aisles. Others climbed from seat to seat, trying to reach the rear and safety. Frantic employees attempted to lower the asbestos curtain which, had they been successful, would have prevented the flames from leaving the stage. The curtain was part way down when something went amiss; it could be lowered no farther. Then the lights went out.

Half an hour later, when the chief of the Fire Department made his way into the theatre he found human bodies piled to a height of seven feet choking every exit. To his call "Is any one alive here?" not a soul responded. Of the 2000 people who an hour before had entered the theatre, 588 left it corpses.

This disaster led to a new theatre code in practically every American city, calling for fire-walls, more numerous exits, unobstructed alleyways, asbestos curtains, non-inflammable scenery, the covering of all lights, and doors opening outward.

December. During 1903 immigration records were broken, 857,046 being granted admittance.

December. The most important scientific announcement of the year 1903 was of the discovery made jointly by M. and Mme. Curie of the new element, radium. Its properties were so subversive of many accepted theories of force and matter as to produce a sensation. The discovery was the more discussed because a woman had done much of the tremendous labor connected with separating radium from the pitchblend in which it is found.

The popular fiction of 1903 included "Lady Rose's Daughter," by Mrs. Humphry Ward; "The Pit," by Frank Norris; "The Little Shepherd of Kingdom Come," by John Fox, Jr.; "The Call of the Wild," a dog story, by Jack London. Andy Adams's standard picture of the old West, "The Log of a Cowboy," appeared this year. A remarkable autobiography, published in 1903, was Helen Keller's.

On the New York stage in 1903 George Ade had two musical comedies and a play. "The Sultan of Sulu" achieved a combination rarely found of real wit, topical allusion, and tunefulness. It was one of the best Ameri-

Mme. and M. Curie, co-discoverers of radium.

can musical comedies of any time. "The Prince of Pilsen" was less good. The refrain of one of Ade's songs was quoted for years:

> It is no time for mirth and laughter
> The cold gray dawn of the morning after.

Ade's "The County Chairman" was one of the best American character plays of the generation. Next to "The County Chairman," or equal to it in funniness, was Henry E. Dixey in the farce "Facing the Music." Lawrence D'Orsay in Augustus Thomas's "The Earl of Pawtucket" was one of the most extraordinary cases of the adaptation of an actor's natural personality to a character that ever appeared on any stage. It ran 296 times.

Ben Greet and an English company, including Miss Edith Wynne Matthison and her marvellous voice, made an old morality play, "Everyman," popular. Later they introduced a vogue of open-air performances of Shakespeare on college campuses. "The Darling of the Gods," a sombre tragedy of old Japan, was as good in its staging as in its art, probably the most worthy production of the early part of 1903.

Henry Irving produced Victorien Sardou's "Dante." Another classic drama of the year was "Ulysses." E. H. Sothern played the poetic and highly romantic "If I Were King," based on the life of François Villon. Forbes-Robertson, with Gertrude Elliott, was drawing big houses and driving a "thriving trade in tear-bedecked pocket-handkerchiefs," as James Huneker put it, in a dramatization of Kipling's "The Light That Failed."

William Gillette played in "The Admirable Crichton"; Richard Mansfield in "Old Heidelberg"; Mrs. Fiske in Ibsen's "Hedda Gabler"; Ethel Barrymore in "Cousin Kate"; Leo Ditrichstein in "What's the Matter with Susan"; Maxine Elliott in Clyde Fitch's "Her Own Way."

Maude Adams played Pepita in "The Pretty Sister of José"; Charles Hawtrey played "The Man from Blankley's"; John Drew, "Captain Dieppe"; Kyrle Bellew, Raffles in "The Amateur Cracksman."

"Way Down East" was called by Broadway "cow and chicken drama," but the country liked it. "The Little Princess" was a lovely play for children.

INDEX